REVOLUTION AND THE MEANINGS OF FREEDOM IN THE NINETEENTH CENTURY

The Making of Modern Freedom

General Editor: R. W. Davis
Center for the History of Freedom
Washington University in St. Louis

REVOLUTION AND THE MEANINGS OF FREEDOM IN THE NINETEENTH CENTURY

≺ ≻

Edited by Isser Woloch

STANFORD UNIVERSITY PRESS
STANFORD, CALIFORNIA

Stanford University Press
Stanford, California
© 1996 by the Board of Trustees of the
Leland Stanford Junior University
Printed in the United States of America

CIP data appear at the end of the book

<>

Series Foreword

THE STARTLING AND moving events that swept from China to Eastern Europe to Latin America and South Africa at the end of the 1980s, followed closely by similar events and the subsequent dissolution of what used to be the Soviet Union, formed one of those great historic occasions when calls for freedom, rights, and democracy echoed through political upheaval. A clear-eyed look at any of those conjunctions—in 1776 and 1789, in 1848 and 1918, as well as in 1989—reminds us that freedom, liberty, rights, and democracy are words into which many different and conflicting hopes have been read. The language of freedom—or liberty, which is interchangeable with freedom most of the time—is inherently difficult. It carried vastly different meanings in the classical world and in medieval Europe from those of modern understanding, though thinkers in later ages sometimes eagerly assimilated the older meanings to their own circumstances and purposes.

A new kind of freedom, which we have here called modern, gradually disentangles itself from old contexts in Europe, beginning first in England in the early seventeenth century and then, with many confusions, denials, reversals, and cross-purposes, elsewhere in Europe and the world. A large-scale history of this modern, conceptually distinct, idea of freedom is now beyond the ambition of any one scholar, however learned. This collaborative enterprise, tentative though it must be, is an effort to fill the gap.

We could not take into account all the varied meanings that freedom and liberty have carried in the modern world. We have, for example, ruled out extended attention to what some political philosophers have called "positive freedom," in the sense of self-realization of the individual; nor could we, even in a series as large as this, cope with the enormous implications of the four freedoms invoked by

Franklin D. Roosevelt in 1941. Freedom of speech and freedom of the press will have their place in the narrative that follows, certainly, but not the boundless calls for freedom from want and freedom from fear.

We use freedom in the traditional and restricted sense of civil and political liberty—freedom of religion, freedom of speech and assembly, freedom of the individual from arbitrary and capricious authority over persons or property, freedom to produce and to exchange goods and services, and the freedom to take part in the political process that shapes people's destiny. In no major part of the world over the past few years have aspirations for those freedoms not been at least powerfully expressed; and in most places where they did not exist, strong measures have been taken—not always successfully—to attain them.

The history we trace was not a steady march toward the present or the fulfillment of some cosmic necessity. Modern freedom had its roots in specific circumstances in early modern Europe, despite the unpromising and even hostile characteristics of the larger society and culture. From these narrow and often selfishly motivated beginnings, modern freedom came to be realized in later times, constrained by old traditions and institutions hard to move, and driven by ambition as well as idealism: everywhere the growth of freedom has been *sui generis*. But to understand these unique developments fully, we must first try to see them against the making of modern freedom as a whole.

The Making of Modern Freedom grows out of a continuing series of conferences and institutes held at the Center for the History of Freedom at Washington University in St. Louis. Professor J. H. Hexter was the founder and, for three years, the resident gadfly of the Center. His contribution is gratefully recalled by all his colleagues.

R.W.D.

Contents

<．＞

Acknowledgments

Several foundations have generously supported The Making of Modern Freedom series, and two in particular have supported this volume. The National Endowment for the Humanities provided funding for planning meetings and also sponsored the autumn 1993 conference where the volume was first discussed. It largely took shape in the sixth of our annual Institutes in the spring semester of 1994. The Institutes, which brought the authors together as Fellows of the Center for the History of Freedom, were fully funded by the Lynde and Harry Bradley Foundation. We are grateful for all the support we have received, including the strong backing we have always enjoyed from Washington University.

R.W.D.

CONTRIBUTORS

István Deák
Columbia University

Laura Engelstein
Princeton University

Raymond Grew
University of Michigan

Richard Herr
University of California, Berkeley
(Emeritus)

Sergio Luzzatto
University of Genoa

Iain McCalman
Australian National University

John M. Merriman
Yale University

James J. Sheehan
Stanford University

Richard J. Walter
Washington University

Isser Woloch
Columbia University

＜ ＞

REVOLUTION AND THE MEANINGS OF FREEDOM IN THE NINETEENTH CENTURY

≺ ≻

Introduction:
The Ambiguities of Revolution in
the Nineteenth Century

ISSER WOLOCH

> Violence is no more adequate to describe the
> phenomenon of revolution than change; only where
> change occurs in the sense of a new beginning,
> where violence is used to constitute an altogether
> different form of government, to bring about the
> formation of a new body politic, where the
> liberation from oppression aims at least at the
> constitution of freedom, can we speak of revolution.
> —Hannah Arendt, *On Revolution*

TO HISTORIANS INTERESTED in the development of freedom in the nineteenth century, revolution imposes itself as a subject for at least two reasons. First, besides forging a model of civic and social transformations in France, the French Revolution and its Napoleonic sequel etched the possibilities and perils of dramatic change in European consciousness. Secondly, the remarkable confluence of revolutions that swept across the Continent in 1848, with a pan-European simultaneity that had no parallel until 1989, demonstrates the centrality of the revolutionary option in the European experience, even if those revolutions did not prove to be a turning point comparable to 1789.

In this volume we are not interested in the revolutionary option per se, but use it as a vantage point for examining contested and alternative notions of freedom in the nineteenth century. In doing so, we have specifically chosen what might appear as the most conventional format for this exploration: a series of chapters on particular countries. We thereby insist on the primacy of national contextualization as against a more abstract thematic approach in the effort to engage the history of freedom in the nineteenth century, a period dominated by strong states and robust if sometimes thwarted national consciousness. By the same token, a number of issues and themes will appear and reappear across the chapters in the volume, and it is one function of this introduction to identify them as we make a first pass at the case studies that follow. (We regret that practical considerations limit the number of chapters that could be included in this volume, so that pertinent histories of places such as Belgium, Greece, Haiti, or Poland do not receive the attention they merit.) Most obvious among these questions are the problematic relationship between revolution and reform, and the related issue of violence. To progress at all in our inquiry we must lay to rest any notion that reform and revolution are simple opposites, yet must equally free ourselves of the converse supposition that they are mere alternatives for accomplishing similar ends. Reform and revolution lie on a complex and ambiguous continuum in the history of freedom.

Revolutions entail avowals that fundamental changes in political institutions or social relations cannot be negotiated against the resistance of existing power structures. In the summer of 1789 the French people and their elected representatives had stumbled into revolution inadvertently, having first mobilized in various ways for a vast if inchoate project of national reform that the king himself appeared to be leading. After 1789 such innocent spontaneity was much less likely on either side. Indeed the possible lessons to be drawn from the outbreak of the French Revolution posed a conundrum for governments in the future: while serious undertakings of constitutional or social reform might preclude or avert more drastic (that is, revolutionary) upheavals, they might also, as evidently happened in France, precipitate them.

Most nineteenth-century rulers, especially the more autocratic ones, ultimately faced that dilemma: to concede or not to concede to popular demands for change; to reform or not to reform? Were a government to negotiate major reform under duress and make timely concessions for repugnant changes, it might thereby salvage the existing polity or it might undermine the power of the ruling circles by diluting their real power, after which anything might happen. Yet the contrary course could appear just as dangerous or misguided. Inflexibly to resist demands from outside or indeed from within the ruling circles, even if they had somehow managed to build substantial support and expectations, was to risk unleashing violence, city streets awash in blood, or even civil war across the land.

Something of a middle course might prove the worst of all choices or could yet turn out to be the best. What if a government went to the brink of resisting demands for change but finally backed away from unleashing the full might of its armed force when popular determination did not shrivel at the initial deployment of such force? That, of course, is what actually occurred in France in the summer of 1789. After first seeming to capitulate to the will of the self-constituted National Assembly—the erstwhile deputies to his Estates General, who had on their own authority, in a supreme revolutionary act, proclaimed themselves the representatives of the sovereign people— Louis XVI ostentatiously deployed troops around Paris and prepared to renege on that momentary concession by overwhelming his rebellious subjects with force. When instead resistance in the capital grew, some troops refused to fight, others were withdrawn to barracks by their nervous officers, while still other units confronted the armed citizens of Paris. At the Bastille, the garrison killed or wounded over 150 Parisians before the crowd captured the royal citadel. At that point the king lost his resolve and capitulated, thereby sealing the triumphs of the revolutionary movement in Paris and the beleaguered deputies at Versailles.[1] This remarkable sequence of political daring by the patriot elites, royal intransigence, popular resistance, and final armed triumph gave unimagined writ and impulsion to revolutionary dreams and ambitions. It is what made the French Revolution truly revolutionary from its inception, and it is a sequence that seemed to unfold in several countries in 1848.

The breakdown of authority and the eruption of popular violence—whether in armed clashes against the forces of order, or spontaneous lynchings of notorious officials—seemed to be one hallmark of a revolutionary situation and perhaps the most immediate reason for wishing to avoid one. Alongside the celebrated military feats of the Parisian crowd on July 14, 1789 and August 10, 1792, the politically motivated lynchings and massacres that followed those events weighed heavily on the prestige of the French Revolution even before the Terror. In 1848, not only would barricades go up in the streets, but the equivalent of *"à la lanterne"* would resound in central Europe—with the lynching, for example, of two reactionary deputies to the Frankfurt Parliament after its acquiescence to the Malmø armistice; the murder by an enraged crowd in Budapest of General Lamberg on his ill-fated mission for the Habsburgs in Hungary; or the lynching in Vienna of Count Latour, the Habsburg war minister.

Around the issue of violence, then, the distinction between reform and revolution would appear to be obvious; yet from a slightly different perspective it can disappear before one's eyes. In the course of his own political career, for example, Edmund Burke himself seemed to draw no line between serious political reform and revolution. Several years before he attacked the French revolutionaries for their abstract radicalism, social effrontery, and violence, Burke rose in the House of Commons to oppose a parliamentary reform bill submitted by Prime Minister William Pitt. In part to appease extra-parliamentary agitation by such groups as the Yorkshire Association, Pitt proposed to eliminate the most archaic rotten boroughs, reallocate a number of parliamentary seats to the counties, and enlarge the franchise by small increments. An ardent believer in the notion of virtual representation, Burke denounced this modest proposal in almost apocalyptic terms that depicted Pitt's bill as a lethal assault on British traditions, values, and institutions. One could scarcely argue from this episode that Burke later pilloried the French revolutionaries only because they had willfully bypassed the alternative of peaceful, gradual reform. In 1785, such reform aroused his ire as much as the radical presumptions and revolutionary violence across the channel four years later.[2] Burke's fervent adherence to an organic view of tradition, including his belief that the fundamental political right of a people is simply the right to be well governed by their elites, aligns him with conservative positions articulated in post-revolutionary Europe by such contrasting minds as DeMaistre and Metternich.

For much of the nineteenth century—until Louis Napoleon and Bismarck each in his own way took a different tack by adapting certain reformist programs the better to preserve state power—conservatives usually opposed political and social reform adamantly (especially in response to popular demands), as tantamount to revolution. They shrewdly understood that the principles of an honest liberalism were open ended and could eventually support unintended constructions, whereas liberals themselves tended to be more sanguine that the application and consequences of their principles could be carefully delimited. A few notable liberals such as Guizot, who grew more alarmed at the radical or democratic potential of liberal reform after his own rise to political power in France after 1830, ultimately abandoned their liberal stance altogether and evolved into outspoken conservatives whose whole purpose in public life seemed to be the defense of the status quo. Where liberals generally constituted "parties of movement" in Europe, and believed that a constitutional framework and a public sphere of free discourse and debate would preclude chaotic and violent revolution, conservatives—the "parties of order" or resistance—feared that with constitutions, a free press, and open elections there would be little to choose from. As Guizot eventually learned, however, such rigidity helped create revolutionary situations in Paris, Berlin, Vienna, Milan, and elsewhere in 1848.[3]

These specific episodes are not our central concern in this volume but they do dramatize its core issue: the struggles in various countries to define, advance, or delimit freedom in the aftermath of the French Revolution. We are really tracing a long durational process— the great transition from traditional, particularist conceptions of liberty to new, universalist ideologies; the concomitant growth of the public sphere; the transformations, in particular national contexts, of political culture. This may or may not have been punctuated by a successful revolution, but even a failed revolution (the fate of most such episodes discussed in this volume) could have a substantial impact on this larger process. The recurrent themes include demands for a constitution and parliamentary institutions in countries without them; campaigns for franchise reform where representative bodies already existed; battles in the courts for a rule of law that would protect individual rights or freedom of expression; and associational movements along professional, cultural, or ethnic lines with veiled political agendas.

Sometimes historic debates within governing circles produced far-reaching innovations (Prussia's "revolution from above" after its humiliation by Napoleon in 1806, or the abolition of serfdom in Russia); but more commonly change was impelled by pressures against existing governments. What might have begun as a campaign to mobilize opinion for reform could erupt into violence and revolution given sufficient frustration and the right circumstances. And like the question of who should gain the franchise in France's July Monarchy (over which Guizot eventually came to grief), social issues usually lay behind such political questions, just as they had during the

French Revolution: Who would control the institutions of a reformed or revolutionized state? Whose privileges would be maintained or effaced, whose disabilities removed or perpetuated? Whose social and economic interests would be served and at whose expense?

For conservatives such as Burke and DeMaistre, the French Revolution appeared as a gratuitous disaster, a free choice and a foolish one—with or without the supposition that it was a conspiracy engineered by freethinkers and other fanatics. In this view, once it was launched on its presumptuous and reckless course, the Revolution's bloody excesses and chaos were inevitable. The first generation of French liberal historians writing during the Restoration took an opposite view on this fundamental question of cause and effect. To Thierry, Guizot, Mignet, and Thiers, the Revolution appeared as an historically-ordained upheaval on mankind's long, arduous, and honorable road toward freedom. That it descended into frightful excesses did not negate its positive, liberating essence because those excesses, unlike 1789 itself, were avoidable and, in the final analysis, incidental.[4]

While these two classic and rather archaic positions continued to influence the unending debate about the French Revolution, they were soon overshadowed by a thicket of more nuanced attempts at comprehension, interpretation, or evaluation. This array of postmortems on the French Revolution indeed forms the indispensable portal into the problem of revolution and freedom in the nineteenth century. In our first chapter, Sergio Luzzatto interrogates the recollections of surviving contemporaries (whether participants, victims, or observers) and the reflections of the succeeding generation. It is not his intention to dissect the cluster of historiographical masterpieces that emerged from this effort (for this has been done many times over with increasing subtlety),[5] but rather to explore the trajectories of memory, myth, interpretation, and literary representation that helped to fix varied images of revolution in French and European consciousness. For while conflicting visions of the French Revolution dominated historiography and politics in France during the first half of the nineteenth century, if not beyond, European writers from England to Russia proved equally fascinated by the commanding event of their times, and engaged it in a variety of forms, some quite ephemeral, others more weighty and influential. This chapter thus has the merit of treating the subject from a European rather than merely French perspective, and of placing an extravagant variety of material within a series of perspectives or visions, rather than simply discriminating between writers "for or against" the Revolution.

In France itself, to citizens of all social classes and degrees of literacy, memories of the French Revolution were as mother's milk. For decades, political allegiances, hopes, and fears fed on such images. In areas of western and southern France, like Brittany or the Vaucluse, where the reciprocal persecutions of the 1790s had cohered into traditions of hatred and ongoing local vendettas, memories of the Revolution had a ferocious immediacy.[6] Less vivid elsewhere, the images still flowed subterraneously, strongly enough to keep Restoration prefects and mayors on edge for any hint of their volatility. These officials often reported "public spirit" to be inert, meaning that people did not seem exercised by public affairs, but they knew that such benign passivity might be precarious. Napoleon, giving a new and extreme application to the Revolution's dream of consensus and a unified national will, had successfully depoliticized France both at the centers of power and in the provinces. But in reality he had simply papered over or given a long respite to the partisan political passions sown or unloosed by the Revolution. The Bourbons had hoped to perpetuate this depoliticization, but their own institutions provided more of an opening than Napoleon had. The Restoration's narrowly but genuinely elected Chamber of Deputies and its modicum of press freedom permitted a nascent liberal opposition some visibility and legitimacy. Moreover, when the ultra-royalists came to power within the Restoration government, their reactionary program had a polarizing effect that was bound to stir up fears and recriminations. Meanwhile, the passing decades widened the spectrum of popular discontent with new responses to the "social question" arising from the problems of labor and poverty in the cities.

From the broadest comparative perspective, France in 1815, along with Britain, was a relatively liberal polity seemingly well positioned to contain political passions: it had a written constitution (whatever the regime); a solid tradition of legality enshrined by the collective volumes of the *Bulletin des Lois* that dated originally from 1793; some form of legislative authority distinct from the governing executive; and a well-established tradition of political pamphleteering and

journalism.[7] Meanwhile, however, political consciousness and clashing ideologies probably ran more deeply in early nineteenth-century
France than elsewhere thanks to the revolutionary legacies of constitutional monarchism, ultra-royalism, liberalism, Jacobin republicanism, Bonapartism (whatever that was), and, now, socialism. Any
of these persuasions might embrace revolution as a necessary strategy for change, and John Merriman's chapter evaluates the ensuing
upheavals, with particular attention to their evolving social contexts.

Liberals were not averse to a mild dose of revolution if that seemed
the only way to slough off the stifling conservatism of the ultra-
royalists that seemed to block the road to freedom charted in 1789.
Emboldened by historians who celebrated the revolution of 1789
(while distancing it as much as possible from 1793) and by aggressive journalists who echoed that view, the liberals ousted the Bourbons in 1830—not in one of those orchestrated conspiracies or military seizures of power in the style of the *carbonari*, but in an un-
planned movement whose momentum mobilized Parisian society.
Later, when their Orleanist regime itself rigidified excessively, some
warily participated in the revolution of 1848. As reluctant revolutionaries, the French liberals resembled continental liberals who preferred the path of peaceful gradualism in their quest for constitutionalism, representative government, and civil liberties, but who ended
up despite themselves in rebellion. How and why this occurred so
often is perforce a central if implicit question in this volume.

It is a particularly poignant question because the stakes in successive revolutionary confrontations in France grew increasingly lethal. To be sure, the fighting at the barricades of July 1830 quickly
ended once the Bourbons had fled, and thereafter the July revolution
progressed peacefully. The liberals might well have regarded it as a
French equivalent of the Glorious Revolution of 1688 in England or
as a revival of 1789 without the problems of the Church, the emigres,
or the war to ruin things. The Orléanist regime was especially intent
on keeping social questions from jeopardizing their juste milieu notion of liberty and civil equality. Still, 1830 was a revolution in our
sense of the term, as conceptualized by Arendt. By blocking the ascendant alliance of throne, altar, and nobility that had emerged during the Restoration, it freed the French polity from the domination
of the erstwhile privileged orders of the Old Regime and from any
further presumption of unchecked monarchical power. The massive

resignations or dismissals of prefects and judges in 1830 signified more than a shift in patronage.

In the 1830s, however, working-class militancy in Lyon generated a new form of revolutionary action in behalf of a very different notion of freedom. Armed uprisings in 1831 and 1834 by silk workers and master artisans against the merchant-capitalists of the silk industry and their governmental allies in France's second city unfolded under such banners as "Live Freely in Work or Die."[8] These violent rebellions for a living wage, for freedom of association, and for social solidarity were no doubt doomed from the start, but Lyon provided a foretaste of how the new "social question" would impinge in 1848 not only in France but in various German towns and in Vienna. The nature and purpose of revolution was growing more ambiguous, freighted with an expanding field of contention about the meanings of freedom.

The revolution of 1848 began in Paris under the impetus of liberals and democrats demanding franchise reforms and civil liberties. Confrontation led to the building of barricades in the capital in February, a brief spasm of violence as in 1830, and the precipitous collapse of the Orleanist monarchy. But the February 1848 revolution immediately produced a democratic republic with universal male suffrage—an outcome that liberals conceded almost without a fight despite two decades of determined resistance to those ideals redolent of the Jacobin republic of 1792–94. The French revolutionary tradition had passed from the hands of the liberals, as the mosaic of activism in the capital burst all familiar bounds. Artisans and workers formed their own associations and political clubs and pressed their own economic and political demands in a kind of "permanent revolution."[9] Where agrarian issues had been the focus of social conflict in 1789, urban workers now forced onto center stage the question of state policy on wages, labor conditions, and unemployment—issues which proved impossible of peaceful resolution.

The situation erupted during the June Days into a class war on the barricades of shattering ferocity. In and of itself, an explosion of revolutionary class hatred into violence was not without precedent in France. After the suppression of the anti-Jacobin "federalist" rebellion in Lyon in 1793, the forces of repression sent from Paris set upon the despised urban elites of the rebellious city with an implacable fury. Then, in the spring of 1795, when desperate Parisian *sans-culottes* in the faubourg Antoine had launched a rebellion to demand "bread and the Constitution of 1793"—a notion of freedom wildly at variance with the new thermidorian consensus—the wealthier sections of Paris turned out in force to suppress the uprising. But in those prairial *journées* of the Year III, the fighting was more limited in scale and the repression less severe than what followed the June days of 1848.

The June Days reflected a type of social consciousness in which the upper classes tended to close ranks against the popular masses—a people whose burgeoning numbers and seeming rootlessness, moral laxity, and presumed criminality caused a social panic in the big cities of nineteenth-century Europe. This growing chasm signified not only the defensive claims of wealth, status, and power but also the pretensions of culture and taste. In its more extreme form, this outlook encouraged a starkly polarized view of society: the respectable and the dangerous, the civilized and the savage.[10] The negative consequences of this outlook for the prospects of a democratic political culture cannot be underestimated.

Yet the French Second Republic survived the social rupture of the June Days in Paris, and more remarkably still, the forces of the left reemerged in the months ahead as a vigorous political movement across the country rallying to the cause of "the democratic and social republic." Ultimately the republic succumbed to the plebiscitary dictatorship of Louis Napoleon Bonaparte, who seized power after the legislature refused to alter the constitution so that he could seek a second term as the republic's popularly-elected president. This dream-killing coup in turn provoked a popular uprising in the provinces rather than Paris—which perhaps explains its relative neglect in the annals of the French revolutionary experience. The insurrection of December 1851 against Louis Bonaparte's coup testified to the profound politicization in certain regions of small town and rural France, particularly in the south, and to the possibility of joint direct action by artisans, peasants, and middle class radicals in behalf of the democratic republic.[11]

Revolutionary activism in France thus did not depend on the building of barricades in Paris. Yet the most searing revolutionary episode in France did come in precisely that form, when the very walls of the capital formed a barricade against the new government of France in Versailles that had emerged after the fall of the Second Empire during the Franco-Prussian war—an early instance of a new linkage in modern Europe between war and the potential for revolution, which could be fatal to a government on the losing side. In the Paris Commune of 1871, at once a revolution and a civil war, the level of violent conflict reached a new intensity, and the depth of the repression that followed the suppression of the Commune—with its summary executions and deportations—exceeded any previous settling of accounts in France, with the exception of the Vendée rebellion during the French Revolution. Here was an attempt not simply to punish an insurgency but to choke off the revolutionary movements of the future.

This litany of revolutions and their aftermath in France begins to sound like a depressing saga of futility. It seems to suggest that the French Revolution's legacy of rationalized and quasi-liberal civic institutions proved ineffective against its other legacy of contending political passions, compounded now by divisive responses to socio-economic change. But that judgment is assuredly premature. Indeed Merriman argues that the succession of popular mobilizations and revolutions contributed significantly to the political settlement and social equilibrium that finally stabilized in the French Third Republic. At least two subsidiary questions with relevance to the other countries under consideration in our volume lay embedded in this history. First, why was freedom of association (the hallmark of a healthy civil society and the prerequisite for a democratic politics) so troublesome to every successive regime after 1789, not only in France but in the rest of Europe? Secondly, how should we evaluate France's precocious and impressive second foray into universal male suffrage, where turnouts during the Second Republic (unlike 1792) proved astonishingly high, and where the results of voting were never predictable—yielding a conservative constituent assembly in April 1848, an ambiguous outcome in the first direct presidential elections anywhere, a conservative majority and a radical minority in the ensuing legislative elections, and finally a dramatic trend favoring radical advocates of "the democratic and social republic" in the by-elections of 1849 and 1850?

Though it had seemed immune to the influence of the French Revolution, neighboring Spain would soon enough generate its own traditions of liberal revolution and populist counterrevolution, whose clashes would dominate Spanish political history for most of the

nineteenth century. King Carlos III (r.1759–88) had initiated a program of modest, state-building reform in his kingdom and, as in Joseph II's Austria and Frederick the Great's Prussia, a tradition of bureaucratic absolutism served by dedicated officials and seconded by
influential writers was developing in Spain. What progress this tradition would have made without the outbreak of the French Revolution we cannot say, but in the event the news from France provoked
a reaction against that reformist tide—another illustration of the
ambiguous relationship between reform and revolution. As the government attempted to insulate the peninsula from the baneful influence of France, it effectively shut down Spain's fragile "public
sphere," the arena of free public opinion that had been struggling to
life in Iberia under the shadow of the far from toothless Inquisition.[12]

If the roots of Spanish liberalism can be traced back to the reign
of Carlos III, this tradition, temporarily buried by the attempt to
quarantine the French Revolution and then by the outlandish vaga-
ries of court politics in Madrid after Carlos's death, faced a great crisis
when confronted with the French occupation in 1808. The *afrancesados* who rallied to the Napoleonic regime hoped to avert the punishments of civil war, and to find in Joseph Bonaparte a king who
would take up the mantle of Carlos III; as Napoleon had misleadingly
reassured his brother, "all the better people are for you." That was of
course anything but the case. Many liberally-inclined Spanish notables turned against the French, and the most determined managed
to convene the ancient parliament or Cortes in Cadiz, where in 1812
they produced an historic constitution. The steps leading to the convocation of the Cortes and the contending notions of liberty that this
event evoked are the focus of Richard Herr's chapter.

One of the early and grand monuments of European liberalism,
which served as a model to European insurgents in the 1820s, the
Cadiz constitution of 1812 was a decidedly revolutionary text, forged
against the background of an armed struggle and of sharp dispute over
the composition, powers, and agenda of the Cortes. The long constitution that finally emerged embodied the liberals' commitment to a
new vision of universal liberty and their repudiation of an older notion of corporate and particularist liberties. Here, in other words,
Spanish liberals faced the classic alternative visions of freedom in
eighteenth-century thought and made a decisive choice. Their choice
was comparable to if not quite as sweeping as the one made by the

French National Assembly in 1789, when the latter repudiated all forms of corporatism and privilege and proclaimed the value of individualism and free competition as the engine of social progress. In the French Revolution national integration and individual freedom alike demanded an end to all forms of the corporate ethos: hereditary privilege, venality of office, corporate exclusivism, professional or intellectual monopolies—whether in national government, local administration, the Church, the professions, business, the handicrafts, or the arts and sciences.

The Spanish liberals showed more willingness to compromise with tradition, especially with Catholicism, and a keen sense of how to maintain effective power in the hands of existing elites while eliminating abusive practices. But these restraints made no impression on the dominant reactionary and populist opinion, to which the Cadiz constitution of 1812 must have seemed as remote and offensive as a copy of the French constitution of 1791. In the short term, the 1812 constitution proved an essentially stillborn initiative (although elections under its auspices were held in 1813), and its authors felt the boot of repression when Ferdinand VII, with support from the military, tore up the constitution after he had regained the throne in 1814. Yet as Herr demonstrates, this experience helped shape the course of Spanish liberalism in the nineteenth century and left some of its votaries willing to resort to revolution ignited by military coups to revive their fortunes, the first coming as early as 1820.

In any consideration of revolution and freedom, Spain would also rank high because it spawned the first sustained and ultimately successful guerrilla rebellion in modern European history. The 30- to 40,000 hard-core guerrilla fighters against the Napoleonic occupation and its Spanish collaborators went to battle for church and king; for an implicit sense of nationhood that had been violated; and, in the epicenters of Navarre and the Basque country, for their sense of historic local liberties (fueros) as well, although these fueros had lost much of their effect long before the French occupation.[13]

The awesome power of populist rebellion from the right had earlier been displayed in western France during the counter-revolutionary Vendée uprising, and again during the French occupation of Naples, where in 1799 a peasant revolt instigated by Cardinal Ruffo in the name of church and king literally crushed the relatively few support-

ers of France's client state, the Neapolitan Republic. The Naples rebellion proved to be ephemeral but in Spain the dogged guerrilla rebellion established a durable patriotic myth and popular tradition.
This mirror-image of a revolutionary tradition mutated into Carlism later in the century, with its locus in the Basque country and
its potent if factitious invocation of local liberties to justify rebellion against seemingly legitimate governments in Madrid, which had
shown a willingness to compromise with liberalism and therefore
lacked the integral character of a traditional monarchism allied with
the Church. One leaves nineteenth-century Spain with an especially
perplexing sense of ambiguity: should we be placing the red beret of
Carlism alongside the red liberty cap of the Parisian *sans-culottes* in
the historical iconography of freedom?

If for a moment we attempt to personify revolution in the western
world, whom would we place between a Thomas Paine, Robespierre,
Wolfe Tone, or Kosciuszko in the 1790s and a Mazzini, Louis Blanc,
Kossuth, or Karl Marx in the 1840s? The answer draws us to Latin
America, an extension of European civilization on the one hand and
a frontier society of the New World on the other. Standing comfort-
ably astride that dual identity, and looming with extraordinary interest as a revolutionary leader, is Simon Bolivar, the successful
"Liberator," who yet failed to forge the new polity he so ardently
envisioned.

Latin America's revolutions exemplify two issues that recur elsewhere in this volume. Do revolutionary states have "natural" or obvious borders once they have been liberated, and if so, how are they
determined: by the accidents of Old-Regime arrangements or by the
volition of revolutionary elites? Are revolutionary states destined
to be united around a strong center or to fragment along regional or
ethnic lines? After ignoring the first question for a year or two, the
French revolutionaries had found it to be perilous indeed and were
drawn into increasingly aggressive formulations including the notion of expanding to France's "natural frontiers" by annexing Savoy,
Belgium, and the left bank of the Rhine. The second question, on the
other hand, they had settled early and decisively. The National Assembly created a new civic order around a unified national state subordinate to a central representative legislature, and rejected any effort to dilute this settlement along provincialist or regional lines—a

stance adopted even more vigorously by the National Convention and then by Napoleon.

In contrast, Bolivar's tenacious military struggle helped oust Spain from the South American continent, but his dream of replacing the old vice-royalty of New Granada (modern Colombia, Ecuador, and Venezuela) with a grand, conservative republic disintegrated under his eyes, and turned instead into a congeries of new nations and a world of unstable regimes. The same experience had already oc-curred in the Rio de la Plata (modern Argentina, Uruguay, and Para-guay) and would be replayed when the vice-royalty of New Spain freed itself from Spanish rule, only to have the southern portion of that huge former colony break away from Mexico and subsequently fragment into the feeble mini-states of today's Central America. Re-gionalism, the tradition of provincial liberties and loyalties—a force to be reckoned with at one time or another in Spain, France, Italy, and Germany as well—asserted itself in Latin America with irrepres-sible force but with extremely ambiguous political results.

A longstanding self-consciousness about an American identity in Spain's New World empire; Enlightenment thought; the example of revolution in North America; the destruction of Spanish naval power by the British—all contributed to the Latin American independence movements.[14] But above all they came as a reaction against Span-ish colonial rule and the collapse of the Spanish monarchy after the French occupation of 1808. The old amalgam of centralized absolut-ism, choking mercantilism, and a disdainful social prejudice which demeaned the native-born creoles stimulated the desire for freedom from Spain. Spanish mercantilism in particular managed to offend the interests of colonial inhabitants as producers, consumers, and merchants alike. But as Argentine resistance to the British incur-sions of 1806–7 in the Rio de la Plata had demonstrated, the thirst for economic opportunity did not alone motivate the creoles.

After fighting off repeated Spanish efforts to reconquer the conti-nent, the first challenge for the Americans was to establish the bound-aries, geographic and political, of sovereignty. As Bolivar pressed for a large super-republic, unitary or at least federal, he was instinctively following Madison's subtle prescriptions in *The Federalist Papers* about the virtues of large political systems in helping to balance par-ticularist interests. When the ephemeral Republic of Gran Colom-bia fragmented first into two states and then into three, just as the

Rio de la Plata had several years earlier, the result was not concord and stability but a kind of chronic instability, even chaos in both regions.[15]

In the political culture of the new Latin American states, liberal republicanism and even democratic sentiments vied for influence, but the authoritarian solution had decided advantages. In the absence of the hereditary rulers and "legitimism" that became the vehicles of European conservatism in the era of Metternich, Latin America produced a new variant of authoritarianism (a kind of penny ante Bonapartism?), or perhaps a very old kind reminiscent of the *condottieri* who sought to become princes. Latin American *caudillos* might guarantee order, but they did not contribute much to the development of liberty. As Richard Walter shows in his chapter, the liberal persuasion had a daunting uphill fight against the rivalry of oligarchic factions and the pretensions of military strongmen.

Post-independence Latin America produced a succession of constitutions but with very few exceptions (Chile's constitution of 1833 for one) none assumed the inspirational or totemic significance, the historical weightiness, of the Cadiz constitution of 1812, which could establish a potential framework for political development in the future. Putting it another way, the struggle for independence from Spain, though perforce a revolutionary movement as well as a military feat, therefore had no specific political outcome inscribed in its success. Without a crystallizing political fulcrum like the French National Assembly of 1789 or the Cortes of Cadiz in 1810, the independence struggle in Latin America did not produce a clear reference point for the political culture of the region, let alone an accepted framework of legality. Walter examines this "limited revolution," with its uncertain sense of what the new regimes should be like, including efforts at constitution making and the role of the press. This nascent political culture also had to accommodate the tensions of a racially complex society. The privileged status of "whiteness" figured strongly in post-independence struggles, especially in Argentina, Mexico, and Brazil—the last bastion of Atlantic slavery. In nineteenth-century Latin America, responses to the racial question distorted the notion of freedom much as the "social question" did in Europe.

In contrast to Latin America, where regional separatism followed independence or liberation from foreign rule, Italy's politics in the nineteenth century fostered the unification of a divided peninsula, a fragmentation perpetuated by outside conquest and oppressive regimes, as well as deeply-rooted localist traditions.

A long period of gestation for the modern Italian notion of freedom began in such enlightened princely courts of the eighteenth century as Habsburg Leopold II's in Tuscany, where precocious plans for reform even contemplated the promulgation of a written constitution that would bind the sovereign as well as his subjects. As in Spain, reformist sentiment was temporarily stymied when the Italian states tried to insulate the peninsula from the contagion of the French Revolution, but French military strategy against Austria spread the revolutionary wars across the Alps in 1796, much to the joy of Italian political refugees and incipient Italian revolutionaries on the ground. Unlike the French armies that had briefly crossed the Pyrenees in 1794, the Army of Italy did not soon evacuate. French victories brought "liberty and requisitions" to northern Italy and then, despite the wishes of the Directory back in Paris, French generals moved down the peninsula to Rome and even Naples. Marriages of convenience between French generals and progressive natives created several Italian sister republics, although only the Cisalpine Republic, with its capital in Milan and the patronage of General Bonaparte, seemed to show substantial viability and popular support.[16]

If the Restoration left Italy essentially as it had been before 1789 politically, the idea of freedom had gained deeper roots from the republican civic experience of the revolutionary decade and the durable administrative reform implanted by the Napoleonic regimes. After 1815, the restored petty autocracies in the north, Austria's reoccupation of Lombardy and Venetia, the benighted Bourbon dynasty in Naples, and the heavy hand of the papacy in central Italy would be on the defensive. As Raymond Grew suggests in his chapter, to many Italians these regimes appeared as artificial as the sister republics of the 1790s. The credibility of these reactionary regimes suffered both from their dogmatic denial of any form of constitutionalism and from the emerging desire for national unity which their very existence precluded.

Conspiratorial revolutions or coups in the *carbonari*, secret society, style during the 1820s made as little impact in Italy as they did in France, Spain, or Russia. More importantly, Italy was the seedbed for a new brand of romantic and nationalistic revolutionary sentiment exemplified in the organizational whirlwind of Mazzini and in the military campaigns of Garibaldi. Both promoted popular involvement in the liberation struggle and promised some form of participation, at least symbolic, in the civic life that would follow upon liberation. This Italian idiom offered Europe a new nexus of revolution, constitutionalism, and liberty distinct from the French revolutionary experience.

In 1848 republicanism and nationalism energized the insurgents in Milan, Rome, Venice, and elsewhere on the peninsula, but most of these revolutions succumbed to the repression orchestrated by a beleaguered Habsburg Monarchy, despite the heroic resistance of the besieged patriots. What contribution, then, did these and other less dramatic revolutionary episodes make to the advance of freedom in Italy? As Grew suggests, the image of revolution had achieved a kind of sentimentalized respectability in Italy. Even if the direct results of its many revolutionary episodes before, during, and after 1848 seemed to be meager (with the concomitant benefit that the bitter polarizations of the French Revolution were largely absent), the symbolic and emotive features of those dramas helped frame the dialectic of the ideal and the actual that has had such resonance in Italian political culture. In particular the strategies of popular mobilization fostered by Mazzini and Garibaldi linked the ascendant nationalist objective to a consensual notion of constitutional liberty.

As several authors in this volume argue, constitutionalism could be advanced by the established governments themselves, but what would impel such concessions? In Italy, rival strategies of nation building—Realpolitik vs. popular uprisings—came to a dramatic moment of confrontation in 1859–60, as Cavour faced Garibaldi. In the resulting synthesis (including the use of plebiscites), the framework for modern Italian political culture assumed its distinctive shape, consonant with the experience of limited revolutions. For as the elites of the peninsula awoke to find themselves citizens of a newly united nation-state, they were certainly not about to lose their status or political influence.

Like the dog that did not bark in the night, the revolution that did *not* occur in England in the 1790s has served as a potent image for historians. E. P. Thompson, for example, maintained that the English working classes of the late eighteenth and early nineteenth century were engulfed by a dual tragedy: the growing economic competitiveness and greediness that eroded customary relations of production, security, and living standards; and the absence of a political revolution that would have mitigated the unresponsive or repressive policies of the ruling classes. "It is in this insight—that the revolution which did *not* happen in England was fully as devastating, and in some features more divisive, than that which did happen in France—that we find a clue to the truly catastrophic nature of the period."[17]

The receptivity of small but significant groups of English and Scottish radicals to the French Revolution is well known, the success of Paine's *The Rights of Man* being only one indication of this sympathy. Alongside older movements advocating democratic reform, the London Corresponding Society and the Scottish Convention movement even appropriated elements of the organizational and political style of the Jacobins. How deep the impetus for some revolutionary mutation in England or Scotland might have been in the 1790s is of course moot, since the government pre-emptively squelched it with prosecutions, effective populist appeals to patriotism, and the combination acts of 1798. But as Iain McCalman argues in his chapter, popular constitutionalism could embody the moral and political equivalent of a revolution in British society. The rich varieties of this tradition in the nineteenth century, their discursive and practical ambiguities, and their contested emphases both in England and (quite differently) in Ireland, form the matrix of his chapter.

It seems clear that Britain did not experience one of the classic stimuli for revolution in the nineteenth century—a blinding antipathy between conservative and liberal elites. English conservatives had already proven adept at mobilizing popular opinion against the French Revolution and Napoleon. Equally important, activist reformers such as the Benthamite Francis Place retained the confidence, even in the least hospitable of times, that reform through Parliament was possible despite the manifest limitations and corruption of the parliamentary system. This belief of the liberals was vindicated in the parliamentary Reform Act of 1832, an antidote to an insurgent coalition between liberals and radicals. But in hardening what had seemed before to be the elastic boundaries that might redefine the political nation, and in gradually restricting the traditional ritualistic involvement of unenfranchised people in electoral campaigns, this reform inevitably disillusioned excluded working class militants. With their radical middle-class allies, they proceeded to fashion their own democratic response in the Chartist platform.

Did Chartism, a variant of an older tradition of popular constitutionalism, challenge the very foundations of Britain's social and political equilibrium? Was Chartism a kind of lawful revolutionary movement from below, whose program would have transformed the British polity beyond recognition? If not, how should we interpret Parliament's adamant resistance to Chartism despite its remarkable associational practices and mass support? For without the heavy handed directness of a Metternich, the British government deftly responded to Chartist agitation as it did to Irish demands for the repeal of the Act of Union, the other contemporaneous mass movement it faced, by effectively criminalizing certain tactics of the campaigns and forcing many of its leaders to spend time in jail, hiding, or exile.

In 1848, coincident with the final climax and collapse of Chartism, revolutions in France, Austria, and Prussia had forced the calling of elections for constituent assemblies on the basis of near-universal male suffrage, while in France the president of the new republic was to be elected by direct popular vote. Overnight, the most liberal parliamentary system in Europe had been eclipsed, as the British ruling class dug in its heels and rejected even a symbolic compromise with the democratic Chartist platform. Yet it is instructive to remember that, when the continental revolutions were suppressed, exiles from France, Germany, Italy, east-central Europe, and Russia converged on London, where the residual liberty of "freeborn Englishmen" could offer a protective umbrella to political refugees as well. Of equal interest, the presence of these revolutionary exiles helped reinvigorate various English radical movements, which had shared in their own way the defeats of 1848.[18] Moreover, it is possible to discern the impact of popular radicalism—of mass agitation that linked political and economic issues—on the emergence of Victorian liberalism. As McCalman suggests from several perspectives, the gap between "revolutionary" Europe and "reformist" Britain was not as definitive as one might suppose.

As much as any country at the time of the French Revolution, Prussia exemplified Europe's Old Regime, from its highly articulated bureaucratic absolutism to its norms of social organization, in which society comprised not individuals but groups or *Stände* whose specific rights and privileges each regarded as liberties. The Prussian nobility dominated the power structures of local and central government, as well as of the army, and upheld traditional limitations on the movement of property and labor in the countryside, while the urban craft and merchant guilds fostered restrictive trade practices and maintained the mechanisms by which masters policed the journeymen in their trades.

In France the National Assembly of 1789 had repudiated all such forms of group privilege and had proclaimed, alongside its doctrine of popular sovereignty and representation, a universal and individualist concept of liberty and civil equality. As if responding to the French challenge (though it was merely a coincidence), Prussia reaffirmed the older tradition in its General Code of 1791—a legal codification initiated by Frederick the Great some years earlier. Alongside enlightened provisions that formally proclaimed a *Rechtsstaat* or rule of law in Prussia, the code legitimized a hierarchical society of orders and particularist liberties:

The rights of a man arise from his birth, from his estate . . . The nobility, as the first estate in the state, most especially bears the obligation, by its distinctive destination, to maintain the defense of the state . . . The nobleman has an especial right to places of honor in the state for which he has made himself fit . . . Noblemen shall normally engage in no burgher livelihood or occupation.[19]

If the French Revolution struck an unequivocal blow against hereditary privilege, corporatism, and localist liberties in France, their persistence outside France, and their resilience in post-revolutionary France itself, remained evident. The European nobility's commanding status in the nineteenth century—to be envied, emulated, respected, feared, or resented as the case may be—and its tangible stake in existing agrarian and political arrangements, formed the most serious structural obstacle to the prospect of liberal constitutionalism and social reform, even if a minority (or in the case of Hungary and Poland, a large number) of nobles joined the ranks of nineteenth-century liberals as they had in 1789. In France itself, where the nobility's loss of formal privileges in the Revolution proved irrevocable, it quickly recovered much of its status and its disproportionate political influence under the Restoration.[20] And in England, where the aristocracy had relatively few legal privileges to begin with, its control of vast landed wealth and its traditional influence in local and national government continued in tandem with its enduring social status. But it was in central Europe above all that the un-

easy yet mutually reinforcing interests of monarchs and their aris-
tocracies held sway. Their alliance would assure, as historian Arno
Mayer contends, that to a certain degree "the old regime" would persist down to World War 1 in that region.[21] Yet as James Sheehan argues in his chapter, although Prussia never had a successful revolution, along with the other German states it assuredly experienced the
general transforming process at work in Europe during the nineteenth century.

Even while reeling from Napoleon's humiliating military con-
quests, Prussia managed, without jeopardizing the position of the autocracy or the aristocracy, to adjust defensively to the challenge—to
"the spirit of the new age, one of mobility, destruction, and creative-
ness, of power and action" as a Bavarian official described it in 1810.[22]
A "revolution from above" allowed the Prussian ruling circles to re-
gain their confidence and effectiveness by 1815, with the added balm
of moral satisfaction from their belated resistance to Napoleonic hegemony. The military and bureaucratic reforms launched by Hardenberg and others stopped short of creating a French-style model of citizenship and civil equality, but did open up the elites (civil and
military) to new, non-aristocratic talent. An infusion of meritocracy,
in the form of sponsored upward mobility for non-nobles, reinvigo-
rated the officer crops and the bureaucracy, and thus the aristocracy
itself. In addition, a new doctrine of German nationhood as an antidote to French domination helped mobilize the German people for
the war of liberation, without spilling over against the existing political and social structures. On the contrary, the decisive military
success of the allies in throwing off Napoleonic domination immediately obviated the need for any further liberalization. As the historian Hans Rosenberg observed: "The War of 'Liberation' from 1813 to
1815 brought liberation from the yoke of Napoleon I, but it also freed
the rulers of Prussia from the practical necessity of making further
concessions of a serious nature to the middle, let alone the lower
classes." Or as Prime Minister Montgelas of Bavaria put it at the
time, in defense of Bavaria's continuing cooperation with Napoleon,
the war of liberation against France offered the prospect of bringing
back old constitutions, rights, property relations.[23]

In the era of Metternich between 1815 and 1848, German liberals,
apart from those in the southern states which retained the rudiments
of constitutional and parliamentary government, proved largely im-

potent in their attempts to revive the cause of reform. Still, as Shee-han argues, the very arrival of these liberals as a public presence on the German scene is noteworthy. The forging of their quasi-political associational networks proved to be an indispensable preliminary to any claim to actual political power. Then, when popular ferment seemed to provide broad support in the streets of Berlin in March 1848, the Prussian autocracy suddenly found itself under siege. The ensuing revolution seemed to be following a script of sorts, a stan-dard procedure for wresting constitutional government and political freedom from a recalcitrant government. But this script covered only the first act, and the remainder of the drama would be determined by actions and choices that could not be predicted. In Germany, the revolutionary movements of the spring also reinforced the chain of events that led to the convening of a "German National Parliament" in Frankfurt, the great liberal triumph which for sheer audacity and historic drama is comparable to the creation of the French National Assembly in 1789 or the Cortes of Cadiz in 1810.

No doubt the clashing visions of the future among the oppositional elements of German society and the resulting turmoil facilitated the counterrevolution—exactly what the French National Convention had precluded when it embraced the Jacobin program of public safety and terror to enforce unity through revolutionary dictatorship. But the German liberals could not become Jacobins, and the radicals did not command enough power, support, or solidarity to play that role either, even if they had wished to.[24] Yet those few months of tur-moil set in motion by the uprisings of 1848 in Berlin and other Ger-man towns gave visibility to social forces and ideological claims that might otherwise have remained opaque. Liberals and radicals, jour-neymen and burghers may have stumbled over each other at cross purposes, but it would be harder for rulers to ignore their presence in the future. Moreover, as in Austria, the most significant, durable change to emerge from 1848 was the abolition of seigneurialism and the remnants of serfdom where they still existed, and we are bound to wonder when and in what form that crucial step to a free society would have occurred without the revolutionary impetus.

By making timely if disingenuous concessions, keeping the army under its control, and capitalizing on conflicts and timidity within the oppositional forces, the party of order in Prussia managed to prevail. Once he regained the initiative, King Frederick William IV scrapped the constitution drafted by a democratically-elected Prussian constituent assembly and promulgated a constitution of his own, unlike his Austrian counterpart who shortly resumed his rule without one. The three-class voting system of this first Prussian constitution retreated from the egalitarian franchise of the assembly's draft, and instead linked the weight of a vote to the citizen's level of wealth. But Prussian liberals might have been satisfied with the existence of a parliament in which the dominance of the elites was assured and the democratic demands they had come to fear in the course of 1848 would be precluded. In its way the king's constitution repaired the fissure briefly opened in 1848 between the state and the liberal wing of those elites.

The rise and fall of the liberal project of national unification in Frankfurt paralleled the fate of the revolutionary movement in Prussia. If anything, at Frankfurt the contradictions and conflicts proved even more intractable. Liberals and a minority of democrats clashed on such matters as the franchise, legislative vs. executive power, and corporatist vs. laissez-faire economic policy for the Reich. One could scarcely seek a forum in which contending notions of freedom were debated more systematically at mid-century. The deputies also faced the morally perilous problem of defining Germany's national boundaries against the aspirations of other ethnic groups that happened to reside within those elastic borders, especially the Czechs, Poles, and Danes of Bohemia, Poznan, and Schleswig-Holstein, respectively.[25] An even more excruciating test for the liberal nationalists came when the king of Prussia declined Frankfurt's proffered "crown from the gutter." The deputies had espoused a lawful revolution, a cooperative if improbable joint venture between sovereign princes and the German people; this rejection put an end to that prospect. To the boldest of the democrats the only possible recourse was a second revolution based on the sovereignty of the people, but this weak and belated republican project succumbed to popular indifference and the Prussian army. How different this progression looks from the French experience between 1789 and 1793, where, among other things, the revolutionaries early claimed control over the royal army, gradually nationalized it, and made their claim good in the face of the defection of two-thirds of the royal officer corps.

In the Habsburg monarchy as in Prussia the army played a decisive role before and during 1848—a role all the more crucial in the face of the monarchy's extraordinary ethnic diversity. Vienna, Prague, Budapest, Milan, Venice, Pressburg, Cracow, Innsbruck, Zagreb . . . Merely to enumerate its administrative centers is to evoke that complexity. Neither German nor Italian self-determination could be realized without confronting Habsburg power. Polish, Hungarian, Czech, Romanian, and South Slav national aspirations likewise clashed with the Habsburgs' supranational imperial order. An often irresolute or even bewildered imperial government in Vienna tried to uphold the status quo among its nationalities and territories, thereby to maintain internal peace and ethnic coexistence. But as István Deák suggests in his chapter, the rivalries of ethnic groups within large swaths of the Habsburg dominions proved as great an obstacle to national self-determination as the claims of Habsburg sovereignty.

The cement for this empire was the Habsburg army, which recruited from all parts of the realm. This in turn meant that each ethnic group could draw on trained veterans for its national cause when the moment came, a factor particularly important in Hungary. But the general impermeability of the Habsburg army to revolutionary sentiments in 1848 ultimately permitted the triumph of the Habsburgs, as the government implemented a more aggressive version of its traditional centralizing policy.

Deák dissects the incredibly complex cross-currents of national identities and political loyalties that both shaped and confused contending notions of freedom within the Habsburg domains in 1848. Apart from the north Italians, who regarded themselves as colonial subjects of Vienna, most ethnic elites in the empire professed loyalty to the emperor-king and sought only some degree of autonomy, hoping to use the legitimacy of the ruling dynasty as an umbrella for their own interests. The Magyars' revolution began in 1848 with that strategy, even if the Hungarian national assembly was eventually driven to declare complete independence as the only way to push through its program. Hungary then defended itself as one sovereign state against another, in effect attempting to undo the outcomes of the Battle of Mohács and the Rákóczi Rebellion centuries earlier.

An extraordinary confluence of demands for freedom descended on the Habsburg government in 1848: rebellion by the dynasty's Italian subjects; demands for autonomy by Czechs, Serbs, Croats, Romanians, and Poles; demands for virtual independence by the numerous Magyar nobility of Hungary; demands for a liberal constitution and for national unification among the empire's German subjects;

and, in the capital itself, a tumultuous democratic agitation by students and workers.[26]

The striking initial success of the Viennese revolution of 1848 drove the process of change forward when it wrested from the emperor the convocation of a consultative assembly for the empire, to be elected by virtually universal male suffrage. This historic assembly, even while troubled with serious divisions in its own ranks, attempted to fashion a new constitution under the eye of the imperial government. Its draft proposal, known as the Kremsier Constitution of 1849, deserves the most careful scrutiny as a landmark in the history of Western freedom, although—like the French constitution of 1793, the Cadiz constitution of 1812, or the Great Charter in England—it was never effectively implemented.

Ultimately all of the revolutions in the Habsburg domains failed. The Czech movement succumbed early-on, when Germans perceived it as a threat to their own national cause in ethnically mixed Bohemia and did not intervene when the Habsburg army bombarded Prague, extinguished the insurrectionary forces in the city, and dispersed the Pan-Slav Congress that had convened there. The Poles' struggle for independence in Galicia barely got off the ground. Habsburg armies defeated the Piedmontese military ally of the Lombard revolutionaries, besieged Milan and Venice into surrender (though it took over a year in the latter case), and bombarded Viennese radicalism into submission in October 1848.

That episode was the pivotal crisis point of the 1848 revolutions in central Europe. The Hungarians and the Viennese had recognized their mutual interests and intended to support each other against the counterrevolution, but for circumstantial reasons could not manage to concert in a timely fashion. What, then, of the Frankfurt Parliament, which lacked an army but still could have wielded great moral force across Germany? Here is how Karl Marx, in the acid prose of his journalistic style, described the situation, not without insight:

When the Viennese insurrection [of October] broke out, there was a host of interpellations, debates, motions, and amendments upon it [in the Frankfurt Parliament], which, of course, led to nothing. [The Central Executive did send two commissioners to Vienna.] The travels of Don Quixote and Sancho Panza form matter for an Odyssey in comparison with the heroic feats and wonderful adventures of those two knights-errant of German Unity. Not daring to go to Vienna, they were bullied by Windischgratz, wondered at by the idiot Emperor, and impudently hoaxed by Minister Stadion . . .

The left side of the Assembly had also sent two commissioners to Vienna, in order to uphold its authority there—Froebel and Robert Blum. Blum, when the danger drew near, judged rightly that here the great battle of the German Revolution was to be fought, and unhesitatingly resolved to stake his head on the issue . . . [H]is plebeian instinct and plebeian energy got the better of his indefiniteness, and, therefore, [of his] indecisive political persuasion and knowledge . . . Thus in Vienna he saw at a glance that here, not in the midst of the would-be elegant debates of Frankfurt, the fate of his country would have to be decided . . . Everybody knows how, after the storming, he was arrested, tried by court-martial, and shot. He died like a hero. And the Frankfurt Assembly, horrorstruck as it was, yet took the bloody insult with a seeming good grace.[27]

Though damaged by the defeat of its potential Viennese radical allies, the Magyars' revolution came closest to succeeding. Indeed Kossuth's leadership of the Hungarians is probably the most interesting case study of the ambiguities of revolution in the nineteenth century, both for his attempt to balance aristocratic ruling traditions with democratic mobilization, and for the resistance of the Magyars to the national aspirations of subordinate groups within Hungary's borders, such as Romanians, Serbs, and Slovaks[28]—a myopia reminiscent of the insistence by Spanish liberals that Spanish America must accept amalgamation with the mother country under a new constitution. Hungary also underscores the role of armed force as the ultimate arbiter of any real power struggle. Even if the Habsburgs could have eventually won their war in Hungary without assistance, the intervention of Russia decisively tipped the military balance against the Magyars. When the last battle ended in October 1849, the integrity of the three autocratic ruling dynasties of central and eastern Europe was undamaged, and Russia in particular had retained its reputation as the immovable bastion of European reaction.

From 1815 onward—with its regime of serfdom, its iron grip on most of Poland's national territory, its spasms of violent rebellion and pogroms, and its repressive secret police—Russia appeared as the very archetype of a rigid autocracy. To a unified chorus of disapproval from liberal Europe, Russia made manifest its resistance to liberalism and national liberation by its forceful military intervention against the Hungarian national revolution in 1849. Yet Russia is far from being a simple counterexample to the rest of Europe. In Russia we find the same forces involved as in most of the other situations considered in this book: the state itself, with its capacity to act as an instrument of transformation or resistance to change; the arena of "public opinion," where the Russian elites held a gamut of positions on the spectrum between revolution and reaction; and finally the popular masses on whom the others cast their eyes if not their sympathies. While the Russian state generally defended the status quo of authority and privilege, Peter I, for example, had turned the status hierarchies of the elites inside out and had recast government institutions to spur a certain kind of Westernization despite the resistance of his subjects.

Freedom or citizenship was another matter. Catherine the Great, by paying lip service to the Enlightenment's campaign for a public sphere of free debate, seemed to create an opening in the shell of the Russian autocracy. In reality little came of her consultative assembly, the Legislative Commission of 1767, or of her limited tolerance for independent writers. Indeed the individuals who were drawn most deeply into the game of critical discourse—Novikov and Radishchev—ended up being thrown into jail by the sovereign when their independence exasperated her. This ambiguity would remain a hallmark of the Russian scene in the nineteenth century. Rarely was the autocracy monolithic in its stance or impervious to internal debate. The bureaucracy itself encompassed a progressive wing of reform-minded officials who competed both with their reactionary colleagues and with the radicals outside the government to shape the nation's public opinion—to create a simulacrum of public life even without foundational civil liberties or representation.

As Laura Engelstein argues in her chapter, the relationship between the radical intelligentsia and a potentially restive if not incendiary populace was also extremely ambiguous. The latter certainly did not depend on the intelligentsia to mobilize spasmodically in popular protests, violent or otherwise, and the radicals were not necessarily deterred by a lack of popular support or comprehension. The first abortive revolutionary episode of the nineteenth century—the failed coup in 1825 by the disaffected aristocrats known as the Decembrists—was in fact an attempt to seize power from within not very different from a traditional Russian palace coup, or for that matter from the military coups by liberals of the 1820s in Naples and Spain.

Thereafter, the intelligentsia began to take as its mission the task of mobilizing the masses for their own liberation. This vision at the least energized the radicals themselves with a kind of personal dedication and idealism that occasionally led to martyrdom. It also aroused the government. But the actual tenor of public life was little affected by this elusive prospect of a dialogue between disaffected elites and the masses. The principal arena of struggle remained the "theater" of elite public opinion, even if it lacked the sparks set off in western Europe by successions of colorful publicists, journalists, and caricaturists. Characteristically, the abolition of serfdom came from above without a constituent assembly to force the issue (as in Prussia or Austria), let alone a transforming autoemancipation through violent rebellion.

The abolition of serfdom did create at least the possibility or precondition for a meaningful dialogue between the radical intelligentsia and the peasants. The most distinctive, home-grown variant of revolutionary ideology in nineteenth-century Russia was thus the romantic populism of the *narodniki*, which espoused a vaguely popular notion of freedom unanchored in the liberal constitutionalist tradition. People who in other parts of Europe might have become Mazzinian liberal nationalists seem to have been driven by social guilt into the populist ideology of "going out to the countryside" in Russia. (Was there ever a more directly influential political novel than Chernyshevskii's *What is to be Done?* ?) The legacy of material and cultural poverty in Russia and Poland that they encountered, however, remained an insuperable barrier to their influence and to their hope of finding a distinctive rural path to national freedom, Russian style.

A more immediate if superficial impact could probably be claimed by the Russian adherents of the anarchist persuasion with their notion of destroying autocracy by individual acts of violence. The small but militant subculture of professional revolutionaries (the Russian equivalent of the Blanquist insurrectionary mentality in France) influenced the shape of the Russian polity disproportionately by forcing it to respond to the specter of subversion through terrorism. Above all, the challenge of terrorism strained the fragile efforts in Russia to establish a rule of law, both substantive and procedural. As Engelstein demonstrates, the courtroom had become one of the chief arenas for the dialogue of the state and its militant opponents, but the autocracy was still free to modify the rules of engagement as it saw fit. Neither the revolution of 1905, despite its incipient constitutionalism and legitimation of political opposition, nor of course the Bolshevik revolution would eliminate that critical prerogative of the Russian state.

This introductory chapter has placed France's succession of nineteenth-century revolutions in the spotlight at the outset, and has concluded with a discussion of Russia. No particular weight, however, should be ascribed to either of those organizational conveniences. As this introduction itself has already insisted, Russia or Germany has as much to tell us as France about the issues raised in this volume: the contending meanings of freedom, the expansion of participatory forces, the contested growth of the public sphere, the ambiguous relationship between reform and revolution—in short, the evolution of political culture in the nineteenth century.

In fact the actual order of the chapters will not follow the sequence of presentation in the introduction and indeed ought to neutralize any implication of either historical primacy or exceptionalism. While we insist on national contextualization as the operative strategy for this undertaking, we are working collectively to analyze a nexus of common themes across geographic and chronological space. After an opening chapter on European visions of the French Revolution, for reasons of chronology and substance we turn next to Spain and then to its American colonies. At that point we make our case against any simplistic notion of exceptionalism by considering England, where conflicting views about freedom, social change, and political participation take on great clarity even if the revolutionary option never actually came into play. We then present four chapters that treat (in no inherently fixed order) the regions of Europe that were swept by revolutions in 1848 but whose broader historical trajectories of course remained distinctive: France, Italy, Germany, and the Habsburg Monarchy. None of those revolutions took root to produce a durable new regime, yet none of them aborted so completely as to obliterate the multiple aspirations for freedom and the ensuing conflicts that propelled them. For reasons of chronology and closure we end with Russia, although one could easily have placed that chapter squarely at the center of the volume.

European Visions of the French Revolution

SERGIO LUZZATTO

AT THE VERY END OF THE eighteenth century, Louis-Sébastien Mercier, renowned in revolutionary France more as a popular novelist than as a member of the National Assembly during the Terror, expressed doubts about the possibility of writing, in the next decades, an accurate history of the French Revolution. According to Mercier, everything in the Revolution had been a matter of individual perspective, both for the actors engaged in the political scene and for the spectators involved in the revolutionary drama. *"Everything is optical* . . . everything is . . . exaggerated out of the visual line."* For the next half-century, Mercier argued, even the most sympathetic observer would find himself lost in the "labyrinth" of the French Revolution.[1]

Despite Mercier's skepticism, writing a history of the Revolution was undertaken in the first half of the nineteenth century, not only by dozens of French *gens de lettres*, but also by some of the most distinguished European writers of the time; and, as we shall see, their efforts eventually led to true historiographical achievements. Still, it is worth keeping in mind Mercier's statement about the pervasiveness of "the optical" in every possible approach to the French Revolution, inasmuch as nineteenth-century interpretations of the historical meaning of the revolutionary and Napoleonic decades were balanced precariously between the authors' claim to a reserved objectivity and their pride in an insightful subjectivity.

Before the mid-nineteenth century historians paid little attention to archival sources related to the period 1789–1815. The European revolutions of 1848 seem to have awakened in them the urge to look into historical evidence at a deeper level than the one they could expect to reach by a close reading of the *Moniteur* and the *Bulletin des lois*. But even after 1848, notwithstanding their rising concern with "objective" sources, historians were interested predominantly in "subjective" ones. Members of the revolutionary generation survived into the middle of the century and beyond, and the story of the Revolution was treated by them as a showcase for various heroes and anti-heroes. As for the spokesmen for the new generation, they tried to collect oral and written testimonies with the passion of heirs to the Revolution, coupled with the coolness of testamentary executors. Ninteenth-century visions of the French Revolution are profoundly shaped, and inevitably biased, by an inter-generational dynamic.[2] No matter their talent or their degree of self-pride, most nineteenth-century historians of the Revolution thought of themselves only as glossarists of or commentators on the actors' memories.

The lasting role of the different and often contradictory perceptions of the events by eye witnesses in shaping nineteenth-century representations of the French Revolution is attested to by the astonishing success of an emerging literary genre, the memoir.[3] This genre flourished both in France and elsewhere in Europe during the first half of the century. The widespread hunger for secret details and piquant anecdotes concerning statesmen's public and private lives had something to do with its success. What Hegel called "the psychology of the valet"—that is, the curiosity about human peculiarities which have no special connection with the historical role of the person involved—may have been common among early-nineteenth-century readers. However, the memoirs had a substantial influence on political cultures.

Furthermore, the rise of another genre, the historical novel, testifies to the operational link between reality, memory, and imagination which framed European nineteenth-century visions of the French Revolution and the Napoleonic wars. As Georg Lukács, borrowing an expression from Karl Marx, has convincingly shown, whatever the proportions of "regeneration and reaction" in individual national movements aroused by revolutionary wars, these movements—real mass movements—conveyed a sense and experience of history to broad masses. The historical novel throve insofar as it succeeded in demonstrating by artistic means that historical circumstances and characters existed in precisely such and such a way. Heinrich Heine, a German exile in Paris, described the appeal of the historical novel to his contemporaries when he wrote: "They demand their history from the hand of the poet and not from the hand of the historian.

They demand not a faithful report of bare facts, but those facts dissolved back into the original poetry whence they came."[4]

Yet almost all of the nineteenth-century writers I will be dealing with were, or at least considered themselves, as much historians as novelists or poets, or journalists, or even philosophers. Walter Scott and Alessandro Manzoni tried their hands at French revolutionary history; the Girondins' historian Lamartine was mainly a poet; John Stuart Mill and Karl Marx conceived projects for a history of the Revolution; Quinet and Taine endeavored to write dramas and novels. Thomas Carlyle, for whom reality was "the only *possible* poem,"[5] described the true history of the French Revolution, "that impossible thing I mean by History" (the very history he was nevertheless to undertake), as the grand poem of his times.[6] And Georg Büchner's *Danton's Death* (1835), the finest attempt at dramatizing the Revolution, was based on a close reading of French pamphlets of the 1790s and historical narratives of the 1820s.[7] By the descendants as well as by the survivors, the events of the French Revolution were offered to posterity as the plot of a tale.[8]

Nevertheless, it would be unwise to drown all European narratives of the French Revolution in a sort of discursive *mare magnum*. In this chapter I wish to identify the most significant and shared nineteenth-century visions of the Revolution, placing them within a specific if tentative framework. In the following pages I will present five interpretative categories, five "lenses" through which nineteenth-century observers looked backward to Europe's recent past. I consider the heroic, the organic, and the messianic "eyes" to be predominant in the European mind during the first half of the nineteenth century; the critical and the pathological ones, during the second half. Each of these visions is informed by a preeminent concern for the relationship between nineteenth-century political and social issues and the essence of the French Revolution, although none of them should be considered—at a given time—exclusive of the others.

Profoundly molded by Napoleon's adventure, the heroic perspective addresses the dynamic of the Revolution primarily as a paradigm of a wider rationale which might explain the place of individuals in history. The organic viewpoint questions the decisive function of the Revolution in giving birth to modern democracy while unmasking the limits of democracy itself. The compatibility of French revolutionary values with the spirit of Christianity puzzles the messianic vision, whose holders are primarily committed to finding a viable solution for the increasingly burning social question. As for the critical perspective, it predominantly stresses the contribution of the Revolution in forging the dull, disenchanted landscape of modernity: world fairs, class struggles, and Caesarism. Finally, observers sharing the pathological vision are especially concerned with the founding role of the Revolution in transforming peasants into criminals.

≺ I ≻

The Heroic Eye

The most important French revolutionary character who survived into the post-Waterloo world was, admittedly, Napoleon himself. Neither in France nor elsewhere in Europe did the relegation of the former emperor to St. Helena mean his eclipse from the political arena. The faraway internment did not prevent Napoleon's admirers and opponents from perceiving him as a Caesar or an Attila, as an Hellenic hero or an oriental despot, in short as either an exciting or a threatening deus ex machina still hanging over the European scene.[9] Judicial evidence shows that political opponents of Restoration France were much more often prosecuted for having invoked Napoleon's name than for having explicitly regretted the First Republic.[10]

Factious activities and popular beliefs worked together in keeping the Napoleonic legend alive. Until Bonaparte's death in 1821, French militants faithful to the emperor skillfully managed to propagate worldwide apocryphal manifestos, crediting rumors about Napoleon's escape from St. Helena or his liberation by Latin-American insurgents.[11] After 1821, the legend of Napoleon—this incarnate symbol of the New Regime—was nourished by the lasting Old-Regime fascination with the figure of the "hidden king": that is, the king who for some reason disappears and is hence reported dead, but who ultimately reappears and makes his subjects happy forever.[12] In France during the 1820s, the memory of the Hundred Days (which had begun in March 1815) promoted almost every year, in March, gossip about Napoleon's return.[13] The vitality of the legend was not just a matter of manipulation, nor was it confined within the borders of France.[14] After all, spurious French propaganda seems unlikely to have reached that obscure Greek peasant who, in the late 1850s, was positive about Leonidas's sacrifice in the famous battle of the Thermopylae, but could still not figure out the destiny of the second hero of the day, General Bonapartis.[15]

The *Mémorial de Sainte-Hélène*, Napoleon's political testament, helped the legend to endure because it presented the emperor as a sort of liberal revolutionary, and furthermore as a republican king. The *Mémorial* was probably the greatest bestseller of the nineteenth century.[16] Yet, the power of the written word would hardly have been sufficient to keep alive the Napoleonic legend if it had not been supported, among French people, by political and social experiences. Again, what seems to have been crucial in shaping the revolutionary tradition of the 1820s is the memory of the Hundred Days: namely, the memory of the *fédérations* of 1815, that is the massive paramilitary political associations that supported Napoleon after his flight from the island of Elba. The peculiar spirit of the *fédérés*, which has recently been defined as "revolutionary Bonapartism," both informed the programs of the political underground and inspired the idiom of the opposition intellectual community during the 1820s.[17]

Moreover, in the early 1820s French republicanism and Bonapartism were drawn together by Louis XVIII's armed intervention in Spain on behalf of Ferdinand VII, who had been forced to accept a liberal constitution. The tyrannical solidarity between the two branches of the Bourbon dynasty fostered the cohesion between the two branches of, so to speak, the revolutionary dynasty. It was only in the late 1820s that the joint effects of Louis XVIII's military success in Spain and the failures of Carbonari in France and Italy were to compel the heirs of the French revolutionary tradition to revise both their tactical devices and their political programs. Grouped around the charismatic figure of Filippo Buonarroti—a survivor of Gracchus Babeuf's famous plot of 1796, the Conspiracy of the Equals—some of the most prominent European revolutionaries would finally work for the separation of the Jacobin legacy from the Napoleonic one.[18] But this is a slightly different story, significant in a post-1830 rather than pre-1830 perspective. It is by no means arbitrary to conclude, with the Dutch historian Pieter Geyl, that a remarkable ideological feature of the first post-Waterloo generation is the association of the Napoleonic legend with radicalism.[19]

Geyl's half-century-old book *Napoleon For and Against* still stands as an important contribution to the bibliography on the subject. A rigid antithesis between ninteenth-century supporters and antagonists of the New Regime is a commonplace among scholars; but it is inadequate to address the French Revolution and its aftermath as a whole (that is, from 1789 to 1815). What is especially noteworthy in reviewing nineteenth-century visions of the French Revolution through the heroic, the organic, the messianic, the critical, and the pathological "eyes," is precisely the fact that none of these visions easily fits in a dichotomic framework.

An example of this general pattern is the attitude of Russian Decembrists towards the French Revolution. As young officers, most of them had actually fought Napoleon between 1812 and 1815, finally entering Paris with the victorious Russian army. Moreover, they had been too deeply influenced by the rationalistic, tolerant, humane legacy of the Enlightenment to ever consider the guillotine a viable solution for civil war. Their favorite French mentors were, indeed, Mme de Staël and Benjamin Constant rather than Saint-Just or Robespierre.[20] Still, Decembrists recalled their military experience in Napoleonic France as the amazing discovery of a new, developed, and after all attractive world.[21] Furthermore, in Alexander I's Russia, the Eastern bastion of the Holy Alliance, the officers engaged in the Decembrist movement ended up delving into the history of the Jacobin and Napoleonic phases of the Revolution in a vein quite comparable to that of Carbonari officers in France. With their Western counterparts, Pavel Pestel and other Decembrist leaders shared both the fascination for a powerful provisional government, somehow fashioned after the example of the Committee of Public Safety, and the dread of its drift towards military dictatorship.[22]

More generally, what was at stake in European thought was the proper evaluation of the role of the individual in history (artistically a characteristic concern of romanticism, politically a characteristic concern of liberalism). The French Revolution had started the process, both welcomed and feared, of democratizing and popularizing heroism. Interestingly, this issue was raised in several memoirs written by former officers, both French and Italian, of the Grande Armée: people, that is, who had personally experienced the social and psychological effects of the so-called amalgam between the units of the old royal army and the new Republican draftees. At a less sophisticated level than the one reached by Thierry, Guizot, and Mignet—

the most discerning among the French historians of the 1820s—
these former officers were dealing with the very same problem. Each
group foreshadowed the need to reconcile two intrinsically contradictory organizing principles dear to nineteenth-century liberalism:
every man a hero, and every man at his post.[23]

The problem of the democratization and the popularization of
heroism also lies at the core of the romantic historical novel. Since
Lukács's pathbreaking study on the topic, research has emphasized
the so-called "mediocre hero" as a distinctive component of the historical novel. Yet, as the literary critic Paul M. Lützeler has cogently
argued, mediocrity is less typical of the romantic novel's hero than is
a low place in the social ladder; likewise, the main character of a
given novel is hardly its sole hero.[24] While in the classic *Bildungs-
roman* the hero unquestionably plays a central role, in the historical
novel of the Restoration individuals are important insofar as their
personal vicissitudes highlight the conflicts of all sorts—between
generations, classes, nations, regions, religions, and institutions—by
which those individuals are surrounded and eventually overwhelmed.
According to Lützeler, both the devaluation and the diffusion of the
romantic hero are related to the experience of the French Revolution
and the Napoleonic wars.[25] This relation is explicit in the finest historical novel of the decade, Honoré de Balzac's *The Last Chouan or
Brittany in 1800* (1829).[26]

Balzac's literary master was Walter Scott, whose tremendous appeal to European writers and readers of the age of Romanticism had
to do with a peculiar capacity to construct plots in tune with the fundamental political, social, and religious preoccupations of the time.
As for France, Scott's fictional treatment of relations between bourgeoisie and aristocracy appeared particularly captivating to the post-
revolutionary generation: for Scott sympathized with aristocratic social values, but he knew a lost cause when he saw one.[27] Reading
Scott's novels, and eventually writing following his example, French
intellectual élites of the 1820s could assimilate Edmund Burke's lesson about the inescapable value of past and the continuity of historical traditions,[28] without yielding to the first and fiercest British critic
of the French Revolution.

Nothing is more distant from Scott's mediocre, devalued, diffuse
hero, than Lord Byron's "demonic" one: the former is a pawn of British history, almost interchangeable with any of his peers; the latter

is a unique figure somehow in touch with divine and diabolic patrons rather than with human characters. While Scott was becoming a mentor for the liberal historians of the French Restoration, who were basically interested in praising the progressive role of the middle classes, Byron was adopted as a muse by Hugo, Lamartine, and other young poets confusingly committed—at least until the middle 1820s—to the eulogizing of legitimism. Still, one might argue that Scott's and Byron's influences on both writers and readers in Restoration France represent the two sides of the same coin: the coin being the widespread intellectual urge to assess the contribution of individuals to French history since the Revolution. To his French audience, Scott illustrated the strength and limits of historical necessity, whereas Byron disclosed a Pandora's box of personal responsibility.

The indelible memory of the Terror overshadowed Restoration France. In 1816, Louis XVIII had banished those among the former members of the National Convention who had both voted to carry out the capital punishment of Louis XVI in 1793 and formally supported Napoleon during the Hundred Days. One-hundred-fifty-three "regicides," out of 206 still surviving, had then had to leave the country, for sad old age in Brussels, Nice, or some obscure Swiss cantons.[29] Despite the Bourbons' hopes, however, the ban of the Conventionnels did not lead France to collective amnesia about the Revolution. On the one hand, legitimist devotees kept publishing lists of *votants* in the decisive sessions of the Convention's rule, and—more royalist than the king—kept tracking those persons they presumed to be responsible for countless revolutionary crimes in the departments. On the other hand, because the Restoration did inherit much of the revolutionary social and political legacy, imaginations were puzzled by the character of the terrorist.

In French people's memories and fantasies, in pamphlets and novels,[30] a short step separated the hero from the criminal, the titan from the monster. The romantic fascination with the role of the individual in the recent national saga helps to explain the success of the gothic novel and the Byronian poem with the French public. Furthermore, such a climate is reflected in the growing importance of the representation of the devil in French literature. One thinks, among dozens of texts, of Vigny's and Balzac's juvenilia, respectively *Eloa* (1824) and *Le Corrupteur* (1827), although the most passionate contribution to this literary vein is probably Claire Destay's *La Fille de Dieu ou l'Héroïne des Pyrénées* (1821), a novel which explicitly deals with the double nature—diabolic *and* angelic—of the French terrorist.[31]

Destay's "daughter of God" is Marie, a charming foundling from a tiny village in the French Pyrenees, who feels sent to redeem through her love Céoli, an apostate Catholic priest overpowerful in that province as commissioner of the Committee of Public Safety, in 1793. Céoli's wild orgies do not inhibit Marie from loving "the Jacobin's beauty," nor does his ruthless revolutionary career prevent her from recognizing in Céoli's crimes a sort of Herculean, desperate attempt to liberate mankind from evil. By the end, a fearless Marie encounters the guillotine, while Céoli (who does not save Marie from the scaffold because he places his Jacobin reputation before love) leaves revolutionary France, to wander aimlessly around the world, both aware of his historical role and upset by his own guilt.[32]

The philosophical *pendant* to this gothic narrative had been published two years earlier by an original Catholic thinker, Pierre-Simon Ballanche.[33] *L'Homme sans nom* is the poignant if dull account of the elderly life of a former Conventionnel, who is driven by his guilty conscience to endure deliberately a strict segregation from the rest of the human race. Unlike other personae molded by writers of the Restoration out of French revolutionary characters, Ballanche's Unnamed is a completely Christian figure, held firmly in the grip of the traditional dialectic between sin and redemption.[34] Admittedly, the author was conscious of the heterodoxy of this representation, for he managed to have only 100 copies of the book published.

One might wonder whether one of the few copies of Ballanche's book fell into the hands of a foreign writer profoundly influenced by French culture, both romantic and Catholic: Alessandro Manzoni, the leading figure in Italian nineteenth-century literature. Although Manzoni's correspondence offers no evidence that he read *L'Homme sans nom*, he does depict a Satanic old man with no name, Innominato, in the central chapters of his masterpiece, the historical novel *The Betrothed* (1827). Some forty years before actually devoting an essay to the history of the French Revolution, and before denouncing the totally gratuitous character of the political breach of 1789,[35] Manzoni explores the gratuitous crimes of Innominato in seventeenth-century Lombardy as a way of probing the essence of sin, the puzzling shift from innocence to guilt.

The novel's setting in the seventeenth century contributes to placing Innominato's wrongs in a broad, providentialist perspective. Yet
ignoring the relationship between the historical problem of French
revolutionary violence and Manzoni's literary account of Innominato's awful career would be somewhat like dismissing the implicit influence of the experience of the Terror in shaping the famous portrait
of the public executioner in Joseph de Maistre's *Soirées de Saint-
Pétersbourg* (1821).[36] In fact, both texts illustrate the endeavor of
some true Catholic believers to exorcize French revolutionary evil,
by ransoming the evil itself through a teleological perspective. Besides, the scene of Innominato's conversion before Cardinal Borro-
meo in Manzoni's novel inaugurated a theme which was to become
common in nineteenth-century literary representations of penitent
revolutionary characters, the climax of this topos being the chapter
on former Conventionnel G. and Bishop Myriel in Victor Hugo's *Les
Misérables* (1862).[37]

Novels, histories, memoirs of the French Revolution: in Restoration France was any of these literary genres perceived as more threatening for the institutions, in other words more "republican," than
the others? In 1827, Achille Roche—the young author of a wary *Histoire de la Révolution française* (1825), who was then rapidly moving towards radicalism—warned writers of historical novels to "submit to the approval of reason" the fantasies to which a "nebulous
imagination" had led them; it was time for historical truth, Roche
maintained.[38] More recently, a scholar has argued that in Restoration
France, there was no better and safer way to endorse the legacy of the
French Revolution than to write a history of the Revolution itself.[39]
Two young friends from Provence, Adolphe Thiers and François Mignet, did it in such a masterly way that the publication of their histories of the Revolution changed their lives, transforming two impatient journalists into left-wing opinion-makers.[40] Editing French
revolutionary memoirs eventually proved to be not safe at all. In
1829, Achille Roche was brought to trial for having transformed a
rough manuscript of recollections by a former Montagnard, René Levasseur, into a four-volume work. Indeed, Bourbon prosecutors were
unlikely to agree with the principle that the counsel for the defense,
Saint-Albin Berville, presented before the court as plain truth: "An
opinion on a historical fact, whatever it be, cannot constitute an offense in the eyes of the law."[41]

Berville was in a position to make this point, for from 1820 to 1828, together with Barrière, he had skillfully edited—without having to face any major judicial consequence—a 56-volume *Collection des Mémoires relatifs à la Révolution française*. This series was not only a commercial success in the sluggish book market of Restoration France; it was, also, an arsenal of liberal propaganda, given that a characteristic of the series was to classify as moderates and constitutionals members of the Convention who would normally have been regarded as extremists and criminals.[42] Under the ultra-conservative French governments of the 1820s, the publication of works by Girondins such as Barbaroux, Louvet, Mme Roland, by Dantonists like Desmoulins and Fréron, even by a banished Conventionnel such as Thibaudeau, was truly a *tour de force*.

Bertrand Barère, another Montagnard exile, did not believe in Berville and Barrière's good faith. The publishers of the *Collection des Mémoires* offered Barère ten thousand francs a volume for his recollections of the French Revolution; but Barère, former spokesman of the Committee of Public Safety, fearing "a trap of the French police,"[43] chose to have his memoirs published posthumously.[44] However, for an historical understanding of European nineteenth-century visions of the French Revolution, Barère's cautious recollections are less important than the tremendously influential reaction they stimulated in an English reader, Thomas Babington Macaulay. In a lurid review of Barère's *Memoirs* (1844), the Whig parliamentarian and historian pointed at Barère as the nearest incarnation—"in history or fiction . . . man or devil"—of consummate depravity:

A man who, having been blessed by nature with a bland disposition, gradually brings himself to inflict misery on his fellow-creatures with indifference, with satisfaction, and, at length, with a hideous rapture, deserves to be regarded as a portent of wickedness; and such a man was Barère . . . Rigid principles often do for feeble minds what stays do for feeble bodies. But Barère had no principles at all. His character was equally destitute of natural and of acquired strength . . . The weakest and most servile of human beings found himself on a sudden an actor in a revolution which convulsed the whole civilized world. At first he fell under the influence of humane and moderate men, and talked the language of humanity and moderation. But he soon found himself surrounded by fierce and resolute spirits, scared by no danger, and restrained by no scruple. He had to choose whether he would be their victim or their accomplice. His choice was soon made. He tasted blood, and felt no loathing; he tasted it again, and liked it well. Cruelty became with him first a habit, then a passion, at last a madness.[45]

≺ II ≻

The Organic Eye

From October 1831 to April 1832, a newly-founded and increasingly influential Parisian magazine, *La Revue des Deux Mondes*, published in serial form an historical narrative by Alfred de Vigny. The novel, *Stello*, soon printed as an independent volume, attested to the extent of Vigny's political disillusionment with legitimism, republicanism, Christianity, Saint-Simonianism. The author took a particularly severe stance on the inter-generational dynamic ongoing in the French political arena, where "ambitious centenarians" pretended to hang upon the doctrine of "beardless boys, their dupes," and "children" hoisted themselves on tiptoe "to exhort grown men." Furthermore, according to Vigny, deeds which had been, since 1789, "the shame of families" were invoked, by 1832, as "a sort of claim to fame (a legacy dear to many a self-made man)."[46]

Vigny was pointing to, and complaining about, a peculiar feature of the French revolutionary tradition, namely the role played by familial networks in keeping the tradition alive. Almost the whole history of republicanism in nineteenth-century France is reflected in the individual stories of countless sons of French revolutionaries, Hippolyte Carnot—the minister of education of the Second Republic—and Auguste Blanqui—the chief of the revolutionary opposition to the Second Empire—representing only the tip of the iceberg.[47] Evidence of the sons' role in reshaping the legend is to be found also across the Channel. While exiled in London during the 1830s, Godefroy Cavaignac, the son of a former Conventionnel, served as an historical consultant to both Etienne Cabet and Thomas Carlyle, who were then preparing their narratives of the French Revolution.[48] A few years earlier, the son of a leading counter-revolutionary propagandist of the 1790s, Jacques Mallet du Pan, acted as a French revolutionary expert for William Smyth, Regius professor of modern history in Cambridge, who was the first Englishman to write on the French Revolution as a professional historian.[49] Conversely, Jacobin parentage could prove to be almost unbearable.[50] The burden of inheriting the name and the blame of French revolutionary fathers is vividly described in nineteenth-century novels such as Balzac's *L'envers de l'histoire contemporaine* (1844–47) and Barbey d'Aurevilly's *Un prêtre marié* (1864).

Let us return to Alfred de Vigny's novel, *Stello*, whose third and main episode, "A Tale of the Terror," opens with a digression on how liberals and democrats were dealing with the political heritage of the French Revolution. Once again, Vigny uses sarcasm: "When they want to make use of the dead, they promptly lend them their systems; everybody makes one up, good, bad, or indifferent; it's a saddle that's good for every horse, and it has to fit. Do you want to ride the Committee of Public Safety? All you have to do is make it wear your saddle!"[51] Despite its inescapably aristocratic and somewhat annoying tone, Vigny's novel deserves extensive quotation, since it contains an accurate analysis of the three left-wing "systems" predominant in France during the 1830s. This analysis is both exceptionally insightful for its day, and particularly functional for my own argument.

The first system Vigny refers to attributes to the terrorists "an edifying project for a continuous mitigation of their own tyranny," crediting them with an unfaltering faith in the triumph of virtue. Clearly, Vigny is thinking of people like Mignet and Thiers, whose liberal interpretation of 1793 contained no denigration of the Jacobin phase of the French Revolution.[52] The spokesmen of the French generation of 1820[53] were interested less in Benjamin Constant and Mme de Staël's historical problem—whether the Terror had been inevitable or not—than in the political rise, through the First Republic and the Napoleonic empire, of the French middle classes.[54] In Vigny's terms, the second system does the terrorists "the honour of ascribing a religious doctrine to them." The author of *Stello* has evidently in mind his friend Philippe Buchez, who was then setting up his own Christian interpretation of the French Revolution.[55] According to Vigny's third system, the French revolutionary leaders in 1793 were "deeply devoted to the interests of the people," and prepared to sacrifice everything "for the progress of humanity." Here, Vigny is concerned with the neo-Robespierrist revival promoted by the seminal books of an old revolutionary, Filippo Buonarroti, and a young one, Paul-Mathieu Laurent (de l'Ardèche): respectively, the *History of Babeuf's Conspiracy for Equality* (1828) and the *Réfutation de l' "Histoire de France" de l'abbé de Montgaillard* (1828).

Mignet and Thiers's interpretation of the Terror as a regime necessitated by the dramatic circumstances of 1793 sounds familiar: it has been updated and reinforced by the scholarly contributions of the

Third, Fourth, and Fifth French republics. In the first half of the nineteenth century, their histories influenced the common reading of the
Revolution by liberating French middle classes from the guilt complex of the Terror and providing them with a strong confidence in the
natural growth of bourgeois society.[56] However, in the short term, the
other two "systems" Vigny was pointing to in 1832 were to mold
even more crucially the current visions of the French Revolution.
Buchez's documentary enterprise, the *Histoire parlementaire de la
Révolution française* (1834–38), offered an historical groundwork to
the "populist religion" that informed much of the French left-wing
propaganda in the late 1830s and the 1840s.[57] Meanwhile, Laurent's
re-evaluation of the most radical phase of the French Revolution kept
infusing the neo-Jacobin revival.[58]

In the late 1820s, both Buchez and Laurent were leading figures
of the Saint-Simonian family (or group, or sect, or whatever we might
agree to call it).[59] Their reflections on the history of the French Revolution need to be put in the context of the configuration of scien-
tism, messianism, and socialism, which a whole cohort of passionate
Europeans learned in the books of Charles Fourier, Saint-Simon, and
Auguste Comte. Profoundly affected by the twin ruptures of the
French and the Industrial revolutions, most of the members of this
intellectual cohort searched for a rhythm of events in human history.
The Saint-Simonians' search, oriented in this matter as much by the
works of Pierre-Simon Ballanche as by the ones of Saint-Simon,[60] actually led to the statement of a law of progressive periodic mutation.
In the Saint-Simonian reading,[61] historical progress relied on an al-
ternating movement of so-called organic epochs—that is, epochs
socially balanced and essentially religious—and of critical epochs—
that is, epochs socially destructive and politically anarchical.

According to the Saint-Simonian doctrine, the French Revolution
came at the peak of a five-century-long critical epoch: it was the welcomed decree executed by history against a European order which
was as old as the Catholic system in religion and the feudal system
in polity. Yet, when Laurent de l'Ardèche asked the French generation of the 1820s to admire the "inflexible democrats" of the National Convention, he did not mean to endorse the democratic legacy of the Revolution. Laurent admired Robespierre and the Jacobins
mainly because their rule had shown the limits of democracy. "An
inherently transitory system," democracy had been muddied forever

by the Terror, and successfully overcome by the Napoleonic empire.[62] By the end of 1828, Laurent had published, in addition to the *Réfutation de l'Histoire de France*, an *Histoire de l'Empereur Napoléon* (richly illustrated by Horace Vernet), which acclaimed the historical role of Bonaparte as Caesar of the modern times.

Except for the books of Laurent, the Saint-Simonian interpretation of the French Revolution did not produce significant historical works, Buchez's *Histoire parlementaire* belonging to the Christian rather than to the Saint-Simonian stage of his ideological career. Nonetheless, in reconsidering nineteenth-century visions of the French Revolution one can hardly overestimate the importance of the "organic eye." The Saint-Simonian historical perspective ended by launching and disseminating a Bonapartist interpretation of the Revolution precisely in Bonapartism's most critical years: those running from the death of Napoleon I at the beginning of the 1820s, to the advent of his nephew Louis Napoleon (the future Napoleon III) on the European political scene in the mid-1830s. Furthermore, during the 1830s some of the most prominent European political analysts—John Stuart Mill, Heinrich Heine, Alexander Herzen among others—were inspired by Saint-Simonianism in looking both backward to the French Revolution and forward to the future of freedom and equality.[63] And a sort of Saint-Simonian filter seems to have been installed, so to speak, on Thomas Carlyle's fish-eye lens, giving a peculiar color to his narrative of the French Revolution.

Carlyle borrowed from his friend John Stuart Mill both the interest in Saint-Simonianism and the project of an essay on the French Revolution.[64] There is strong evidence of the impact of Saint-Simonianism on Carlyle's philosophy of history, particularly in his exposition of the laws of progress in *Sartor Resartus* (1833–34), as well as in almost all his historical works of the 1830s. In *The French Revolution: A History* (1837), the interpretation of the period 1789–99 as the final destruction of feudalism instead of a time of constructive faith, and the conclusion that democracy and anarchy are synonymous, are consistent with the Saint-Simonian doctrine.[65] By stressing the revolutionary contribution to the downfall of the Old Regime, but also the revolutionary drift into the cul-de-sac of political democracy, the *Lectures on the History of Literature* (1838) and the essay on *Chartism* (1839) reiterate the Saint-Simonian exegesis of the French Revolution as the negation of a negation. Carlyle's belief in the epochal

role of individuals in history, as it is firmly stated in his lectures of
1840, *On Hero, Hero-Worship and the Heroic in History*, appears to
be consistent with such premises. The following passage on Napoleon, for example, sounds literally Saint-Simonian: "To bridle-in that
great devouring, self-devouring French Revolution; to *tame* it, so
that it may become *organic*, and be able to live among other organisms and *formed* things, not as a wasting destruction alone: is this
not still what [Napoleon] partly aimed at?"[66]

Interpreting the French Revolution as the negation of a negation
induced Saint-Simonian observers to evaluate the Napoleonic rule
as the resulting positive product: a few years prior to Carlyle's lectures on hero-worship, Heinrich Heine defined Napoleon as "a Saint-
Simonian Emperor."[67] Images of power and marble hands taming anarchy abound in Heine's writings of the decade: they suggest that it
was via Caesarism rather than via republicanism that he was looking for a solid link between the issues of religion and equality.[68] As
historian George G. Iggers has convincingly argued, political disillusionment after the dismal revolution of 1830 made Heine aware
of the social and economic foundations of politics; and the Saint-
Simonian request for equal economic opportunities, combined with
its authoritarian emphasis on the hierarchical structure of society,
harmonized Heine's democratic convictions with his unfailing faith
in monarchy and his fundamental distrust of the masses.[69]

A thousand miles east, Alexander Herzen, a young member of
the Russian enlightened gentry, could hardly agree with Heine's ap-
praisal of Napoleon: to his great pride, Herzen was born in Moscow
in 1812, the very year of the Great Patriotic War. Still, insofar as the
distances and the censorship allowed him, Herzen undertook, in the
early 1830s, a nearly Western training in philosophy of history and in
history.[70] After having devoured Schelling's works, he enthusiastically read, among others, those of Michelet, Guizot, and Thierry.
Moreover, he carefully studied Buchez's *Introduction à la science
de l'histoire* (1833), devoting to this book an essay which circulated
among his fellows at the University of Moscow. Above all, appalled
by the outcomes of the July revolution of 1830 and the Polish revolt
of 1830–31, Herzen espoused the Saint-Simonian doctrine, along
with the Saint-Simonian diagnosis on the merits and limits of the
French Revolution.

"We feel . . . that the world is waiting for a renewal; that the revolution of 1789 is broken, and that a new era must be brought about through *palingenesis*. European society must be given new foundations, based more firmly on right, on morality and on culture. This is the actual meaning of our experiences—this is Saint-Simonianism": the well-known letter of Herzen to his friend Nicolai Ogarev[71] attests to the precocious development of an "historiosophical" arsenal which Herzen would employ endlessly over the years.[72] Among its weapons, this arsenal included the Saint-Simonian idea that the French Revolution was an end and not a beginning, the Saint-Simonian skeptical attitude about the achievements of Western democracy, and the jargon borrowed from Ballanche[73] about the final palingenesis which was still to come. Furthermore, Herzen was preparing himself to use the romantic analogy between nations and organisms, and the consequent comparison between "old" and "young" peoples, to the advantage of such recent arrivals in history as the Slavs.[74]

≺ III ≻

The Messianic Eye

During the 1830s, the same themes occurred again and again in the European literature concerning the legacy of the French Revolution. The diffusion of particular ideas and images could be attributed to the physical mobility and intellectual prestige of single individuals (one thinks of Ludvig Börne and Heinrich Heine, whose reportages on July-Monarchy Paris molded the "sentimental education" of German youth during the whole decade) as well as to the wide circulation of printed materials such as *Le Globe* and *La Revue encyclopédique*.[75] Yet, one can perceive resonant accents in texts which had no access to each other. When the Italian revolutionary Giuseppe Mazzini wrote, in his political credo *Faith and Future* (1835), "The past is fatal to us. The French Revolution crushes us,"[76] he was unlikely to know that the German agitator and poet Georg Büchner had avowed to his girlfriend, in a letter of January 1834: "I studied the history of the Revolution. I felt myself crushed under the frightful fatalism of history."[77]

The title *Faith and Future* tells us much about the ideological priorities of Mazzini, the leading revolutionary in post-1830 Europe. Insofar as religion was concerned, the "fatalist" interpretation of the

Revolution—as it had been set by the French historians of the Restoration—proved to be, if consoling for some revolutionary heirs,
unbearable for others. Indeed, secularization was one of the mixed
blessings that posterity received from the French Revolution. The
traditional dichotomy of supporters and adversaries of the French
revolutionary tradition does not explain the cross-fertilizing influence of writers like Maistre and Ballanche in orienting nineteenth-
century reflections on secularization. Like the legitimist thinkers,
the admirers of the French Revolution believed, to a greater or lesser
extent, that the social world of free and equal individuals, as it had
emerged from 1789, had failed to found a political community based
solely on the unitary will of its members.[78]

European literati were not yet prepared to face openly the nexus
between the heritage of the French Revolution and the demystification of the Western world. Like other doctrines related to so-called
utopian socialism, Saint-Simonianism (a cause that both Mazzini
and Büchner embraced for a while) reflected the urge for an all-
encompassing response to the political, social, and religious threats
inherited from the French Revolution. After the sudden decline of
the Saint-Simonian dogma, the search for a viable solution to the
problems posed by the revolutionary legacy took mainly the form
of a providential interpretation of the events of 1789–99, in which
Girondins and Montagnards alternatively played the role of prophets.
Many European intellectuals of the 1830s and 1840s tried to cast the
French Revolution within a messianic framework.

For France, Philippe Buchez's career is almost archetypical.[79] Buchez discovered the Gospels in the middle of the 1820s, while still
a young leader of the Carbonari movement. Later on, the espousal
of the Saint-Simonian faith oriented this former militant atheist toward a re-evaluation of Christian moral values. By the time Buchez
edited the *Histoire parlementaire de la Révolution française* (1834–
38), whose dozens of volumes in octavo were to replace the yellowed
and rare copies of the *Moniteur* on the bookshelves of European intellectual élites, he was ready to assert the Catholic nature of popular
sovereignty of 1793. According to Buchez, the revolutionary notion
of popular sovereignty was essentially Catholic, since it meant that
each be subject to all; likewise, this notion was Catholic since it proceeded directly from the influence of the Church.[80]

In his study on populist religion and left-wing propaganda in July-

Monarchy France, the historian Edward Berenson has demonstrated that while the culture of the *juste-milieu*, which was incarnated in Guizot, Thiers, and Mignet, found how to keep alive the secular tradition of the Enlightenment and the Revolution, the left-wing intellectual opposition to Louis Philippe increasingly turned towards Catholicism in looking for a critique of the Orleanist regime.[81] From Felicité de Lammenais's *Paroles d'un croyant* (1834) to Victor Considérant's *Démocratie pacifique* (1840), from Quinet's *Le Christianisme et la Révolution française* (1845) to Lamartine's *Histoire des Girondins* (1847), from Alphonse Esquiros's *Histoire des Montagnards* (1847) to Pierre Leroux's *Démocratie et christianisme* (1848), those works which put the history of the French Revolution in the broader perspective of the history of Christianity and secularization were based on the hope for a republic built on "fraternité" rather than "liberté" or "égalité."[82] Jules Michelet himself, no matter the depth of his commitment to lay culture, set as the main goal of his *History of the French Revolution* the conversion of his readers rather than the elucidation of the past.[83]

For the French republican propagandists, if not for their popular audiences,[84] claiming the Catholic essence of the Jacobin credo and disguising the social outcomes of the 1790s as a comforting interclass achievement were a way of taming the political implications of actual social conflicts. The most striking example of this attitude is offered by Etienne Cabet's *Histoire populaire de la Révolution française* (1839–40), which was written in London during the author's five-year banishment due to his political opposition to the Orleanist regime. Chiefly, Cabet stressed the joint contribution of the middle and lower classes to the decisive episodes of the Revolution, including the massacres of September 1792 in the Parisian prisons. Far from being a ludicrous parody of justice, a horrible butchery, these massacres were—according to Cabet—a sort of Catholic festival, an eighteenth-century happening much more meaningful than the ones that occurred during the sixteenth-century wars of religion: "[The September massacres] showed the strength of the popular feelings . . . the mistrust for immorality, the love of justice, the respect of innocence, the unselfishness . . . They showed the presence of humane feelings that were absent in St. Bartholomew Day."[85]

After the failure of the conspiracy plots of the 1830s, the 1840s marked a change in the methods of republican propaganda within

France. On the one hand, the 1840s witnessed—at least in Paris—a new form of public teaching of the French Revolution, thanks to Michelet's and Quinet's well-attended lectures at the Collège de France.[86] On the other hand, this decade experienced a commercial boom in politically-oriented almanacs, a literary genre which since the Revolution had been considered the most proper tool to achieve a mass diffusion of the democratic ideals.[87] Yet, while coupling the glorification of the *sans-culottes* with the denunciation of the miserable conditions of workers' lives in July-Monarchy Paris, the almanacs did not produce a significant renewal in the content of republican propaganda. The authors of and contributors to the almanacs represented the élite of the French left-wing *demi-monde*—Cabet, Blanqui, Laponneraye, Carnot, Daumier, Michelet, Quinet, Sand. None of them, however, openly faced the main problem of political messianism; that is, the paradox of a doctrine which claimed to be both revolutionary and traditional, both factional and ecumenical.

Moreover, during the 1840s non-written political messages related to the First Republic—songs, engravings, statues—gradually became commonplace.[88] The revolutionary tradition became banal as well as diffuse. A knowledgeable young Swiss traveler in Paris, Jacob Burckhardt, was right when he noted, in June 1843: "One only gets a mythical notion of the first Revolution; on the whole, Paris is far more absorbed in an anxious care for the future than in recollections of its past, although the individual memorials are legion."[89] Had Burckhardt spent a few more months in the French capital, exploring the amazingly rich collections of the Bibliothèque Royale, he would have met in the library another German-speaking traveler, who was also 25 years old when he first arrived in Paris, in October 1843: Karl Marx. These two *rats de bibliothèque* had almost nothing in common but their hard-working habits and a critical stance towards the role played by the French revolutionary vulgate in shaping nineteenth-century political culture.

Marx, Arnold Ruge, and other Young Hegelians fleeing Germany because of the severity of local censorship carried into France a personal reputation for atheism which did not help them establish productive relationships with the leaders of the French republican movement.[90] Evidently, not just individual choices about religious issues were at stake; so were different philosophical approaches to the French revolutionary heritage. Writing in the socialist journal *La Revue indépendante* in November 1843, Louis Blanc warned the Young Hegelians against the pernicious influence of atheism in recent European history; namely, the materialist nature of the bourgeois order established in 1789 France by the heirs of the *philosophes*.[91] Marx replied with his well-known essay *The Jewish Question* (1844), underscoring the illusory character of any revolution which purports to overcome social conflicts by investing politically in a new state, instead of abolishing the state itself. Thereafter, Marx turned his attention to Britain, focusing mainly on economic matters and giving up his project of a history of the French convention.[92]

The abandonment of such a project looks all the more understandable from a 1848 standpoint, for young Marx's failure to achieve an historical critique of Jacobinism should be considered, as much as the result of his intellectual evolution, the reflection of his militant career. Unmasking the illusory nature of the Jacobin investment in politics would have been a tactical mistake in the context of the European revolutionary dynamic of the 1840s. Authoritative studies have indeed stressed the "Jacobin" character of Marx's involvement in the Rhenish revolution of 1848–49. In the Rhineland, which had been annexed to the Grande Nation during the Napoleonic years, the memory of the French Revolution was surprisingly vital and extremely popular. Following the example of the revolutionaries of the 1790s, the Rhineland democrats of 1848–49—and particularly Marx, despite his reputation as leader of class struggle—successfully created cross-class coalitions against monarchy and state bureaucracy.[93]

Until the publication of the *Communist Manifesto* in March 1848, Marx did not play a significant role on Europe's political scene. In mid-1840s Paris, the center of the exiles' stage was occupied by the Polish poet Adam Mickiewicz. A close friend of Quinet and Michelet, Mickiewicz was by no means an historian of the French Revolution: from 1840 to 1844, he gave passionate lectures on Slavic literature at the Collège de France. Still, Mickiewicz did find his way into a public teaching of the Revolution, depicting the latter as an extraordinary manifestation of the Christian spirit in action.[94] In Mickiewicz's view, the historical evidence of the dechristianization of 1793 was not sufficient to prove the anti-Christian temper of sans-culottism. While murdering priests and destroying churches, he argued, French revolutionaries gave Jesus Christ the title of *sans-culotte*: "An ignoble title to be sure, but the most noble of those that people held at the time."[95]

Neither Quinet nor Michelet, the two most perceptive historians of the Revolution of the time, agreed completely with such an interpretation of sans-culottism. Quinet criticized the Jacobins for missing an historical chance, that of revitalizing the social body by introducing Protestantism in France; whereas Michelet recognized, in the dechristianization of 1793, evidence of the limits of the lay religion inaugurated by the federation movement of 1790. Nonetheless, the two professors of the Collège de France shared with their colleague Mickiewicz the conviction that the French revolutionary legacy had to be relaunched not by stressing its social and political divides, but by reaching that sort of religious unanimity which the revolutionaries of the 1790s had failed to attain.[96] The underlying rationale of such an approach might be summarized as follows: the best revolution is one everybody can agree with and take advantage of, any other revolution being inevitably ill-fated.

The spirit of the great histories of the French Revolution that were published in 1847 (Lamartine's and Esquiros's whole narratives, Michelet's and Blanc's first two volumes) somehow anticipated what was to be the behavior of their authors in 1848: it prefigured their naive delight in the peaceful February revolution, and their total inability to understand the frightening dynamic of June. Again, Jacob Burckhardt deserves attention, for his antipathetic stance towards left-wing European intellectuals had the benefit of foresight, in the days of the Polish upheaval in Galicia and of the communist challenge on both sides of the Rhine. Writing from Basel in February 1846, Burckhardt pitied the foolishness of those bourgeois intellectuals who trusted their own capacity for controlling the flow of popular grievances: "They are the Feuillants of the coming movement, which like the French Revolution will develop as a natural phenomenon, involving everything that is hellish in human nature."[97]

The events of 1848–49 disclosed both the existence of crude social antagonisms within the borders of France and the unlikeliness of a unanimous revolution on the continental scale. After the revolution of February 1848, the sober domestic policies of the French Second Republic, largely opposed to the radical ones of the First in confessional and economic matters, did not prevent the tragic Parisian in-

surrection of June. Meanwhile, as a political leader of the Second Republic, Lamartine (the historian of the Girondins, the most bellicose
faction in the National Convention of 1792) undertook an extremely
cautious foreign policy, well-described by the title of his poem *La
Marseillaise de la paix*. Italian revolutionaries fighting for the unification of their country, as well as Polish exiles striving to bring the issue of independent Poland high on the international agenda, discovered the ultimate truth about political messianism: however
Christian in its premises and aims, the struggle for revolutionary values implied, in Holy-Alliance Europe, the necessity of bloodshed;
and fifty years after the battles of the Grande Nation, the blood of
Frenchmen belonged solely to France.[98]

≺ IV ≻

The Critical Eye

The terrible violence and the dismal outcomes of the European revolutions of 1848–49 led the continental intelligentsia to share a
mournful judgment on the viability of all the political traditions inaugurated by the French Revolution: liberalism, Jacobinism, legitimism. One could recall here the obvious names of political analysts
such as Marx, Tocqueville, Bagehot, though no quotation from their
writings would be more eloquent than Charles Baudelaire's "We all
celebrate some funeral."[99]

Baudelaire might have been right, if others had not celebrated triumphs. Both in France and in Germany[100] during the 1850s and the
1860s, historians backed up politicians by separating history's great
men from history's steady course, isolating them and raising them
into myth.[101] Ironically, Caesarism became a milestone in the trend
towards the democratization of politics.[102] One year before Louis
Bonaparte's coup d'état of December 1851, Auguste Romieu, an obscure publicist of the Bonapartist entourage, achieved continental
celebrity by writing *L'ère des Césars* (1850), an endeavor to legitimize—before the fact—the seizure of power by the nephew of Napoleon I. After the coup d'état, French writers hostile to republicanism felt all the more able to praise the peculiar form of popular sovereignty embodied in Louis Bonaparte's plebiscitary democracy. The
content of the historical works on the French Revolution written

by the supporters of the Second Empire is hence predictable. These works depicted the revolutionary dynamic as a pitiful sequence of aristocratic conspiracies, political betrayals, and social failures, until the welcome advent of Napoleon in Brumaire Year VII (November 1799).[103]

The fall of the Second Republic warned the republicans too of the fragility of the French revolutionary tradition, which had attempted to remain faithful to two contradictory principles: universal male suffrage and the right of insurrection.[104] Understandably enough, the results of the plebiscites nourished in the purist republican souls an increasing mistrust for politics; yet, the fiery reaction to the Napoleonic coup by a significant portion of the French peasantry kept feeding their obsession with politics. The combination of these two elements, mistrust for and obsession with politics, gave the literature produced by the opponents of the Second Empire (most of whom were exiled) its unique imprint. In their books and articles, poems and dramas, journals and letters, the republicans still dreamed of a new 1789; but they now knew that any 1789 is followed by a new 1793, and any 1793 by a new 1799.[105] They had learned that there is no revolution without terror and dictatorship.

As a result, the *enfants terribles* of French republicanism did not hesitate to share with their foes an ambiguous fascination with Bonapartism, and a scorning contempt for the revolutionary heritage: "The whole French Revolution," Pierre-Joseph Proudhon wrote, "is a true mythology, where men and things look bigger than they are because nothing is true."[106] Nevertheless, the Proudhonian circle enriched the continental debates on the coup d'état with something more valuable than paradoxes. By stressing the carnivalesque nature of the popular support of Napoleon III, Proudhon's own works of the early 1850s—conceived and written in jail—contributed significantly to an ideological understanding of Caesarism;[107] his essay of 1861 about the foreign policy of the Second Empire, *La guerre et la paix*, was to leave an indelible if indirect mark on nineteenth-century culture by inspiring the title and some themes of Leo Tolstoy's literary masterpiece, *War and Peace* (1865–69).

Why did the French republic fail, in 1851 as well as in 1799? During the 1850s, some republican thinkers and agitators from abroad proved able to address this question with more subtlety than their French peers. Giuseppe Ferrari, an Italian exile who was closely associated with Proudhon, devoted himself to a thorough analysis of the revolutionary foundations of Bonapartism, which he saw as deeply rooted in the Jacobin "double equivocation over religious and economic freedom."[108] Despite their rhetorical overtones, Ferrari argued, the French revolutionaries of 1793 had not entirely rejected the legacy of the Old Regime in terms of religious hierarchies, social distinctions, and political privileges. Proceeding from the Jacobin example, the rule of Napoleon I had been the triumph of duplicity: secular education and the Concordat, economic freedom and the Continental System, republicanism and monarchy.[109] According to Ferrari, Napoleon III was simply the heir of this contradictory revolutionary tradition, appallingly reflected in 1848–49 events such as the June Days and the Second Republic's armed intervention against the Roman Republic on behalf of Pope Pius IX.[110]

A friend of Ferrari and a collaborator in Proudhon's newspapers,[111] Alexander Herzen (who had emigrated from Russia on the eve of 1848) based his own interpretation of the French Revolution precisely on a critique of the Jacobin policies in the domains of religion and property.[112] As for religion, Herzen eloquently denounced the limits of the revolutionary contribution to the secularization of French society. The festival of the Supreme Being, what an ironic ceremony for the zealots of a credo advocating the weaning of mankind from all sorts of prejudices! By choosing deism as opposed to atheism, Robespierre had hypocritically avowed his belief in the disciplining role of religion. As for property, Herzen pointed to the fate of the Babouvist conspiracy as the sample of a general pattern: the French revolutionaries' incapacity to think of a world freed from all tools of social discrimination and class dominance.[113]

Herzen furthermore assailed the tendency of European liberals and revolutionaries towards an abstract, formalist, bookish approach to the economic problems of the poor and the political needs of the masses: "[They] always lived in large towns and small circles. They were men of books, journals, clubs; they did not know the people at all; they studied with immense profundity from historical sources, antiquities, not in the villages and the market place."[114] One might consider such a statement as the announcement of what was to become the motto of Russian populism: "Going to the People." In any case, Herzen's harsh attitude against revolutionary formalism explains his refusal to join Ledru-Rollin, Ruge, and other European agitators, who had signed—in July 1850—the manifesto of the European Central Democratic Committee, Giuseppe Mazzini's latest creation. Herzen's appreciation of Mazzini's integrity did not prevent him from drawing skeptical conclusions about the prospects of the Committee: "These are epilogues, not prologues . . . Where is our progress since the Mountain of '92? These men are the Bourbons of the revolution: they have learned nothing."[115] France could rise again only through a radical economic revolution, "a 1793 of socialism."[116] But according to Herzen, a socialist revolution was much more likely to occur in Russia, where the archaic traditions of the rural commune had preserved the peasants from both the burden of oriental despotism and a misleading Westernizing liberalism.

In the aftermath of 1848–49, Herzen traveled back and forth from Switzerland to Piedmont before settling in London, in August 1852. His pamphlets and articles were published and reviewed in several Western languages—German, French, Italian—shaping the ideas and eventually orienting the political action of a few left-wing extremists in southern France and northern Italy.[117] In the long run, Herzen's reflection on the failures of the French revolutionary tradition and the prospects of the Russian commune affected the entire history of nineteenth-century socialism, insomuch as it contributed to shifting the horizon of expectation for the next revolution to the east.[118] During the 1850s and 1860s, however, deep-seated Western prejudices about the social backwardness and moral inferiority of the Russian peasantry largely prevailed.[119] Conversely, Herzen became the most passionate critic of both the weaknesses and the deeds of the democratic approach to the French revolutionary tradition.

Herzen could not deny the consistency of Michelet's and Quinet's struggles for social progress and political democracy: until his death in 1870, the Russian exile was to count the two French historians among his best friends. Yet, in an open letter to Michelet—*The Russian People and Socialism* (1851)—Herzen accused the author of *Pologne et Russie. Légende de Kosciusko*[120] of having immolated the revolutionary hopes of millions of Russian peasants on the altar of his unfailing faith in the primacy of French republicanism and Frenchmen; worse, of having slandered the Russian rural commune. Herzen's reply to the leading French historian of the day was straightforward: "Your history . . . provides us with certain lessons, but no more: we do not consider ourselves the legal executors of your past."[121]

Some fifteen years later, Herzen would claim that the historical treatment of the rural question in Quinet's *La Révolution*, including some bitter pages on the Babouvist conspiracy, resulted from the author's fear of the outcomes of Russian peasant communism.[122]

Herzen ended rebuking the whole historical literature produced by the adversaries of the Second Empire. The demystification of Napoleon I had become, not unnaturally, one of the main goals of the intellectual opposition to Napoleon III. Two French exiles in Belgium and Switzerland, Marc Dufraisse (a Proudhonian, and former representative in the National Assembly of 1848) and Jean-Baptiste-Adolphe Charras (the former deputy minister of war in the Second Republic), undertook the challenge of demonstrating—respectively—the peaceful essence of the French revolutionary movement until Brumaire and Napoleon Bonaparte's usurped reputation as a military chief. The arguments of Charras's *Histoire de la campagne de 1815* (1858) and Dufraisse's *Histoire du droit de guerre et du droit de paix de 1789 à 1815* (1867) proved sound enough to reshape the ongoing continental debate on Bonapartism, particularly by influencing the political thought of Karl Marx and the historical reflection of Jacob Burckhardt.[123] Yet, Herzen described Dufraisse, along with Quinet, as the prototype of the French intellectual surviving to the ruinous end of his enchanted dream. The exiles who used the history of the French Revolution against Caesarism were—in Herzen's view—the Daniels of the modern time, who pronounced their sentence knowing that it would not be carried out.[124]

Nostalgia may describe the attitudes towards the French Revolution in the 1850s and 1860s. On the one hand, the gloomy consequences of 1848 made republican writers yearn for the revolutionary world they had lost. On the other hand, political changes, technical innovations, and artistic fashions combined their effects, leading some of the most influential intellectuals of the day to reject the French Revolution and, vice versa, to long for the Old Regime. As for politics, the rise on the continental scene of Cavour and Bismarck, monarchical counterparts of the plebiscitary figure of Napoleon III, was eventually seen as the result of a trend initiated by the French Revolution: that is, the tendency of modern political systems to transform the demand for democratic participation into an offer of bread and circuses.[125] As for technology, the development of new methods of reproducing images (daguerreotypes, then photographs)

led to a new relationship between the inherited and the lived experience of the past.[126] As in art, the evolution of the European historical
novel and the new tastes of connoisseurs indicated an increasing interest in anachronism and exoticism, while testifying to a declining
concern for chronologically recent and spatially close events such as
the French Revolution.[127]

No study of the nineteenth century revolutionary legacy can ignore the massive presence of the Old Regime in literature.[128] As literary critic Francesco Orlando has brilliantly demonstrated, European
novels were filled—especially after 1848—with accurate descriptions
of a variety of useless objects: time-worn stuff, domestic rubbish
whose unique value was that it dated back to the Old Regime.[129] Gustave Flaubert's novels *Madame Bovary* (1856–57) and *The Sentimental Education* (1869) contain some of the most telling specimens.[130]
As well, Flaubert's correspondence of the 1860s, particularly his letters to George Sand,[131] hints at another component of his nostalgia,
that for the Enlightenment. During the second half of the decade,
while reading extensively about the French Revolution, Flaubert repeatedly polemicized with the lay mysticism of the interpretative
tradition founded by Philippe Buchez and carried on by Louis Blanc:
an approach to the eighteenth-century heritage which Flaubert considered a flagrant betrayal of the ideas of the Enlightenment.[132]

Two good friends of Flaubert and leading literati of the Second
Empire, the brothers Edmond and Jules de Goncourt, committed
themselves to a systematic reconstitution of the manners and ideas
of the epoch of Louis XV, as opposed to those of the French Revolution. The Goncourts' acclaimed books, the *Histoire de la société
française pendant la Révolution* (1854), *Histoire de la société française pendant le Directoire* (1855), *Portraits intimes du XVIIIe siècle*
(1857–58), and *Les Maîtresses de Louis XV* (1860), built a paper
monument to Old Regime nostalgia.[133] Furthermore, because they
were outraged by the leveling effects of the French Revolution, because they despised the lower classes as sordid animals and the bourgeois as vulgar philistines, the Goncourts transformed their mansion
in the outskirts of Paris into a shrine of Old Regime souvenirs: furniture and jewelry, but also fashion manuals, address cards, invita-
tions to masked balls, boxes of all shapes and sizes, tapestries, engravings, pastels, candelabra.[134]

In 1862, the brothers Goucourts' regretful *Histoire de Marie-*

Antoinette (1858) was fiercely reviewed in the columns of a radical Russian journal, *Russkoe Slovo*.[135] The author of this and other reviews[136] of current French books about the French Revolution was Vassili Popov, a young officer who was then serving in the same military academy of St. Petersburg in which the founding father of the Russian populist movement, Nikolai Chernyshevsky, had taught before being arrested and banished by the tsarist government. Writing during the season of reaction that followed Alexander II's reforms of 1861, Popov praised Robespierre and other Jacobin leaders for having undertaken radical social reforms in the countryside: free elementary schooling, alongside of land redistribution and poor relief. Later on, Popov's successor at the *Russkoe Slovo*, Dmitrii Pisarev (a prisoner in St. Petersburg's notorious fortress of Peter and Paul), moved from the reading of French historical bestsellers to elaborate a political program for Russian left-wing activists.[137] The *Histoire de la Révolution française vécue par un paysan* (1868–69), an extremely popular historical novel by Emile Erckmann and Alexandre Chatrian,[138] inspired Pisarev's theory about the need for social mediators in the Russian countryside. To triumph against the forces of reaction, Pisarev argued, Russian democrats had to take care of the political apprenticeship of the peasants as effectively as the French *minorité agissante* of 1789–94 had educated the local peasantry.

Popov's and Pisarev's contributions to the *Russkoe Slovo* are worth recalling, since they point to the ultimate fate of nineteenth-century literature about the French Revolution. In the last decades of the century, the reflection on the social origins of the French Revolution was more likely to play an ideologically crucial role in those countries which were facing the historical problem of economic backwardness:[139] Russia and Italy, rather than England or France.

≺ V ≻

The Pathological Eye

After the tragedy of the Parisian Commune of 1871, which to some appeared as the last episode of a nearly century-long French revolution, the two most popular novelists in France, George Sand and Victor Hugo, decided to try their hands at current affairs via the historical events of the 1790s. Their two works, respectively *Nanon* (1871) and *Quatre-vingt-treize* (1874), can be read as the novels of a forth-coming republican conciliation.[140] Conversely, other French *maîtres-à-penser* found in the shattering events of 1870–71 new reasons for devoting themselves to an old practice: that is, the semiotic search for "le mal de la France," the illness fatally rooted somewhere in French social tissue or body politic. One thinks, first, of Ernest Renan's gloomy diagnosis and tentative prognosis, *La Réforme intellectuelle et morale de la France* (1871); and also, of Hippolyte Taine's harsh critique of universal suffrage, *Du suffrage universel et de la manière de voter* (1872).

During the difficult beginnings of the Third Republic, Taine—whose reputation as philosopher, literary critic, and art historian was already established—undertook to write a general narrative of the French Revolution. He performed it, according to his own expression, as an exercise in "moral zoology," by attempting an history which would couple a positivistic concern with an ethical stance.[141] In fact, as regards the use of "objective" sources, by no means did Taine's *Origins of Contemporary France* (1875–93) attest to an improvement in nineteenth-century historiography on the French Revolution. Much of the evidence that Taine accumulated against the Jacobins in his six-volume work was, rather, based on "subjective" sources, such as pamphlets, journals, and letters of the Thermidorians and counter-revolutionary émigrés. Explicitly, he defined the testimonies of eye witnesses as the most solid foundation of any historical understanding.[142]

Taine's ideological prejudices and methodological weaknesses triggered the reaction of Alphonse Aulard, the very republican first professor of the history of the French Revolution at the Sorbonne. Before writing (some fifteen years after Taine's death) a severe critique of the *Origins*,[143] Aulard promoted the publication of countless monographs, anthologies, editions of revolutionary texts, and archival records. During the 1880s and 1890s, this professional historian untiringly worked at giving solid foundations to the Third Republic interpretation of the French Revolution as a landmark in the history of Western civilization. Yet, Hippolyte Taine was probably—on a continental scale—the most influential writer of his time. It was primarily through Taine's irate narrative that the European intellectuals of the late nineteenth century found their own way towards an historical understanding of the French Revolution.

However biased by the author's hatred of Jacobinism and mistrust for democracy, Taine's enterprise had, admittedly, at least one merit: it delved into the eighteenth-century history of the French country-side.[144] The privileged position of peasants within Taine's conceptual framework explains some extraordinary adventures that occurred to his narrative of the French Revolution: namely, the eager reception of the *Origins*—this monument of political conservatism—by Petr Lavrov and Petr Kropotkin, leading characters among the Russian democrats in exile; the accurate translation of Taine's volumes by Herman Lopatin, another Russian exile closely associated with Lavrov; and the tremendous impact of Lopatin's translation on the Russian liberal intelligentsia of the 1880s.[145]

Nicolai Kareev and Ivan Luchitsky, the most talented Russian historians of this generation, were both influenced by Taine's lesson on the centrality of the peasant question and upset by his conclusions about the pernicious effects of the eighteenth-century development of the French countryside. They moved from the liberal academic circles of Moscow and Kiev[146] to the archives of Paris and provincial France and produced pioneering works on the social origins of the French Revolution.[147] The most evocative testimony of Taine's influence on nineteenth-century Russian democrats, though, would come later, from the *Memoirs* of Vladimir Debagory-Mokrievich, who had been, in his young days, a militant of the populist movement:[148]

We learned through [Taine] that the French peasants began to revolt several decades before the Revolution. In his history, we were able to see these revolts burst, grow, become more frequent and more widespread in a given province, and finally see the entire France surging at the time of the Revolution. Taine gave examples of peasants wreaking their anger upon the public officers and landowners, and committing all sorts of excesses while shouting *Vive le Roi!* But next, this very king was beheaded on the public place . . . The whole picture of the rise of the Revolution was so enticing to us, and some of its details reminded us so much of our own history, that it was very difficult to resist the temptation of taking the comparison to its end. We did take it to the end.[149]

Meanwhile, Taine's arguments against the Jacobins were used as a tool of political propaganda by the supporters of tsarism—particularly by conservative newspapers after the assassination of Alexander II, in 1881. According to the reviewer of *Rossiia*, the readers of Taine's *Origins* were led to forget that the book was about eighteenth-century France, for they recognized in the French Jacobins the hideous traits of nineteenth-century Russian nihilists.[150] Moreover, *Novoe vremia* depicted sexuality as a calamitous phenomenon infusing vice in Old Regime French aristocrats, transforming the Bourbon kings in effeminate caricatures of themselves, and finally causing their ruin.[151] These Slavophile publicists claimed that sexuality had played a particularly ruinous role during the Terror, when a devouring libido had driven the French revolutionaries in their furious competition for power; the Napoleonic wars were explained as the further result of French males' desire to please their sexual appetites.[152]

One has to recast such questionable assumptions in the scientific configuration of medicine, law, and criminal anthropology characteristic of the cultural landscape of late Imperial Russia. Among the mentors of Russian professionals and scientists was the Italian forensic psychiatrist Cesare Lombroso.[153] And Lombroso's works—extremely influential in Italy, France, and elsewhere in Europe during the last two decades of the nineteenth century—were strongly concerned with an historical perspective.[154] As for political crimes, Lombroso elaborated a theory based not only on physiognomical deductions and statistical records, but also on the distinction between "revolutions" and "revolts." The former, Lombroso argued in *Il delitto politico* (1890), were physiological phenomena, resulting from the political, social, and ideological evolution of a given country in a given time, whereas the latter were pathological phenomena, resulting from the deviant behavior of individuals. Despite its name, the French Revolution was a perfect historical example of a revolt: it had been announced by the proliferation, in the French countryside, of vagabonds, thieves, and murderers; it had been supported by women; it had been guided by alcoholics—the true inspirers of sansculottism.[155]

Lombroso himself acknowledged how heavily his interpretation of the French Revolution, and more generally his degeneration theory, relied on the lesson of the author of the *Origins of Contemporary France*: "Taine was truly my master," Lombroso declared in 1897.[156] During the 1880s and 1890s, other leading Italian social scientists and political analysts pointed to the French historian as the muse of their intellectual apprenticeship. Among them was a young friend of Lombroso, Gaetano Mosca; Taine's "wonderful volumes" on the French Revolution, Mosca wrote, imbued his devastating critique of parliamentary democracy, *Sulla teorica dei governi e sul governo parlamentare* (1883).[157] Both Mosca and his brilliant peer Vittorio Emanuele Orlando used the saturnalia of the French Revolution as an anti-democratic argument in the debate on the extension of electoral suffrage.[158] On the other side of the political spectrum, the influence of Taine's *Origins* and Lombroso's *Delitto* is apparent in the founding text of modern crowd psychology, Scipio Sighele's *La folla delinquente* (1891).[159] Sighele was the most brilliant disciple of criminologist Enrico Ferri; and Ferri—another young friend of Lombroso—had made his national reputation as socialist leader by pleading on behalf of northern Italian peasants arrested for incitation to civil war.[160] It was not the least irony of Taine's fate that his arguments about the irresponsibility of the French Jacobins proved instrumental in the defense of the Italian left-wing activists of the 1880s.

The "pathological eye" resembled the visions of the French Revolution previously predominant in the European nineteenth-century mind in one major respect: observers still defined the French revolutionary experience as natural or artificial, original or conventional, according to ideological bias rather than historical evidence. The continental success of Taine's narrative was a significant mark of this cultural continuity.[161] Nonetheless, it would be inappropriate to underestimate the extent of some ongoing changes, scarcely veiled by the persistency of old patterns. During the last three decades of the nineteenth century, the European relevance of the French revolutionary tradition was weakened by the "German crisis of French thought,"[162] threatened by the growing influence of Marxism,[163] and eventually overwhelmed by the Leninist re-appropriation of the Jacobin legacy.[164]

The desperate endeavor of the Parisian Communards and—after the Bloody Week, of May 1871—the stubborn attempt of the Blanquist diaspora at revitalizing the Jacobin example proved inspiring only to small and esoteric circles.[165] True, from the 1880s on contrasting approaches to the history of the Revolution kept nourishing the political life of the French Third Republic, especially insofar as foreign policy was concerned.[166] Yet, professors rather than intellectuals engaged in such discussions;[167] the study of the French Revolution was hence professionalized, becoming a matter of academic controversy rather than a source of political debate. A symptom of such a shift was the publication of the last posthumous memoirs of former Conventionnels in scholarly journals instead of commercial series.[168]

The failing interest of the audience in histories and memoirs of the French Revolution testified to a generational turnover. After the passing away of the sons and daughters of the eye witnesses of the French Revolution and the Napoleonic wars, nothing could be "optical" anymore in the cultural apprehension of these historical events. Indeed, the late nineteenth century experienced the unraveling of the linkage between memory, history, and legend of the Revolution, which for half a century had constituted the most peculiar feature of the French revolutionary tradition.

The Constitution of 1812 and the Spanish Road to Parliamentary Monarchy

RICHARD HERR

MOST OF THE PERSONS who struggled to achieve constitutional and democratic governments in the nineteenth century were inspired by one or another of the visions of the French Revolution so well described in chapter 1. This was less true of Spaniards, however, because they initiated their own revolutionary tradition during their war against Napoleon. Alone in Europe in this era, Spaniards undertook a radical domestic revolution while fighting a desperate struggle to preserve their independence against French armies. Out of it came the liberal constitution of 1812, which headed the country on its road to parliamentary government.

In the eighteenth century Spain enjoyed one of its brightest eras, recovering remarkably from its sorry state under the later Habsburgs. The new Bourbon dynasty charted reforms in the peninsula and the colonies, the population rose, the economy grew, and the empire expanded. The kings had a knack for choosing capable ministers, and they manipulated effectively the royal councils they had inherited from the Habsburgs, of which the most important was the Council of Castile. It combined supreme administrative, judicial, and legislative functions in one body. The *fiscales* of the council were of critical importance, for they received petitions and projects and formulated the proposals that the council considered and then submitted to the king for his approval and publication as *cédulas* or decrees. Carlos III (1759–88) in particular appointed intelligent and energetic men to be *fiscales*.

Beneath this enlightened absolutism lay a tradition of regional liberties typical of early modern monarchies. Indeed, there was no country legally called Spain. The monarch's decrees identified him as king of Castile, of León, of Aragon, of Valencia, of Navarre; as

count of Barcelona, lord (*señor*) of Vizcaya; and as ruler of other
places inside and outside the peninsula, some of which had long ago
been lost. (The first "King of Spain" was to be Napoleon's brother
Joseph.) The kingdom of Castile had its parliament (cortes) made up
of deputies from the leading cities. To the east of Castile, the realms
of the Crown of Aragon had sided with the Habsburg pretender in the
War of the Spanish Succession, and the victor, Felipe V, the first Bourbon king of Spain, had abolished their liberties (*fueros*), and their
cortes had disappeared. In the eighteenth century, their major cities
sent deputies to the cortes of Castile, whose name remained un-
changed although they now were the cortes of Spain. Navarre and
the Basque provinces, which had supported Felipe V, preserved their
fueros. They had their own laws, voted their own taxes, and raised
their own troops.[1]

Outside Navarre and the Basque provinces no one had a constitutional basis for opposing the edicts of the king, but this did not
leave him a despotic ruler. At the local level, especially in the south,
municipal governments maintained much control over their affairs.[2]
Many of the *regidores* (municipal councilors) owned their offices outright, their ancestors having bought them from the king. The king
lacked an adequate network of officials who could enforce his edicts
and relied on these councilors, who obeyed as they found convenient
and ran their communities rather as local aristocratic republics.

Their power became evident when Carlos III, in a major effort at
reform, sought to increase agricultural production by distributing
public lands to the peasantry. Like many enlightened thinkers, his advisers accepted the "yeoman myth" that independent peasants were
the most productive farmers and best citizens. Large landowners in
southern Spain feared a loss of authority, however, and resisted the
royal orders. The king attempted to penetrate their bastions by creating new municipal officers elected by all heads of household; but
from what we know, the measure had very limited success in making
the towns more democratic or more amenable to royal authority.[3]

The king also had to reckon with the spiritual and economic power
of the Church. The Catholic faith was the only one allowed, and
the Inquisition sought out anyone who questioned its beliefs. Spain's
churches, monasteries, and religious endowments owned land that
produced perhaps one fifth of the agricultural income of the country,
and they collected in addition tithes on grains and some other har-

vests. To strengthen royal authority over the Catholic church within the Spanish dominions, Carlos III expelled the Jesuits, asserted his control over the Inquisition, and nominated for bishops clergymen who favored improving discipline within the regular orders and restricting extravagant forms of worship and religious display. Clerics who supported such purification of church practices were known as "Jansenists," and among them were some of the finest minds in eighteenth-century Spain. The monastic orders and conservative bishops did not challenge royal authority, but resentment brewed among them.[4]

These attempts of Carlos III at reform inevitably produced tensions. Nevertheless the prestige of the king was high: he was admired for his dedication to the problems of government, his relatively modest life style, and his chaste loyalty to the memory of his wife. His was not the kind of charisma that inspired passionate adulation, but it was powerful enough to keep to a tiny minority the number of people who dreamed of changing the structure of the monarchy. Indeed most enlightened Spaniards looked to the king and his counselors as the source for a better future for the country.

≺ I ≻

The Last King of the Old Regime

Carlos III died in 1788. Under his son and successor, Carlos IV, the situation changed radically.[5] Carlos IV was a well-meaning ruler, but he lacked the strength of character and dedication of his father. Worse, his queen, María Luisa, appeared to have an inordinate influence over him, and she seemed to be guided by her passions. In 1792 Carlos IV named Manuel Godoy, a debonair 25-year-old guardsman, to head his government, placing him above men of mature age and experience. Rumors soon had it that Godoy owed his position to the favor of the queen, and this because he was her lover.

Honors continued to shower on Godoy. For his negotiation of peace with France in 1795, he received the title the Prince of the Peace. The title rankled because traditionally there was only one prince in Spain, the heir to the throne, prince of Asturias, whose brothers were called infantes. Yet the honors continued. In 1801 Godoy became generalísimo and commander of the armies, and soon he was also admiral with command of the navy, although he had never been to sea.

After 1800, Fernando, the prince of Asturias, became the focus of those who opposed Godoy. Little was known about him, and both partisans and opponents of reform believed him to be on their side. Both looked forward to his accession, since Carlos IV was in poor health. Stories circulated that Queen María Luisa and Godoy were plotting to set the young prince aside and take over themselves after Carlos IV's death. Aristocrats spread the story, but Godoy believed the clergy to be his worst enemies, preaching hatred of him from the pulpit.

The Spanish public had before it not only the scandals circulated about the court. The revolution in France also inevitably made some Spaniards think about their own political system. They had materials to work with. Under Carlos III the universities had introduced courses in the law of nature and of nations. Although drawing on pre-Enlightenment authors, they taught that every monarchy had its fundamental laws, which it was unjust or illegal for kings to violate. The subject seemed related to the history of Spain, a topic that had become popular among the eighteenth-century Spanish reading public. Some persons argued privately that liberty had existed in Spain in the Middle Ages, with parliamentary bodies and restrictions on royal authority. According to this view, which we may term the "liberal tradition," the Habsburg rulers had destroyed Spain's liberties.[6] The cortes, if powerless, were not dead, however. They met at the accession of each new king in the eighteenth century except Fernando VI in 1746 to swear allegiance to him and to recognize his heir as prince of Asturias. Furthermore they provided the approval of the kingdom for fundamental laws, such as the laws of succession. In 1713 Felipe V called on the cortes to accept the Salic Law denying the right of women to inherit the throne; in 1759 Carlos III asked them to recognize his son, who was born in Naples, as prince of Asturias, thus violating the law of 1713 which denied the throne to one not born and educated in Spain; and in 1789 Carlos IV had them abolish the Salic Law (for diplomatic reasons the abolition was not published at the time). Joint decrees of the king and cortes were called *pragmáticas* and were the highest law in the land. Occasionally a king issued a *pragmática* on his own, but he attached to it the phrase "as if it had been made in Cortes." Finally a standing body called the

Diputación del Reino, originally established in the sixteenth century, in theory represented the kingdom before the king when the cortes were not in session. It consisted of four, and later six, deputies chosen by lot from the cities with a vote in cortes. Unlike France, whose Estates General had not been convoked since 1614, in Spain the cortes remained a living if docile institution.[7] Few Spaniards wanted to imitate the French Revolution, but news of it reinforced their loss of faith in the Crown and opened doubts about their own political system.

People of such a mind especially disliked the Inquisition. It constantly threatened to discover and discipline a Jansenist priest or enlightened layman reading prohibited books brought under cover from abroad. Very few Spaniards questioned their Catholicism, for the skepticism of the Enlightenment found barren soil in Spain. But many were impressed by the Civil Constitution of the Clergy of 1790, which made the French church independent of Rome, and they began to dream of abolishing the Inquisition and returning its authority in matters of faith to the bishops' courts, which they expected to be more sympathetic to their views.

The French Revolution also produced a response among the Spanish opponents of reform. Spain was at war against the French republic from 1793 to 1795, and Spanish priests and friars excited the common people against the revolutionaries in the name of religion, king, and country. Those unhappy with Carlos III's policies, which Godoy was imitating as well as circumstances allowed, were able to preach effectively that the new ideas of the century could lead to horrible anarchy.

The wars of the French Revolution and natural disasters combined to bring suffering to the people. In 1796 Spain declared war on Britain, which had been attacking Spanish shipping. The British navy effectively cut off trade with Spain's colonies in America, ruining its export trade and shrinking royal revenues. In addition, yellow fever ravaged southern Spain after 1800, and the worst famine in over a generation caused distress from 1803 to 1805. To pay the costs of war and disaster relief, the king resorted to selling off properties of religious endowments, embittering clergymen who thought he had overstepped his authority.

Although an impartial observer might conclude that international developments and acts of God were to blame for Spain's sorrows, many Spaniards held the royal favorite to be responsible. The rivalry between Godoy, Prince of the Peace, and Fernando, prince of Asturias, took on epic proportions in the public mind. The young Fernando had become heir to the royal charisma that had been lost with the death of Carlos III. Carlos IV seemed a duped and complacent cuckold, incompetent to right the wrongs of his people. One may recall that the reputation of Marie Antoinette for sexual perversion and immorality was a major factor in discrediting the French court before 1789.[8] In both countries casting shame on the queen and thus on the male honor of the king became a potent factor in the fall of the absolute monarchy.

In November 1807, the armies of Napoleon and Carlos IV cooperated in an attack on Portugal to force it to join the continental blockade against Britain. The Portuguese were rapidly defeated, and their royal house escaped to Brazil, yet French troops lingered on in northern Spain. They aroused hostility among the Spanish people, but word got around that the French might be coming to save Fernando from his mother and her lover, and for the moment this calmed the suspicions.

In mid-March 1808 the events began that were to end the Old Regime in Spain. As the French army approached Madrid, rumors circulated that Godoy planned to take Carlos IV and his entourage, including María Luisa and Fernando, to Andalusia, headed for America like the Portuguese rulers.[9] By the evening of March 17 crowds gathered in Aranjuez south of Madrid, where the royal family was wintering, apparently drawn there by the partisans of Fernando. Intending to prevent a royal flight, they assembled outside the palace crying "Long live the king of Spain!" "Long live the prince of Asturias!" "Death to Godoy!" Royal guards surrounded Godoy's house, and when one of Godoy's hussars fired on them, the crowd was drawn to the scene. Growing more heated, well after midnight, the people broke into the house and sacked it in their fury, but they searched for Godoy in vain.

Carlos IV and María Luisa were up all night, terrified by the mobs. Ignorant, like everyone else, of Godoy's whereabouts—he appeared to have fled—and desperate to prevent further tumults, Carlos the following day dismissed Godoy as generalísimo and admiral. The news of Godoy's dismissal brought crowds into the streets of Madrid, singing and dancing and embracing each other throughout the city.

On the morning of March 19 Godoy, who had hidden himself in a roll of matting in the attic, came out after over thirty hours, desperate for water. The soldier he approached turned him over to the guards, and while being taken to their barracks, he was attacked by the mob, who nearly blinded him in one eye and tore open one hip. The king and queen appealed to Fernando to save Godoy, and the prince did so, going out to quiet the people. By now thoroughly unnerved and concerned over the fate of his favorite, and according to some accounts pressured by Fernando and his follows, Carlos reached the decision to abdicate.

The news of the accession of Fernando sent the crowds into the streets of Madrid for the second day. They murdered the minister of finance and attacked the palace of Godoy and the houses of his relatives and some associates, casting their belongings into bonfires. Rioting continued for two days, ending with the sacking of food stores and taverns, while neither the police of Madrid nor the soldiers made any effort to stop the mobs.[10]

It was now the turn of the new king, Fernando VII, to seek to restore peace. In various decrees he confiscated all the property of Godoy, promised to indemnify those whom Godoy had harmed, informed his subjects that he continued the policy of friendship with France and its soldiers should be welcomed, and promised to come to Madrid as soon as the people restored order.[11] He finally arrived on the 24th amid the acclamations of an immense crowd. In the words of the French ambassador, "One could say that all the people of this capital came together before the prince to show their devotion."[12]

From Madrid news of Fernando's accession traveled at a gallop along the Spanish roads. Everywhere it produced scenes of exaltation, celebrations for the new king.[13] A collective hysteria gripped the country elated by the prospect that Fernando "the Desired One" would end its troubles.

≺ II ≻

Napoleon and the Revolt of the People

What had occurred would not normally be labeled a revolution, for the crown had passed to the legitimate heir. Nevertheless Spain had entered a new age, one in which public violence would be regularly used to achieve political aims. In a masterful article John Elliott made a structural analysis of early modern European revolts. According to him, these contained two distinct forces, at one level the "political nation," and below them the common people. The first consisted of the nobility, urban patricians, men of letters, and clergy, conscious of the rights and privileges of their communities and defending them against the increasing centralization of the monarchies. The second, the common people, responded rather to material hardships, frequently combined with an innate xenophobia. Revolts usually began with a popular rising in protest against the authorities of the state. The political nation then had to make a choice: to support the people in defense of their common interests, or oppose the people, conscious that they could turn their anger upon the upper sector. If they supported the common people, as in Catalonia in 1640, the rising would successfully produce changes in the state. If they sided with the government, as in Naples in 1647, then the rising would eventually collapse.[14] Elliott's paradigm is useful in understanding the events in Spain after the spring of 1808, because it shows both continuity with the past and also how the political world was changing.

It is not immediately apparent, however, that the paradigm applies to the change of reign. Rioting by the common people in Aranjuez and Madrid destroyed the power of Carlos IV and Godoy, but there is no sign of hesitation among the political nation, most of whom also disliked Godoy. No one openly opposed the accession of Fernando. Nevertheless, the sight of violence in the streets has always caused anxiety among peaceful urban dwellers, and this was even more true in the early modern period, when the well-to-do lived cheek by jowl with the common people. Persons then alive could recall other scenes of violence. In 1766 three days of demonstrations in Madrid had forced Carlos III to dismiss an unpopular minister, and the troubles had spread to at least 69 other towns and cities. Nevertheless, the royal government had not lost control of the situation. On the contrary, it had responded with public executions.[15] It was a hundred years since force—and that in a foreign war—had been used successfully to achieve political control.

After Aranjuez, the Prussian ambassador described Madrid society as including "the sensible people, the good Spaniards, whose national pride is hurt [by the French troops] but who remain quiet," and

in contrast "the people, the public" which can be led by agitators,
and along with them "the most vile populace," who want free food
and to pillage houses and insult the rich.[16] The French and Russian
ambassadors wrote in a similar vein.[17] Their observations provide
good evidence that even if the "political nation" shared the common
people's joy, they would have been impressed by the danger from the
popular fury.

As soon as quiet returned to Aranjuez, Carlos IV regretted his abdication, and he directed a protest to Napoleon, denying its validity
because it was signed under duress.[18] The events had aroused the
imagination of the French emperor. He ordered Carlos IV, the queen,
and Godoy brought to France. Fernando sensed that as long as Napoleon did not recognize his accession, his throne was insecure, and
he accepted Napoleon's invitation to meet him in France. When Napoleon had the royal family together in Bayonne, he pressured the
son into returning the crown to his father, and the father into ceding
it to him. He then bestowed it on his brother Joseph, currently king
of Naples and Sicily. To Napoleon, this accomplishment no doubt
seemed the successful trick of an astute poker player, and he counted
on another new king, openly dedicated to bringing the benefits of
the Napoleonic system to the people of Spain, also finding a warm
welcome.

The Spaniards did not respond as he anticipated, however. The
departure of Fernando aroused anxiety among the subjects who had
just rejoiced at his accession, despite the young monarch's continued assurances that the French emperor was a friend. Through April
there was a tense quiet in Spain, with sporadic attacks on French
soldiers. However, when the French commander ordered the remaining children and grandchildren of Carlos IV to be driven north to
France, he provoked a violent outburst in Madrid on May 2, 1808.
News of the rising, brutally put down by the French soldiers, led to
demonstrations in some other cities. The Supreme Junta of Government, which Fernando had left in charge with his uncle at its head;
the Council of Castile; and local authorities all ordered Spaniards to
keep the peace and denounced the attacks on French soldiers. A tense
calm returned.

In its issues of May 13 and 20 the official *Gazeta de Madrid* carried the texts of the transfer of the crown to Napoleon, validated by
the Council of Castile. These produced violent risings in favor of Fer-

nando VII in different cities of Spain, this time not to be quieted. The crowds rejected the official pronouncements, and they threatened the officials who published them. Three provincial governors and two captains general were killed.[19] In Valencia the mob, harangued by a friar, attacked the fort in which the local French residents had taken shelter and killed three hundred of them.[20]

The local authorities' hesitation to reject the change of dynasty, even if lasting only a few hours, or at most a day or so, indicates that they were of two minds. Many no doubt were angered by Napoleon's duplicity, but they were disciplined to accept orders from Madrid. They sensed the power of Napoleon's war machine and believed resistance could ruin Spain. On the other hand they were intimidated by the angry crowds outside their windows screaming for action against the French. They resorted to a practice taught them by the last kings, the creation of ad hoc juntas to deal with urgent issues. To meet the recent crises of epidemic and famine, for instance, Carlos IV had named juntas of health and of charity, central ones in Madrid and local ones in the provinces, manned by persons of distinction.[21] In cutting themselves off from the Council of Castile, local authorities followed this pattern. After setting aside those persons who had too openly committed themselves to accepting the abdications or were known to be partisans of Godoy, they established supreme provincial juntas of armament and defense. Bowing to the popular demand, the juntas recognized Fernando VII as their rightful sovereign and began to organize military opposition to the French.

This has been interpreted as the moment of revolution in Spain, taking power from the constituted authorities into the hands of the people.[22] Drawing on Elliott's paradigm, however, one can see it in a different light. The people who made up these juntas consisted of leading local figures, including captains general (military commanders), corregidores (royal representatives to city governments), intendants (of the Crown), regents of the audiencia (local high court), bishops, archbishops, and representatives of the nobility, the religious orders, and the merchants. In them one finds the spokesmen of the authorities and established sectors of local society, the political nation. The crowds in the streets belonged to the lower level.[23] There is evidence that in some places, Oviedo for example,[24] conspirators had agitated them, but this does not keep them from being popular uprisings. Driven by their enthusiasm and under the leadership of the provincial juntas, in the summer of 1808 Spaniards undertook a war against Napoleon's armies that was to last five years. It would sap the strength of Napoleon's empire and be accompanied by irreversible changes in the Spanish political culture. A violent popular uprising that brings in the political nation to give it leadership and direction fits very well Elliott's formula for a successful early modern revolution.

≺ III ≻

The Rule of the Juntas

After acquiring the Crown of Spain, Napoleon convoked in Bayonne an assembly of representatives of the Spanish nobility, clergy, and commoners and had them ratify a constitution that he had drawn up for their country. The constitution of Bayonne was the first written constitution of the Spanish world. The troubled state of Spain meant that it was never applied, but its existence was to have a significant impact on the Spanish political scene. Modeled on the Bonapartist constitutions created for France, it abolished privileges but not nobility, and established cortes with representatives of the three estates. These could not initiate legislation but would discuss and approve decrees coming from the king and the Council of State. Napoleon was conscious that Spaniards saw in the French Revolution the enemy of religion. The first article of the constitution of Bayonne established the Catholic religion as the religion of the country, with none other tolerated.[25]

Napoleon and Joseph appealed successfully to a minority of the Spanish people, who became known as *afrancesados*.[26] Some hoped for a revival of the enlightened absolutism of Carlos III. Others admired Napoleon or distrusted the common people and feared their fury. But the majority who swore allegiance to Joseph, at least at first, did so out of the habit of accepting royal orders, or simply to keep their government jobs. They had no way of knowing that resistance would not be rapidly crushed. Those who rose against the French labeled the afrancesados traitors to their country, but they were certainly not so in spirit. They were to offer a foil against which the patriots identified themselves and measured their policies.

When King Joseph arrived in Madrid in July 1808, he had a full-blown war on his hands. The provincial juntas were raising troops, and Spain's standing army had engaged the French. The army of Andalusia trapped and defeated a French force at Bailén on July 19. When he learned the news, Joseph fled north to Vitoria, where he stayed until he was saved by his brother at the head of a large army in December. By now lukewarm Spanish partisans had begun to desert him.

As soon as Joseph left Madrid, the Council of Castile, conscious that its acceptance of the new dynasty had earned it the opprobrium of those loyal to Fernando, declared the abdications of Bayonne null and void.[27] It invited the provincial juntas to send deputies to meet with it to organize the representation of the nation. When the juntas did not reply, it issued a public manifesto claiming that it had tenaciously resisted cooperation with Napoleon and Joseph. It had refused to approve the new constitution, arguing that only "the Nation" could determine a change in the legal succession to the throne or ratify the constitution. The council denied that it or the Bayonne assembly represented the nation, which only the cortes could do.[28]

The juntas did not welcome this move to take over leadership of the resistance. In response they hastened to create a supreme body of their own. They sent deputies to Aranjuez, away from the Madrid officialdom, who met on September 25 and took the name of Supreme Governing Central Junta of the Monarchy, ruling in the name and with the powers of Fernando. The Council of Castile meekly recognized it as the supreme authority,[29] but the council's claim that only elected cortes could legitimately hold final authority, stilled for the moment in the heat of the war, would not be buried. One is reminded that the highest court of France, the Parlement of Paris, by insisting that only the Estates General could abolish the tax privileges of the nobility, had forced Louis XVI to convoke that body in 1789. Again the highest court of an absolute monarchy had issued a pronouncement that was to become an invitation to revolution.

Although the war was the primary concern of the juntas, they continued to fear the threat of popular disturbances.[30] The Central Junta addressed the problem in a royal order of November 22, 1808. In a messianic tone, the order proclaimed Spain to be the liberator of Europe. In eight days, it said, Spaniards, despite the corrupt state of the nation from the effects of "a perverse favorite," possessed by an "enthusiasm as burning as it was patriotic," determined to die or to defeat the tyrant. But to succeed, besides fighters, the nation needed "faithful corps, devoted to preventing disorders, and capable of repressing troublemakers, bandits, deserters, and the lawless." For this purpose it established an Honorable Militia. It would consist of volunteers who would provide their own uniforms and arms. "They may not include . . . those persons whose subsistence depends entirely on their own personal daily labor," but only "those who have fixed wages, salaries, or incomes . . . the most distinguished and wealthy residents of each town, in whom one can anticipate more enlightenment, more patriotism, and greater interest in the preservation of public order." Except in fortified places, their sole purpose would be "the preservation of the public peace and the apprehension of delinquents."[31]

The leaders of Spain's rising were watching the behavior of the common people with a wary eye, but they were not to respond to the afrancesados' appeals to join them against the rabble. In a few towns, rowdy groups did harm Spanish citizens.[32] On the whole, however, there was little to fear of a popular attack on the upper classes, for those piping the tune, many of them priests and friars, kept the public hatred mobilized against the French and their partisans, not loyal Spaniards of any class. The rising continued to follow Elliott's formula for success.

Nevertheless, the rising soon took turns that reveal that Spain had entered a new age. The absolute monarchy had destroyed most of the local charters that sixteenth- and seventeenth-century revolts had sought to defend. The provincial political nation was interested in preserving the established social order, but the juntas that represented it would have to resort to different justifications for their opposition to Madrid.

The local authorities who had accepted the royal abdications argued that they were obeying the orders of their legitimate rulers. The governor of the audiencia of Valencia, for example, told the supporters of Fernando that Carlos IV had the authority to give his crown to Napoleon.[33] In the heat of the moment, those who overturned these authorities did not seek to defend their acts on philosophical grounds. They simply took it for granted that Fernando had the right to the throne. The junta of Seville, which until the meeting of the Central Junta claimed leadership of the whole Spanish monarchy, published a "Declaration of War on the Emperor of France Napoleon I" headed simply "Fernando VII King of Spain and the Indies, and in his name the Supreme Junta of Both."[34]

Very shortly, however, the defenders of the rising, including some juntas, began to offer a new justification for their acts. Not the reigning monarchs but the people had the right to determine who would rule them. One of the first was the aged Bishop Pedro Quevedo y Quintano of Orense in northwest Spain, a person destined to play a major role in coming years, who refused an invitation to the assembly at Bayonne because of his age, but published what he said he would have told the assembly, to wit, whatever decision is taken on the disposition of the Crown, it must be ratified by the Spanish nation, through its cortes. "Let the nation itself, with the independence and sovereignty that belongs to it, choose as its legitimate king him whom nature and law and the circumstances call to the throne of Spain."[35] The junta of Valencia was soon calling itself "The Supreme Junta of the Kingdom which assumes sovereignty by the will of the people."[36] When the junta of Seville sent deputies to the Central Junta, it told them, "The people resumed its uncontested rights, and created the juntas, and gave them all its power to defend and preserve the Patria."[37] Their statements had a revolutionary tenor, but none of these was revolutionary in spirit. One need not see the origin of their argument in the Enlightenment. One can find it in medieval Thomism. *Vox populi, vox Dei.* The Spanish theologian Francisco Suárez had developed the theory in the sixteenth century,[38] and shortly thereafter the popular historian Juan de Mariana wrote that "the power of the king is only legitimate when it is set up by the consent of the citizens."[39] In 1808 the theory of popular sovereignty was given voice by authorities who represented the privileged sectors struggling for control of a movement that had been started by the popular classes.

The Central Junta had as its immediate task organizing armies and raising money to supply them. At first it did not bring up the question of the origin of its power. Its announcement of its installation simply said that it was "the depository of the authority of our beloved Fernando VII."[40] From the outset, however, it labored under the shadow of the need for cortes to embody the expressed will of the people to oppose Joseph. Divisions of opinion on this issue began to surface and were to solidify in the next years. The junta itself, with its more than thirty members sent by the provincial juntas, could claim to represent the will of the people and to be a kind of cortes.[41] Its rules of governance, adopted in early October 1808, stated: "The members that make up the Supreme Junta of the Kingdom meeting together represent the entire Nation and not individually the Provinces from which they are deputies."[42] The rules of governance indicated that the junta would undertake to reform the country. One article read: "The Commission on Grace and Justice will busy itself constantly proposing methodical and uniform plans of studies for public education that will reach even the most indigent classes, and in improving the administration of justice and of our Constitution."[43]

When the war turned against the Spanish insurgents in November 1808—Napoleon entered Spain at the head of a large army and marched rapidly toward Madrid, defeating the armies that the Central Junta had organized—the Central Junta fled before the threat of capture and took up residence in Seville at the beginning of 1809. Members of the Central Junta who favored convoking the cortes now became bolder. They accepted the "liberal tradition" that Spain had once had a constitution that guaranteed freedom from arbitrary rule through its cortes. The constitution needed to be revived. The most prestigious member of this persuasion was Gaspar Melchor de Jovellanos, a leading royal counselor whom Carlos IV had imprisoned. After some hesitation, he denied that the Central Junta could act in place of legitimate cortes, and insisted that real cortes should be organized into separate legal orders as in Spain's "constitution." Jovellanos admired the structure of the English parliament, with its upper house of clergy and aristocracy.[44] Persons of this moderate persuasion believed Spain's proper constitution gave authority to persons of responsibility, screening out the common people.

Partisans of a more democratic approach also existed in the Central Junta, but the expressions of this position were voiced primarily by persons who were not members of it. Most conspicuous was Manuel José Quintana, editor of the *Semanario Patriótico,* a new journal that was openly political. As the Central Junta was about to meet, an article in it, presumably by Quintana, called on the junta to convoke cortes that would give Spain a

constitution adapted to our circumstances . . . that will make of all the Provinces that compose this vast Monarchy a Nation truly one; where all are equal in rights, equal in duties, equal in burdens. With it there should vanish from sight the differences among Valencians, Aragonese, Castilians, Basques: all

should be Spaniards. And who is not proud today of bearing that name! . . .
Only when this great task has been accomplished can we congratulate ourselves on having garnered all the fruit of the present crisis. Then we shall
have borne ourselves like men, and shall deserve the attention and the interest of the world that has its eyes placed on us.[45]

Quintana was shortly thereafter named to the staff of the Central
Junta.[46]

The junta established a commission on the convocation of the
cortes, which Jovellanos headed. He managed to convince his colleagues to announce in May 1809 the summoning of cortes, the
structure to be determined after hearing the opinion of the councils,
provincial juntas, bishops, universities, and "the learned and enlightened persons."[47] No one appeared to think the eighteenth-century
form of the cortes suitable for the present crisis.

The request called forth a flood of replies that shows how burning
the question had become during the war. The junta received back
some 180 responses, 39 of them from civil and religious authorities,
including seven from provincial juntas. The rest came from private
individuals. They were a confused mass of manuscripts, of which
about one hundred were to the point.[48] This collection of documents
can be compared as a source for the state of public opinion to the lists
of grievances that were sent with the deputies to the Estates General
in France in the spring of 1789. Their variety can be appreciated from
the words of a member of the junta who was assigned to review them.
He reported that all the memoirs and reports show "good and praise-
worthy desires and a general commitment to improving our moral
force, reforming political and legal abuses by means of a national representation that will assume the authority to direct this important
task." Some wanted cortes in a purely monarchic form, others a
mixed form, others a democratic form. "Some want only reforms,
others regeneration; others annihilation of all our institutions; others the reconciliation of our ancient laws, usages, and customs with
those that are to be newly constituted."[49] The junta was left without
much guidance in formulating the convocation of cortes.

Napoleon had left Spain in January 1809, and his armies did not
obtain a decisive victory during that year. So long as this was the
case, the junta headed the government successfully. At the end of
1809, however, the French broke through to the south, and in January
1810 they marched into Andalusia. The Central Junta now hurried

through the very contentious subject of how the cortes were to be convoked. The great issue, reminiscent of 1789, was whether they should be unicameral or have separate representation for the nobility and clergy. The moderates, led by Jovellanos, favored the latter; the more radical, led by Lorenzo Calvo de Rozas, a merchant who was a delegate for Aragon, feared that two upper houses would outvote the "third estate." Although the majority voted in favor of all three orders meeting together with the representatives of the *pueblo* forming a majority, in the confusion of January 1810, Jovellanos, almost singlehandedly, was able to convince a rump meeting of the junta to approve two houses for the cortes, with the affirmative vote of both needed to sanction laws, very like the British system he admired.[50]

The junta decreed that the deputies of the people were to be elected by a very democratic franchise. Their number would be proportional to the population of their provinces; male parishioners over 25 could vote for electors of the *partido* (judicial district), who would then choose the deputies. Provision was made for temporary substitute deputies for provinces occupied by the French and for the American colonies. The instructions went out to elect deputies of the people on January 7, 1810,[51] but the instructions prepared for the grandees and the bishops (the only people in the upper house) were not issued. The reason for this has not been determined. Lack of a proper list of addressees, confusion and loss of papers, and intentional negligence by the staff of the junta have been suggested as possible reasons.

As the French forces advanced, the Central Junta moved to Isla de León, next to Cadiz. The departure of the junta from Seville, followed by the other government bodies, was seen by the population of Seville as a flight. Reports circulated that the Central Junta was sailing from Cadiz with the treasures and jewels of the state. A violent rising erupted in Seville beginning January 24. The mob established a council of regency, made up of men who were believed to be opponents of the junta.[52]

Once again the common people had taken the initiative. The situation was different from May and June of 1808, however. The revolt produced no echo outside Seville, in part because within days Seville fell to the forces of Joseph. A greater reason, however, is that the prospect of cortes had produced anticipation throughout free Spain, and people were prepared to await them. Moreover, for more than a year the common people had been aroused against the French, and public opinion had buried domestic discord. By now perhaps 40,000 Spaniards were engaged as guerrillas, harassing and consuming the French armies.[53]

For the Central Junta, the events in Seville showed how shaky its authority had become. It had been under pressure for some time to establish a regency to substitute as executive for the absent king. Meeting in Isla de León, the junta approved the proposal of its democratic colleague, Lorenzo Calvo, that it name a regency and give over authority to it, thus upstaging the regency created in Seville. The Council of Regency of five members was to be headed by Bishop Quevedo of Orense and would include a member from America.[54] With this act, the life of the Central Junta came to an end. After sixteen months of ruling war-torn Spain, it disbanded under a cloud that left its members bitter and disillusioned. One of its major weaknesses was the lack of a leading figure who could capture the imagination of the country as Fernando had done. But its great achievement and hope was that it had provided for a meeting of the cortes that would remake the constitution of the country.

While the Central Junta wanted reforms and undertook some of its own, its majority was not democratic in outlook. Its members believed in the sovereignty of the people, but its creation of the Honorable Militia shows how nervous it was over the threat of the uncontrolled mob. In this it was not out of tune with most provincial juntas. So far the people who had obtained authority in the summer of 1808 had been able to keep things under control. They would get out of control in 1810, because of the way the cortes were called, and because of the rising power of the press.

≺ IV ≻

The Cortes of Cadiz and the Constitution of 1812

The Central Junta required the members of the regency to swear to bring about the meeting of the cortes in two houses and also to maintain freedom of the press "as one of the most appropriate ways not only to spread general enlightenment but to preserve the political and civil liberty of the Citizens."[55] By this order the junta resolved a burning issue that had long plagued it. The anarchic conditions that had existed since the beginning of the uprising allowed Spaniards to make free use of the press. The juntas that sprang up in the provinces and cities printed their proclamations, clerics intoned and published sermons calling for a war for religion, and private individuals wrote tracts urging resistance to "the tyrant" or published songs and poems with patriotic motifs.[56] In this the press reflected the spontaneous nature of the rising against Napoleon. The Central Junta soon became aware of the importance of the press to the war effort. In the instructions in which it formulated the concept of a guerrilla war, for which the Spanish War of Independence was to become famous, the junta also called on "all educated persons . . . to print and publish continuous short speeches to maintain the public opinion" and uncover the lies of the French.[57] Although the war was to reach almost all parts of Spain, with attendant inconveniences, requisitions, suffering, and death, most Spaniards undoubtedly saw printed flyers and pamphlets more frequently than armed conflicts.

From early on the patriotic press also took up questions of popular sovereignty, the cortes, and the role and powers of the juntas. Journals sprang up around the country, Quintana's *Semanario Patriótico* being the best known, and their content was frequently political. The press thereby presented the Central Junta with a thorny issue. How far should it, or could it, go in trying to control what was printed? A bare week after the junta first met, it ordered the Council of Castile to enforce the existing laws calling for prior censorship of all publications, because, the order said, their non-observance could be exploited by the enemy.[58] The other body that dealt with dangerous publications was the Inquisition. It had become leaderless because the inquisitor general had gone over to Joseph. The junta sought to revive it by appointing Bishop Quevedo of Orense inquisitor general, but conditions did not permit it to act.[59]

In contrast to the anxiety of their majority, several members of the Central Junta became avid campaigners for an end to prior censorship if the country were to get the full benefit of the reforms to be instituted. Lorenzo Calvo proposed freedom of the press shortly after the junta met, and a year later, in Seville, he brought the matter up again. He argued that "the country is interested in being enlightened about everything that can lead to the improvement of its laws and its institutions, and this cannot happen without a free press . . . We have never needed it more than now when the cortes are to place a repairing hand on our old and sad public travails."[60] The junta did not vote on the proposal, but its partisans obtained the instructions to the Council of Regency to allow a free press.

The regency had many things to worry it. The French army soon stood across the bay from Cadiz, within cannon shot of Isla de León, and elsewhere in the peninsula French troops faced little organized military opposition. In the American colonies the news of the flight of the Central Junta from Seville was taken to mean that Spanish resistance had collapsed. To avoid falling under French domination, in Buenos Aires, Caracas, and elsewhere in America, the colonists created supreme juntas on the Spanish pattern, loyal to Fernando VII but not to any current government in Spain. The unoccupied parts of the monarchy were falling apart.

The support of the British navy permitted the Spanish line to hold before Cadiz. The regents could communicate with the unoccupied parts of Spain by sea, and gradually the periphery of the peninsula was tied to Cadiz. In May Bishop Quevedo of Orense arrived and took over the presidency of the Council of Regency. His letter refusing to go to Bayonne had been widely circulated and had made his name popular in free Spain. Now 72 years old, he was strongly monarchical in outlook, and the prospects of cortes had no attraction for him. Neither did they for Miguel de Lardizábal, the American member of the Council of Regency. Nevertheless that summer the regents finally were convinced that the cortes must meet by the alarming news from America, along with pressure from the many refugees in Cadiz. In unoccupied Spain elections were held and deputies set out for Isla de León. For those parts where elections were not immediately possible, their residents who were present in Cadiz elected temporary deputies (*suplentes*). The Central Junta had declared the colonies in America integral parts of the monarchy, and they too were to hold elections. Meanwhile suplentes for them were also chosen in Cadiz.

By the last week of September 1810 enough deputies were present to open the General and Extraordinary Cortes, as they were officially termed. The procrastination of the regency had lost it the opportunity to include an upper house. Failure to do so could be justified by the fact that both clergymen and titled nobles were being elected as representatives of the "Nation" and the Cortes could decide after meeting if they should divide into separate bodies.[61] When the Cortes met, out of a total of 102 deputies (eventually the number would reach 223), 46 were *suplentes*, 28 of them for overseas provinces.[62] Although a third of the final total of deputies were clergymen, only five were bishops. Perhaps another third were *hidalgos* (untitled nobles), but only six were titled aristocrats.[63] There were a number of royal bureaucrats, persons who had accompanied the Central Junta and its government in their peregrinations. They and the Jansenist priests became part of a majority in the cortes strongly committed to remaking the country, turning it into a democratic parliamentary monarchy.

It was precisely the anticipation of this kind of cortes that had caused anxiety among the moderates of the Central Junta. The threat of revolution no longer came from mobs but from enlightened laymen and Jansenist priests who were eager to take the destiny of the country in their hands. Their ideological origins were in the enlightenment of Carlos III, but they were a new generation, radicalized by two decades of national disasters, rule by a favorite, and news of developments in France. Soon they were to become known as "Liberals"; those deputies who opposed their reforms were to be labeled "Serviles." The first name was destined to enter universal political parlance; the second expired with the Restoration of 1814.

The first act of the Cortes was to declare that they represented the nation, that sovereignty resided in them, and that the cession of the crown to Napoleon was invalid[64] "not only because of the lack of freedom [of Fernando] but most importantly because of the lack of the consent of the nation."[65] They voted to continue the regents in office provided they took an oath to the Cortes as sovereign. Four caused no problem, but Bishop Quevedo wrote the Cortes denouncing their declaration of sovereignty, "as if the Cortes had been called to decide on the rights of the king in conformity with the general will of the Nation," without attention to the oath taken to Fernando VII as hereditary prince or the legitimate representation of the "principal arms." He accused the Cortes of turning the king into "the vassal of the Nation" and creating in themselves an omnipotent power that "would consummate the ruin of the Nation, and even offend Religion."[66] The Cortes responded to the challenge by confining the bishop to a monastery, where he remained until he finally took the oath to the Cortes as sovereign six months later. It was a pyrrhic victory for the Cortes, for a popular bishop questioning the legitimacy of the Cortes in the name of religion was ominous for the future.

One of the first legislative acts of the French National Assembly in 1789 was a declaration of the rights of man and the citizen. The immediate agenda of the leaders of the Cortes was more limited but equally significant for them. It was the freedom of the press, which they took up at the end of the third week. One deputy proclaimed, "The freedom to publish one's ideas is a right, the most legitimate of man in society,"[67] and another called it a guarantee against despotism in the manner of Godoy.[68] In the next days the deputies enacted a law establishing the freedom of the press. It stipulated that everyone had "the liberty to write, print, and publish his political ideas" without prior review or license. Matters of religion needed the prior censorship of the bishops, according to the Council of Trent, and laws would provide for the punishment of publications that were libelous, indecent, or "subversive of the fundamental laws of the monarchy."[69] With this the Cortes fulfilled the dream of the more advanced members of the Central Junta and opened up the press for active discussion of national reforms. In its first major act, the Cortes of Cadiz had established one of the most significant of modern freedoms, whose absence had characterized Spain for centuries. The next step would be the achievement of popular sovereignty.

The Cortes named a commission of fifteen members to draw up the project for a constitution. The liberal leaders Diego Muñoz Torrero and Agustín Argüelles provided its inspiration. They presented their project to the Cortes in August 1811, and the discussion and enactment of it took seven months. The Cortes proclaimed the constitution on March 19, 1812, the fourth anniversary of the riots of Aranjuez that made Fernando king. They felt no need to submit the document to popular ratification. In this, as in all their measures, they were acting as absolute as had the king, whose authority they claimed to have in his absence.

The constitutional commission accompanied the draft with a lengthy "preliminary discourse."[70] The words "Nation" and "liberty" filled its pages; the need to unite the two was its main burden. The term "Nation" was a sign of the times; in the eighteenth century the cortes spoke of themselves as representatives of the "Kingdom" (*"Reino"*).[71] Used already in 1808 by the Council of Castile and the Central Junta, the word "Nation" was now in everyone's mouth when speaking of their country.

The draft constitution, the preliminary discourse said, restored

Spain's ancient freedoms destroyed by the foreign houses that had ruled in recent centuries. It argued that all the provisions of this "liberal Constitution" could be found in past and present codes and practices of the various Spanish realms, although they were modified to fit the European "advance in the science of government." The discourse was an expression of the liberal tradition that had developed at the end of the eighteenth century. Precedents for limits on the power of the monarch did indeed exist, but not for an amalgamation of all the realms on both sides of the ocean into one uniform state, or popular voting for delegates to a national parliament. The "advance in the science of government" was a euphemism covering a new, untried system. The constitutional commission no doubt sensed that they would be accused of imitating Joseph Bonaparte and the French. They convinced themselves, however, and the liberal tradition became a staple of the constitutionalists of the nineteenth century, providing a domestic revolutionary tradition that did not need to look back to 1789.

The constitution of 1812 is a long document, 384 articles. It defined "the Spanish Nation" as "the union of all Spaniards in both hemispheres"[72] and declared it free and independent, not the patrimony of any person.[73] "Sovereignty resides essentially in the Nation," it said.[74] Laws were to be the same for all regions and all citizens on both sides of the Atlantic and in the Philippines.[75] Freedom of the press, freedom from arbitrary arrest, and the right of property were guaranteed.[76] But Spaniards also had obligations: to support the country in proportion to their property and to defend it with arms[77] and, with the idealism of the Enlightenment: "Love of the Patria is one of the principal duties of all Spaniards, and also to be just and beneficent."[78]

The form of government was what the commission called a "moderate monarchy."[79] The cortes were to be unicameral with indirect elections for deputies. All male citizens could vote except servants, bankrupts, criminals, and those without known means of support.[80] Except for those who had voted for the present Cortes, Spaniards had no experience with elections for national representatives, and the constitution spelled out in prolix fashion the dates and procedures for the various steps.[81] Deputies had to be 25 years old, could not be members of the regular clergy, and had to have an adequate income derived from their own property, although the "preliminary discourse" declared that the property qualification would be suspended until property could be freely exchanged.[82] There was to be a division of powers. The king could veto a bill two years running; if the cortes passed it a third time, it became law.[83] He could appoint the "secretaries" (ministers), but these were responsible to the cortes for the constitutionality of their acts.[84] The authors intended no repetition of Godoy. And, a measure of the debt owed to Carlos III, the constitution opened all municipal offices to election by the voters, abolishing hereditary municipal councilors.[85] With this reform, the Liberals threatened the very marrow of local oligarchic rule, the stumbling bloc of the enlightened reformers of the previous century. They were self confident men indeed.

A comparison of the text with the French constitutions of 1791 and 1795 shows that its authors took some of the articles from these models.[86] They have been accused of being disciples of the French Revolution, but in similar fashion one could find British and American precedents for the French constitution of 1791. All were part of what R. R. Palmer has called the "age of democratic revolution." "Liberty" was the touchstone against which the Spanish Liberals defined the abuses they sought to eliminate. Equality was not a word they used, but in fact the Spanish constitution created a more centralized, more egalitarian and democratic nation in the Rousseauan sense than other projects of this period, except the stillborn Jacobin constitution of 1793.

≺ V ≻

The Abolition of the Inquisition
and the Fall of the Liberals

The Cortes had come in under a wave of anticipation, and they had fulfilled their mission. Conservatives might not be happy, but most bit their tongues. Not so Bishop Quevedo. He stated publicly that in taking the oath to the constitution, he was not swearing to the truth of its principles. Sensing another challenge before public opinion, the majority of the Cortes declared him unworthy of the Spanish name and exiled him from Spain. Bishop Quevedo took refuge in a parish of his diocese located in Portugal and responded with a well argued "representation." Citing Rousseau against those he called

Rousseau's disciples, he pointed out that the Cortes could not be sovereign because the nation could not divest itself of its general will, so that to impose the constitution on the people without their sanction was to make slaves out of free men. He accepted it as law but added, "The bishop does not love the Constitution because he does not believe it useful or suitable but rather prejudicial and contrary to the good of the nation." The "representation" was published in Galicia, Cadiz, and Madrid.[87]

Not satisfied, and still in exile, in April 1813 he added a "Manifesto of the Bishop of Orense to the Spanish Nation," which elaborated his arguments. For the constitution to be valid, it must be ratified by newly elected deputies and the king must approve it, or "Is Fernando VII no longer king?" And, he added, almost as an afterthought, now the Cortes have even refused to hear the bishops on such a serious question as the Inquisition.[88]

Tensions that had festered for half a century were bursting forth. The constitution proclaimed the Catholic religion to be that of the Spanish nation, which "protects it by wise and just laws and prohibits the exercise of any other."[89] Religious freedom held no appeal for the Cadiz Liberals; nevertheless, religious issues were to dominate the remaining life of the Cortes. Their social legislation was relatively moderate. Its major piece was the abolition of seigneurial jurisdictions (señorios) and the fiscal privileges that went with them, thus placing every Spaniard directly under royal jurisdiction. The Liberals had no love for monks and friars, and they considered closing small monasteries, but the dream that moved them most was the freedom to read and write, and that involved the future of the Inquisition.

Two works helped urge them on. In 1811, Antonio Puigblanch published The Inquisition Unmasked, an account of its methods and history.[90] He argued that it offended religion and must be eliminated. An even more authoritative work came out in Madrid. King Joseph had abolished the Inquisition, and he gave Juan Antonio Llorente, a former inquisitor, access to its archives. In 1812–13, Llorente published for the first time an authentic story of the early procedures and trials of the holy tribunal[91] and followed it with an account of the Spanish authorities who had protested against its establishment.[92]

Despite the attempt of the Central Junta to activate the Inquisition, the confusion of war had halted its activities. The Cortes referred the question of its revival to its constitutional commission. It reported in November 1812 that the secret procedures of the Inquisition were incompatible with the constitution, and it should be abolished.[93] The ensuing debate was the most heated of the Cortes.[94] The Liberals argued that Christ had never needed the Inquisition to defend His doctrine. Perhaps the most original indictment came from Antonio José Ruiz de Padrón, a censor of the Inquisition. He told how once in Philadelphia he had succeeded in convincing the immortal Benjamin Franklin and more than twenty Protestant ministers that Catholicism was the true faith until one of them pointed to the Spanish Inquisition. Ruiz de Padrón was forced to admit that the Inquisition was founded by men full of evil. Franklin challenged him to say this in public. He did so in the Catholic church of Philadelphia, and the result, he said, was that many Anglo-Americans converted to Catholicism when they learned the Inquisition was alien to it. At least six editions of Ruiz de Padrón's speech to the Cortes were printed in 1813, including one in Mexico City.[95]

The Cortes abolished the Inquisition in February 1813, but with a reduced majority. They issued a manifesto to the nation explaining that the better to protect the Catholic faith in Spain, they were giving back to the bishops' courts jurisdiction over cases of religious belief. Drawing on the recent histories, the manifesto revealed the names of outstanding Spaniards who had suffered at the hands of the Inquisition and cited the protests against it by cortes in the sixteenth century. It will be difficult for posterity to explain how such a tribunal was ever established in "the noble and generous Spanish Nation," the manifesto said.[96] The Cortes ordered the manifesto and the decree to be read on three successive Sundays in all the parishes of the monarchy.

By now an ever increasing flow of periodicals and pamphlets was debating the issues before the Cortes. They appeared in many places. Cadiz was most active, while La Coruña supplied northern Spain and Palma de Mallorca the Mediterranean coasts. Although conservatives disapproved of press freedom, they exploited it actively, with clergymen in the lead. The Liberal writers were more sparkling, showed more intelligence, but undoubtedly reached a smaller audience.[97]

The abolition of the Inquisition gave the conservative clergy the cause they had been looking for. The bishops of Galicia announced that they were not going to read the decree abolishing the Inquisition in their churches because it was being exploited by persons who boasted that the popes had lost their influence in Spain.[98] The bishop of Segovia had already published his protest to the Cortes against the act,[99] while eight bishops who had taken refuge in Mallorca issued pronouncement after pronouncement against the dangers that freedom of the press was presenting to religion. They reminded their readers that Joseph Bonaparte had abolished the Inquisition. Were Spaniards at last driving out the French only to find that the system they had fought was being adopted by those who claimed to speak for the sovereign nation? [100]

In response, the Council of Regency, headed by the archbishop of Toledo, addressed a letter to the prelates and cathedral chapters urging them to stop their campaign.[101] The bishop of Barbastro published his support of the abolition of the Inquisition,[102] and 115 persons in Mallorca signed a "congratulation to the Cortes."[103] Nevertheless, against the torrent of papers denouncing the act of the Cortes, the pamphlets expressing support were a small stream. Passions over what kind of church Spain should have were driving a wedge through the political nation.

By 1812 the French forces were on the defensive. Madrid was lost by them in August 1812, recovered, and then lost again. British, Spanish, and Portuguese forces under the duke of Wellington defeated the French at Vitoria on June 21, 1813, and Joseph and his Spanish followers had to flee across the Pyrenees. The General and Extraordinary Cortes moved to Madrid, where they adjourned in September 1813 having remade Spain in the image they desired, at least on paper.

In October 1813 the first regular Cortes elected under the constitution came together, with the Liberals in a far smaller majority. Reports had been reaching the Cortes of troubles in the elections of the municipal councilors according to the constitution.[104] The local oligarchies were up to their old tricks to maintain themselves in power, and they must have welcomed the activities of the conservative clergy.

The burning question became how Fernando would respond to becoming a constitutional king. In December 1813 Napoleon freed him, got him to sign an alliance against the British, and sent him back to Spain. The Cortes instructed him to return directly to Madrid to swear to the constitution before taking any official act, but

Fernando went instead to Valencia, where he received pleas from the Servile deputies to overthrow the constitution. After finding the local commanding general in sympathy with a restoration of the old order, on May 4, 1814, Fernando VII declared the convocation of the Cortes illegal and all their legislation null and void. The government of Spain would return to the form it had before 1808. The liberal deputies attempted to rouse a public response to this coup, but only a few small disturbances in Madrid answered them. The Liberals, for all their intelligence and zeal, lacked a charismatic figure who could excite the common people as Fernando, or in his absence Bishop Quevedo, did. In Seville the fall of the Cortes produced great rejoicing, and the return of the young king for whom they had fought a long war was welcomed almost everywhere. Local ruling groups resumed their authority; the Inquisition, again active, sought out Liberals, Jansenists, and the freemasons who had accepted Joseph's invitation to join his lodges. Muñoz Torrero, a priest, was confined to a convent and Argüelles was imprisoned in a presidio in Africa.

The events of this period show how Spain and, by extension, how Europe were evolving since the seventeenth century described in Elliott's paradigm. In the first instance, the political nation chose to support the rising of the common people in defense of the hereditary king, and they managed to keep the violence of the people directed against the foreign enemy and intruder king, avoiding the possibility of a social upheaval. Elliott's formula for a successful rising.

The most obvious difference with the seventeenth century was that the juntas justified the rising by an appeal to popular sovereignty. At least as indicative of a new era, however, was that the political nation rapidly became divided along ideological lines, hardening disputes that had their origin in the previous century. The traditionalists claimed to defend Spain's Catholic faith, and thus its national past, defined in struggles against Muslims and Protestants. They abandoned popular sovereignty in favor of absolute monarchy. This was novel, since both the conservative clerics and the local oligarchies had objected to the royal reforms of the eighteenth century. The Liberals, also paradoxically, looked to Spain's past instead of enlightened reason for their authority. Adopting the liberal tradition, they claimed to be reviving ancient liberties. They were almost reverting to the seventeenth-century defense of charters, except that they substituted the "Spanish Nation" for the traditional kingdoms.

Although heirs of Carlos III's enlightened rule, they seemed to partake unconsciously of the fascination with the medieval world that marked the burgeoning romantic movement.

Their program embodied in the constitution of 1812 offered a true revolution. As their allies they looked to the common people, who would recognize the benefits to accrue to them in the new society. They gave the vote to all men of any substance, imagining a yeoman society like the ideal that had inspired Carlos III's reformers. Freedom of the press and universal education would be their major weapons, and the constitution provided for both. As it turned out, the press helped the traditionalists more than the Liberals, but on both sides it was drawing the common people into the public sphere.

≺ VI ≻

The Gospel According to 1812

Fernando VII could abolish the constitution of 1812, but it remained very much alive in the minds of liberal Spaniards, and for a decade it served as a model for revolutionary movements outside Spain. Fernando had drawn the military into politics by relying on generals to overthrow the constitution. In the years after 1814 army officers of a different bent joined civilians in several attempted coups to restore constitutional government. Finally, on January 1, 1820, General Rafael del Riego, commanding a force that was supposed to embark to quell rebellion in the American colonies, proclaimed the constitution of 1812 and marched through Andalusia. He became the inspirational figure the Liberals had lacked. Acting in sympathy, important cities restored their constitutional governments, and Fernando VII, indecisive as always, then accepted the constitution, abolished the Inquisition, and convoked cortes.

The revolution of 1820 in Spain immediately inspired supporters of constitutional monarchy in neighboring countries. The Portuguese king had remained in Brazil after 1814, leaving the reactionary Englishman Marshal Beresford in control of Portugal. In August 1820 a military rising in Oporto expelled Beresford and arranged for a national assembly that enacted a constitution providing like Spain's for a one-house legislature, but with direct elections for deputies. João VI returned home to accept it.[105] Southern Italy, which had a long history of association with Spain, also responded to the Spanish example. A small military revolt in Naples forced Ferdinando I of the Two Sicilies in July 1820 to adopt the Spanish constitution of 1812, with modifications to be made to fit the local situation. Eight months later Vittorino Emmanuele I of Piedmont abdicated in the face of a civilian and military rising. Prince Carlo Alberto, appointed regent, promptly accepted the demand of the revolutionaries for the Spanish constitution.[106]

Spanish American revolutionaries also had the constitution before their eyes, for it had made the Indies an integral part of the Spanish nation. Fifty deputies from America had debated and signed it. In the first decade of their independence Gran Colombia, Venezuela, Argentina, Uruguay, Chile, Peru, and Mexico adopted constitutions that incorporated many of the provisions of the constitution of 1812, hoping thereby to strengthen the legislature and the central government against the centrifugal forces of their revolutions.[107]

The Holy Alliance, driven by Prince Metternich, moved to restore order. In 1821 Austrian arms drove the Italian liberals into exile, and in 1823 a French army entered Spain to restore Fernando to absolute rule. This time there was no popular rising against the French, and the Cortes, having fled to Cadiz, had to surrender. In Madrid General Riego was condemned to death and dragged to his execution before a jeering mob in a pannier behind a donkey. The common people of Spain had fought Napoleon to defend their king and their faith; they did not fight a French army to defend a constitution. The French commander, however, conscious of European sentiment, did not let Fernando revive the Inquisition. In Portugal, the opponents of liberal monarchy took the opportunity to force João VI to revoke the constitution.

The first international revolution of the Restoration era had failed. The Spanish constitution of 1812 had offered a beacon for the seekers of constitutional government. With the image of the French Revolution clouded by the memory of the Jacobins, the Spanish document had the merit of having been enacted by a people whose struggle against Napoleon had won the admiration of their contemporaries. The defeat of the constitutional regimes brought an end to the moment of Hispanic revolutionary inspiration. European liberals began once more to look to France, and in Spanish America Benjamin Constant, Jeremy Bentham, and later Alexis de Tocqueville were taken up as the prophets.[108] Spanish liberals, however, having located their model in their past history, proceeded at their own rhythm toward parliamentary monarchy. Political movements would defend, reject, or modify the constitution of 1812, but it would remain a standard against which they judged their programs. Spain has one of the longest histories of constitutional government in Europe.

≺ VII ≻

Expropriating the Revolution

During the war against Napoleon, the dominant sectors of Spain, which drew their income primarily from the land, with the clergy in the lead, used what seemed revolutionary weapons—at first popular sovereignty, then a free press—to halt a revolution. In the next half century the majority of this kind of people came to accept a constitutional regime. In this, they were helped by a split that developed among the liberals. The failure of the common people to come to their support in 1814 had destroyed the democratic enthusiasm of many liberals. During the "Revolutionary Triennium," 1820–23, such persons became known as Moderados. In the next decades they attracted support from the mercantile interests as well as people who secured their positions by entering into newer capitalistic activities: industry, railroads, public utilities, urban expansion, commercial agriculture. After the end of the first Carlist war in 1839, the Moderados succeeded in attracting to their side the less doctrinaire partisans of royal absolutism, both clergy and laymen, to create a conservative parliamentary monarchy that offered satisfaction to both sides.

Those liberals who remained closer to the ideals of 1812 were called Exaltados, and later Progresistas. They appealed primarily to an urban constituency: professionals, shopkeepers, craftsmen. The Jansenist clerics had been punished and silenced, and the new generation of priests, trained in seminaries controlled by the conservative bishops, were less intellectual and not liberal.[109]

The army became involved in all political disputes. The war against Napoleon and the enactment of the constitution of 1812 had politicized many officers. The Carlist war of the 1830s, in which the liberals successfully defended constitutional government against its enemies, further involved the army deeply in domestic politics.

Spain and Portugal were the only European countries to experience prolonged civil war in the nineteenth century. The Spanish army became virtually independent of civilian control, while numerous generals became members of the legislature. Riego had shown that military intervention could determine the nature of government. Military leaders came to conceive of themselves as the proper arbiters of the national fate, although they were not all of the same mind. Generals could be found to place their troops behind almost every political persuasion, and civilian politicians welcomed their support. Pronunciamientos contributed a distinctive military form of violence to political life although the actual fighting was usually modest. Military interventions brought the Progresistas to power with a palace coup in 1836 and revolutions in 1854 and 1868. On the other side, in 1843, 1856, and 1875 conservative generals overthrew the regimes inaugurated by these revolts.[110]

In the process new constitutions were enacted. The Crown, working with the Moderados, issued a "royal statute" in 1834; the Moderados produced a constitution in 1845; and the Progresistas and their allies enacted constitutions in 1837, 1856, and 1869. A brief republican regime fathered a stillborn constitution in 1873. Finally the Conservatives, heirs to the Moderados, introduced the second restoration with the constitution of 1876.[111] It brought an end to the revolutionary upheavals introduced by the riot of Aranjuez in 1808. Although the constitution of 1876 was suspended by a military takeover in 1923 and elections produced the Second Republic in 1931, not until the Civil War of 1936–39 would force of arms again overthrow an established government. By then the evolution of Spain's economy and society and newer international ideologies would make the conflict different from the constitutional struggles of the nineteenth century.

Although the constitutions reflected strong political differences, one element of 1812 proved too dear to be touched. Except for the brief royal statute of 1834, every constitution guaranteed the freedom of expression.[112] At first the right applied to the printed word; in 1869, speech was included. Freedom of assembly and of association and the inviolability of the mail all were added in 1869 and were preserved in 1876.[113] The drafters of 1812 had considered establishing the jury system, which they admired in England and found present in medieval Spain, but had left it for future cortes.[114] The progresista constitutions of 1837 and 1856 introduced it for cases of freedom of the press, and that of 1869 extended it to political crimes;[115] but the 1876 constitution omitted it. Trial by jury was an ideal of the left; the right did not want it. Given the political realities of the time, however, the printed word was not immune to government pressure, whatever the constitutions said.

Gradually freedom of expression was expanded to include religious freedom, as the ban on non-Catholic faiths included in the constitution of 1812 was eroded. The constitutions of 1837 and 1845 maintained Catholicism as the religion of the Spanish nation.[116] Protestant missionaries were nevertheless making conversions, and the constitution of 1856, in part to curry British favor, for the first time gave Spaniards the right to hold other religious beliefs, provided they did not exhibit them in public.[117] This constitution never took effect, and by the 1860s Spain was the only European state that still allowed only one religion. Religious freedom had now become a demand of the left, and the constitution of 1869, while maintaining state support for the Catholic church, permitted public observance of other faiths.[118] More radical, the republican draft of 1873 would have separated church and state and allowed the free observance of all cults.[119] The 1876 constitution reasserted that Catholicism was the religion of the state and allowed only Catholic worship in public, but it preserved the right of Spaniards to hold other faiths.[120] Religious toleration, which had not crossed the minds of the authors of 1812, had finally become accepted, although conservative Catholics still denounced it. Spain's long history of war against Muslims and Protestants had made religious toleration perhaps the hardest of modern rights to achieve, in contrast to freedom of political expression. Until after the Civil War of 1936–39, the proper place of the Catholic faith and church in Spanish life would remain the most bitter bone of ideological contention.[121] Spain's road to modern freedom was indeed unique.

If individual freedoms experienced a steady growth, the democratic elements of 1812 gradually lost ground. Before parliamentary monarchy could be stabilized, the dominant elements of society had to become reconciled to it: the Crown, the upper classes, both old and new, and the Church. The result was the "moderado order" that took shape in the middle of the century.[122] The restoration of 1875 mellowed its harshest features but preserved it into the next century.

The Crown became an ally of the Moderados as a result of a dynastic conflict. In the decade after 1823, clerics and others who believed religion was in danger from the loss of the Inquisition gathered around Fernando's brother and heir, Don Carlos. In 1830 Fernando had a daughter, Isabel. To assure her right to the throne he finally published the revocation of the Salic Law by the Cortes of 1789. Don Carlos rejected the legitimacy of this act and on the death of Fernando in 1833 he went to war to assert his claim to the throne. Isabel II's mother as regent turned to the Moderado leaders. Together they produced the royal statute of 1834, conceived to attract the Old Regime elites and those erstwhile supporters of 1812 who had come to fear universal suffrage. It included provision for an upper house of bishops, grandees, and appointees of the Crown, and a lower house elected by voters who paid a stipulated property tax.

The later constitutions, even the republican draft of 1873, preserved the two houses of the cortes, called the Senate and the Congress of Deputies. The progresista documents put the choice of senators in the hands of the voters, but the moderado system, firmed up in 1845, gave the monarch the right to appoint senators for life from among grandees, bishops, generals, leading politicians, and men with a large income. It thus institutionalized a tacit alliance of the queen, the army, the aristocracy, the clergy, and the nouveaux riches. Jovellanos's wish for a second house had been fulfilled, though not with the results he had anticipated.

A broad suffrage remained the policy of the Progresistas, but the Moderados placed tight property requirements on voting. By itself this did not assure them local control, for the progresista constitution of 1837 followed 1812 in making municipal officials elective (its leading author was Agustín Argüelles, of 1812 fame), and the Progresistas soon controlled the major cities, where they were in a position to influence the elections for national deputies. After 1845 the Moderados gave the ministry the power to appoint the mayors of all but the smallest towns, either directly or through the provincial governors. To back up the mayors against any popular threat, in 1844 the Moderados established a police force called the Civil Guard. If the Inquisition had been the bogey of enlightened persons in the Old Regime, the Civil Guard became that of advanced elements, anarchists, and urban revolutionaries in the nineteenth and twentieth centuries.

The final guarantee of local oligarchic control was outside the realm of constitutions and laws. It involved an unofficial system of rule that took shape in the decades after 1845 and became notorious under the name of "caciquismo." *Caciques* were local political bosses who developed control over their districts with carrots for their clients, and the Civil Guard and courts as sticks for those who challenged them. They had no official position, but their power, derived from serving the local elite and responding to informal orders from the government in Madrid, gave them more authority than the officially appointed mayors and judges. Caciquismo was the linchpin of the moderado order, and it existed in large sectors of Spain well into the twentieth century.[123]

The Church remained to be converted to the system. In the Carlist war of the 1830s the conservative clergy as a whole had supported Don Carlos against Isabel II. The beginning was not propitious. The Moderados retaliated by closing male and female religious orders and reviving Carlos IV's policy of selling church properties to pay the national debt. During the rest of the century the long process of *desamortización* allowed private individuals to acquire most ecclesiastical buildings and lands. In 1856 the Progresistas added many municipal and royal properties to the sales. In the end the sectors behind the moderado order became the principal beneficiaries.

In making peace in 1839 the Carlists abandoned their clerical allies, opting instead to defend local privileges of the Basque provinces and Navarre. The Moderados saw here an opportunity to attract the clergy, but the conservative clerics could not be reconciled to the new system without concessions. The Moderados rose to the challenge. They won the support of Pius IX in 1848 by sending troops to fight the revolutionary Roman republic. Their government then signed a concordat with the Vatican in 1851. In it the Church recognized the sale of its properties, but got the right to acquire property in the future. Two male religious orders were reestablished, a third was to be named, and nuns were permitted back. Most critical, the bishops were given the authority to watch over all levels of education to see that they remained in line with Catholic doctrine. This was not the Inquisition, but it was a new way to determine what Spaniards would read, at least in their formative years. And for the time being Catholicism remained the only religion tolerated in Spain. Although the state's enforcement of the concordat's terms disappointed the more militant Catholics, the Spanish church became a central member of the constitutional monarchy. Carlism had ceased to be the church's cause.[124]

The Carlist war of 1833–39 was one of the bitterest of nineteenth-century Europe. The Carlists conceived it as a continuation of the struggle for God and king that went back to the war against Napoleon and had been refocused against the Cadiz Liberals after 1812. At its outset the Carlist cause found support in wide areas of Spain. Gradually its active followers were reduced to the Basque people, especially the peasantry, tied together by a language no outsider could understand, fear of central authority, and dislike of liberal culture.[125] Peace was made when the army of Isabel II promised to guarantee the Basque and Navarrese *fueros*, which had survived the absolute monarchy but disappeared in the uniform structure of the constitution of 1812.

Defense of local charters recalls a past age, and Elliott's paradigm again comes to mind. But again one perceives that this was a new era. Charters had been the cause of the "political nation." Now the political nation was divided, for Basque merchants and some large landowners supported Isabel II. *Fueros* were the cause of the Basque peasantry and the common people of the Basque cities, who fought paradoxically both for them and for royal absolutism.

Eventually the rights of the ethnic nation would replace the *fueros* as the basis for Spanish regionalism. After mid-century the Catalan intellectuals experienced a cultural awakening similar to those taking place in central Europe. It would be joined after 1876 by a political movement demanding autonomy for Catalonia and the official use of its language. Because the Carlists at first had little following among the educated class of Basques, a movement to defend Basque culture did not develop until the twentieth century. The Catalan and Basque leaders glorified their earlier *fueros*, but in fact their "nationalities" embodied the new democratic ideal of popular self determination.[126]

Democratic ideas contributed to the rise of another thorn in the side of the oligarchic monarchy, a product of the changing economy and the expanding population, what became known as the "social question." This involved the politicization of the lower classes of urban centers. From the outset the constitution of 1812 had excited some support among the lower class in the cities, although the partisans of Fernando's absolutism were at first more successful in ap-

pealing to the common people. The liberals had attributed their defeats in 1814 and 1823 as well as the rising of the Carlists largely to
the machinations of the clergy, especially the friars and monks. By
the time of the Carlist war, the liberals' message was being heard by
the lower urban class. In 1834 and 1835 popular crowds in Madrid,
Barcelona, and elsewhere attacked and murdered friars and monks.
In 1854 the urban proletariat of Madrid joined the progresista revolution with barricades, and many common people of the major cities
welcomed the revolution of 1868. The Progresistas, however, could
not count on solid backing from the lower class. Beginning in the
1840s, workers, especially in Barcelona, the most industrialized city,
were forming labor unions. The political instability following the
revolution of 1868 gave an opportunity for disciples of Marx and
Bakunin to preach their messages in Spain. Small but active groups
began to turn to socialism and anarchism. The horror inspired by the
Paris commune among the European middle class reached into Spain,
and after the restoration of 1875, the "social question" both concerned and frightened the supporters of the constitutional monarchy.

The division that had appeared in the political nation was spreading down to the common people, but along geographic rather than
class lines. Those living in urban centers were in touch with the political world, through newspapers or word of mouth, and came to rest
on the left, whether republican, socialist, or anarchist; while those
living in small places, rural peasants, remained on the right, influenced by the clergy and by the power of local *caciques*. Elliott's paradigm assumes that the political nation and the common people each
was politically fairly uniform in the early modern period. The democratic transformation that began at the end of the eighteenth century
had split both levels into different political camps, divided over the
meaning of liberty and popular sovereignty. Regionalist nationalism
and proletarian movements were new developments since the time
of Napoleon, outgrowths of the doctrine of popular sovereignty. They
would become strong threats to the parliamentary monarchy as Spain
moved into the twentieth century.

The restoration of 1875 had concluded the transformation that
began with the rising of 1808. The final result enabled the privileged
sectors to take command of the country by exploiting constitutional
forms that had originally been aimed at their power. Carlos III had
tried to restrain the rural oligarchies, improve the conditions of the

peasantry, and limit the power of the clergy. Those whom he opposed relied on passive resistance and control at the local level. The constitutional monarchy proved much more serviceable to the upper classes than the absolute monarchy revived in 1814 because now the central power as well as local authority was in their hands. The timing and issues were Spanish, but this story is not unlike that in other Western countries, where the privileged sectors also learned in the nineteenth century how to exploit the achievements of the liberals to enhance their own control. The Spanish case is a prime example of the ambiguities that dotted the nineteenth-century road to civil liberty and parliamentary democracy.

Revolution, Independence, and Liberty
in Latin America

RICHARD·J. WALTER

THE REVOLUTIONS THAT OCCURRED in Latin America at the beginning of the nineteenth century differ in significant ways from
the other revolutions discussed in this volume. First, they began as
trans-Atlantic struggles for independence by the American colonies
of France, Spain, and Portugal at a time when the mother countries
themselves were undergoing revolutionary turmoil. Second, the successful outcome of these anticolonial struggles produced a score of
separate independent states stretching over an enormous area, from
California to Tierra del Fuego. Third, the Latin American revolutions took place in societies where racial divisions were particularly
marked and particularly significant and had a great bearing on the
course and outcome of these struggles. Black slavery existed throughout the entire region and was particularly prominent in Brazil, Cuba,
and Haiti. Exploited Indian populations could also be found throughout Spanish and Portuguese America and were especially numerous
and important in Mexico and Peru, the two main centers of Spanish
colonial power. Fourth, they generally lasted longer and were more
destructive of lives and property than their continental counterparts.
Finally, in many ways the Latin American revolutions represented a
sharper break with the past than their European or even North American counterparts, as the revolutionaries sought to establish new forms
of government radically different from the colonial institutions and
practices that had ruled them for more than three centuries.

Along with these differences, there were also certain similarities
and certainly many connections with developments on the European
continent and elsewhere. Occurring within the larger context of the
"Age of Democratic Revolutions," the struggles in Latin America
were much influenced, directly and indirectly, by the ideas of the Eu-

Latin America in 1830

ropean Enlightenment. In addition, the Latin American wars of independence were significantly affected by the events in Europe involving the spread of liberal ideas and most notably the impact of the
French Revolution and its consequences. Indeed, it is doubtful that
the Latin American revolutions would have occurred when and how
they did without those events.

The struggles and their aftermath, too, were marked by developments that are main features of other cases treated in this volume: the
emergence of a vibrant and influential press, the appearance of issues
revolving around the relationship among differing social classes as
major factors in the revolutions and in the attempts to develop viable
nation-states, and the efforts to establish suffrage and elections as
instruments to legitimize governments and to express the popular
will. As with most of the other examples in this volume, the results
of the Latin American revolutions were ambiguous, as democratic and
constitutional aspirations confronted social-economic realities and,
more often than not, dictatorial solutions. With turbulent change
there was considerable continuity, especially with regard to persistent
elite domination of society, leading many to question at the time, as
well as a century and a half after the fact, just how "revolutionary"
were, in fact, the Latin American struggles for independence.

≺ I ≻

Background to Independence

Covering a period that extends from the mid-eighteenth century to
the 1830s and trying to deal with three colonial empires and the
numerous states that resulted from the independence movements
requires painting an historical picture with broad strokes. For the
most part, this chapter will concentrate on the Spanish empire, the
Spanish-American fight for independence, and the states that resulted. Not all of the states that emerged after independence can
receive equal treatment. Basically, I shall limit myself to discussion
of Mexico, Argentina, Chile, Peru, Colombia, and Venezuela. While
Spanish America will receive the bulk of my attention, some consideration of French America (Haiti) and Portuguese America (Brazil)
will also be included.

To place the Spanish American revolutions in context, and to understand the ambiguous nature of their results, it is necessary first to sketch the background of colonial rule and experience against which they were directed. That rule was established soon after the European discovery of the New World by Christopher Columbus and the ensuing conquest of the Caribbean and the American mainland that continued from the late fifteenth to almost the end of the sixteenth century. As discovery and conquest progressed, the Crown sought to develop a system that would allow it to protect and profit from its new-found empire while at the same time prevent the development of a powerful, autonomous nobility in the New World composed of the *conquistadores* (conquerors) and their heirs. The administrative system put in place was hierarchical and centralized, with the monarch at the top of the governmental pyramid, exercising a supreme authority by "divine right."[1] This monarchical power, in turn, was buttressed in Spain and the colonies by the predominance of scholastic thought, a system of belief that reinforced the infallibility of divinely-sanctioned authority.[2]

   To handle the details of colonial policy and government, the Crown created the Council of the Indies in 1524. In the colonies themselves, the principal official was the viceroy, appointed by the Crown to govern the two main administrative divisions of the empire, those of New Spain, with its capital in Mexico City, and of Peru, with its capital in Lima. In the eighteenth century two more viceroyalties were created, that of New Granada, with its capital in Bogotá, in 1739, and that of the Río de la Plata, with its capital in Buenos Aires, in 1776. The viceroyalties, in turn, were subdivided into smaller units governed by *audiencias*, which combined judicial and legislative functions. The *cabildo* (city council) served as the principal body of municipal government.

   Most of the crucial administrative positions were limited to persons from Spain, or *peninsulares*; creoles, persons of European background born in the New World, were generally excluded. There were at times certain important exceptions to this rule; but of the 170 viceroys appointed over the course of the colonial period, for example, only four were creoles.[3] Unlike the British colonies of North America, few governing institutions, based as they were on an appointed hierarchy, allowed the creole colonists opportunity for or experience in self-government. The one governmental body in which creoles did participate—and even predominate—and which occasionally possessed some autonomy and some democratic features, was the municipal *cabildo*. By the end of the colonial period, however, most *cabildos* either had proved inefficient and ineffective and had been replaced by other institutions or had become the exclusive domain of the local elite, which controlled elections and passed positions down from generation to generation.[4]

Within the larger administrative system, the Crown sought to regulate colonial production and trade in ways that would provide maximum benefits for Spain. Adhering to mercentalist theory, imperial policy considered the colonies essential sources and producers of raw materials—gold, silver, agricultural goods—to be shipped exclusively to Spain, which in turn would supply the Americas with manufactured goods. As a result, colonial industrial development was discouraged. The colonies were to trade only with the mother country and were prohibited from economic interaction with one another. The Crown established an elaborate system of monopoly ports and regular fleet sailings to try to assure its monopolistic control over commerce.

In both the political and the economic realms, however, practice often deviated from theory. Many cracks existed in the supposedly hierarchical and authoritarian system. Viceroys, for example, often found that the laws created in Seville had little applicability to the situations they encountered in the Americas. Therefore, they often adopted the flexible attitude of "Obedezco pero no cumplo" ("I obey but do not enforce") when confronted with edicts they believed made little sense. Moreover, as early as the mid-sixteenth century the Crown began the practice of selling offices in the colonial administration as a way to raise revenues. This practice not only diluted the quality of bureaucratic office-holders, it also opened up positions for creoles wealthy and influential enough to purchase them. Almost half (44 percent) of the audiencia appointments between 1678 and 1750, for example, went to creoles.[5] With regard to the theoretically highly regulated and controlled system of trade, enforcement proved difficult from the beginning. The lengthy coastlines and vast interior of the Americas made any serious oversight of economic transactions almost impossible and contraband contacts among colonists and between colonists and traders of other European nations and colonies flourished, especially in the peripheral areas removed from the centers of colonial authority. Regulation became even more difficult to enforce with Spain's economic and military decline in the seventeenth century. In addition, Spain's laggard manufacturing and its consequent failure to keep up its end of the mercantilist bargain impelled the colonists to deal with representatives of other nations that could supply manufactured products as well as to develop some small-scale industries of their own.

With all its flaws and inconsistencies, the Spanish imperial system had sufficient vitality to persist for better than three hundred years. Part of this persistence was due to what John Lynch and others have described as the development of a kind of colonial compromise and consensus that evolved as local elites were able to penetrate the administration of their own affairs and as mechanisms and practices allowing for some decentralization and flexibility that were acceptable to both rulers and subjects emerged.[6]

Another crucial ingredient in imperial longevity was the Catholic church, from the time of the conquest the preeminent religious institution in Spanish America. Controlled by and tied to the Crown by the *patronato real* (royal patronage) established in the early sixteenth century, the church and the various religious orders associated with it converted the native Americans to Christianity, aided settlement on the frontier, and dominated social welfare and education. Over time, too, the church accumulated considerable wealth in both property and capital. Gradually, creoles came to predominate numerically within the church, although *peninsulares* continued to control most of the highest offices. Overall, the church and Catholicism provided an important institutional and philosophical support and coherence for the entire imperial system.[7]

The Spanish-American social structure during the colonial period (and after) was a hierarchical one, based primarily on race, occupation, and wealth. At the top were *peninsulares* and creoles, men and occasionally in some areas women who owned mines or large estates or who exercised a profession or engaged in commerce. Below the *peninsulares* and creoles were the *castas*, notably *mestizos* (mixture of Indian and European) and mulattos, who composed something of a middle strata in the overall social structure. The lower classes, by far the largest elements of colonial society, were occupied by the Indian masses, whose numbers had been devastated by conquest and disease in the sixteenth century but who began to recover in the seventeenth and eighteenth; and by black slaves, brought over by the millions from the early sixteenth century to the mid-nineteenth century. While opportunities for mobility were few, some Indians were able to advance into skilled occupations and the professions and a substantial number of slaves gained their freedom before 1800.[8]

To protect the ideological underpinnings of its empire and as leader of the counter-Reformation movement in Europe, the Spanish Crown sought to prevent the infiltration and circulation of what it considered "radical" ideas into its dominions. The best-known instrument in this regard, of course, was the infamous Inquisition, established on the peninsula in the late fifteenth century and extended to the colonies in the sixteenth. Designed to censor and prohibit "subversive" ideas and behavior and to assure religious conformity, the Inquisition was neither as effective nor as pervasive as its many critics have charged. Though it no doubt did dampen and discourage creative thought and critical inquiry,[9] by the mid-eighteenth century the ideas of the European Enlightenment began to circulate widely throughout the empire. Increasingly, a substantial number of creoles became exposed to and familiar with the works of men like Voltaire, Rousseau, Montesquieu, Adam Smith, and others. In contrast to the dogmatism and authoritarianism of scholasticism and the divine right of the monarchy, Enlightenment thought stressed the importance of the use of reason and the senses to gain knowledge, the value of experimentation, and the inherent rights of the individual.

Enlightenment ideas entered Spain and its colonies in a variety of ways. Increasingly in the late eighteenth and early nineteenth centuries, well-to-do creoles traveled to and studied in Europe, where they absorbed these new concepts. Others, many of whom had never been to Europe, assembled substantial private libraries filled with the volumes of Enlightenment figures. These libraries, in turn, served as locales for informal discussion of the new currents in salons and tertulias. At the same time, foreign visitors toured Spanish America, spreading new ideas, especially in the scientific realm. The best known of these was Alexander von Humboldt, the famed German scientist and traveler, who spent five years (1799–1804) in a lengthy expedition throughout Spanish America shortly before the wars of independence.[10] As the eighteenth century progressed, Enlightenment influence could also be seen with growing frequency in colonial universities, especially in the study of science and medicine.[11]

The development of a public press aided the diffusion of new ideas. Various newspapers and magazines began to appear in Spain itself in the second half of the eighteenth century. While many were short-lived and limited, they served to disseminate political and economic information and offered a sounding board for criticism of the status quo.[12] This development in the homeland soon spread to the colonies, where newspapers and periodicals began to appear with increasing frequency from the 1760s on. By the turn of the century, despite constraints imposed by the Inquisition, many had become organs for Enlightenment ideas. These included the *Gaceta de Literatura* (1788–95) in New Spain, the *Mercurio Peruano* of Lima (1791–95), the *Gazeta de Guatemala* (1797–1810), the *Papel periódico de Bogotá* (1791–97), and the *Papel periódico de Habana* (1790–1804).

While clearly significant, the impact of Enlightenment ideas and of the press on the course of Spanish American independence should not be exaggerated. Newspapers and magazines of this period had limited distribution and circulation, rarely reaching more than a few hundred readers in a society where literacy did not extend much beyond the creole and peninsular elite. It is far from certain that even those readers all reacted favorably to the thoughts expressed. Some rejected these ideas altogether while others used them to argue for reform of the existing system rather than any revolutionary break from it. Nonetheless, ideas concerning the promotion of individual rights and liberties, faith in reason, and representative government did have a considerable influence on the elite that eventually led the movements for independence. Moreover, the newspapers and magazines that helped to spread these new ideas grew substantially in number (from a handful to several hundred) and in circulation (from a readership of a few hundred to one of several thousand in most major colonies) and played an ever-increasing and important role in the struggles for independence and the attempts to establish new nation-states that followed.[13]

Of greater significance to the overall course of Spanish American independence than the direct impact of Enlightenment ideas on certain key individuals, it can be argued, was the indirect impact of these ideas as transferred through the so-called "Bourbon reforms" to colonial society as a whole. These reforms followed the War of the Spanish Succession (1700–1713) and the replacement of the Habsburgs with the French-connected Bourbons through the reigns of

Philip V (1700–1746), Ferdinand VI (1746–59), and Charles III (1759–88). The new monarchs, inspired by French advisors, sought to revitalize Spain and the empire through a series of changes that would restore the glory of both to the "golden age" of the sixteenth century following the disastrous decline of the seventeenth.

One of the most important changes involved a new conception of the relationship between the monarch and his subjects. Instead of the Habsburg demand for blind, unquestioning obedience, the Bourbons argued that the monarch should be respected and revered according to the material benefits he provided.[14] Unfortunately for the Bourbons, this new concept of the relationship between ruler and ruled placed them in a tenuous position. On the one hand, it opened them to severe criticism and loss of support if they failed to perform as promised as judged by the new criteria they had established. On the other hand, many colonists rejected altogether this new justification for the Crown and adhered to the Habsburg theory of the absolute state.[15]

The most important specific reforms of the Bourbon period, with the greatest implications for the wars of independence, occurred during the reign of Charles III. Responding to the British capture of Havana in 1762, the Crown determined to bolster its military capabilities in the Americas by incréasing substantially the size of its standing armies there and by allowing and encouraging for the first time the creation of colonial militias. This decision allowed creoles greater access to military equipment, training, and experience—and a growing confidence in their own military capabilities—that would eventually be turned against the Spanish armies themselves. But the expansion of the military also encouraged a new wave of *peninsulares* to reach the Americas and to assume the choice positions not only within the standing armies but also in the militias, further exacerbating creole-peninsular antagonisms.

In 1767, seeking to reinforce royal authority and to add to the royal treasury, the Crown determined to expel the powerful and influential Jesuit order from America and to confiscate its assets. An order that had long refused to recognize royal over papal authority, the Jesuits had played an important role in advancing the frontier, converting and protecting the Indian population, and promoting education. In the process, they had acquired vast and valuable properties throughout the region.[16]

As was the case with many of the Bourbon reforms, creole reaction to the expulsion was ambivalent. Creoles associated with rival orders or resentful of Jesuit protection of Indian labor that they might otherwise have been able to exploit were pleased with the edict. Moreover, some wealthy creoles were able to acquire some of the best landed properties owned by the order before 1767. Many creoles, however, saw the expulsion as a blow to an order that included a majority of American-born members, another example of arbitrary Crown behavior to favor *peninsulares*. Finally, the expulsion of the Jesuits was just the first salvo in a Bourbon campaign to limit the power and privileges of the Church throughout the colonies, a campaign that alienated many churchmen, especially of the lower clergy, a substantial number of whom would join the revolutionary cause.[17]

In the economic realm, efforts were made to enhance production, especially in the mining sector. Encouraging the introduction of new organizational methods and new techniques, the Bourbons helped to stimulate a boom in silver and gold mining that resulted in record-setting volumes in the latter part of the eighteenth century, particularly in Mexico. At the same time, the Crown gradually lifted most of the restrictions on trade between the colonies and within the empire, producing a dramatic increase in exports from the Americas. Increased production and trade, in turn, led to an unprecedented prosperity in much of the Americas. Nonetheless, for many creoles engaged in and benefiting from this prosperity, there were still restrictions and still resentments against Crown policy. Most of the wealth continued to flow out of the colonies to the mother country. The freedom to trade within the empire only whetted the creole appetite for totally unrestricted trade with the wider world.[18]

Few Bourbon policies produced as much resentment among the colonists as attempts to increase and improve tax collection. From the 1760s on, there was resistance and often violent opposition to these efforts, resistance that intensified as the eighteenth century progressed and the demands of imperial defense and Spain's involvement in European conflicts increased the Crown's reliance on colonial revenues. In December 1804 the Crown issued its most controversial revenue-raising decree, the *consolidación*, which demanded that assets held by religious and charitable funds in the Americas be seized and sent to Spain. Since many of these assets were in the form of loans to landowners and merchants, the measure had wide repercussions. In Mexico, where the decree was felt most profoundly, it led to a severe contraction of credit and produced widespread resentment among many creoles.[19]

In the social sphere, Bourbon policies aimed to improve the lot of Indians and blacks, partially in the hopes of developing allies among these exploited peoples as a counterbalance to the creoles. Under Charles III, the Crown abolished the *encomienda* (grant of authority over Indians), *mita* (forced labor draft, usually for mining), and *repartimiento* (distribution of Indian labor) systems, all of which had long been used to abuse and exploit the Indian population. Other reforms aimed to open up some areas of local administration to Indians as well as to increase their wages and make some educational institutions accessible. Various decrees sought to limit and prohibit some of the worst treatment of black slaves, such as the practice of branding them. Other measures sought to undercut aristocratic privilege through taxes aimed to curtail primogeniture and entail and by allowing skilled laborers to aspire to positions of nobility. While well intentioned, these measures, especially those concerning Indians and blacks, were rarely enforced and did little to ameliorate the conditions of the lower classes. On the other hand, they served to alienate further creoles sensitive to any measures that threatened to reduce the distance between themselves and colored masses.[20]

Social reforms were also a Crown response to growing unrest and rebellion among the lower orders of society, especially the Indian and *mestizo* population. In the Andean region the number of indigenous revolts against abusive conditions increased steadily from the 1740s, culminating in the massive insurrection in Peru in 1780 led by José Gabriel Condorcanqui (Tupac Amaru II), a Jesuit-educated descendant of the Incan nobility. This rebellion, which began as a tax revolt with some participation by poorer creoles, soon became a strictly Indian protest movement. Ultimately suppressed by Spanish and creole forces, this movement cost some 100,000 lives. In 1781, in New Granada (Colombia and Venezuela) another uprising, the so-called *comunero* (literally, "commoner") revolt, also began as a protest against Bourbon tax and other fiscal policies and soon acquired support from *mestizos* and mulattos and began to take on the dimensions of a radical, mass-based movement. When that happened, the creoles, as in Peru, joined the peninsular authorities in opposing and eventually suppressing the uprising. In this instance, as in most others of its type, the Crown emphasized the danger of revolution from below not only to the imperial system but also to the relatively privileged status of the creoles themselves. The creoles, in turn, rallied to the Crown and in Peru in particular the memory of the Tupac Amaru rebellion helped make that colony the last to declare and win its independence from Spain.[21]

Among the various reforms of the Bourbon period, none caused more resentment among creoles than those that took place in the administrative realm. Seeking to improve governmental efficiency overall, the Bourbons, beginning in the 1750s, abolished the sale of public office and tried to appoint officials on the basis of loyalty and ability. The most important structural change was the introduction of the *intendant* system, creating a new set of bureaucratic offices with considerable power designed to enhance Crown authority at the local level and in the countryside.[22] From the creoles' point of view, the most objectionable aspect of these changes was their own exclusion. With an end to the sale of offices, that avenue of access to the upper ranks of administration was closed. Moreover, the Crown made it a policy again to favor *peninsulares* in making bureaucratic appointments. Most *intendant* positions went to Spaniards and the system itself largely supplanted local institutions, like the *cabildo*, where creoles had once predominated. From 1751 to 1808, the eve of independence, only a little better than one in five *audiencia* appointments went to creoles, drastically curtailing the presence of Spanish Americans in this important institution. As a result, the tacit consensus between Crown and colonist over the centuries of Habsburg rule began to unravel.[23]

Other developments contributed to this unraveling. During the period of the Bourbon reforms, a new generation of Spanish *conquistadores* had arrived in the New World and a few had made fortunes in the millions during the economic boom of the late eighteenth century. Some had become established merchants, who usually enjoyed greater financial success than their creole counterparts. In Mexico, among the wealthy elite whose fortunes were based on mining, agriculture, and finance, creole-peninsular antagonisms were muted through marriage and the nature of business relationships.[24] Not all *peninsulares*, of course, gained fortunes. Nonetheless, many creoles, growing in number, saw positions in an expanding bureaucracy that they felt should be theirs going to *peninsulares*. In addition, successful *peninsulares* often married the most attractive and well-to-do creole women, adding one more element to growing creole discontent.[25]

As creole resentments of peninsular privileges peaked at the turn of the century, they coincided with and contributed to a growing sense of creole nationalism, which had been slowly evolving throughout the latter colonial period. This nationalism was based, naturally enough, on the fact of American birth and permanent residence as opposed to the transience of the *peninsulares*. In the late eighteenth century it was reinforced by a growing American literature that focused on the history and abundant resources of the New World.[26] Increasingly, many creoles preferred to call themselves "Americans" instead of "creoles" and certainly instead of "Spaniards." Nonetheless, the Spanish American empire was too vast and communication among its component parts too infrequent for a strong sense of a truly "American" identity to emerge. Most "Americans" more commonly identified themselves with their particular homeland rather than with the continent as a whole. This sense of separate identity had been strengthened both by geography and by the Crown's awareness of regional differences in establishing its governmental system.[27]

As creole nationalism and a desire for greater self-determination grew, fueled by resentment of the Bourbon-inspired "re-peninsularization" of the Americas, external events continued to contribute to the climate and the circumstances that would culminate in independence. First, the former British colonies of North America won their independence in the early 1780s, providing an important model and inspiration for the Spanish Americans. The principal ideas and documents of the newly-founded United States circulated among sympathetic creoles, a number of whom were able to visit the fledgling northern republic and view first-hand its attempts to establish democratic government. The U.S. constitution would have a significant influence on a number of Spanish American republics. Moreover, in the late eighteenth and early nineteenth centuries, links of trade and cultural and scientific exchange between the U.S. and the Spanish American colonies increased substantially, enhancing the impact of the North American example.[28]

The French ideas of liberty and the rights of man after 1789 also had a powerful appeal to those creoles attracted to the liberal concepts of the Enlightenment. There were many, too, however, who were ambivalent about the Revolution's emphasis on equality and its anticlerical aspects. As its more radical aspects became clearer, many creoles saw it less as a hope for greater freedom and more a potential threat to their own status. During the course of the wars of independence themselves, a few creoles did associate with the more radical traits of the French experience. Most, however, rejected what were considered revolutionary "excesses" and selected only those elements they found most appropriate. For others, the French model was one most decidedly to be avoided. As one Argentine publication put it, "If the French Revolution, with all the genius and civilization of its people, deceived all those who had had faith in it, and a ferocious soldier came to occupy the throne of the kind, but arbitrary, Louis, that example helps the present generation to avoid following its steps."[29]

The revolution in the former French colony of Haiti, a consequence of the revolution in the homeland, also caused unease and misgivings among many creoles. Initiated by a slave revolt in 1791, the movement for independence and abolition of slavery finally culminated in a French defeat in 1804, after a long and violent struggle, and the creation of a black republic.[30] Spanish colonial authorities responded to the Haitian revolution, which included the extermination of whites and an attack on the slave trade, with attempts to assure that it did not spread to its possessions, especially Venezuela. For neighboring Cuba, the Haitian revolution was particularly sobering. With a large slave population of their own and constantly concerned with black uprisings, the Cuban creoles determined to avoid the larger revolutionary movements of the early nineteenth century.[31] As a result, Cuba remained a Spanish colony until 1898. The Haitian experience was also influential in Portuguese Brazil, another colony where blacks were numerous and where slavery undergirded the entire economy. Fears of an uprising similar to that which had occurred in the Caribbean, "A dread of what was termed *haitianismo*," affected the way in which independence was achieved there and helped to keep the colony unified.[32]

As these various events evolved, Spain became enmeshed in a tangled web of European war and diplomacy. Immediately following the French Revolution, the shaken Spanish Crown joined with England in a coalition against the radical new regime. As the Revolution moderated, however, the coalition weakened and by 1798 Spain had determined to ally with France against the second coalition of Russia and England. England, in turn, retaliated by cutting off trade between Spain and its colonies. For Spain, alliance with France, combined with a series of inept leaders after the death of Charles III, spelled disaster, underscoring the nation's overall decline.

Confronted with Napoleon's ascendancy on the Continent in the early 1800s, the British devised a strategy that included encouraging revolution in the American colonies of Spain, France's ally. A British expeditionary force invaded and occupied Buenos Aires in June 1806. Upon hearing of the impending invasion, the Spanish viceroy fled for safety to Córdoba. The creoles, however, organized a resistance and forced the British from Buenos Aires in August. In early 1807 the creole militia was again successful in defeating a second British expeditionary force from Montevideo.

The British invasions had clear implications for the process of independence in the Río de la Plata region. While British control was fleeting, it did provide for a brief period of unregulated free trade, a particularly important consideration in this area, and increased the creole appetite for more of the same. Although the flight of the viceroy underscored the flaws and ineptitude of Spanish rule, the fierce creole resistance to the British underscored their unwillingness to substitute one form of colonial subordination with another. Third, and most importantly, the successful creole struggle against a powerful foreign invader gave the American colonists a sense of pride and confidence in their own abilities not only to defend their home territory but also, eventually, to manage their own affairs.[33]

The most fateful of the external events to induce the Spanish American wars of independence occurred in 1807–8, when Napoleon invaded and took direct control of Spain and Portugal. In May 1808, he forced the newly-proclaimed Spanish king, Ferdinand VII, to abdicate and to suffer enforced exile in Bayonne while he placed his brother Joseph on the throne in Madrid. The Portuguese monarchy was more fortunate, spirited away to Rio de Janeiro by British intercession before French troops could capture the royal family.

≺ II ≻

The Wars of Independence

The Napoleonic invasion and takeover of the Iberian peninsula provided the proximate cause for independence in both Spanish and Portuguese America. On the peninsula, resistance to the French, led by ad-hoc juntas, began almost immediately. In the Americas, as soon as news of Iberian developments reached its shores, creoles throughout the region formed their own juntas and sought to assume governance of their respective regions. In Brazil, thanks to the presence of the monarchy, Rio de Janeiro became the official seat of the Portuguese empire. There, too, the changes introduced by the transfer of power, combined with a steadily evolving gap between creoles and *peninsulares*, would lead to independence. In Spanish America, most creoles began their efforts with the rather modest goal of achieving greater autonomy and freedom within the empire, an aim that seemed both reasonable and realizable in the early stages. When the Crown was restored in 1814 and rejected this possibility, however, the creole leadership, for the most part, saw total independence from Spain as their only option.

The wars of independence, which pitted creole against Spaniard, lasted from 1808 to 1825. By 1825, all the former Spanish and Portuguese colonies with the exceptions of Cuba and Puerto Rico had won their freedom from imperial control. It was, in many respects, a continent-wide movement, with the principal leadership, especially that of General José de San Martín in southern South America and Simón Bolívar in northern South America, aware of the fact that independence could not be secured in any one place unless all Spanish troops were defeated and Spanish authority destroyed throughout the region. Therefore, they led campaigns of liberation that extended well beyond their respective homelands of Argentina and Venezuela. This aspect of the struggle, in turn, provided the wars with a coherence and a uniformity that they otherwise might not have had. At the same time, however, each region and resultant nation had its own particular characteristics and history, wherein the course of the independence struggle took on unique features. Space does not permit a treatment of each of these cases, which have been described in some detail in other sources.[34] Therefore, I shall limit myself to a few general remarks and features that bear on the principal concerns of this chapter.

The revolutions were led by a relatively small sector of the creole elite, men who sought primarily to replace the *peninsulares* as the leaders of government and commerce. Not all creoles favored independence. As in the North American revolution, many remained passive and apathetic throughout the struggle. Others stayed loyal to the

Crown and even after independence advocated some kind of monarchy within an orderly, imperial structure. Others shifted with the prevailing tides, backing or opposing independence as circumstances dictated. Few, except perhaps for the most radical, were entirely clear and consistent as to just what they foresaw as the appropriate and preferred forms of governmental and societal organization in place of the monarchy once independence was achieved. Even one as steadfast in his commitment to independence as Simón Bolívar espoused often conflicting and contradictory ideas when faced with the task of governing emerging states.[35]

Mestizos, Indians, blacks, and mulattos also played important roles in the struggle, be they the *gauchos* (cowboys) of Martín Guemes in northern Argentina, the *llaneros* (horsemen) of José Antonio Páez on the plains of Venezuela, or the Indian masses who followed Father Miguel Hidalgo y Costilla and José María Morelos in Mexico. For the most part, with the exception of certain *mestizos*, the lower orders did not have leading positions in these movements, usually serving under the direction of creole leaders. As with the creoles, some fought for the Crown or changed sides as conditions and the balance of forces shifted. Probably most preferred to stay out of the conflict altogether, although this was often difficult to do in the middle of a continent-wide process that lasted almost two decades.

While independence-minded creoles generally welcomed support from below, they also were very wary of it. Whatever their fluid and uncertain views on the course of the struggle and its results, all but the most radical creoles were totally opposed to any kind of massive social uprising that smacked of the Tupac Amaru rebellion or the Haitian revolution. This was abundantly clear, for example, in the case of Mexico, where independence was initiated on September 16, 1810, by an "enlightened" creole priest, Father Miguel Hidalgo, in the parish of Dolores, northwest of Mexico City. Gathering tens of thousands of Indian supporters, Hidalgo led his hordes on a rampage toward the capital, along the way sacking the rich silver-mining city of Guanajuato. There, Hidalgo's unrestrained forces slaughtered the Spanish garrison and while creoles were generally spared the worst excesses of killing and looting, they did suffer momentary imprisonment and loss of property.

These events terrified most creoles throughout Mexico. As the revolt proceeded, those who had initially favored independence either backed the *peninsulares* or remained neutral. This alienation of the creoles sealed the fate of the Hidalgo uprising. Failing to attack Mexico City, the revolutionary priest was captured and executed in 1811. His struggle was carried on by another priest, José María Morelos, who also was eventually captured and executed. Independence in Mexico would not be achieved until creoles could be assured of their total control of the process.[36]

As in the pre-independence period, the press articulated and spread the views of creole revolutionaries. In Mexico, Hidalgo created *El Despertador Americano* ("The American Awakening") to publicize his positions and programs. This was one of several publications in support of the insurgent cause.[37] In Buenos Aires, the revolutionary junta in 1810 created a periodical entitled the *Gaceta de Buenos Aires*, which became an important sounding board for the government, especially its most prominent figure, Mariano Moreno, the junta's principal exponent of free trade.[38] Similarly, in Chile the revolutionary government founded a number of newspapers, the most important of which was *La Aurora de Chile* ("The Dawn of Chile"), under the editorship of Father Camilio Henríquez.[39] A unique publication was a monthly review entitled *El Español*, published in London between 1810 and 1814. The editor, a Spanish exile, José María Blanco y Crespo (known more widely as Joseph Blanco White), used *El Español* to argue for a more accommodating Spanish policy in recognizing the autonomy of the insurgent American colonies and thus retaining the integrity of the empire through a confederation of states. Excerpts from *El Español* appeared in the American press and the ideas on its pages influenced the thought of many revolutionaries.[40]

The Church and churchmen were also crucial factors in the struggle. For the most part, the Church hierarchy, mostly peninsular, supported the royalist cause. In Mexico, the Church establishment made clear its disavowal of the social radicalism of Hidalgo and Morelos by both condemning their movements and excommunicating them. Even at the higher levels, however, some bishops sided with the patriots. At the lower levels, where creoles predominated, even more adherents to and participants in the revolutionary cause were found. In addition to Hidalgo and Morelos and scores of others in Mexico, numerous priests associated with independence movements from Guatemala to Argentina.[41] In New Granada, a number of former royalist churchmen became enthusiastic supporters of the patriot cause as the pro-independence forces fought their way to eventual victory.[42]

The Bourbon reforms and Enlightenment thought had done much to sow the discord within the Church and to weaken the ties between church and state that surfaced during independence. However, while revolutionary creoles might criticize the Church's alliance with the Crown, few mounted an attack on Catholicism itself. When independence was finally won in Mexico, for example, the first article of the "Three Guarantees" that assured it declared that "the religion of the country would be Roman Catholicism, with no toleration of other faiths."[43] In the Río de la Plata region, even such an Enlightenment liberal and revolutionary firebrand as Mariano Moreno remained a devoted Catholic, who, while a staunch devotee of Rousseau on most matters, wrote that Rousseau "had the misfortune of speaking foolishly on religious matters."[44] In Venezuela, one historian argued, the ideas of the French Revolution had little influence "because they ran counter to religious beliefs."[45]

Overall, however, there is little doubt that independence substantially weakened the power of the Catholic church. Closely allied with the Crown for better than three centuries, the church could only suffer when ties with the monarch and Spain were sundered. Unlike the Crown, however, the church remained deeply implanted in the Americas and, while battered by the revolutions, still commanded considerable spiritual and material resources. How to accommodate the church to new forms of political organization and state power would be a major issue of the post-independence period.

During the course of their struggle the creole revolutionaries benefited from a substantial amount of external assistance. The governments of both the United States and Great Britain showed sympathy for the patriot cause, provided considerable if sporadic material aid, were the first to recognize the new nations that emerged from the wars of independence, and sought to protect them from reconquest. In addition, private citizens of these two nations sold goods and arms to the rebels and some enlisted directly in the military campaigns themselves. The best-known foreign contributor was the famed British sea captain Thomas Cochrane, who played an important part in the naval engagements that secured the liberation of Chile, Peru, and Brazil.[46] In northern South America, Bolívar was able to recruit some 3,000 mercenaries, mostly well-trained and well-equipped Napoleonic war veterans from England, Ireland, and Germany, men who were crucial to his ultimate military triumphs.[47]

A military establishment both created and was created by the wars of independence. Most of the creoles involved in the fighting, with the exception of General José de San Martín, the leading military figure of the southern South American campaigns, and a few others, had had little formal training or been exposed to rigorous discipline. In many ways, they were citizen soldiers, who took up arms out of conviction and necessity, not because they were professionals.[48] Given their lack of experience, they could take some considerable pride in their impressive victories over the adversities of nature, terrain, and the generally better-trained and -equipped enemy. At the same time, however, the more battle-hardened civilians-turned-soldiers became, the more resentment among them grew over what they perceived to be the failures of civilian-dominated governments fully to either appreciate or support them. These resentments grew after battles were won and the armies disbanded, only to return to devastated homesteads and inadequate compensation. In sum, by the 1820s a new, large institution had emerged on the Latin American scene (Bolívar's army of Gran Colombia may have had as many as 36,000 men[49]), one that by wielding its superior physical force could ultimately determine the political destiny of any new state. Just how the grievances of the military would be resolved and just how it would interact with the larger society and new governments being formed would be another prominent issue of the post-independence era.

The events in Spain during this period as described in chapter 2 had a major impact on events in the Americas. On the peninsula, the various juntas organized to resist the French occupation established a central governing body, first in Seville and later in Cádiz. In Cádiz, in 1812, they produced a liberal constitution which established a constitutional monarchy with a severely-constrained monarch. That document, drafted by delegates among whom were colonists, also created a cortes that would allow for American representation, seemed to go a long way toward meeting the goals of most creoles, and, at the least, promised greater autonomy and flexibility within a reformed imperial system. These hopes were dashed, however, with the end of French rule and the restoration of Ferdinand VII to the throne in 1814. Ferdinand rejected the constitution of 1812, reversed liberal advances that had occurred in his absence, such as the abolition of the

Inquisition, and even rescinded reforms enacted under Charles III. As part of his general conservative reaction, in 1815 he dispatched an expeditionary force under peninsular war veteran Pablo Morillo to crush the creole insurgency in Venezuela, a task that was accomplished in relatively short order. In the south, however, the gains of independence held and under San Martín spread from the Río de la Plata to Chile. By 1817, Bolívar had re-entered the fray and began a series of campaigns that would liberate Colombia and Venezuela. Meanwhile in Spain dissatisfaction with the king culminated in January 1820, in a refusal of troops to depart for the colonies. As a consequence, Ferdinand was forced to accept the constitution of 1812. Three years later the absolute monarchy was again restored, but by then whatever the Crown did, absent a massive deployment of force, could not forestall Spanish American independence.

Were the Latin American revolutions inevitable? Conceivably, if Ferdinand had sought to accommodate creole desires for greater autonomy rather than to confront them, the colonists, many of whom were clearly unsure and ambivalent about outright independence, might well have accepted a compromise that gave them greater freedom within some sort of revised governmental structure and preserved the basic imperial framework. Moreover, while the role of heroic individuals ought not to be over emphasized, Bolívar, San Martín, and other creole revolutionaries were clearly exceptional personalities and their early removal from the scene by disease, a stray bullet, or some other circumstance might well have altered the course of events in the Americas. While these things, of course, did not happen, counterfactual speculations suggest the tenuous nature of the independence struggle and the extent to which the final outcome depended upon a delicate mix of personalities, forces, and events both at home and abroad.

The wars of independence in Spanish America were lengthy, destructive, and disruptive. Stretching from 1808 to 1825, with some regions ravaged by almost constant warfare, the Spanish American revolutions lasted three times longer than their North American counterpart. Hundreds of thousands of lives were lost, either in battle or as a side effect of the conflict. Fields were destroyed, flocks of livestock plundered to feed contending armies, and mines sabotaged and abandoned. The most severe damage to persons and property probably occurred in Venezuela and Mexico, two centers of intense and continuing conflict, while other areas experienced lesser damage, and still others, like Paraguay, very little at all.[50] The interruption of trade and the demands of financing the war produced a fiscal crisis throughout the region. As a result of this disruption, destruction, and dislocation, it was clear in most of Spanish America that after the wars considerable attention would have to be given to economic reconstruction and that economic difficulties would prove major obstacles to successful state-building.

≺ III ≻

State-Building After Independence

From 1808 on, the creole leadership wrestled as much with problems of political organization as with gaining military victory—perhaps more. And this struggle was as intense, confused, and complex as anything waged on the field of battle. One of the main issues for certain leaders in certain regions was the basic one of the geographic and territorial extent of the new nation in formation. In the Río de la Plata region, the *porteños* (of the city of Buenos Aires) hoped to develop a state that would more or less encompass the original viceroyalty. This plan fell apart with the eventual creation of the separate states of Paraguay and Uruguay, whose inhabitants showed themselves as adverse to *porteño* pretensions of domination as they had been to the rule of the Spanish Crown. Similarly, Bolívar's scheme to retain the essential shape of the viceroyalty of New Granada in the form of the republic of Gran (Greater) Colombia was shattered when Colombia, Ecuador, and Venezuela determined to go their separate ways. The enormous new nation of Mexico also succumbed to division when the provinces of Central America first formed a separate republic and then broke into individual nations. For the most part, these new states corresponded roughly to administrative units established by the Spanish empire.

The failure to retain the integrity of these large colonial governing units underscored certain major realities and major problems of the post-independence period. For most inhabitants of the region after independence, their strongest attachments were to their immediate localities—their towns and villages—or regions, not to the new nation or its capital. This usually meant, too, that their strongest political loyalties were with local, not national, political leaders. Even at the higher levels, inhabitants of one region or nation often felt a sense of separateness and distinction from those of another, even though they shared the same language, religion, and heritage. One of the factors involved in the breakup of Gran Colombia, for example, was the sense of superiority Venezuelans felt over Colombians, whom they regarded "as a band of backward mountaineers."[51] Similar sentiments of difference could be found throughout the continent at all levels. These sentiments, in turn, were accentuated by the enormous geographic obstacles and barriers that divided newly-established nations, regions, and smaller localities one from the other, making travel from one locale to another a lengthy, costly, and often life-threatening experience.

These realities produced one of the principal political conflicts and debates of the independence years; namely, should the governments formed accommodate this strong localist sentiment through a loose federal system that would allow for a considerable amount of autonomy, or should they be strongly centralized so as to prevent further splintering. Related to this question was whether the new states should be constitutional republics modeled generally after the United States or constitutional monarchies similar to that of Great Britain—or, as Bolívar proposed, some combination of the two that included an elected legislature and a life-term president.[52]

The idea of a constitutional monarchy had little appeal, in part due to the difficulty in finding acceptable candidates. One exception was Mexico, where monarchist sentiment was strong and where the main figure of the final stages of independence, American-born Agustín Iturbide, ruled briefly (1821–23) as emperor before succumbing to republican sentiment.[53] The other major exception was Brazil where, despite some similarities with Spanish America with regard to the background causes of independence, the circumstances were significantly different. Most importantly, with the transfer of the royal family to Rio de Janeiro, there was a viable monarchical candidate in place. In April 1821, after fourteen years in Brazil, King João VI set sail for Portugal to resume the throne there, leaving his son and heir, Dom Pedro I, to rule as prince regent. A year and a half later, backed by Brazilian creoles, Dom Pedro declared the colony's independence, which was won after a brief period of comparatively minor military combat. A constitutional monarchy was soon established, designed to provide continuity, prevent the disintegration of the large and diverse new state, forestall the abolition of slavery, and avoid the anarchy and disorder into which so many Spanish American republics had already drifted. Although Dom Pedro I followed his father to Portugal in 1831, his own son, Dom Pedro II, served as emperor of Brazil until 1889 and the end of the monarchy.[54]

Most Spanish American creoles favored some form of constitutional republic, which they considered the wave of the future and which emerged from their exposure to Enlightenment thought. Frank Safford has identified two stages in the growth of Spanish American constitutionalism in this period. The first stage, from about 1810 to 1815, was marked by "liberal constitutionalism," wherein new governing documents were based on popular sovereignty—the "general will" of the people—assured basic individual rights, established relatively weak executives, and allowed for significant local autonomy.[55] Often drafted in the heat of battle, however, none of these initial attempts at a decentralized, federalist form of government survived the pressures to provide coherence and order in these turbulent years.[56] Accordingly, most constitutions of the second stage, after 1815, sought to establish a strong central authority. During this period, the examples of the U.S. and French constitutions continued to provide inspiration. In addition, as they developed, constitutions in one Latin American country often had influence on those in other nations. Also important was the example of the Spanish liberal constitution of 1812, many provisions of which showed up in direct or modified form in Latin American charters.

Unlike the liberals of Cádiz, however, the creoles crafting post-1815 documents looked to expand rather than to constrain the power of the executive. In most cases, for example, the president was given considerable authority to appoint local officials. Moreover, most of the constitutions of this period gave the executive special powers to suspend individual rights and guarantees during occasions of "external threat or internal disturbance." In Gran Colombia, for example, Article 128 of the constitution of Cúcuta "permitted the Executive to take emergency measures under a state of virtual martial law in any region threatened by foreign invasion or internal rebellion."[57] Similar provisions could be found in constitutions throughout the region; indeed, the executive's power to suspend the constitution and declare a "state of siege" that temporarily suspends individual guarantees persists to the present day. In many nations, the executive still enjoys considerable authority to appoint local officials (mayors of capital cities, for example), and to intervene directly in the management of state or provincial governments.

All constitutions, whether federalist or centralist, for the first time in Latin American history provided for the popular election of public officials. Popular democracy rather than divine right would provide the legitimacy of the new system. This principle coincided with the common assertion accompanying independence and written into most constitutions that all inhabitants of the new nations were free and equal citizens. The creole elite drafting these documents, however, imposed severe limits on the suffrage, assuring that the "popular" electorate did not extend much beyond their own number. The constitution of Cúcuta in Gran Colombia gave the vote only to adult male citizens who owned at least $100 in real property or who were "engaged in some business, trade, profession, or useful industry, having a house or place of business and not being dependent upon another as a day laborer or as a servant."[58] In Brazil, the constitution of 1824 that provided for a parliament to rule with the emperor set income requirements for voters and prohibited workers and domestic servants from participating in elections.[59] The fact that most elections were indirect (as in the Cádiz constitution of 1812), with most systems based on a carefully-controlled system of choosing local electors for higher office, enhanced elite control and further restricted popular participation.

Many Spanish American constitutions included provisions for the abolition of black slavery. In other instances, legislation was enacted to achieve that end. While the process was slow and gradual, by the 1850s slavery in independent Spanish America was generally a thing of the past. Similarly, some attempts were made to extend the concept of equality to the Indian population and to end some of the abuses to which they had been subjected. In Gran Colombia, for example, colonial restrictions on the right of Indians to hold public office were abolished.[60] There and elsewhere efforts were made to encourage the Indians to abandon communal landholdings and to become individual property-owners who could, therefore, be more easily assimilated into the larger society.[61] In practice, however, blacks, even when freed, and most Indians remained at the bottom or the margin of society, lacking the essentials of education, property, and income that would allow for political participation. Full equality for them remained more theory than fact. Even Mexican liberals rejected any democratic system that allowed for Indian participation.[62]

Most constitutions after 1815, as before, guaranteed freedom of the press. In the 1820s and 1830s, newspapers and magazines continued to flourish, expanding in number, size, circulation, and influence. In his study of Bolívar's political thought, for example, Víctor Andrés Belaunde lists three dozen Peruvian periodicals of the period related to political and ideological issues.[63] While most publications before independence served primarily to spread Enlightenment ideas or promote the insurgent cause, after independence they came to represent the competing interests of political factions that fought to have their points of view prevail in the formation of the new states. In Mexico, the newspaper *El Sol* ["The Sun"] was in 1821 and 1822 the main organ opposing Iturbide.[64] A few years later, leading Mexican liberal José Luis Mora became the editor of *El Observador de la república mexicana* (1827–30), which he used as an instrument to diffuse his ideas as to how Mexico should be governed.[65] Mora's conservative counterpart, Lucas Alamán, used *El Tiempo* and *El Universal* to express his opinions.[66] In Gran Colombia, various publications appeared to advocate either centralism or federalism, to defend or to attack the prevailing government.[67] In Chile, the editor of *El Tizón Republicano* ["The Republican Brand"] proclaimed "that the chief role of newspapers was to keep watch over all the activities of government, and in particular to 'combat public abuses and bad conduct on the part of magistrates.'"[68] For the most part, these publications were, like their predecessors, of limited circulation and longevity.

Scores of constitutions were written in Latin America during the quarter of a century after 1810, and while no single country's experience in this regard can be considered strictly typical of the region as a whole, the example of Chile provides a useful case study of the general trends. Between 1811 and 1833, Chilean creoles, in a process similar to that described for Italy in chapter 6, crafted nine different governing documents. The first, that of 1811, provided in its nineteen articles for a weak plural executive and a congress that would rule in the name of the king. A second, in 1812, following closely on the first, also recognized the authority of Ferdinand VII, but called on him to rule by way of a constitution formulated by the "representatives of the people" in the same manner as "that of the Peninsula [the Spanish constitution of 1812]."[69] This document also included articles to insure certain individual rights. The third, that of 1814, showed the shift to centralism, concentrating most governing authority in the hands of a "Supreme Director"; the fourth, of 1818, extended these executive powers even more, in essence ratifying the virtual dictatorship of revolutionary hero Bernardo O'Higgins following independence from Spain.

These four documents were essentially provisional charters, created in the passion and turmoil of the independence struggle. The first *real* constitution of Chile was that of 1822, consisting of 248 articles that laid out in some detail how the country should be governed and generally reaffirming the centralist trend. Three others in this decade, those of 1823, 1826, and 1828, reflected the ongoing struggle between centralists and federalists to have their views prevail. By the end of the decade, the press began to play an important role as a sounding board for competing factions, especially in the deliberations involving the constitution of 1828. Finally, the centralist position prevailed with the drafting of the constitution of 1833, a culmination of the previous eight charters and a document that with its 168 articles remained effective and in effect until 1925.

While these various documents often differed substantially one from the other, they shared certain basic features. They were much influenced by other examples, including, depending on time and circumstance, the constitutions of the United States, France, and Spain; various constitutions of the Río de la Plata region; the Mexican federalist constitution of 1824; and each other. All reaffirmed the primacy of the Roman Catholic church, making it the official religion of the state and excluding any other. They were also much concerned with the fair and equitable administration of justice, the lack of which under Spanish rule had been a major complaint of the Chilean creoles and a main force behind their commitment to independence. Considerable effort was made to construct a judicial and legal system that guaranteed all Chilean citizens equality before the law and protected them from arbitrary abuse of their rights. These rights were detailed in article 12 and chapter 10 of the 1833 constitution and included the right to reside and to move freely about the republic, the right to own property, the right to personal security within the home, the right to hold public office, and the right to petition constitutional authorities for redress of grievances.[70]

Almost every document, beginning with that of 1812, guaranteed freedom of the press and of expression. For the most part, these were unrestricted freedoms, although the pertinent clause in the 1833 constitution allowed for legal judgments to be brought against those who abused them. The 1833 constitution also abolished slavery and prohibited Chileans from engaging in the traffic of slaves. It included provisions for regulating a public educational system that, according to earlier constitutions, was to see the state establish primary schools in all towns and parishes. It also established that all persons born in Chile and their children were automatically citizens of the nation and laid out procedures and provisions for becoming naturalized citizens.

While the stipulations with regard to rights and citizenship were broad and generous, one of the major rights of a citizen in a constitutional democracy, the right to vote, was severely limited. None of the documents of the period included universal male suffrage, and the constitution of 1833 was no exception. To vote, a male citizen had to be 25 years of age or older if single (21 if married), be literate, and own property or receive income from industrial or artisanal activities. In practice, these provisions in a nation where perhaps 90 percent of the population was poor and illiterate limited the suffrage to the creole elite.

The constitution also created a powerful president, chosen by a select group of electors for a five-year term with provisions for reelection to a second term. The president had the power to appoint almost all the governing officials in the republic and the right to declare a state of siege virtually at will. He governed with a bicameral legislature composed of a directly-elected Chamber of Deputies and an indirectly-chosen Senate, bodies that in effect could do little to check executive authority even if they had been inclined to do so.

The Chilean constitution of 1833 was exceptional in Latin America not so much for its provisions as for its longevity. It remained the country's effective governing document, with some amendment, for almost a century, a notable record in a region where constitutions were often changed, abandoned, or ignored at whim. Constitutional continuity, in turn, contributed to a nineteenth-century history for Chile that was generally freer of the scores of rebellions, civil wars, and dictatorial rule that afflicted the rest of Spanish America. The success of constitutionalism in Chile, too, might be traced to provi-

sions in 1833 that subordinated the armed forces to civilian authority, provisions that were firmly enforced by President Manuel Bulnes
(1841–51), himself a former military officer.[71] But above all else, the
Chilean constitution prevailed because it, like most others in Latin
America, was designed primarily not to guarantee individual rights,
which in practice were often violated, but rather to serve the interests of the dominant creole elite.[72]

With Chile a notable exception, governments operating under
centralist constitutions were no more effective than their federalist
predecessors in bringing order, stability, unity, or democracy, however limited, to the emerging republics of Spanish America. While
most constitutions were exquisitely detailed and included the no-
blest aspirations, most regimes either ignored many provisions or
were too weak or disinterested to enforce them. In most of the region,
chaos reigned as localism, factionalism, and personalism predominated. In the year 1820 alone seven different governments tried un-
successfully to bring order to Argentina. With only a few exceptions,
the transition from an authoritarian government based on an all-
powerful hereditary monarch to one whose political legitimacy was
expressed through popularly-elected officials proved virtually impossible. Bolívar, whose attempts to bridge the gap between liberator
and ruler in the manner of George Washington had ended in total
failure, proclaimed bitterly near his death that America was ungov-
ernable and that "Those who served the Revolution have plowed
the sea."[73]

The contrast with the North American experience after independence is striking and, given the geographic propinquity, often noted.
However, the former British colonies had been exposed to constitutionalism and certain forms of self-government long prior to independence, while the Spanish Americans had not. Moreover, in the
United States the first governments were able to establish early on
the rule of law, a successful balancing of powers, and the subordination of the military to civilian authority thanks, in large measure, to
traditions and circumstances that were largely absent in Latin America.[74] Indeed, given the enormous change constitutional government
represented for Spanish America, a change attempted within the context of an area devastated by almost two decades of war and within
sharply divided societies, lacking much in the way of infrastructure
and with, for the most part, isolated, illiterate, and indifferent popu-

lations, the successful establishment of democratic forms would have bordered on the miraculous.

The general failure of constitutional government and the widespread breakdown of law and order throughout the region after independence set the stage for the emergence of the Latin American caudillo (strong man). Usually local leaders with devoted followings, caudillos often seized power by force and ruled through violence, fear, and terror. For their opponents and victims, they were no more than vicious tyrants. For their supporters they were heaven-sent saviors who reestablished order and stability. Juan Manuel de Rosas, a proto-typical caudillo who ruled Argentina from 1835 to 1852, was called "Bloody Rosas" by his enemies and the "Restorer of the Laws" by his backers.[75]

Caudillos shared certain general characteristics. Many had fought in the wars of independence. Most displayed in abundance the masculine traits of personal courage and physical ability widely admired in societies where *machismo* was predominant.[76] Most developed and sustained an extensive network of personally loyal supporters, drawing on patron-client relationships and family connections. Most had magnetic, charismatic personalities. Most, too, while often identifying with one faction or one trend as circumstances might dictate, were usually quite pragmatic, using whatever idea or tactic might help them gain and retain power.

With regard to social origins, caudillos were more diverse. Some, like Rosas of Argentina, General Tomás Cipriano Mosquera of Colombia, and Antonio López de Santa Anna of Mexico, were creoles of the upper class. Others, like Rafael Carrera of Guatemala and various Mexican leaders, were *mestizos* of humble origins. José Antonio Páez of Venezuela rose from poverty to wealth through his leadership in the wars of independence and his control of the country from 1830 to 1846. Some caudillos, like Rosas and Páez, were able to establish a continuous dominance that lasted almost two decades. Most caudillos, however, enjoyed shorter and more uncertain tenures. Santa Anna served as president-dictator of Mexico on nine separate occasions between the 1830s and 1850s. This meant, of course, that in some countries caudillos were able to establish a considerable amount of order, stability, and predictability and in others they were not. Some, too, came from military backgrounds and used the standing army for support, while others depended on local militias or their own personal bodyguard.

While they might occasionally pay lip service to them, caudillos were little concerned with constitutions or with respecting the individual rights and liberties such documents theoretically guaranteed. Nor did they have much use for elections unless results favorable to them could be assured. Nonetheless, many caudillos clearly enjoyed popular, even majority, support, often from a broader and more diverse social base than any "democratic" official of the period could claim. In many ways the caudillos were the logical figures for the transitional period between monarchy and democracy, in their persons exercising "naturally" the authority of the former while also incarnating the aspirations and values of the people at large. But whatever the popular and populist traits of the caudillos, ultimately most served as defenders of elite interests against the masses. In John Lynch's term, they were "necessary gendarmes," who in the era of uncertainty and danger and at a time when constitutions had little force used their personal authority to preserve the social status quo.[77]

The emergence of caudillos in the post-independence period owed something to the Spanish colonial legacy. In many ways, caudillos were a throwback to the original conquistadores, with whom they shared many characteristics. Richard Morse has argued that caudillos were part of the "patrimonial" structure deeply implanted in Latin America during the colonial period and reinforced by loyalty to kings and viceroys.[78] Lynch, on the other hand, sees the caudillos as essentially a new form of leader, "a child of war and a product of independence."[79] Whatever the origins, caudillos predominated in Spanish America until about 1870 and persisted in one form or another for better than a century after that.[80]

From the viewpoint of the creole elites, who appreciated the caudillos' "gendarme" quality, the great weakness of this style of rule was its personal, often arbitrary, and unpredictable nature. Gradually, they began either to co-opt or supplant caudillos, restoring some semblance of constitutional government and reinstituting elections, albeit under strict controls and with limited participation. The struggle to expand the electorate and to achieve meaningful democratic government in Latin America was a slow, painful, and difficult process, frequently interrupted by old and new forms of authoritarianism.

≺ IV ≻

The Legacy of Independence

In 1968, Samuel Huntington, drawing on Hannah Arendt, defined a revolution as "a rapid, fundamental, and violent domestic change in the dominant values and myths of a society, in its political institutions, social structure, leadership, and government activity and politics."[81] If judged by these standards, the Latin American wars of independence fall far short of being full-fledged revolutions. Indeed, over the past 30 years or so, most scholars have argued that independence was basically a movement engineered by a few ambitious creoles intent primarily on supplanting the *peninsulares* in positions of political and economic power. As Safford points out for the region as a whole, it was the creole upper class that benefited most from independence and that came to fill or to control the most important and prestigious positions in the new and expanding governments they themselves created.[82] Once in power, the creoles brooked little challenge, encouraged little change, and refused to recognize the principles of full equality for all the nation's citizens proclaimed in the very constitutions they had drafted.[83]

The idea that independence effected little fundamental change in Latin America has been a main theme of much of the scholarship on the area, especially since the 1960s. Proponents of this point of view were much influenced by new studies of the social and economic history of the region, the widespread presence of "bureaucratic-authoritarian" regimes from the 1960s to the 1980s, and the belief that Fidel Castro's Cuba represented the only genuine revolution in Latin American history. Accordingly, they highlighted the many continuities of social structure, political practices, and economic behavior from Spanish colonial times to the contemporary period, underscoring the persistence of elite dominance, authoritarian forms of government, dependent export-oriented economies, and colonial value systems. They also argued that the viewpoints and positions of the upper class had changed the least over time.[84]

From the perspective of the 1990s, at a time when democratic governments are the norm throughout Latin America, it seems clear that independence, despite these continuities and while perhaps not "revolutionary" in all respects, did bring with it some substantial changes. Most obviously, the former American colonies of Spain and

Portugal became sovereign nation states, liberated from direct imperial control. As a result, the new national leaders were free to determine their own destinies and to make their own decisions. Among those decisions, with some exceptions, was the choice to establish liberal democratic institutions based on written constitutions. However limited, incomplete, futile, and often half-hearted the attempts to achieve democracy, post-independence state-builders established a goal toward which most Latin Americans would aspire with considerable determination and dedication.

Independence swept away most constraints, such as the Inquisition, on the free flow of ideas. A generally free press emerged from the struggle and expanded significantly over the course of the nineteenth and twentieth centuries. In Argentina, Uruguay, and Chile, new state-supported national universities and national libraries were created and they and existing educational institutions at all levels were opened up to the free exchange of ideas and information. The responsibility of the state to provide free public education to all its citizens was also established in principle if not in practice. The opening up of commerce to all nations contributed to the overall atmosphere of intellectual freedom. From time to time, various caudillos sought to interrupt or even reverse this process, but usually with only short-term effects on the general long-term trend of greater openness.

Another consequence of independence, reversing colonial policy, were attempts by the leaders of the new nations to attract foreign immigrants from throughout the world to settle in their fledgling republics, bringing with them their capital, their resources, and their skills. Immigration, mostly from Europe, began in the 1820s but did not become a major factor in the region until later in the nineteenth century, when millions of foreigners, primarily from southern Europe, settled in Latin America and dramatically affected the historical development of nations such as Argentina, Brazil, and Uruguay, which received the bulk of them.[85]

Other socio-economic changes were more ambiguous. With independence, the practices of entail and primogeniture along with granting noble titles were eliminated, an apparent undermining of the privileges of the creole elite. The elimination of Crown control and constraints over economic activity and rights, however, allowed many creoles, especially those who already had capital, to acquire even more property, wealth, prestige, and power after independence than before. Most notably, they were able to amass enormous quantities of land in a few hands, reinforcing and expanding a pattern of ownership (*latifundio*) with colonial roots. Attempts were also made to limit the strength and authority of the church and the army by eliminating the *fueros* they had enjoyed during the colonial era. Both institutions, however, managed to weather these and other attacks and to maintain and even enhance their power in the post-independence period. The armed forces, in particular, emerged as the dominant political actors in much of Latin America from the time of independence until the 1980s.

Slavery was abolished in Spanish America as a consequence of independence and some *mestizos* and mulattos achieved prominence in national life that would have been impossible before 1825. In the second half of the nineteenth century in Mexico, for example, Beníto Juárez, an Indian, and Porfirio Díaz, a *mestizo*, assumed the presidency of the country. Overall, however, with only a few exceptions, little changed fundamentally from the colonial pattern of the whites at the top of the social pyramid and the mixed and darker races distributed towards the bottom, depending on skin color.

With independence, too, the leaders of these new nations were free to make their own decisions with regard to economic policy. Faced with serious fiscal crises, they developed new tax systems, renovating the colonial structures that had caused so many resentments. In addition, of course, after independence the revenues collected remained at home rather than being shipped abroad. On the other hand, as was generally the case throughout the region in the 1820s, when tax revenues were insufficient to meet governmental expenses, foreign loans were floated. Repayment of these loans, in turn, meant that government monies again flowed into foreign coffers.

The main economic change with independence was unrestricted free trade, one of the principal goals of the revolutionaries. Opening up their economies to contact with the rest of the world had many consequences. Among the first to establish commercial links with liberated Latin America were United States and British interests, with the latter predominating. British merchants in particular contributed to new consumption patterns that emphasized the alleged superiority of foreign-produced goods to domestic manufactures, patterns that persist to the present day.[86] In addition, as early as the 1820s, many governments began to seek direct foreign investment in their economies, particularly in the areas of infrastructure development and mining.

Critics point out, with some justification, that in the economic realm, as in the political, the changes wrought by independence were more apparent than real. After winning its freedom from Spain and Portugal, Latin America continued to be primarily an exporter of raw materials, often of one particular product, and an importer of manufactured goods. At liberty after independence to industrialize, most Latin American nations were slow and often reluctant to do so. Increasingly dependent on external markets for their exports and on foreign goods, investment, and loans, they seemed to have moved from a formal colonial status under Spain and Portugal to an informal "neo-colonial" status under Great Britain in the nineteenth century and the United States in the twentieth. While these relationships provided for substantial economic growth, especially in the latter part of the nineteenth century, and, perhaps, more of the benefits remained at home than would have been the case under direct colonial control, it was far from the "golden age" of autonomous, balanced, and vital economic development many leaders of independence had envisioned.

In sum, with independence not all changes were immediately beneficial for the majority, nor were all revolutionary promises fulfilled. But the disappointing results did not make independence any less of a major break with the past. After 1825 Latin America was something quite different from what it had been before. With independence came the freedom for Latin Americans themselves to chart their own destinies and craft their own aspirations.

Popular Constitutionalism and Revolution in England and Ireland

IAIN MCCALMAN

MODERN ENGLISH-IRISH RELATIONS have been said to pivot on the fact that the English remember no history whilst the Irish forget none. Surveying British responses to revolution from the 1770s to 1870, one is struck rather by the persistence of seventeenth-century revolutionary memories in both countries; the problem is that Protestant English and Catholic Irish remembered their constitutional history very differently. No one embodies this contradiction better than the man regarded as the father of British revolutionary theory, Edmund Burke. It is a truism of modern British historiography that Burke's prophetic *Reflections on the Revolution in France* of November 1790 succeeded in imposing new and opprobrious meanings on the word revolution. The word's rather literal association with an astronomical-like return to states of former virtue—embodied in the English constitutional freedoms of 1688 and the American colonial resistance of 1776—was replaced by connotations of Gallic political violence, social anarchy, cold rationalist theory, fanatical enthusiasm, irreligion, and sexual license. Against this nightmarish Jacobin philosophy Burke counterposed a scrubbed version of English constitutional prudence that became the intellectual foundation of the English counterrevolution and ultimately of modern British conservatism.

≺ I ≻

Burke's Revolutionary Legacies

The anti-historicist character of much modern Burke criticism has blurred the ambiguities, tensions, and contradictions in his writings on revolution. It has not been generally noticed, for example, that he simultaneously advanced at least two contradictory positions on revolution during the 1790s, depending on whether he was speaking for England or Ireland. As an Irishman of old Catholic stock whose father seems to have made a reluctant and humiliating conversion to Anglicanism under pressure from the penal laws against Catholics, Burke retained a heartfelt sympathy with the plight of Irish Catholicism.[1] In England, however, he carried the taint of the Irish colonial, the rootless intellectual, the flunkey of grandee Whiggery, the expedient Anglican, the crypto-Catholic, the parvenu country gentleman. These smears were some of the sources of his "rage" and of his conservatism.[2] One English political tradition in particular crystallized these contradictions and at the same time precipitated his uneasy dualistic views on revolution in the 1790s. This was the body of doctrine or rhetoric associated with Puritan libertarian anti-popery—the old seventeenth-century idea of England as divine bearer of Protestant civil, religious, and political freedoms against the forces of servile, tyrannical, and popish European absolutism.[3]

The contradictions between Burke's commitment to Whiggish constitutional liberty and his sympathy for Irish Catholic aspirations for religious emancipation emerged in 1778–79 when Lord North's Tory government tried to stimulate Highland and Irish recruitment for the American wars with the bribe of a Catholic relief act.[4] Though politically torn, Burke committed himself to support Catholic freedoms and so set himself in searing confrontation with his former friend and political ally, "mad" Lord George Gordon, champion of a neo-Puritan campaign in favor of American revolution and against collaboration with domestic or international popery. By the end of 1780 Burke's life, family, and property had been threatened in the worst riots of the century; he had lost his parliamentary seat of Bristol at the instigation of a hostile dissenter faction, and he had become the butt of Protestant Association propagandists. Like few other Whigs he thus exulted in the strengthening of the monarchy's martial powers as a consequence of the Gordon riots.

This, then, was the true genesis of Burke's *Reflections*, the source of his vivid imaginative evocation of mob violence and of his profound hostility to the anti-papal tendencies of Whig politicians like Lord Shelburne, rational dissenting preachers like Dr. Price, and early French Revolutionary edicts like the November 1789 annexation of church property. Above all, he feared the blend of enlightenment radicalism and Puritan fanaticism espoused by Lord Gordon—

Scots Presbyterian enthusiast, instigator of the anti-papal riots, cor-
respondent of the French National Convention, and notorious
politico-pornographic libeler of Queen Marie Antoinette.[5] Burke
smelled in the early French Revolution a modern-day secular revival
of Britain's Puritan Revolution, which is why in his *Thoughts on
French Affairs* he compared it with the Reformation rather than the
Glorious Revolution of 1689: "It is a Revolution of doctrine and theo-
retick dogma. It has a much greater resemblance to those changes
which have been made on religious grounds, in which a spirit of
proselytism makes an essential point."[6]

He could not apply this same analysis to Ireland, where his sympathy for popery and hatred of the Protestant ascendancy produced
an opposite formulation. There the bigoted and corrupt ruling class
was as much anti-papal as anti-Jacobin, whilst his oppressed Catholic brethren looked to the French Revolution to somehow alleviate
their plight. Throughout the 1790s Burke thus found himself advancing ideas and political programs for Ireland which contradicted his
counter-revolutionary crusade in England. We find him arguing in
1792 that the spirit and purpose of the Glorious Revolution had differed fundamentally in the two countries. In England it had been a
movement of liberty to free "the great body of people"; in Ireland, an
imposition by "a small faction . . . at the expense of the civil liberties
and properties of the far greater part, and at the expense of the political liberties of the whole. It was, to say the truth, not a revolution,
but a conquest."[7] In December 1796—the same month that a French
invasion fleet landed in Ireland—we find him criticizing an Irish
friend, Father Hussey, for preaching passive obedience to intolerably
oppressed Catholic parishioners: Burke reminded the priest that Irish
Jacobinism, as distinct from the wanton English strain, stemmed
from terrible hunger, distress, and injustice. If such sympathy did not
push Burke into becoming a republican revolutionary like Irish Whig
counterparts Arthur O'Connor and Wolfe Tone, he verged on com-
plicity. He retained intimate connections with the Irish Catholic
Committee in the mid 1790s, despite its mounting pro-French militancy, and he backed the new Whig Lord Lieutenant Fitzwilliam's ill-
fated crusade of 1795 to emancipate Irish Catholics and purge ascendancy corruption.[8] Because Burke died in 1797, the year before the
bloody Irish rebellion and English repression of 1798, we cannot
know whether the counter-revolutionary or revolutionary strands of

his divided personality would have prevailed in the face of that great sectarian watershed.

Not only has this seminal Anglo-Irish political thinker transmitted contradictory legacies of revolution; he also personifies the destabilizing effects of considering England and Ireland in relationship. To introduce Ireland into an analysis of the meanings of revolution in nineteenth-century Britain is to generate not so much Burkean "reflections" as multiple refractions and inversions. Burke embodies the intricate polarities of attraction and repulsion between the two countries. His country of birth was at once a subject colony and a colonializer by virtue of the immigrant communities it exported to England and America, who exerted their own complex effects on English and Irish politics. Moreover, Ireland's own cultural and religious divisions reverberated within and in response to the mother state: radicals and nationalists oscillated between mimicry and loathing of England, between enmeshment in English affairs and an ardent wish for separation; alternately fighting for England and courting her enemies.[9]

Recent writing on British popular politics in the nineteenth century has focused on the constitutive power of language as creator of meaning: "constitutionalism" is depicted as the fluid, pervasive, "master narrative" through which British responses to domestic and international struggles for freedom, reform, and revolution were mediated and articulated.[10] Whilst endorsing the centrality of British constitutionalist idioms and rhetoric, this chapter argues that Ireland complicates, extends, and sometimes subverts the "master narrative" by polarizing its central and abrasive contradiction—the legacy of Puritan libertarian anti-popery. The conflicting meanings of this seventeenth-century memory, implanted in Burke's writings on constitution and revolution, pervade English and Irish politics during the period from Waterloo to the Second Reform Act, thereafter becoming part of the divided inheritance of modern British democracy.

≺ II ≻

The Bulwark of the Constitution:
Radicalism and Reaction, 1810–22

Three months after the "Peterloo massacre" of August 16, 1819, in which armed yeomanry attacked a Manchester crowd petitioning for radical franchise reform, the Tory home secretary Lord Sidmouth introduced the notorious Six Acts, designed to restrict popular assembly, publication, and expression. It was necessary, he said, "to create a fence around the Constitution; and a bulwark to protect it against those spurious rights which were foreign to its sober genius." Recent scholarship has seen the Six Acts as the most sweeping and comprehensive of a series of legal attempts by Tory governments to redefine and restrict the rights of those entitled to participate in the political nation.[11] Beginning in the 1790s, these included libel campaigns and punitive newspaper taxes, intermittent suspensions of habeas corpus, the passage of several treasonable practices and seditious meetings acts and the combination acts against trade unions in 1799, as well as legislative attempts to restrict dissenting ministers' licenses in 1810–11. Sidmouth's famous circular of 1817 calling on provincial magistrates to prosecute hawkers caught peddling blasphemous and seditious publications was only one of several executive means for further limiting popular constitutional claims; others included the mounting of *ex officio* legal prosecutions, withdrawal of publicans' licenses for hosting radical meetings, and packing juries to ensure pro-government verdicts.[12]

Ironically, the Tories' legal "bulwark" of 1819, designed to check the threatened torrent of radical reform, was justified by a broadly shared, if fiercely contested, intellectual inheritance. Tories, Whigs, and radicals in early nineteenth-century England disputed the boundaries of legitimate political nationhood by drawing on a diffuse constitutionalist idiom inherited from the seventeenth and eighteenth centuries. Derived from a melange of "Country," Commonwealth, civic humanist, common law, American republican, and Protestant Reformation traditions of thought, it evoked such foundational texts as Magna Charta, Locke's *Treatises*, the 1688 settlement, and Blackstone's *Commentaries*. "Constitutionalism" stressed balance between monarch and Parliament—a concept that even Charles I had articulated in 1642—as well as elimination of executive corruption, influence or unfair taxation; and the political rights of the virtuous, independent, propertied citizen. Reformers inherited a "radical" formulation from elderly Major Cartwright, who had sought since 1776 to restore a popular democratic government of mythical Saxon origin. Calling for a restoration of the lost "historic" rights of universal suffrage and annual parliaments, this radical program was thought by most of the governing class to imply demands for social equality. Often couched in rhetoric as "transformational" as that of the French revolutionaries of the 1790s, radical constitutionalist versions of the idiom possessed considerable capacity for mobilization and transcendence, and were potentially revolutionary.[13] Conversely, radical constitutionalism could provide a defensive "bulwark" against ruling-class attacks on traditional popular liberties, particularly when patriotic loyalism prevailed as in the French and Napoleonic wars. From the late 1790s counter-revolutionary propaganda, combined with wartime anti-Gallican patriotism, considerably discredited reform politics in Britain. Thanks partly to Burke and other anti-Jacobin writers, partly to United Irish and English insurrectionary plots of 1802–3, the French Revolution became synonymous with treasonous, violent, and un-English underground activity. Loyalists continued throughout the Regency years to blacken reform programs of Whigs, radicals, and reformers by linking them to French Jacobinism. Under these circumstances the ambiguous and inclusive idiom of popular constitutionalism offered vital legal and rhetorical shelter.

Historians—long blind to Burke's Irish radicalism—have similarly overlooked the emergence in England during the Napoleonic wars of an Irish emigré underground which helped to restore an effective rhetoric of oppositional resistance and to organize a popular political counterattack against Tory loyalism. That former "Irish Rebels" should have formed a stubborn knot of resistance to wartime English patriotism is not surprising: the promise of emancipation which had lured Catholics into supporting the Act of Union of 1801 had, as they believed, been treacherously broken. Though nominally part of Britain after this act, Ireland's population remained subject to exceptional religious and political disabilities and to draconian law-and-order provisions that would have been unthinkable on the English mainland. Republican separatism and other variants of subversive sectarian doctrine had been widely disseminated by the clandestine United Irish and Catholic Defender societies in the 1790s, aided by brutal government suppression of Catholic rebels after the 1798 rising. To avoid capture in Ireland numbers of United Irish revolutionaries slipped into England and attached themselves to constitutionalist opposition movements.

It was thanks in part to the ferocious propaganda and the electoral campaigning of ex-rebel emigrés like Peter Finnerty, Patrick William

Duffin, and Roger O'Connor that English popular radicalism began in the 1810s to recapture lost ideological ground by developing a version of "patriotic" constitutionalist rhetoric that exploited resentments of wartime taxation, economic distress, military tyranny, and political corruption. Their oral, literary, and graphic attacks on government wartime corruption and ineptitude, on prison and military abuses, and on the savage repression of Irish rebels furnished a journalistic staple for William Cobbett's libertarian critique of "Old Corruption." They masterminded radical baronet Sir Francis Burdett's electoral successes and lofty public image after 1807 as "a man of the people" and "hero of liberty" in combat against a despotic state, and they helped to politicize a new generation of liberal romantic poets, critics, and writers such as Shelley, Byron, Moore, Hazlitt, and Leigh Hunt.[14]

By 1815 popular radicals and reformers had consequently advanced a long way towards re-appropriating libertarian patriotism from Tories and loyalists. Peace with France and postwar economic recession further increased their political purchase. Over the next five years radicals were able to deploy defensive and offensive constitutionalism as a source of political legitimacy in the face of intensive legal and executive attack. Despite their differing social backgrounds, merchant Henry Hunt, self-made yeoman William Cobbett, and ex-artisans Thomas Wooler, Thomas Evans, and Richard Carlile fashioned themselves into orators, journalists, and activists within a common radical culture. As rhetorical "bricoleurs," they tacked together political defenses and critiques from the seemingly contradictory languages of civic independence, Enlightenment freethought, Christian communitarianism, and natural rights theory. They asserted traditional "historic" and natural rights to preach and prophesy in dissenting chapels; to express their opinions in debating clubs, reading circles, and alehouse convivial gatherings; to compose and perform songs, toasts, burlesques, and ballads; to defend themselves in courts of law before a jury of their peers; and to gather in meetings and marches to petition the king and Parliament for reform or redress.[15] They worked in effect to construct and defend a radical "counter public sphere" of discourse pitted against both government and parliamentary party and they promised legitimate participation in the political nation.[16]

On occasion, popular participation in the public sphere could swell to uncontainable proportions; in "the Queen Caroline affair" of 1820–21 it swept away the conservative bulwark of the Six Acts erected only a few months before. This agitation, which arose from the Prince of Wales's attempt to divorce his estranged wife through a Bill of Pains and Penalties in the House of Lords, is acquiring a position in British historiography akin to the Diamond Necklace affair in pre-revolutionary France.[17] Both incidents saw the state's legal apparatus of repression overwhelmed by "public opinion," manifested in a torrent of print, oral discussion, visual caricature, and public theatrical performance. Both "affairs" generated sensationalist and melodramatic moral narratives. In England, Whigs and radicals expanded their constitutionalist idiom to incorporate Caroline as "the people's queen," a figure comparable to Saxon Alfred or Protestant Elizabeth: at once a legal monarch and a popular choice. The long and highly political pre-history of her struggle with her husband and his courtier mistresses was also cast into a powerful melodrama. Disregarding Caroline's own checkered past, it represented her as an innocent princess lured by a gross voluptuary into a cynical and mercenary marriage, subjected to a drunken rape on her wedding night, ensnared in a gothic plot to smear her morals by the Prince's "seraglio" of aristocratic courtesans, torn from the company of her late beloved daughter, forced into lonely continental exile and deprived of her constitutional rights to serve as the people's monarch.[18]

Just when radical printers, publishers, and newspapers had been seemingly crushed by the Six Acts' new series of licensing curbs and legal restrictions, including a penalty of transportation for those convicted more than once of seditious and blasphemous libel, a flood of scurrilous pro-Caroline propaganda engulfed the government. Cobbett's twopenny *Peep at the Peers* was said to have sold 100,000 copies; his pseudonymous *Queen's Letter to the King*, two million copies in Britain and a half million in the United States.[19] Pro-Caroline squibs and burlesque handbills exploded with satirical and parodic tropes borrowed from plebeian as well as polite literary genres. William Hone's brilliant shilling satires, illustrated with woodcuts by George Cruikshank, were instantly translated into French for Parisian consumption. A huge cache of Queen Caroline satire even found its way to the distant antipodean city of Melbourne. The tycoon of St Giles street literature, Jem Catnach, is said to have made a fortune in less than twelve months from sale of pro-Caroline ballad sheets and chapbooks.[20] Petitions flooded in from every corner of England. In remote and supposedly loyal hamlets, village bells tolled and windows blazed for Caroline. In London, the new restrictions on public assemblies were brazenly flouted. Lord Sidmouth, who had calmly dismissed the dangers posed by mass radical meetings after Peterloo or by Arthur Thistlewood's plot to assassinate the Cabinet in early 1820, expressed fears that Caroline had brought the country to the verge of revolution.

The social reach of the Caroline affair matched its methodological plurality. "It was the only question I have ever known," wrote Hazlitt, "that excited a thorough popular feeling. It struck roots into the heart of the nation; it took possession of every house and cottage in the kingdom."[21] It swept up women as diverse as Jane Austen and the London prostitute who warned a group of soldiers that if they did not salute the queen, "you shall not come to bed to me. I am for Caroline. I am a whore and if she has had a whore's stroke is that any reason she is not to be queen." To the government's chagrin, soldiers and guardsmen, previously immune from democratic contagion, were all too often seen saluting or toasting the queen. The clause in the Six Acts against influencing military personnel proved as ineffectual in the face of the popular agitation as any of its other provisions. Journalist Henry Mayhew's interviews with street folk in the 1850s unearthed a crossing sweeper and a ballad singer who vividly recalled their involvement in the pro-queen ferment.[22] Conversely, the artist and diarist Joseph Farington attended a dinner at Cowes in August 1820 when a group of highly respectable and usually reticent provincial ladies had passionately defended the queen's cause. Although such populist eruptions often proved volatile and short-lived—the Caroline affair died with the queen in August 1821—they signalled that the state had little more control over the politically-conscious nation in 1820 than it had in June 1780, when the mob had ruled the streets of London for a week.

< III >

The Rise of the "Mass Platform," 1822–32

Eruptions of popular anti-establishment sentiment did not always prove as evanescent as the Caroline affair. By 1819 constitutionalist reformers already possessed in the "radical platform" a methodology capable of channeling anti-establishment sentiment into the achievement of major political change.[23] Only suitable leaders were lacking; the emergence—significantly in Ireland in the early 1820s—of the most formidable democratic orator, agitator, and organizer of the nineteenth century changed this at a stroke.

Though in some measure a child of the Enlightenment, Daniel O'Connell was scorched by an early brush with the French Revolution whilst studying at St. Omer; this, and a close shave during the government's roundup of Irish rebels in 1798, seem to have shocked him into embracing constitutionalist idioms and tactics. Godwinian and Benthamite utilitarianism always informed his liberal principles but marriage to his pious cousin Mary turned him into an increasingly devout Catholic who abhorred violence and illegality. Like that of others of old Catholic gentry lineage, his radical political ideology grew out of the vigorous tradition of Anglo-Irish Whiggery. Unlike many European and Latin American reformers whose constitutionalism sought to overthrow the evil past by enshrining natural rights in fixed and codified form, O'Connell harked back to an historic Christian "golden age" of saints and scholars prior to the Protestant invasion. He was also prone to cite the Treaty of Limerick as an existing constitutional bulwark of Catholic rights and to evoke the example of Earl Grattan's "independent"—albeit Protestant—Irish Parliament of 1782. In short, O'Connell shared the English lawyer's typical reverence for common law principles and the English radical's typical faith in nostalgic historicism, seeking civil and religious liberties for his countrymen similar to those espoused by many reformers on the mainland. As brilliant a platform orator as he was a court lawyer, O'Connell made himself a legend as "the people's Counsellor"—the Irish equivalent of English libertarian heroes Wilkes or Burdett—through his masterly exploitation of legal disputation, newspaper propaganda, and public performance.[24] And as Burke had found in the 1790s, seemingly unexceptionable political stances could develop explosive implications when transferred to the subordinated Catholic majority of Ireland.

Moreover, O'Connell introduced two crucial methodological innovations which transformed the demagogic platform. The first was to open up his elite Catholic Association to penny membership in the early 1820s, giving the mass of peasantry a stake in a cause which could otherwise bring them little practical benefit, as well as providing funds to mount a formidable newspaper propaganda. The second was to mobilize the priesthood into acting as the first modern electoral machine. It was they who at the Waterford and Clare elections of 1826 and 1828 organized, pledged, and directed the votes of the Catholic forty-shilling freeholders so as to break the back of Protestant landlord political control in Ireland.[25] Even this might not have been enough to overcome entrenched Tory and royal opposition to Catholic emancipation had O'Connell not also been able to gesture menacingly towards Ireland's seething agrarian violence. It did not matter that the sources of this endemic lawlessness—the maiming, carding, houghing, burning, kneecapping, and killing by Whiteboy secret societies—were essentially conservative and economic or sectarian in origin, nor that O'Connell and the priesthood hated Whiteboyism as heartily as did the Tory Irish secretary, Robert "Orange" Peel. It was enough that Ireland's network of agrarian secret societies represented a cauldron of incipient nationalist violence and alternative law that the British government could not contain. For much of the 1820s and early 1830s the government effectively lost sovereignty over large parts of Leinster and Munster.[26] Were this agrarian underworld to link up with O'Connell's formidable constitutionalist machine, civil war might result. Such a specter was enough to chill even the unflappable duke of Wellington. Catholic emancipation passed into law in 1829, smashing in one blow the Anglican confessional state and the English Old Regime.[27]

O'Connell's dramatic success, coupled with the example of the bloodless French and Belgian revolutions of 1830, helped to revive an English popular reform movement which had flagged under the combined effects of economic recovery and legal repression. In England, as in Ireland, agrarian unrest provided a necessary prelude to reform. The "Captain Swing" riots generated by agricultural laborers in the southeast of England in 1830–31 echoed Ireland's "Captain Rock" and "Ribbonmen" agitations of the 1820s. True, English landless agricultural laborers expressing customary moral economic concerns about low pay and underemployment looked innocuous beside their ferocious Irish counterparts, but the English ruling class was deeply shocked that this most deferential and docile sector of the populace had been infected by democratic unrest. Occasional displays of radical and internationalist sympathy by individual "Swing" rioters partly explain the Whig government's harsh suppression of the movement.[28]

The English extra-parliamentary reform organizations that grew up in the aftermath of Swing espoused a variety of franchise programs ranging from household to universal suffrage but agreed for the most part in using the constitutionalist tactic of the mass platform. Part of the platform's appeal derived from ambiguity over its reformist or revolutionary intentions. Through Whig precedents of 1689, it could be presented as a legitimate gathering of petitioners entitled to elect representative delegates in a convention, and even to arm for purposes of self-defense. Yet massive simultaneous meetings across the country, supported by an array of banners, flags, and caps of liberty, were at the very least intimidating, especially when small pockets of ultra-radicals aspired to make them a springboard for armed rising. Such neo-Jacobins also envisaged the mass platform as a potential national law-making body similar to the French National Convention. By 1830 even non-conspiratorial English radicals were prepared on occasion to flaunt the menacing symbology of the Revolution, including pike, bonnet rouge, and tricouleur, often combined ambiguously with constitutionalist icons and slogans.[29] Popular radical rhetoric also began to incorporate "class" language, using "productive versus parasitic" social and economic definitions as well as claims for the value of labor derived from the writings of Ricardian-influenced social thinkers such as William Thompson and Thomas Hodgskin.

Some more sophisticated "Unstamped" radical newspapers, including Henry Hetherington's *Poor Man's Guardian*, showed a continental tendency to draft elements of the middle classes such as "millocrats" and "shopocrats" into "Old Corruption's" ranks of parasitic kings, priests, aristocrats, fundholders, and stockjobbers. At the same time their analyses often used Christian and Saxon historicist justifications for schemes of smallholder agrarian redistribution along lines advocated by Thomas Spence and his postwar followers.[30] Political reformers of all stamps—parliamentary Whigs, moderate "middling class" members of the National Political Union or the Birmingham Political Union, radical artisans from the National Union of the Working Classes: all mimicked O'Connell's tactic of controlled menace. Each sought to apply enough pressure to carry their program without provoking outright rioting or a feared government backlash.

Within Parliament, the debate turned on whether reform or resistance would best preserve Britain's aristocratic form of government. Invariably such arguments were refracted through the twin lenses of French Revolutionary and seventeenth-century English historiography. For the young Whig intellectual Thomas Babington Macaulay, both histories pointed to the wisdom of moderate reform. Timely concessions would, he argued, have produced the Glorious Revolution of 1688 in England and the benign constitutional revolution of 1830 in France without the needless and bloody extremism of 1641 and 1793. For the Tory historians Archibald Alison and J. W. Croker, history told an opposite story. Reform led invariably to revolutionary extremism: just as constitutionalist Presbyterians had been succeeded first by moderate republican Independents and then by bloodthirsty Fifth Monarchists, the French Constituent Assembly had given way to Girondins and then Jacobins.[31] Significantly, both sides drew extensively on Burke's ideas, as had O'Connell in Ireland, though it was Burke's liberal Whig, rather than Jacobite or Irish radical, legacy that prevailed. In the Reform Act that received royal assent on June 7, 1832, the propertied, "independent," middle-class male gained formal access to the English political nation.

≺ IV ≻

The Revolutionary Era and the
Decline of the Mass Platform, 1834–48

The bulwark that the Tories had attempted to erect around the public political sphere in 1819 was set in place more systematically and solidly by the reforming Whigs of the 1830s. That Whig reforms were often presented in the language of political economy and utility rather than constitutionalism may have been one source of the considerable resistance they generated in both England and Ireland. The administrative imperatives of rationality, uniformity, and accountability underpinning such legislation as the New Poor Law, the Anatomy Act, and the Municipal Corporations Act looked like aggressive centralist attacks on traditional freedoms, rights, and customs, in keeping with the spirit of a government that crushed the Swing riots, transported the harmless agricultural unionists of Tolpuddle in 1834, and introduced harsh coercion acts in Ireland.[32] Recent scholarship has also suggested that the Great Reform Act of 1832 worked to contain as much as expand the popular political nation. Gains in new, albeit narrowly defined, urban constituencies such as Tower Hamlets and Oldham were offset by greater practical restrictions in areas like South Devon.[33] Revisionist historians have also argued for the considerable dynamism and vitality of the old unreformed electoral political system, particularly in its informal electoral operations.[34] At the local level, too, the Municipal Reform Act of 1835 actually enfranchised propertied males at the expense of the traditional informal participation of unpropertied women and laborers.[35] It was thus perfectly logical for popular radicals to continue to use a political and constitutionalist rather than social and economic analysis of their plight when working to defeat the Whig state.

This resentment of Whig interventionism was doubly true of Ireland, given the persisting government temptation to use it as a social and political laboratory for testing out novel and potentially controversial legislation, often cast in starker forms than would have been tolerated in England. Such a double standard informed the Reform Act of 1832, which left Irish rotten boroughs intact and introduced a derisory handful of new seats, as well as the Grand Jury Act of 1837, which strengthened the legal powers of Protestant JPs, and the Irish Municipal Corporations Act, which abolished most corporations and set high property franchises. The country was also subjected to exceptional and coercive law and order legislation—often including suspension of habeas corpus—throughout the first half of the 1830s and for most of the 1840s.[36]

O'Connell's campaign to repeal the Act of Union of 1800 aspired to end this colonial relationship and to restore the mythical parity of Grattan's independent Parliament of 1782. The fact that such a restoration would have excluded the whole Catholic nation was glossed over; 1782 gave O'Connell the justification he needed to pit a mass movement against the legally constituted state. Abandoning his innovative post-emancipation tactics of factional bargaining and brinksmanship within Westminster Parliament, he returned in the early 1840s to his earlier extra-parliamentary methodology of platform protest, adding a new emphasis on Catholic Gaelic cultural symbol and a new vastness of scale. His "monster" repeal meetings represented the *ne plus ultra* of the mass platform. Several meetings are said to have attracted more than a million followers, figures unequalled anywhere in the nineteenth century. Such size necessitated the complex sinews of an alternative state: priests and repeal wardens carried sophisticated powers of financing, organizing, and policing. To succeed, such tactics of bluff and brinksmanship needed to convey a genuine sense of the possibility of revolutionary violence; but by 1843, when the government forced O'Connell to call off his monster meeting at Clontarf, his essential pacifism was known.[37] He also faced a stronger, more prepared and self-confident state than had existed a decade earlier. In one blow at Clontarf the English government eliminated the mass platform from the repertoire of nineteenth-century Irish politics, ironically hastening the triumph of the gun.

Across the seas another Irishman, Feargus O'Connor, nephew of the United Irish plotter Arthur and a former member of O'Connell's parliamentary party, simultaneously pinned his faith on the mass platform. Though Feargus O'Connor, "the Lion of Freedom," and Daniel O'Connell, "the Irish Liberator," were to become inveterate enemies, they had much in common. Both were democrats of authoritarian disposition from old Irish gentry stock; both felt a strong, instinctive sympathy for the small peasant landholder and cottier; both were big, sensual, flamboyant men with prodigious stamina, a pronounced sense of dignity, and the charismatic ability to articulate, dramatize, and embody their respective causes. Both were incorrigibly companionable, inept with money, and, as it turned out, equally wedded to constitutional "moral force" methods.[38] Yet O'Connor's task in mobilizing and controlling the popular movement of Chartism was probably more difficult, if only because his constituency was incomparably more diverse. Striated by occupational, regional, ethnic, religious, educational, and gender differences, the Chartist movement incorporated an enormous body of overlapping, competing, and conflicting goals and tactics. The six points of the Charter—universal male suffrage, annual parliaments, secret ballot, equal electoral districts, payment of members, abolition of members' property franchise—which had been formalized by the moderate radical London Working Men's Association in 1838 ostensibly did little more than gather and endorse basic radical political principles laid down in 1776 by veteran reformer Major Cartwright. However, "the people's charter" also constituted a symbolic program that stretched to encompass a plethora of subsidiary goals: educational and moral, phrenological and mesmeric, Christian and infidel, temperance and convivial, prophetic and pietistic, trades unionist and internationalist.[39] It was O'Connor's great achievement to hold this baggy, creaking movement together for most of a decade by deploying the fluid, inclusive idiom of radical constitutionalism in literally thousands of platform speeches around the country, in the columns of his newspaper artery the *Northern Star,* and in his elaborate political iconography of dress, banner, and parade.

A constitutionalist in an often troubled economic climate, O'Connor inevitably came under pressure from more militant followers eager for confrontation with the government. He wavered between espousals of nonviolence and a melodramatic language of menace and martyrdom. To what extent this rhetoric of "ulterior methods" was responsible for provoking individual groups of Chartists into uncoordinated and futile risings, such as those in London and Newport in 1839,[40] is unclear. At no point, however, did the government and its cool Northern army commander, Charles Napier, seem to have been seriously intimidated either by the mass petitions, the Chartist Convention, or the sporadic riots and insurrectionary outbreaks.[41] O'Connor's bluff was repeatedly called—finally and most poignantly at Kennington Common on April 10, 1848, when thousands of volunteer special constables stood ready to enforce order and protect property against the mass meeting called to present the petition to Parliament. When parliamentarians felt safe to snigger at the gaucheries of the nearly two million genuine signatories of the petition, the Charter's day seemed done.

≺ V ≻

Constitutionalism as Public Culture, 1832–48

Although at Clontarf in 1843 and Kennington Common in 1848 the Irish Repeal and British Chartist movements failed spectacularly to achieve their avowed goals, those abortive gatherings should not be seen as the sum of their achievements. Modern historians of Chartism have focused on its transformative effects as a culture which challenged and extended the public political sphere. For many of their followers Chartism and Repeal may have been more important as participatory processes than instrumentalist movements.[42] Measured in size of following, both can be reckoned amongst the largest and most inclusive democratic organizations of the nineteenth century. Chartism's best selling and longest lasting newspaper, the *Northern Star*, attained a peak circulation of 50,000 and an estimated readership of 2,500,000.[43] Likewise, O'Connell's "monster" repeal meetings regularly attracted half a million attendants and may have several times topped the million mark.[44] Both Chartism and the Repeal movement reached into remote geographical corners of their respective islands and recruited followers with an astonishing diversity of occupations and educational attainments. The columns of Chartist newspapers record a vital participatory culture that encompassed schools, nurseries, charities, tea parties, dances, debates, reading and scientific circles, shops, coffee houses, taverns, churches, dispensaries, cooperatives, trades societies, benefit clubs, and women's groups.[45] Their polymathic libertarian endeavors extended to campaigning against flogging, capital punishment, prison and workhouse abuses, dissection, slavery, and foreign tyranny of all kinds—and these were only some of the Chartist meanings of freedom. In all this "we catch a glimpse," argues David Jones, "of an alternative society—egalitarian, humane, and harmonious."[46] Arguably, the vestiges of Harrington's seventeenth-century republican conception of freedom underlay Chartist efforts to fashion a democratic civil society made up of virtuous and active public citizens. The Repeal movement likewise developed a vital educative and recreational cultural dimension expressed through networks of "Liberal" and "Independent" clubs that sprang up especially in Leinster and East Munster during the 1830s; a decade later these were to flower in the remarkable cultural renaissance of Young Ireland.[47]

Not everyone had equal access to this democratic culture. Ernest Jones, a major leader of late Chartism, admitted that though the movement had redefined the nature of democracy by challenging every facet of the status quo, it had neglected one key asset—the enormous enthusiasm and support tendered by women and children. Male leaders had failed to heed Helen Maria Williams's warning that "the Charter will never become the law of the land until we women are fully resolved that it should be so."[48] This is not to say that women had been completely excluded from participation. In parts of Lancashire and Scotland, for example, women's political activity drew legitimacy from a Nonconformist ethic of mutuality and piety.[49] Anna Clarke has recently also argued that women radicals and Chartists in the early nineteenth century pushed beyond the conservative evangelical language of domesticity to assert a distinctive and militant domestic ideal. Eliding conventional distinctions between the public political and the private domestic sphere, they justified radical activism as wives and mothers defending the right to a wage capable of feeding and educating their families.

Whilst some middle-class women might see domesticity as a shelter from the public sphere, Chartist women sought to politicize the ideal.[50] Their activities in Chartist, anti-slavery, anti-poor law, and factory reform associations helped win substantial concessions from the state and also contributed to decisive changes in masculine radical manners and morals. Feminine ideals of domesticity and respectability challenged older, often misogynistic, artisan recreational patterns built around casual theft, gambling, drunken conviviality, and prostitution. Ex-artisan Francis Place testified from his own experience to the spread in the 1830s and 40s of more mutualist, home-centered and self-improving mores.[51] Despite a pervasive nostalgia for the days of smallholder and pre-industrial cottage industry, male Chartists adopted the powerful melodramatic language of domestic dislocation and hardship that sanctioned women's involvement in public political activity. Between 1818 and 1848 women radicals and Chartists generated independent reform associations in the Midlands and North, incurred prison sentences in defense of political and religious freedom, led food riots, marched in protests, assembled in mass platform meetings, petitioned Parliament and monarchy in defense of Queen Caroline, and participated in all facets of radical journalism and publication.[52]

This activism was to have ambivalent results. By representing themselves as wives and mothers forced reluctantly into the public economic and political sphere, Chartist women helped to force the passage of regulating legislation which enshrined the ideal of the male breadwinner wage and so subsumed their political rights within those of their husbands.[53] The increasingly formal and institutionalized levels of organization evident in both the Chartist and Repeal movements seem likewise to have eroded the participation of women.[54] Recent feminist critics have argued that the very process of radical democratization during the early nineteenth century worked to differentiate and marginalize women. Radical constitutionalists of the 1830s and 40s sought to redefine the basis of popular citizenship from independent property-owning to new forms of legitimacy grounded in notions of historic right, or of property in labor and skill, or of the ability to command a household of dependents such as servants, women, and children.[55] Ultimately, popular constitutionalist movements such as Irish Repeal and Chartism could thus accommodate women only in auxiliary roles, forcing some to look to revolutionary republican movements based on natural rights or to Owenite utopianism for more adequate recognition of their rights to active political citizenship.

≪ VI ≫

Revolutionary Visions: Republicans,
Socialists, and Romantics, 1832–48

Even before the setbacks of Clontarf and Kennington Common, both the Repeal and Chartist movements had sparked critics who were impatient with the apparent ambiguities, limitations, and evasions of popular constitutionalist discourse and strategy. Some of these sought to revive and extend a supposedly purer, more principled, and "revolutionary" political language derived from enlightenment republicanism and rationalist deism. Originally disseminated through Tom Paine's best-selling *Rights of Man* and to a lesser extent his *Age of Reason*, this tradition had gained a firm purchase in the English popular political culture of the 1790s, notwithstanding the fact that the new natural rights paradigm often supplemented rather than supplanted older historicist theories of popular constitutionalism. Paine joined a pantheon of heroes of popular liberty such as Hampden, Sidney, Wilkes, and Burdett. From the mid 1790s Burke's counter-revolutionary critique of French Enlightenment violence, license, and irreligion, combined with wartime anti-Gallican patriotism and United Movement insurrectionism, did much to discredit Painite ideas. However, peace and economic hardship in 1815–19 set the scene for a major revival at the hands of an ex-tinmaker journalist, Richard Carlile, who published numerous cheap editions of Paine's political and theological works as well as republican-rationalist classics from America, France, and Britain. Imprisoned for blasphemous and seditious libel in 1819, Carlile orchestrated a national popular movement in defense of freedom of inquiry, discussion, and publication. For the next five years hundreds of artisan shopmen and women clashed with the government and loyalist prosecuting societies in London's courts and jails, supported by networks of provincial "Zetetic" or radical knowledge societies who furnished volunteers, subscriptions, and articles for Carlile's remarkable jail publication, the *Republican*.[56]

Painite republican rationalism eschewed historic rights and fictional constitutions by asserting the freedom and equality of human beings grounded in nature and equipped with reason. Denouncing the mystifications and oppressions of monarchy, aristocracy, and church, it espoused an American anti-statist republicanism based on universal suffrage and accompanied by rationalist political free thought or "infidelity." Its rationalism looked to transcend the ambiguities and fictions of politics, art, religion, and language by applying pure unmediated reason.[57] Like the French Jacobins, Zetetics aspired to pure transparency, denying all authority other than nature and believing in the possibility of discovering nature's laws through objective scientific inquiry.

Republican-rationalists worked tirelessly during the 1820s and 30s to apply the implications of their rationalist critique to all realms of human knowledge. Suspicious of the contingency and particularity of history and of local or national attachments, they aspired to a universalist and cosmopolitan citizenship of the world based on the diffusion of individual reason. They championed slave risings in the West Indies and the liberal "revolutions" of the 1820s in Spain and South America. During the 1820s numbers of them also pushed beyond Paine's limited deism to embrace a more thoroughgoing French materialism derived from Helvetius and Holbach. Like Godwin and Mary Wollstonecraft during the 1790s, belief in natural rights led some artisan republicans to espouse sexual equality and the political rights of women: freedom of opinion extended to freedom of love. Rejecting marriage as a Christian imposition, Carlile began in the mid twenties to advocate and practice "free moral" relationships supported by birth control.[58] He also campaigned for freedom of scientific inquiry, popularizing "Surgeon" William Lawrence's famous rejection of Hunterian vitalist life theory in favor of a resolutely materialist/mechanist approach to human physiology. According to science historian Adrian Desmond this popular rationalist milieu nurtured revolutionary French Lamarckian and Geoffrist theories of evolution and anatomy with far-reaching implications for British medicine and science.[59]

Even so, this republican-rationalist idiom of revolution attracted only a small minority of adherents. Reverence for intellectuality and scientific knowledge sometimes congealed into pedantry and elitism as artisans remade themselves into intellectuals and men of letters. Such men were often drawn to utilitarian principles or to Ricardian political economic theories based on strongly individualist notions of enlightened self-interest. Their resultant espousal of Malthusianism, birth control, and dissection outraged the customary values of more traditional readers. Carlile's extreme rationalism also alienated him from the powerful legitimating force and allusive emotional appeal of vital religion, spirituality, and romantic art. Dissenters attracted by his pugnacious anticlericalism and advocacy of religious toleration balked at outright infidelity. By the early 1830s this abstract brand of ultra rationalism was being challenged by more romantic freethinking or mystical enlightenment movements which, in the manner of French theophilanthropy, combined sectarian structure and ritual with universalist theology and millenarian rhetoric.[60] By the time of his death in 1842 Carlile had become a licensed Unitarian minister preaching a unique brand of mythological Christian rationalism. His direct intellectual legacy passed to the Victorian republican and secular movements led by former disciples such as G. J. Holyoake and Charles Bradlaugh; other former followers gravitated to the rival popular movement of St. Simonianism or Owenism where rationalism was purveyed in messianic language, accompanied by sectarian ritual and a communitarian social organization.

The philanthropic cotton-spinner Robert Owen developed his utopian vision of moral, social, and economic revolution as a reaction against both the political excesses of the French Revolution and his own experiences of industrialism in the textile industry. By the early 1830s the resultant popular movement—designed to transform individual and social character—was being described as "socialist." Like republican-rationalists, Owen disliked the ambiguities and compromises of political democrats, believing that representative institutions, popular sovereignty, and radical programs of financial retrenchment could not remedy existing distress or confer social justice in a corrupt, competitive industrial society. Institutions of church, school, Parliament, and family—he believed—warped human nature by instilling superstition, selfishness, and competition. He aimed to revolutionize society through small-scale participatory communities based on an equality of men and women committed to implementing a cooperative economic and social ethic.

Between the 1820s and 1840s Owenite "socialism" generated social and intellectual experiment, sometimes in the teeth of opposition from Owen himself. It included practical "cooperative" trading organizations, a phase of syndicalist general unionism in the mid-1830s, a body of anti-capitalist political economic theory propounded in influential "Unstamped" radical periodicals of the 1830s, and a series of cooperative communities dedicated to eliminating Christian education and patriarchal marriage.[61] Owenite utopianism projected a future harmonious moral world based on complementarity of the sexes and the adoption of "feminine" values of love, compassion, and mutuality.[62] Yet like republican-rationalism, Owenism's infidel reputation alienated potential popular support. Its powerful strain of Enlightenment and Puritan perfectionism also limited it to small-scale sectarian or communitarian forms. The inability of communities in Britain, Ireland, and America to sustain these moral ideals led to widespread disillusionment, culminating in the much-publicized failure of the Queenwood community in 1846.[63] Owenite men often succumbed to the attractions of the masculine wage and the sexual double standard, whilst women found themselves unable in practice to shake off responsibilities to children and family. Owenite economic analyses failed ultimately to supplant older constitutionalist theory that simply absorbed any compatible elements, such as the stress on inequities of exchange and distribution.[64] Both rhetorically and practically, Owenite "social revolution" failed to supercede democratic politics.

Inevitably the limitations of both rationalist and utopian variants of revolution opened the way for the revival of insurrectionary models derived from the French Revolution and its Irish Toneite counterpart. This trend was also stimulated by the intermittent setbacks of constitutionalist politics and by government suppression of traditional outlets of protest, as in England in 1817, 1819–20, and 1831, and in Ireland for most of the 1830s and 40s. Insurrectionary attempts by small groups of London ultra-radicals at Spa Fields in 1816 and Cato Street in 1820 revealed shadowy connections with French and Irish emigrés.[65] The early twenties also saw a quickening cultural interest in French revolutionary theories and models amongst young English romantic intellectuals like Percy Bysshe Shelley and William Hazlitt. Their poetry and criticism proclaimed that the excesses of the French Revolution had been the result of provocation and inexperience, and that the Revolution instituted major libertarian advances on the oppressions and inequities of the Old Regime.[66] The European revolutions of 1820 and 1830 further kindled Jacobin revivalism in artisan radical circles. During the Reform Act agitations of 1831–32 several unstamped periodicals associated with the National Union of the Working Classes advocated a French- rather than Whig-style national convention. Over the next five years the influential *Poor Man's Guardian*, co-edited by another brilliant Irish emigré, Bronterre O'Brien, popularized Babeuf's conspiracy, extolled the Jacobin Constitution of 1793, and began to rehabilitate Robespierre as an incorruptible social and political egalitarian.[67]

As editor of the *Northern Star* and leader of the Fraternal Democrats in the mid-1840s, G. J. Harney championed a minority current of French insurrectionary thought against the popular constitutionalism and land-reforming ideals of Feargus O'Connor. This insurrectionary rhetoric reached its zenith in the charged atmosphere of the year of European revolutions, 1848, when Harney persuaded the National Charter Association to endorse participatory lawmaking by direct vote at primary assemblies, and to present an address of support to the provisional government of Paris. The extent of Chartist commitment to European libertarianism and democratic constitution-making in the 1840s is only now being recognized.[68] Meetings, addresses, and resolutions from all over Britain declared fraternal support for the forces of freedom in Spain, Italy, France, Mexico, and Poland; denounced the repressive Old Regimes of Austria and Hungary; and praised the enlightened constitutions of Switzerland and Norway.

This Gallic insurrectionism appealed primarily to a London demimonde of alienated intellectuals and emigrés, including Marx and Engels, many of whose works Harney translated. Rank and file Chartists were inclined to regard Harney as a hot head and O'Brien something of a scholarly crank.[69] Harney admitted to having no stomach for the reality of insurrectionary violence, and his romantic Gallic images of street-fighting and barricades seemed doubtfully relevant in a country of factories, mines, and chapels. He conceded privately that the ingrained libertarianism of British workers recoiled from the military-style authoritarianism of continental and Irish insurrectionary organizations. Though Feargus O'Connor was not above citing the odd French Jacobin example to enhance Chartist rhetorical menace, he trumpeted his dislike of Babeuvist and Blanquist socialism. His own social prescriptions centered on the Land Plan, a pastoral vision to restore a virtuous yeomanry through individual smallholdings,[70] which probably owed a great deal to early experiences as a Cork landlord. The largest British insurrectionary attempt of the period—the Welsh rising of 1839 in Newport with links to Birmingham, Bradford, and Newcastle—seems to have owed little to foreign rhetoric or example.

As in Burke's day, Ireland proved more hospitable to French revolutionary insurrectionism, generating a romantic nationalist revolutionary movement in the European mold. Its incubator was Young Ireland, a group of young, mainly Protestant, intellectuals and writers of professional background who clustered in the early 1840s around Thomas Davis, the charismatic editor of the *Nation*. Davis's troubled Anglo-Irish identity attracted him to Prussian romantic models of cultural and national regeneration. Through the *Nation*'s columns he fashioned Bardic mythology, Gaelic language, and ancient Irish warrior traditions into a redemptive vision of cultural and racial nationhood pitted against a satanic and materialistic English oppressor.[71] The hot prophetic spirit of Thomas Carlyle's *History of the French Revolution* found eager Irish readers in this circle. Under the goad of O'Connell's tactical failures and intransigent legalism, these evocations of historic violence gradually transmuted into concrete plots. Jon Mitchel, editor of the *Nation* after Davis's death in 1842, began to graft Toneite United Irish traditions of militarist, oathbound, cellular organization onto this fervent cultural nationalism. The year 1848 thus saw a restoration of the old Jacobin triangular alliance between revolutionary Paris, Mitchel's newly-named Irish Confederate movement, and elements of physical-force Chartism in England. John Saville's recent detailed study of 1848 cites extensive plans for a coordinated armed rising between Leinster Confederate groups and Chartists in London, the Midlands, and the North.[72] In the event the government's intelligence network proved too good: a swift wave of arrests smashed the revolutionary cadres and prevented a serious rising. Hundreds of Irish and English leaders were imprisoned or transported.

In truth the revolutionaries of Young Ireland and the Confederate movement had been riven by ambiguity and contradiction. Romantic attachment to violence as a source of moral redemption and political virility clashed with intellectual squeamishness and sensitivity. Their literary and linguistic nationalism stood remote from the concerns of the mass of Catholic peasantry smashed by economic poverty and famine, and who anyway often regarded English as a path to material self-betterment.[73] Moreover, as Dorothy Thompson has recently argued, Mitchel's Confederate movement actively sought to eclipse the early democratic universalism of the Toneite-Jacobin tradition in favor of a narrower, more particularist, and racially-based brand of separatist nationalism.[74] For most of the 1840s it was not the Irish romantic revolutionaries but the Irish constitutionalist radicals, Daniel O'Connell and Feargus O'Connor, who came closest to embodying and articulating the political hopes of the British and Irish masses.

≺ VII ≻

Legacies of European Revolution:
Divergence and Convergence, 1848–67

British Marxist, labor, and social historians generally agree that the year 1848 marked a decisive turning point in British popular politics, inaugurating a shift away from revolutionary "class-conscious" politics in favor of collaborative mid-Victorian liberal reformism or at least an era of more atomized sectional and local politics. Explanations for this shift vary. One interpretation stresses changes within the disposition of the leadership of working-class politics. The debacle of Kennington Common supposedly exposed the divisions, weaknesses, and uncertainties of Chartist leadership and goals, exacerbated by the emigration or transportation of many "physical force" Chartist leaders, and paved the way for the dominance of liberal, moral improvement strands of radicalism and trade unionism exemplified by moderate figures like William Lovett, Robert Lowery, Henry Vincent, George Howell, and Robert Applegarth.[75] The large-scale enrollment in 1848 of workers and middle-class volunteers to protect property revealed the dangers of class politics and enhanced the confidence of the British governing classes. One consequence was the passage of more consensual social legislation designed to lessen working-class social ills, encouraging in turn a changed view of the law and the state as potentially neutral and ameliorative. Economic revival, the long-term stabilization of industrialization after a disruptive transitional period, and some partial improvements in living standards are seen to have underpinned this political change. New structural patterns of industrial dependence and loyalty within the work force, as well as the uneven distribution of industrialism within the British economy, are also thought to have contributed to the growth of consensual politics and labor relations.[76] Historians committed to the notion of class struggle as a fundamental feature of capitalist society have usually associated mid-Victorian class collaboration with the emergence of a "labor aristocracy" of pacers and taskmasters who cooperated with management in exchange for superior wages at the expense of semi- and unskilled workers.[77] The spirit of this new, self-improving, and accommodative labor elite is said to be revealed in the industrial bargaining of "New Model" craft unions and the politics of popular liberalism.

Recent work has doubted both the extent and direction of this mid nineteenth-century shift in popular politics and labor relations. Several detailed local studies question the existence of a distinctively new mid-Victorian labor aristocracy and of a correlation between wage levels and political militancy.[78] Others dispute whether 1848 was experienced as the fiasco of legend; they stress instead the continuity of both Chartist and Owenite activities during the 1850s. Margot Finn's new study of mid-Victorian popular politics argues that 1848 actually intensified political divisions between working-class and middle-class radicals in the short term. The end of O'Connor's leadership, the failures of constitutional tactics, and the ferocity of state repression led remaining Chartist leaders such as Ernest Jones and G. W. M. Reynolds to place greater emphasis on social revolution in the French mold. Democratic socialist theories from Proudhon, Cabet, Saint Simon, and particularly Louis Blanc circulated amongst post 1848 Chartists more extensively than labor historians have allowed. This resulted in a widespread adoption of what John Merriman in the French context calls the *democ soc* ideal. Margot Finn glosses this as "insistence upon the interrelation of social and economic spheres and the conviction that political institutions could transform the character of economic relations."[79] Chartists, she believes, began to grope towards new popular conceptions of positive liberty. Conversely, the June insurrection in France, combined with this increased Chartist emphasis on social justice, alarmed middle-class radicals and liberals who sought as a result to limit political and national definitions of freedom both at home and abroad. They denounced socialist experiments like those of exiled Louis Blanc and stressed the primacy of laissez faire in the economic sphere. Meetings in the Midlands and North in support of Kossuth and Hungarian revolution in August-September 1849 revealed mounting tensions and acrimony over these competing definitions of political and social freedom.

Within a decade this trend had been reversed: divergence gave way to convergence, but not, Finn stresses, because of worker "embourgeoisement," labor-aristocrat collaboration, or the displacement of domestic tension by pan-European libertarian enthusiasm.[80] True, radical leaders such as G. J. Holyoake and Ernest Jones became more willing to cooperate with middle-class and liberal domestic political movements in support of political reform and European national freedom. Yet compromises cut both ways. In the long term 1848 sobered the parliamentary parties as much as the unenfranchised Chartists: common lessons had been learned from the militancy. Ruling-class moves to rectify social grievances disclosed by Chartism are manifested in a new spirit of administrative reform, as well as in legislation such as the Repeal of the Corn Laws (1846), the Mines Act (1844), the Factory Acts (1847), the Public Health Act (1848), and the Industrial and Providential Societies Act (1853). A new imaginative sympathy for the working classes surfaces in the works of liberal writers and artists such as Mrs Gaskell, the Pre-Raphaelites, the Christian Socialists, and John Stuart Mill.[81] Mill replied to Lord Brougham's Burkean-style attack on European revolution by defending 1848 as a critical libertarian moment in world history. Mill's qualified support for socialist cooperation also foreshadowed his later moral criticisms of profit-motivated society. The 1850s and 60s saw a softening of doctrinaire Manchester School politico-economic dictums and a greater willingness to contemplate state intervention for social amelioration, particularly amongst younger parliamentarians involved in the National Association for the Promotion of

Social Science or influenced by Comtean postitivism. Middle-class liberals began to absorb the rudimentary notions of "positive liberty" and social democracy implicit in the rhetoric of old Chartists and Owenites.[82]

Significantly, evocation of seventeenth-century struggles for freedom against papal tyranny helped reconcile and mediate tensions between English radicals and liberals. If campaigns in support of continental nationalism furnished an arena for cooperative activity, radical constitutionalism endowed these foreign revolutions with shared meaning. We find the pressman-Chartist G. W. M. Reynolds espousing Louis Blanc's "rights of labour" to counteract the historic effects of the Norman yoke.[83] Liberals and Chartists repeatedly compared Kossuth and Garibaldi to the "Great Protector" Cromwell. Garibaldi re-engaged the libertarian anti-popery tradition within radical constitutionalist discourse by reminding eager English audiences of Albion's historic mission to crush the "immoral monstrosity" of the papacy;[84] he was hailed in traditional English patriotic language as a "man of the people" and "hero of liberty." A "British legion" of Scots, Nonconformist, and republican volunteers formed in 1860 to aid his Sicilian campaigns against a brigade of Irish volunteers fighting for the papal army. Republican and Secularist leader Charles Bradlaugh denounced popery's international conspiracy against liberty[85] in accents little different from those Lord George Gordon had used against Burke nearly a century earlier.

By the 1860s this common heritage of political language based on the richly ambiguous tradition of popular constitutionalism had elided many of the differences between plebeian Chartists and middle-class Liberals. Recent scholarship represents mid-Victorian popular liberalism not as the enshrinement of bourgeois ideology but as an institutionalization of the old plebeian radical language and program. Core ingredients of Gladstonian liberalism had been foreshadowed in earlier radical constitutionalist movements. Common ideals included anti-statism, anticlericalism, anti-corruption, retrenchment, free trade, liberty of conscience, open government, franchise reform, moral independence, rule of law, and freedom from arbitrary intervention at home and abroad.[86] James Vernon's analysis of several militant mid-Victorian working-class constituencies and Eugenio Biagini's broad survey of liberal political rhetoric reveal a pervasive nostalgia for a lost "golden age" of Saxon democracy and pastoralism centered on the moral virtues of the small independent landholding citizen. Both ideals inform the land reform programs of Bright and Mill. Nonconformist religious ideals and sensibilities also surface in the 1860s agitations over unionism and labor laws, in radical attitudes to Irish nationalism, and in popular moral criticisms of laissez-faire individualism.[87]

Speeches and writings of liberals and radicals resound with references to Bunyan, Milton, and Cromwell, set within a prophetic framework of loss, struggle, and restoration. Gladstone's evangelical belief in the superior moral virtues of the poor and the vices of the rich struck a deep chord with radicals like Jones, Edmond Beales, Joseph Cowen, and William Newton. Gladstone appealed beyond the selfish confines of class to a broad collective identity of "the people"—those excluded from the political nation by privilege and aristocratic monopoly. His creed of moral entitlement to representation, though a retreat from the universal male entitlement advocated by Chartism, exploited rhetorical ambiguities over the connotations of "independence" which now became identified with morality, manners, and character.[88] Free trade was equated with the ancient populist ideal of cheap bread; financial retrenchment stood for the end of old corruption. The Reform League, destined to play so large a part in ensuring the admission of urban artisans to the franchise in 1867, blended Gladstonian ideals of moral citizenship with the anti-old corruption and libertarian constitutionalism popularized by Cobbett in the immediate postwar years.[89]

International events between 1853 and 1865 further stimulated this process of popular moralization. The struggles of Mazzini, Garibaldi, and Kossuth against Old Regime despotism attracted extraordinary popular adulation in Britain, as well as Europe. Their romantic images as heroes of "the long European struggle for liberty," their Christian moral idealism and fervent anti-socialist rhetoric sacralized liberal politics and helped divert interest from Louis Blanc's socialist workshop schemes.[90] The American Civil War—once thought to have divided old anti-capitalist and new liberal radicals—seems equally to have rekindled the political commitment of both generations of radical leadership. It revived old republican and Painite ideals of America as a democratic paradise, and installed "Honest Abe" Lincoln, abolitionist, in the pantheon of British working-class heroes.[91]

Even the supposedly irrationalist populist movements which

erupted in mid-Victorian Britain, such as David Urquhart's Russo-phobic foreign policy committees and the extraordinary mass following, in the 1860s, of the "Tichborne claimant"—a Wagga Wagga butcher who claimed to be the missing heir to the Earl of Tichborne's estate—have recently been interpreted as extensions of old plebeian radicalism operating within the popular constitutionalist idiom.[92] At the heart of the rococo politics of Tichbornism stood a plebeian radical concern for fair play and social justice, pitted against aristocratic influence and privilege. Tichbornism's chief agitational method even continued the supposedly defunct radical tactic of the mass platform. As in earlier radical movements, charismatic Irish oratory and leadership style gave moral coherence, purpose, and identity to the Tichborne movement—this time in the form of Cork lawyer, demagogue, and campaign leader Edward Kenealy.[93] Kenealy, Gladstone, and Bright can be seen as heirs to the charismatic platform styles of "constitutionalist" demagogues such as Burdett, Hunt, O'Connell, and O'Connor. All helped induct mass democracy into the values of the traditional Chartist ethos of politically active citizenship.

<< VIII >>

*Irish Exceptionalism: Fenian
Revolution and English Anti-Popery*

The appeal of popular liberalism, however inclusive, could not accommodate Irish grievance, which resurfaced most dramatically in a separatist, republican revolutionary movement inaugurated in New York in 1853. Known popularly as the Fenians, or under its later official title of the Irish Republican Brotherhood, this tightly structured, armed secret society was built out of the shards of the failed Confederate insurrection of 1848 and the bitter emigrant exodus after the famine. Connections with the Parisian revolutionary underground inspired a Carbonarian structure and a Babeuvian cult of violence; the immigrant ghettos of the United States provided funds and a methodology of flamboyant public gesture used, for example, in the abortive invasions of Canada of 1866 and 1870–71. This Franco-Irish-American meld, though sometimes uneasy, produced the first effective modern terrorist movement. By 1864, the ruthless underground organizer James Stephens claimed to have 80,000 sworn members in branches all over Ireland. American-generated public rituals such as the relocation and reburial in Ireland of former United Irish conspirator Terence McManus in 1861 also multiplied Irish sympathizers, including numbers of usually hostile Catholic clergy. Arguably, Fenian publicity successes impelled Gladstone to adopt policies of Irish land reform, disestablishment of the Church of Ireland, and Irish Home Rule.[94] More divisive of English radical and liberal opinion was the portentous export of Fenian terror to the shores of England in the mid-1860s. Police deaths incurred through a bungled prison rescue attempt initiated a cycle of English legal repression and Irish penal martyrdom which in 1867 contributed both to Matthew Arnold's famous jeremiad on the threat to English liberal civilization, *Culture and Anarchy*, and to A. M. Sullivan's heart-wrenching nationalist hymn, "God Save Ireland."[95]

Support for Fenianism amongst the famine-swelled Irish immigrant communities of mid-Victorian England compounded existing economic, religious, and racial hostilities, as well as widening political divisions originating in earlier rivalry between O'Connell and O'Connor.[96] An upsurge of anti-popery rhetoric in the wake of Mazzini and Garibaldi's triumphal tours also contributed to dissension between English liberals/radicals and Irish immigrants. Tensions frequently erupted into open conflict. Irish poverty, lack of skill, ghetto living conditions, alien religion, and national attachments could easily be represented as threats to the free-born libertarian English political nation, particularly when discord was actively exploited by the virulent anti-popery of the Orange Association, the Protestant Electoral League, and the Tory party. Old Puritan idioms of papal despotism, sacerdotal servility, and priestly perversion were skillfully reconstituted in order to exacerbate the anxieties and anger of northern industrial working-class communities. The 1850s and 60s saw endemic anti-Irish tension, as well as periodic rioting, in Stockport, Oldham, Preston, Blackburn, and Rochdale. Tory populists used constitutionalist rhetoric to represent the liberals as "haughty, hypocritical and effeminate snobs,"[97] and even internationalist-minded ex-Chartists were sometimes won over by emotive slogans like "Queen or Pope." Just as pro-Irish Burdettite radicals had appropriated patriotic populist sentiment during the 1810s, the Tory platform now appropriated libertarian and chauvinist anti-popery, helping to win

them notable working-class gains in the extended electorate following the Reform Act of 1867.

≺ IX ≻

The Challenge of Tory Populism

The ability of mid-Victorian Tories and other movements of popular
conservatism to refashion elements of constitutionalist rhetoric to
their own advantage has been seriously under-recognized in the burgeoning recent scholarship of popular liberalism. We have seen that
the strain of Puritan anti-popery in the English constitutionalist idiom that had caused Burke such discomfort during the late eighteenth century also repelled many of his mid-Victorian counterparts,
especially the substantial Irish Catholic immigrant minorities in
London and the Midlands. Others of the working class disliked the
piety and Nonconformist moral zeal which underpinned both Gladstonian popular liberalism and more leftward leaning socialist and
internationalist groups. A considerable popular urban constituency
remained strongly attached to the unrespectable, convivial, and masculine culture of sport, beer, baccy, and bawdry. Since Burke's day and
earlier, popular patriotism had contained strains of racial chauvin-
ism and bigotry, which resurfaced with a new vigor during the Crimean war, the Sepoy Rebellion of 1857, and the controversy over
Governor Eyre's treatment of Jamaican rebels at Morant Bay in 1865.
On these and other imperial and racial issues radicals and liberals
tended to replicate the divisions of the wider society.[98] Though Ernest Jones gave firm support to the Indian uprising and Harney opposed the Opium War with China, they were frequently opposed by
fellow liberals and radicals in the Reform League. Neither did this
side of politics remain immune to the growing mid-Victorian cult of
monarchy centered on the personal appeal of Queen Victoria.[99]

Such unresolved strains and tensions can be seen, for example, in
the ambiguous political and social journalism of G. W. M. Reynolds,
sometimes known as the mid-Victorian Cobbett. Reared in the military middle class, Reynolds served his political apprenticeship within
the culture of French republican journalism in the 1830s. Having
emerged opportunistically as a leader of London Chartism in 1848 by

appealing particularly to London's unskilled poor,[100] he championed French-style republican socialism throughout the mid-Victorian period. He was also perhaps the best-selling British novelist of the century, specializing in sensationalist quasi-pornographic imitations of the *feuilletonistes* Eugene Sue and Paul de Kock. Socialist-republican principle warred with sensationalist commercialism throughout Reynolds's newspapers. His angry nihilistic portraits of urban poverty failed to conceal a voyeuristic fascination with aristocratic vice, fashion, and etiquette.[101] Here was a "darker side" of mid-Victorian populism, open to conservative as well as radical implications.

England's diverse populist constituency of the socially insecure or politically neglected—including rough sporty artisans and uneasy lower-middle urbanites—reveled in the Tichborne claimant's much-publicized prowess as fighter, drinker, and libertine. Theirs was a culture which construed Nonconformist respectability as effeminate, and celebrated the masculine virtues of drink and virility.[102] Tichbornism thus foreshadowed later links between Toryism, brewing interests, and rough masculinity. The claimant's connections with the world of pubs, music hall, and popular journalism testify to the impact on popular politics and culture of the rapid commercialization of leisure in mid-Victorian England. The moral strenuousness of liberal/radicalism could not always accommodate the hedonistic and democratic excess celebrated in music hall and similar spheres of this mass commercial culture.[103] Such excess may in part represent subconscious attempts to recapture lost popular freedoms—displacements, perhaps, of the stifling of expressive, theatrical, and participatory dimensions of earlier popular politics by the growth of institutionalized political parties, uniform franchises, electoral laws, and "rational" legislation such as the Ballot Act of 1872.[104] By this account the Reform Act of 1867 parallels its precursor act of 1832 in closing down as much as opening up popular participation in the political nation.

≺ X ≻

Viewing the Paris Commune

Notwithstanding the portentous rise of democratic Toryism, British responses to the Paris Commune of 1871 symbolize the persistence of the constitutionalist idiom within English popular politics, for on the whole this remarkable expression of foreign revolution and workers' democracy seems to have been viewed in England with either hostility or indifference. Such popular support as it gathered reflected approval for the restoration of lost rights rather than for socialist revolution.[105] Radical gatherings in London, Bradford, and Newcastle depicted the workers of Paris as friends of liberty fighting to achieve what the British working class had already won. In the spirit of Burke, English endorsement of the Commune was filtered through the language of 1689 and 1776 rather than 1793. The struggle of the Communards was likened to that of the Puritans, and legitimized in Lockean terms of just resistance. The radical secularist G. J. Holyoake said it all when he called the Commune "the most English thing" that the French have ever done.[106]

Looking back, this might seem to signal the final triumph of the counter-revolutionary project that Edmund Burke had launched eighty years before. English radicals and labor activists were once again viewing French revolutionary aspirations through the lenses of historicist constitutionalism. Yet this constitutionalism was scarcely less ambiguous in the 1870s than in the 1790s. Holyoake's response to the Commune, however parochial, cannot simply be read as conservative. If the history of the intervening years had shown anything, it was the inability of any one political group to fix or monopolize popular interpretations of the constitution. Popular constitutionalism had done its work over eighty years of social ferment, less by displacing or domesticating English democratic energies than by channelling them towards politically productive ends. In England, as in Italy, revolution had come to mean popular participation in the transformation of political culture. The success of popular constitutionalism had derived from its protean ability to appeal to diverse constituencies, to absorb foreign and domestic revolutionary ingredients without seeming to do so; to persuade as much as intimidate its political opponents through a rhetoric of reasonableness; to thrive on apparent failure by infiltrating the values and ideology of the classes who appeared to have triumphed most decisively in 1832, 1848, and 1867. English historiography conventionally tells a story of popular accommodation to middle-class liberal ideals and programs in the aftermath of 1848, but perhaps the claim should be inverted. If constitutionalism was the master narrative of nineteenth-century En-

glish politics, the common people—and the Chartists in particular—
wrote much of the script that Gladstone marketed so triumphantly
as his own. The supposedly failed movement of Chartism left a deep
imprint on the successor movement of English popular liberalism by
instilling it with new understandings of social justice, social space,
civil life, and participatory democracy, though the transition also
muffled earlier ultra-radical, feminist, and populist constitutionalist
aspirations.

At another level, too, Burke's dilemma of the 1790s remained unresolved by the 1870s, for one element of that fragile construct, the
British nation, persistently eluded the reach of the constitutionalist
master narrative. Significantly, it was Ireland's implacable Fenian
residue who, in the wake of yet another smashed and abortive insurrectionary attempt in 1867, drew consolatory inspiration from the
Commune's reenaction of Parisian revolutionary violence.

Contested Freedoms in the French Revolutions, 1830–1871

JOHN M. MERRIMAN

JUST FIFTEEN YEARS AFTER Napoleon's defeat at Waterloo, there began the first of three revolutions that toppled apparently well-entrenched regimes in nineteenth-century France. As much as if not more than their grand predecessor, the revolutions of 1830, 1848–51, and 1870–71 shaped the relationship between state and citizen in modern France. Liberty was arguably the most important motivating force in each of these revolutions, but the meaning of "*Vive la liberté!*" depended on who was shouting.

The different meanings of freedom for the French were sometimes complementary, sometimes conflicting. The revolution of 1830 demonstrated that the liberal quest for an extension of the suffrage and for a free press stopped well short of republicanism and conflicted with freedom as defined by the search for universal rights in the tradition of the Enlightenment and the French Revolution. Likewise, the idea of freedom held by workers of the skilled trades clashed with laissez-faire liberalism, as did that held by peasants seeking return of collective rights in the forests. After the February Days of 1848, the ideal of freedom embraced by many workers proved incompatible with that of moderate republicans. And before and during the Commune of 1871, the quest for freedom, particularly with regard to the role of the state, engendered fiercely conflicting conceptions of what liberty meant.

An expansion of the public sphere was one of the crucial changes in nineteenth-century France. Partially defined by the collective memory of the great divisions of the French Revolution, political life already extended beyond the narrow limits of the electoral franchise, engaging the interest of people who could not vote. Most notably, newspapers and voluntary associations brought more and more French men and women into political life. The nineteenth-century

French revolutions thus were part of an extended process of politicization as they brought demands for more freedoms.

With each revolution, social conflict intensified after the initial seizure of power, spreading from Paris into the provinces.[1] The goals of groups in the successful revolutionary coalitions thus proved incompatible. Initial victory was followed by dissension. Liberals are reluctant revolutionaries and, as forces on the left vigorously put forward their claims for greater social and political change, moderates became conservatives. *Mouvement* became *résistance*. Following the revolution of 1830, the left faction of the liberal coalition that had mounted an assault on the last Restoration government withdrew its support from the new regime. Within a year, amid demonstrations and riots, a republican opposition had formed, increasingly forced to operate clandestinely. Republican values of *"liberté, fraternité, éqalité"* were adapted to emerging socialist ideology.[2] After the February revolution of 1848, the parting of the ways between liberals, satisfied with a conservative republic, and strong republicans and socialists was even clearer. And, following the declaration of the republic in 1870, the ongoing Franco-Prussian War and the siege of Paris accentuated the ideological differences between former allies.

Why did France continue to be so revolutionary? France had been politically unified since the time of Louis XIV and was exceptional in Europe in already possessing a strongly centralized state. Since the Revolution ended Old Regime privileges—including noble exemption from many kinds of taxation, corporate guild monopolies, and certain municipal privileges—there had been a universally applied law, though women, as the Napoleonic Code would insist, were less equal than men. In this way, too, the Revolution left a powerful heritage for republican and socialist rhetoric, including the claims of popular sovereignty and equality before the law, shaped generally by Enlightenment discourse. Louis XVIII's Charter, however limited in scope, nonetheless guaranteed the "essential liberties" of the French.

The French Revolution had left a strong sense that the state was open to criticism, indeed overthrow, if it failed to act in a way that was considered reasonable or just. During the middle decades of the nineteenth century, many people in France shared a sense that revolutionary political change was always possible. For conspiratorial groups, revolution seemed an option when irreconcilable ideologies clashed. Groups in power, for the same reason, anticipated that they, too, might be sent packing (or worse). One of Louis-Philippe's daughters explained that she always kept some of her valuables ready for a quick departure "should we fall."[3]

France's high degree of centralization may have facilitated revolution. But it also facilitated the subsequent repression by solidifying and enhancing the role of the state. The state was never neutral in the political struggles that followed the initial seizure of power; once the state apparatus had been commandeered by the strongest element in the victorious coalition, it was easily turned against other contenders. The *commissaires* of the Jacobin republic of 1793–94 lacked the relentless efficiency of a well-oiled, tested bureaucracy of prefects and subprefects, *procureurs-généraux* and *procureurs*, division commanders and sub-division commanders. For many ordinary French men and women, the three parts of Gaul seemed the ministries of the interior, justice, and war, and their employees.

After the Orleanists, a moderate republic, followed by the princely republic of Napoleon Bonaparte and Adolphe Thiers's provisional government, held the reins of the state. The army not only backed but played the major role in the subsequent repression: putting down insurrections in Paris and Lyon in the early 1830s; beating back insurgents during the June Days of 1848 with the help of the garde mobile; and crushing the Communards in 1871.

Each of the three regimes was insufficiently prepared militarily for the determined nature of armed resistance. In 1830 and 1848, insurgent crowds overcame inadequate numbers of troops who quickly became demoralized and ineffective. The case of 1870–71 is more complicated, because of the ongoing, losing war against Prussia. The reeling empire fell on September 4, 1870, to a crowd of modest size. The Commune began with the defense of cannon on Montmartre against the arrival of a small force sent by the provisional government to seize them.

Revolutionary tradition, the concentration of political power in Paris, and what appear in retrospect to have been foolishly abysmal military preparations did not by themselves bring three more revolutions to France. Economic hardship played at least some role in mobilizing opposition to each regime: the depression of 1826–27 that followed harvest failure swelled liberal political opposition; that of 1846–47 probably contributed to interest in political reform; and the suffering engendered by the Prussian siege of Paris that began in September 1870 generated indignant opposition to the prospect of a monarchist majority electing the new National Assembly.

Anticlericalism contributed to each revolutionary mobilization. For most Restoration liberals, *quarante-huitards*, and Communards, "liberty" included freeing France from the Church's institutional stronghold. Here, again, the response of France was complex, reflecting regional variation. In some regions—notably the Bourbonnais, Limousin, and much of the Ile de France—religious observance had declined, or had never been high to begin with. However, in parts of the Midi, Brittany, Flanders, the mid-Pyrenees, Alsace, and the Lower Massif Central, religious practice and allegiance remained strong. Complicating matters even further, anticlericalism and dechristianization were not the same phenomenon. The utopian socialism of the 1830s and 1840s in some places infused popular radicalism during the Second Republic with religiosity—the theme of "*Jésus le Montagnard*," the socialist.

Workers in the skilled trades were particularly evident in the *journées* that made the three nineteenth-century revolutions. In the 1960s, historians took these revolutions as a barometer of working-class consciousness. From claims of participation (in the case of 1830 and February 1848) and records of deaths and arrests (the June Days and the Commune), they charted the entry of the "working class" into the political arena. William Sewell, Jr., de-emphasizes economic interpretations of the origins of artisanal radicalism. Instead he privileges shifts in language, specifically the adoption of a revolutionary language of class, in explaining the emergence of a sense that many craftsmen, especially members of *corporations*, had of belonging to a "confraternity of proletarians," the producers of wealth. Skilled workers shared a "corporative idiom" which "expressed and informed the workers' aspirations for a moral community of the trade."[4] Amid the protest of craftsmen in the wake of the revolution of 1830, as well as the social demands of workers after the revolution of 1848, the origins of working-class socialism can be found.

≺ I ≻

The French Revolution of 1830

The revolution of 1830 grew out of a political crisis that centered on a debate over government-imposed limitations in the public political sphere. The charter granted by Louis XVIII in 1814 limited the electoral franchise to men at least 30 years of age paying a minimum of 300 francs in taxes. Thus the franchise included only the 100,000 wealthiest men in France, in a nation of about 30 million people. Benjamin Constant, who contrasted France's repressive regime with Britain's constitutional monarchy and free press, provided liberals with a political program, insisting that the franchise be extended.

Many opponents of the regime denounced its close link to noble and ecclesiastical interests. An 1825 law indemnified émigrés who had lost their property in the Revolution, paid for by lowering the interest rate paid to holders of government bonds, most of whom were drawn from the middle class.[5] Although there were minor conflicts between the state and the Church, which had to live within the perimeters of Napoleon's 1802 Concordat, to the ecclesiastical hierarchy the halcyon days seemed to have returned with the religious orders which returned to France in force during the Restoration. New confraternities and devotions reflected a revival of religiosity in some parts of the country. The observance of Sunday and church holidays became obligatory in France. Ecclesiastical authorities sent a preaching order into most provincial towns to undertake "missions," several days of ceremonies and fire and brimstone sermons intended to restore or reaffirm religious faith, followed by the erection of mission crosses. Charles's coronation in May 1825 in the Cathedral of Reims, his ludicrous attempt to cure several people afflicted by scrofula with the royal "healing touch," and a law making sacrilege a capital offense symbolized the alliance of altar and throne.

The economic crisis may also have helped turn some businessmen, as in the metallurgical and cotton industries that were particularly severely hit, toward liberalism. Indeed liberals enjoyed their greatest political appeal in *départements* with considerable manufacturing, including the Seine and several in north and northeastern France.[6] Not all businessmen agreed that the government's policy of raising tariffs on imports benefited them. Furthermore, in some cities political controversies pitted influential middle-class residents against noble mayors who spent most of their time in countryside châteaux and paid little attention to the condition of the cities over which they presided.[7] Yet, to be sure, some businessmen rejected economic liberalism.

During the grain riots in the hard winter of 1826–27, "freedom" thus took on two very different meanings.[8] Landowners with grain to sell and merchants with enough money to buy it at inflated prices insisted on the freedom of the market. Many consumers, however, wanted to be able to purchase grain at a price they could afford— the old opposition between laissez-faire economics and the Jacobin "maximum" during the Revolution.

Following liberal gains in 1827,[9] the year the king disbanded the national guard of Paris, François Guizot presided over the organization awkwardly called "*Aide-toi, le ciel t'aidera*," which had members in many *départements*. Its goal was to encourage more eligible voters to register, while identifying cases in which men entitled to vote were not being allowed to register to do so. Liberals also formed an association to refuse to pay taxes in protest of the government's policies. The liberal newspaper *Le Constitutionnel* had 20,000 subscribers. The appearance of *Le National* early in 1830 mobilized opposition to the ministry of Jules Polignac, whom the king provocatively named president of the Council of Ministers—in 1815 he had been one of two deputies refusing to swear an oath of allegiance to the Charter. Adding to the tension, a series of mysterious fires broke out in Normandy. Peaking in the first half of 1830, these conflagrations convinced both liberals and conservatives that adherents of the other side were responsible for them.[10]

Meanwhile, romantic writers, rejecting what they considered classical constraints, turned a quest for another kind of freedom against the Polignac ministry. In his remarkable preface to *Hernani*, Victor Hugo in 1830 clearly set the freedoms associated with liberalism and romanticism, denounced by some nobles and churchmen, against the established order of the restored monarchy.

Young people, have courage! However difficult they make our present, the future will be beautiful. Romanticism, so often badly defined, is, on the whole . . . nothing less than *liberalism* in literature . . . Liberty in art, liberty in society, that is the double goal toward which the efforts of all consistent and logical people must tend . . . literary liberty is the daughter of political liberty. That is the principle of this century, and it will prevail . . . in revolution, every movement is a step forward . . . For a new people, a new art.

The opening night of *Hernani* on February 25 led to scuffles in the theater. If no direct connection can be made between the defiance of classicism and the outbreak of revolution, *Hernani* may have deepened the political division between conservative apologists for the Restoration and the bourgeois liberals, a debate that centered on freedom.

On March 2, 1830, the king included in his address from the

throne to the Chamber of Deputies a warning that he intended to maintain order "if criminal maneuvers raise up obstacles against my government."[11] In response to what appeared to be a threat to dissolve the Chamber, 221 deputies signed a stern protest. Charles's dissolution of the Chamber brought more liberal triumphs in the subsequent election. News of the capture of Algiers in June failed to still the opposition.

On July 26, the king promulgated ordinances intended to restrict France's political and public sphere. They dissolved the newly elected Chamber of Deputies; disenfranchised almost three-quarters of those currently eligible to vote, leaving political power in the hands of the wealthiest property-holders, many of whom were nobles; ordered new elections under the newly restricted franchise (which would have reduced the number of electors to about 23,000); and muzzled the press.

Demonstrations became revolution during the "*Trois Glorieuses.*" Fired on in the street and pelted by rocks and tiles thrown from rooftops, General Marmont's 10,000 troops could not break through barricades to reach the hôtel de ville. On July 29 the insurgents controlled most of Paris, with a "municipal committee" behaving like a provisional government.[12] In the provinces, word of the events in Paris sparked some confrontations and even fighting (notably in Nantes, Besançon, and Bar-sur-Aube). Anticlerical incidents following news of events in Paris ranged from attacks on mission crosses (as in Reims) to the pillaging of seminaries in Nancy and Perpignan as hurriedly constituted local committees tried to keep the peace.[13]

The campaign led by the ambitious liberal and historian Adolphe Thiers for Louis-Philippe to become "citizen-king" succeeded. The duc d'Orléans could be seen as representing a monarchical accommodation with the constitutional heritage of the revolution. Despite revolutionary origins and the return of the tricolor flag, the new regime won relatively quick acceptance from the other European powers precisely because it fell considerably short of being a republic. Not long after the revolution, Guizot gently chided the king for joining with crowds in singing "*The Marseillaise.*" "Do not concern yourself, Minister," came the retort, "I stopped saying the words long ago!"[14]

The Orleanist regime guaranteed personal freedom and that of the press. The electoral law of April 19, 1831, doubled the number of eligible voters to 166,583 men, about .5 percent of the population, by lowering to 200 francs the minimal annual tax payment on which eligibility was based. The new Charter allowed the use of juries in political trials, including those involving the press; and proposed new legislation on the freedom of education.[15] Yet ministers remained responsible to the king, not to the Chamber of Deputies. The nobility and the clergy never again enjoyed the status they enjoyed during the Restoration. Louis-Philippe refused to be crowned at Reims and Catholicism ceased to be the official religion of the state, although it remained the nominal religion of the vast majority of French men and women.

The utopian socialist Louis Blanc insisted that the bourgeoisie had stolen the victory of "the people." To Karl Marx, the revolution brought to power "bankers, stock exchange kings, railway kings, owners of coal and ironworks and forests, a section of landed proprietors that rallied around them—the so-called financial aristocracy."[16] From the other side of the political spectrum, Vicomte Louis de Bonald, Restoration political theorist, denounced the "bourgeois monarchy" ruling on behalf of "a sovereign bourgeoisie." Scornful nobles dubbed Louis-Philippe "the king of the barricades," the "shopkeepers' king." To Alexis de Tocqueville 1830 marked "the triumph of the middle class . . . definitive and so complete that all political power, all prerogatives, the whole government found itself enclosed and as it were huddled up within the narrow limits of that single class." This made him uneasy: rule by the "people" might not be far away.[17]

Did contemporaries like Tocqueville get it all wrong? The claim that 1830 brought a "bourgeois revolution" has been challenged and nuanced by a generation of revisionist historiography.[18] Yet some reality remains behind the tired image of the "bourgeois monarchy."[19] Elections under the expanded franchise sent to the Chamber of Deputies lawyers, officials, and men of other middle-class professions. This significantly increased middle-class representation in the legislature, changing the social composition of the Chamber. Land continued to be the source of most wealth in France. But the Orleanist regime helped business by increasing the role of the state and its functionaries in French economic life, for example by improving roads and developing the main trunk lines of the railroad.[20] The regime liberalized banking and credit policies and made it easier to form joint-stock companies. Bankruptcy laws were rewritten to be somewhat less devastating. Tariff policies benefited business. The

revolution of 1830 helped create a "culture of capitalism" that trumpeted economic progress.[21] Furthermore, Louis-Philippe's commitment to maintaining order at all costs helped restore business confidence and encouraged investment.

The revolution's greater significance may lie in its role in expanding a revolution in the public sphere. About ten times more people
read newspapers in Paris than were eligible to vote during the Orleanist regime.[22] The revolution quickly accentuated the taste for print
culture. Political caricature blossomed, encouraged by Charles Philipon's Maison Aubert publishing house. The law of October 8, 1830,
ended—at least temporarily—the censorship of caricatures, although
drawings that were found to be offensive could result in prosecution
and a jury trial.[23]

Philipon and his colleagues shaped posterity's view of the regime
that Alfred Cobban once memorably damned as "being so lacking
in principle that it could only be named by the month of its founding."[24] The king's sizable jowls gave his head a pear-like shape that,
combined with his somewhat ponderous trunk, delighted caricaturists.[25] Philipon, Honoré Daumier, and Jean-Ignace Grandville presented Louis-Philippe as a ridiculous, greedy, and mean-spirited pear,
king-like only in title. He quickly became "the pear of France,"
Louis-Philippe's initials corresponding nicely to Le Poire. Le pair de
France and le poire de France also made for nice plays on words; "the
first fruit of France" could not be easily forgotten.[26]

Following the revolution, new political associations sprang up,
demanding further reform.[27] Perhaps no other regime in French history so quickly lost a significant proportion of its support. Aide-toi
demanded extension of the suffrage, but stopped short of republicanism. Republicans led the attack on the Orleanist monarchy, claiming
to represent the will of the people and France's revolutionary heritage, protesting against rampant electoral corruption that made the
censitaire system even more unfair.[28] Newspapers brought government policies under the critical scrutiny of public opinion.

Republican associations formed close contacts with workers' organizations.[29] For the most part, members of these groups were young
and bourgeois; they often were lawyers, although students and artisans were prominent in number. Organized by Godfroy Cavignac,
the Société des Amis du peuple met first on July 30, 1830. But as its
Jacobin pedigree attracted the immediate hostility of the new Or-

leanist regime, the Friends of the People went underground. The Société des droits de l'homme grouped more determined republicans.
Police repression forced members to adopt secrecy as an organizational principle; and the society, which at its peak had at least 163
sections with something like three thousand members, remained a
loose federation of republican enemies of the regime.

Guizot, the first Orleanist minister of the interior, seemed almost
surprised when he noted in 1831 that "The July Revolution raised
only political questions . . . Society was by no means threatened . . .
What has happened since then? Social questions have been raised."[30]
If the extent to which the revolution itself was a social revolution
can be questioned, there is little question that it served as a catalyst
for the development of workers' demands and organizations, as artisans embraced the discourse of freedom. New ideologies developed
in response to increased concern with the social effects of poverty.
Utopian socialism, social Catholicism, and democratic and social republicanism gained adherents during the July Monarchy.[31]

Workers in the skilled trades quickly parted company with master craftsmen and other employers, as well as the regime itself, because the former had a different conception of "liberty" than economic freedom.[32] To such workers, liberty meant control over their
trades and better working conditions. Printers shouted "*Vive la liberté!*" while smashing mechanical presses.[33] The Le Chapelier law
of 1791 had banned workers' associations in the name of economic
freedom. Workers now demanded the right to strike and to organize.

But economic crisis produced new aggravations. A number of
banking and commercial enterprises failed; employers dismissed
workers. In August and September 1830, workers from the skilled
trades took to the streets to demand higher piece rates and wages, better working conditions, shorter hours, protection against the competition of foreign workers, and, as with Parisian printers, the banning
of some mechanized production. Three self-proclaimed working-class
newspapers began to appear late in September.[34]

Reflecting the ambiguities of freedom, the government declared
that state intervention in industrial disputes was "contrary to the
laws that have established the principles of the freedom of industry."
But to skilled workers, "The freedom to associate with others was a
classic component of liberty, along with freedom of conscience, of

speech, of industry, of religious belief, of the press, and so on." Associations would allow workers peacefully to "overcome the tyranny of private property and themselves become associated owners of industrial enterprises."[35] Many workers' *corporations* were recast as "associations," and then, particularly in 1833, as producers' cooperatives.

Thus, according to Sewell, the idea of a "confraternity of proletarians" was born: the freedom of an individual master or employer to exploit his workers was "egoism"; socialism was the freedom of workers to defend their own collective interests by forming associations and making demands on the state.[36] Workers and the state thus embraced two very different meanings of freedom: "What was a regulation for the good of the trade to workers was a violation of the liberty of industry in the eyes of the legal code; what workers regarded as a brotherhood for mutual assistance was an illegal coalition in the eyes of the state." The prefect of the Seine expressed astonishment that the workers "had lost sight of the fact that the *liberté du travail* is no less sacred than all our other liberties."[37] The break with the July Monarchy came quickly: workers from the skilled trades believed that associationism could come to fruition only in the context of a republic.[38]

Ordinary people attacked *octrois* (urban customs' barriers), ripped apart tax registers, and rioted against the high price of grain. In doing so, they transformed the victory of "liberty" into the quest for freedom from what they considered unjust impositions.[39]

The mountainous *département* of the Ariège in the central Pyrenees provides an interesting example. There many poor people depended for their existence on access to the forests, pasturing sheep and gleaning wood for fuel and to repair their houses.[40] Until about the middle of the eighteenth century, the Crown and the *seigneurs* alike had freely granted rights of pasturage and gleaning, in some places specifying a traditional yearly allotment of wood and fuel. But generally the peasants had taken what wood they needed and pastured their flocks as they pleased. Collective rights of usage had been challenged only rarely, even if the actual deeds or grants themselves no longer existed or could not be found. The difference between ownership and usage did not seem important until state and property owners insisted on the absolute right of property, a process that the French Revolution dramatically accelerated.[41]

But all that changed as the price of wood rose in the 1820s with the development of the local metallurgical industry. The state and the owners of private forests sent guards and *charbonniers*. A new forest code of 1827 put all woods and forests belonging to the state, the Crown, and communes under the strict control of the forest administration.[42] Tribunals were kept busy with prosecutions for violations of the code or of the private property of the rural *notables*. Many peasants lost their most significant, indeed, for many, their only resource.

The "demoiselles" first appeared during the winter of 1828–29. These were "groups of armed men disguised as women," with the "shirt out, and darkening the face with red and black," or, more often, wearing a white linen-cloth shirt, giving the impression of a woman's skirt or gown, combined with some form of headwear.[43]

Pronouncements from the pulpit, stern warnings posted on village *mairies*, more guards, the arrival of troops, and even a royal decree in August 1829 restoring the right to pasture sheep in certain areas for a period of one year did not stop the "demoiselle" incidents. When the bishop of Pamiers ordered his priests to preach against the "demoiselles," he received a letter sent from someone in the commune of Massat, signed "Jeanne Grané, le chef des Demoiselles." This letter reflected not only the violent rhetoric of popular anger but a sense of history as well:

We insurgents, under the mask of the women called Demoiselles: Garchal, curé of Biert, and Sères, of Soulan, have had the imprudence to preach against us . . . You are unrelenting, but we will know how to teach them . . . the lesson given to the clergy and to the nobility in 1793. Their houses will be torn down and burned, their properties pillaged and burned, their bodies torn to pieces, their limbs sent by the parishes of the arrondissement to better set an example.[44]

The disguise, while making each peasant anonymous, fostered a collective identity to give the impression of a well-organized, invincible armed group. Furthermore, the peasants' masking in this "*carnival enragé*" mocked the inversion or violation by outsiders of what the community considered justice, but with deadly seriousness of "doing justice."[45]

The nature of the peasants' struggle changed after the revolution. Peasant communities appeared as petitioners to the new administration intent on wresting concessions in the name of liberty from the owners of the forests and from the state.

On August 22, 1830, a crowd invaded the *mairie* of Ax, almost as far south from Paris as one can go and still be in France, and demanded, in the name of liberty, that the marquis d'Orgeix restore to them the use of his forests which they had enjoyed 50 years ago, that the project of establishing the boundaries of the royal forests be abandoned, and "that there be no more forest guards and that the taxes on beverages no longer be collected, all under the threat of death and fire." The mayor made promises he could not keep, sending the satisfied peasants on their way after midnight. The commander of the gendarmerie for the troubled arrondissement of St. Girons remarked on September 1 that "the public says resolutely that it has conquered liberty and that it wants to gain from its conquest; woe to he who would want to prevent it."

Despite some temporary concessions, and a general amnesty for those accused or convicted of violations of the forest code before the revolution, the hope that the new regime would act to meet their grievances gradually evaporated. The forest commissioner in Toulouse in early November determined that the peasants' claims were "without foundation." Some peasants saw this coming. At the end of August, a letter from a "captain" of the demoiselles warned the new officials and the clergy that an insurrection would follow the example of Paris and conquer "liberty." The forest guards and *charbonniers* returned to the forests and so, the next spring, did the demoiselles, in full disguise. The one-sided war against capitalism and the state went on, albeit intermittently, until 1872; it lost impetus as the Ariège began to depopulate, as many rural people moved out of the mountains to find a livelihood elsewhere.

As Orleanist liberalism faced demonstrations and insurrection, it became overtly conservative. Although the first wave of workers' demonstrations in Paris subsided by the end of November 1830, crowds rioted in December when Charles X's former ministers were let off with prison sentences. On February 14, 1831, while legitimists held a solemn funeral mass in the church of Saint-Germain de l'Auxerrois commemorating the assassination of the duc de Berri in 1820, protesters sacked the archbishop's palace nearby. In November of that year, thousands of Lyonnais silkworkers rose up in a bloody insurrection after national guardsmen fired on a delegation going to the prefecture amid bitter negotiations over the workers' demand of a return to a minimum price for their work. Fighting lasted for two days before the workers capitulated. By the end of May 1832, political divisions were so deep in France that 134 deputies signed a petition warning, "The Restoration and the revolution are once again in confrontation; the old struggle that we had thought was over is beginning anew."[46] A week later, on June 5, 1832, the funeral of the popular republican General Lamarque, a cholera victim, led to insurrectionary riots in which about 800 people were killed or injured. Outbreaks of legitimist counter-revolutionary activity in the west briefly evoked fears of another bloody counterrevolution. The government put four western *départements* under state of siege.

The second Lyon insurrection shook the regime in April 1834. Silkworkers, organized into associations of *mutuellistes*, rose up after a massive strike that shut down the jacquard looms in the tall apartments of the Croix-Rousse. With banners proclaiming "Live free or die fighting!" they battled soldiers and national guardsmen stretched out to defend the *beaux quartiers* below. At least 320 were killed in the fighting. On the second day of fighting, Louis-Philippe signed the Law on Associations, restricting one of the freedoms for which those who had brought him to power had fought.[47]

An insurrection by members of the Société des droits de l'homme in Paris in support of the Lyon silkworkers failed miserably. A few barricades went up, notably near the church of Saint-Merri in central Paris; before the next day troops smashed them down. On the Rue Transnonain, soldiers or guardsmen sent to destroy a barricade entered number 12, from which shots that had killed an officer were believed to have come. They shot to death a dozen of the occupants, including an elderly man and a baby, an incident immortalized by Daumier's lithograph of which Baudelaire wrote "only silence and death reign."[48]

Louis-Philippe, who proudly posed in his national guard uniform for two official portraits,[49] also moved his family from the Palais-Royal to the more imposing and defensible Louvre, with a moat dug around it. In 1833, amid a wave of strikes, the government proposed to fortify the capital by constructing a wall around the circumference of the city, and a number of *forts détachés* beyond it.[50] Preliminary work began even before expenditures had been budgeted.[51] Thiers claimed that their purpose was to assure that never again would the capital fall to foreign armies, as had occurred in 1814. To republicans, their case bolstered by a number of military experts,[52] the placement of the forts suggested that their principal purpose was to turn their guns, if necessary, on working-class quarters and faubourgs, the *embastillement* of revolutionary Paris, the aggressive encirclement of freedom.[53] Early in the July Monarchy, deputy Saint-Marc Girardin announced in the Chamber of Deputies that "the barbarians that threaten society are in the faubourgs of our manufacturing towns, not in the Tartary of Russia." Images of social and geographic marginality began to merge, adding a revealing spatial dimension to the contemporary myth of the "dangerous and laboring classes."[54]

Orleanist laws constraining liberty limited political opposition. In March 1834, just before the second Lyon insurrection, the Chamber of Deputies passed a new law requiring associations with more than twenty members to obtain government authorization. Every member of an association declared illegal was subject to a jail sentence of up to one year and a fine of up to a thousand francs. Members of any association considered seditious could be tried by the Chamber of Peers, not by a jury.[55]

The pens of caricaturists also felt the heavy weight of repression. Confronted by popular revolt, the Chamber of Deputies, despite Article Seven of the new constitution, had passed four laws between November 1830 and April 1831 that raised the stakes of attacking the regime.[56] Philipon, who reminded one jury that caricature had helped bring down Charles X and the Bourbons, went to jail twice in 1831 and 1832, once for six months. Courts heard more than 300 prosecution cases against Paris newspapers during the first three years of the Orleanist regime; more than a third of them resulted in convictions, with judges meting out sentences of more than 50 years in prison and 300,000 francs in fines. The government ordered the seizure of *La Caricature* 28 times between March 1831 and June 1832.[57] A stricter law promulgated in February 1834 forced hawkers and peddlers to obtain government permission before selling prints or lithographs on the streets. Shortly thereafter, police in Paris clubbed people gathering to look at prints mocking the government. Another law made anyone distributing a print responsible for purchasing a stamp, required for all newspapers; that stamp had to be placed directly on the caricature itself.[58] The 1835 press law forced Daumier and his colleagues to abandon overt political caricature for safer, but equally popular, social themes.

Orleanist liberalism had left only small loopholes for free expression. One of these, political banquets, in 1840 and again in 1847–48 would help mobilize proponents, including republicans, for electoral reform, and in February 1848 lead to the end of the July Monarchy.

≺ II ≻

Revolutionary France, 1848–51

The dialectic of radicalization and repression was even more apparent after the revolution of 1848. Popular political mobilization reached unprecedented levels, generating a repressive response from the centralized state. An essentially urban movement for electoral reform had led to revolution in Paris in February. Guizot banned a large banquet planned to celebrate the cause of political reform. Besieged, and relatively unprepared militarily, another regime fell.

As after the 1830 revolution, the expectations of the groups that made up the victorious revolutionary coalitions were fundamentally incompatible. Again different interpretations of what freedom meant clashed. For republicans, freedom meant the right of all adult males to vote. For artisans and workers of the skilled trades, it meant the "right to work," including the right to form trade associations and the right to government assistance for them; but in the short term, it meant freedom from want through the establishment and maintenance of national workshops. Freedom had other meanings, as well: for industrial workers in the Nord, an end to the competition of Belgian workers; for their counterparts in the Loire, among other places, freedom from what they considered unfair competition from girls and young women working for minuscule remuneration in convents; for abolitionists, the end of slavery (which the provisional government hurriedly proclaimed) in the fledgling French colonies; for a precocious group of feminists, women's political rights; and for many peasants, freedom from chronic indebtedness, a lighter tax burden, and the return of forests rights.

Republicans were but one political group seeking to fill the power vacuum left by the fall of the Orleanist regime. Legitimists, demanding a Bourbon Restoration, enjoyed a popular following in some of the west and in parts of the Midi. The Orleanists, too, could not be counted out, for Louis-Philippe had several able sons in exile and retained support among some *notables*. Furthermore, Napoleon Bonaparte's nephew, Louis Napoleon, had a coterie of supporters.

Republicans were divided between those who had systematically opposed the Orleanist regime all along, and those who accepted the republic as a fait accompli. Socialists—*démoc-socs* or Montagnards—hoped that the republic would be but the first step toward a "democratic and social" republic. Parisian workers defiantly proclaimed that they were the source of all wealth and happiness.[59]

France was already politically "unified" in 1848, as the French state had over the centuries imposed its rule over Bretons, Basques, Catalans, Provençals, Alsatians, and other peoples with their own language and cultural traditions. But the February revolution unleashed a groundswell for social reform, aided by universal manhood suffrage and the restoration of the freedoms of the press, assembly, and association. When George Sand, the celebrated novelist and activist for female rights, was locked out of her apartment, she discovered that all three of the neighborhood's locksmiths were at club meetings.[60]

In Paris, more than 200 political clubs formed and 171 newspapers appeared between February and the middle of June.[61] Clubs sprang up also in many provincial cities. The clubs had grand goals: to educate citizens in their civic duties and obligations, and at the same time to work for the election of strong republicans in the April elections. The clubs, visible and noisy, were a mixed bag of lower- and middle-class members, with educated bourgeois leaders capable of flowery oratory.

The freedoms of assembly and association were linked in the minds of the increasingly conservative government. A placard on a barricade at the Porte St. Marcel during the June Days had defined the "democratic and social republic" as "democratic in that all citizens are electors . . . social in that all citizens are permitted to form associations for work."[62] The 1848 republic seemed only the first step toward a republic of economic and social justice. That is what worried many people of means. Auguste Blanqui recalled, "None of the citizens who lived in Paris [in 1848] will ever forget the long processions of workers, who carried sinister placards and seemed pledged to a perpetual strike."[63]

To workers, the "right to work" clearly was based on the "right to associate" as the economic extension of the right of popular political assembly. During the 1840s, faith in association had remained perhaps the central theme of the social program of most republicans. Association was seen as a peaceful means of freeing workers from the horrors of the capitalist economy. The declining fortunes of many workers in skilled trades because of the flooding of those trades, following the abolition of the guilds, and the economic crisis begun by the harvest failure of 1846 and intensified by the February revolution helped shape faith in association, lending a sense of urgency to workers' demands.

The economic crisis widened the gap between moderates and radicals. Unable to secure credit, many businesses closed. Government bonds plunged in value and the Paris stock exchange temporarily shut down. More than half of the Parisian work force was unemployed. Twenty-four thousand of the younger and more marginal workers were enrolled in an auxiliary para-military police force, the Mobile Guard, designed to help maintain order. Needing money, the provisional government imposed an emergency surtax of 45 centimes on every franc paid in direct property taxes, a disastrous levy that compromised support for the republic.

The provisional government opened "national workshops" in Paris, paying unemployed workers to repair roads and level hills for minimum wages. It also agreed to one of the workers' demands by restricting the workday to a maximum of ten hours in Paris and twelve hours in the provinces. At the request of the socialists, the provisional government also established the "Luxembourg Commission" to study conditions of work.

By throwing into question existing political structures, the 1848 revolution in France also initiated a critique of the gender-based order upon which they were formed. Women supported demands for better working conditions and government assistance. In Paris, they attended political gatherings and formed a number of clubs. *La Voix des Femmes* and several other newspapers started by women called for reforms, including the equality of women before the law and the right to divorce (legalized during the Revolution, and then abolished in 1816). Petitioners demanded that the electoral franchise be extended to women. Jeanne Deroin announced that she would stand for election despite the fact that women were ineligible to do so or to vote.

All of this frightened the upper classes. A national guard demonstration in March to protest the admission of workers into its ranks was followed by a counter demonstration of workers. Many property owners in Paris, and other cities as well, saw "communism" in the faces of workers wandering about without employment. In some cities, participation in the national guard became a hotly debated issue.

The April elections, in which an amazing 84 percent of the eligible voters cast ballots, brought a monarchist majority to the National Assembly in Paris. Many rural people resented the workers of the cities who demanded low bread prices and whom the provisional government seemed to be subsidizing through the national workshops. In Limoges and Rouen, workers, angered by the election of a monarchist-dominated Assembly, seized power before troops arrived. The euphoria of February gave way to the anxiety of the spring.[64] On May 15, an inept attempt by leftists to dissolve the Assembly and declare a "social" republic of the people failed. The new government began to arrest radical republicans.

With the provisional government rapidly running out of money and credibility, the Assembly first voted to halt enrollment in the national workshops and, over the vigorous protests of workers' associations and some political clubs, declared on June 23 that the national workshops would be closed in three days. Unmarried men in the workshops were to be drafted into the army and married workers sent to work in the provinces. When word of the dissolution decree leaked out that morning, Parisian workers rose up again.

For four days civil war—the "June Days"—raged in the workers' quarters of central and eastern Paris. General Georges Cavaignac brutally put down the uprising, using regular army soldiers, the Mobile Guard, and national guard units, some of whom arrived from conservative provinces by train and steamboat, symbols of a new age. In the climate of social tension, fed by rumors that the insurgents were sawing in half captured mobile guardsmen and raping women from the wealthy quarters, between 1,500 and 3,000 insurgents were killed, some summarily executed. Afterwards, the provisional government deported more than 4,000 workers to Algeria or other colonies and imprisoned thousands of people.[65]

The National Assembly then passed laws limiting the freedom

of assembly, restricting that of the press, and abrogating the recent law reducing the length of the workday. After specifically forbidding women from joining them, the government had banned political clubs in the wake of the June Days. The Luxembourg Commission quickly disbanded. Cavaignac became provisional chief executive of the republic.

Louis Napoleon's crushing victory in the presidential elections of December 10, 1848, not only reflected the extent of the cult of Napoleon in France. It also demonstrated the conviction of many influential *notables* that Bonaparte's nephew could restore political stability. Marx had it right when he wrote that because Louis Napoleon stood for nothing, in that little was known about him except his magic name, he could appear to be everything. Louis Napoleon also won the support of many people who were for the republic, including some who knew that he had published *The Extinction of Pauperism* (1844).[66] But with his election, many republicans and most socialists had reason to worry.

By 1849, many if not most *notables* viewed Louis Napoleon as the savior of property and family; they now formed "the Party of Order." At the same time, Louis Napoleon increasingly made the centralized administrative, judicial, and military apparatus his own, constricting the freedoms won in 1848.

Yet the Montagnards enlarged their constituency, not only among radical bourgeois and artisans but also among many unskilled workers and peasants attracted by their calls for social reform. Clubs were reconstituted as electoral organizations in preparation for the May 1849 elections for the National Assembly. The *démoc-socs* effectively used newspapers, brochures, pamphlets, almanacs, lithographs, and engravings to reach ordinary people. Many of the mayors appointed after the revolution, as well as school teachers, supported radical candidates in the election. The left called for the establishment of a progressive income tax, the abolition of the tax on drink, the creation of credit banks for peasants, free and obligatory primary schools, a campaign against usury, as well as the "right to work."

In parts of France, traditions of popular religion helped the Montagnards. Democratic-socialist propaganda portrayed Christ as a Montagnard concerned with the plight of the poor and doing good works on earth. Building on a strongly religious current within utopian socialism, the *démoc-socs* added to their ranks in the Rhône valley and the north, regions that had maintained a relatively high religious practice.[67] Elsewhere, such as in the Limousin and Bourbonnais, the Montagnard movement was stridently secular, indeed anticlerical.

Montagnard electoral success encouraged the radical Ledru-Rollin to organize a demonstration against French military intervention in Rome on behalf of Pope Pius IX, who had been expelled from the city by republicans. The French action violated the new constitution, the preamble of which proclaimed that the French republic "never employs its forces against the liberty of any people." The June 13 demonstration turned into a small insurrection, the failure of which further discredited the left. French intervention in Rome earned Louis Napoleon the gratitude of many Catholics. Yet the left won the majority of seats in the by-elections of March 1850, held to replace the deputies imprisoned or exiled after the June insurrection.

Montagnard newspapers appeared in at least 56 *départements* during the period of the republic. Some co-opted that contemporary popular feature, the *feuilleton*, to preach a political message: in *L'Ami du peuple*, "A *chouan* exploit" recalled the counter-revolutionary insurrection, the Vendée, against the earlier republic. *L'Union républicaine* of Auxerre harped on the drink tax, a lively issue in the surrounding cantons, particularly that of Chablis; the Lyon *démoc-soc* papers emphasized the "right to work" and discussed working conditions in the silk industry. Despite modest circulations (*Le Peuple* of Marseille, 2,000; *Le National de l'Ouest*, 1,000; *Le Démocrate de Vaucluse*, 600; *Le Démocrate de Saône-et-Loire*, 400), newspapers reached many times the number of people that circulation figures would suggest. Many of them sometimes printed extra copies and simply gave them away. More than this, cafes subscribed to papers, which sometimes were read aloud to illiterate listeners.[68]

There were also attempts at repression of the radical press beginning when seals were placed on the presses of eleven papers in Paris on June 25, 1848. In August the "caution" laws that had been in effect during the July Monarchy were reinstituted, requiring newspapers to put up money against possible future political offenses. The Paris uprising in June 1849 provided another pretext for new press laws, which made any written attack on the president a crime, raised the caution money, revived the 1835 law requiring all political papers to print government decrees and notices, and forbade the printing of "erroneous or inaccurate facts likely to disturb the peace."[69]

. The war between the conservative republic and the press was one sided. There were 335 court cases involving 185 newspapers in 77 cities and towns between December 12, 1848, and the end of 1850; 240 involved provincial papers.[70] Convictions, despite many cases of juries unwilling to follow the dictates of prosecutors, took their toll. Editors and publishers were legally liable for anything printed that was considered seditious, for example violating the article banning the publication of any text that could "excite one group of citizens against another," including any reference to "[17]93" or discussion of the "right to work" or any other aspect of the "social economy." When the *République du peuple/Volksrepublik* of Colmar editorialized that "the land belongs to everyone" and discussed "the right to work," its editors were charged with supporting *idées partageux. Le Progrès du Pas-de-Calais* confronted a jury at least 28 times between the June Days and the second anniversary of the February revolution, despite the prosecution's relative certainty that the Montagnards would always manage to "get to the jury."[71] Printers willing to take radical newspapers as clients faced prosecution.

Some editors formed joint-stock partnerships in order to raise funds to continue to publish, thus linking the freedom to publish with that of association. But the law specified that all shareholders elect the director of a joint-stock partnership. One newspaper's director had been elected by a board of four, in violation of the law. But what if all shareholders should gather to elect the director, which seemed theoretically possible? The minister of justice instructed his subordinates to consider such a gathering a club, or a meeting that might compromise the public peace. Furthermore, how could several thousand people all actually know each other? If they did manage to get together, the society would necessarily be "anonymous," and not a partnership. The statutes filed at the prefecture would therefore be neither "lawful" nor "serious."[72] The state of siege imposed on the Lyon region after the attempted insurrection of June 1849 and on the Cher, the Allier, and the Ardèche in 1851, following disturbances in those departments, eliminated such legalities.

Some Montagnard newspapers, however, survived. Crowds jammed courtrooms to watch their lawyers publicly raise fundamental questions about the regime and its war on the freedom of the press. Despite some failures, a number of Montagnard papers were started in 1851. As rumors of a coup d'état spread, *La Tribune de la Gironde* continued to protest the destruction of the republic, despite a 20,000 franc fine. Four articles from the constitution appeared at the top of each edition, despite the efforts of the *procureur-général* of Bordeaux to stop this protest.

The seemingly "incessant, mysterious, and almost unseizable" political pamphlets, brochures, almanacs, engravings, printed songs, and Montagnard "catechisms" inundated rural France. As many as 60,000 copies of a brochure circulated just in the Dordogne alone.[73] The work of the popular novelist Eugène Sue and of Pierre Joigneaux, master propagandist and deputy from the Côte d'or, and the songs of Pierre Dupont reached a wide audience. Joigneaux's *La Feuille du village* (first appearing in October 1849) reached seemingly every canton with denunciations of the salt and drink taxes and discussions of pasturage rights, the plight of rural schoolteachers, and the promise of universal suffrage. It included various "how to" articles, news of agriculture, and notices of fairs and markets. Several convictions and soaring caution money put it out of business in February 1851.[74]

Although surveillance and the arrest of hawkers and peddlers had some impact, political literature also moved with the normal flow of ordinary people on the move—traveling artisans, harvesters, seasonal workers, itinerant musicians and song merchants. During the summer of 1851, it seemed to officials that more printed material was circulating in rural France than at any time since before the elections of May 1849. Montagnard papers, brochures, pamphlets, and printed songs continued to appear until the coup d'état.

The decree of July 28, 1848, regulated the clubs. While nominally recognizing the right of assembly, the decree stipulated that the clubs publicize their meetings, notify the police 24 hours in advance, and allow police to be present. After many clubs reappeared in the guise of electoral associations before the May 1849 elections, which returned Montagnards to about a third of the seats in the National Assembly, a new law ordered the clubs closed, although electoral gatherings, provided they were not convened on regular occasions, were tolerated.[75] The effect of the new law was that, for example, between June 19, 1850, and May 5 of the following year, police prevented at least 110 political meetings and 74 banquets from taking place.

Middle-class circles and popular *chambrées* also fell victim to police repression. Prefects dissolved many such associations in the Midi.[76]

In July 1848 the National Assembly allocated three million francs for producers' associations. So many associations (586) requested funds that a form letter was prepared to speed up official responses.[77] About 300 such Parisian associations drawn from 120 trades and approximately 50,000 members started up during the four years of the republic. Most were victims not so much of the repression as the refusal of the government to provide follow-up assistance to those receiving funds. Furthermore, these associations lacked the required experience, tradition, managerial skills, credit, and customers.[78]

Consumers' cooperatives began in Lyon, Nantes, and Reims—in the last the Association Rémoise, undertaken by Dr. Agathon Bressy. It began as a mutual aid society (Société rémoise d'assistance fraternelle) and a consumers' cooperative, which published a newspaper. Its "corporations réunis" included 21 corporations, each of which hoped to transform itself into a separate producers' cooperative.[79]

The freedom of association, which seemed so uncontroversial in the heady spring of 1848, disappeared. "For the party of order in 1850," writes Maurice Agulhon, "popular organization was . . . a veritable obsession. It refused to distinguish between peaceful organization and conspiratorial organization, between the organization of work and that of combat; all free association seemed an evil, a danger which had to be smashed."[80] As gradually the illusion that most Montagnard workers had been "corrupted" by misguided bourgeois faded away, workers' associations seemed even more dangerous.

Workers' associations with wider goals felt the weight of repression heavily because, the prefect of the Rhône asserted, "[they] are founded on the principle of association; their goal is to substitute the workers themselves, organized into societies, for the boss, the master, and the entrepreneur."[81] The Association Rémoise was prosecuted as a political organization because it sought "solutions for the social economy." With official concern mounting that the association had developed influence and even branches in the Ardennes, Moselle, and Vosges, the minister of the interior dissolved the association's mutual aid organization in June 1850. Six months later the government banned the "corporations réunis" and thus the Association Rémoise ended its existence, although its organizers continued to work on behalf of the "democratic and social republic" in the hope of recapturing the freedom of association.[82]

Of the freedoms gained in 1848, none seemed more essential to the republic's survival than universal manhood suffrage. Noting that the workers of Rouen had voted "as one man" for the Montagnards and fearing that further economic deterioration might convert the peasants of the Seine Inférieure to socialism, the state prosecutor set out clearly one of the most essential ambiguities of freedom of the Second Republic: "When it consented to the periodic renewal of political power by election, society committed a type of suicide by offering . . . the communists the possibility of becoming kings one day by a 'coup de scrutin.' We have provided irresistible encouragement for the propagation of their doctrines [and] . . . the country will continue to be in the hopeless and ruinous grasp of the social evil delivered to us by 1848."[83] Surprising Montagnard successes in by-elections early in 1850, notably Eugène Sue's victory in Paris and the defeat of Louis Napoleon's personal secretary in the Haute Vienne, demonstrated an increase in Montagnard influence.

The law of May 31, 1850, ended universal manhood suffrage. It stipulated that all electors had to have resided at least three years in their communes and must be "eligible" to pay some personal tax. Because many workers moved often, the law eliminated almost a third of the men who had been eligible to vote in the May elections.[84] In the industrial Nord, about two-thirds of potential voters lost the right to vote. A massive petition campaign collected more than half a million signatures in 78 départements to protest the end of universal manhood suffrage. Yet until the coup d'état, Montagnards remained hopeful of a sweeping electoral victory in 1852.

A purge of minor officials facilitated the return of the "men of order" to power in France. Half of the newly elected mayors and deputy mayors after the revolution were new to their positions.[85] Mayors were responsible for enforcing laws regulating hawking and peddling, passports, festivals, and the hours of cafes and cabarets. Many were caught between state demands that they enforce counter-revolutionary legislation and the wishes of people in their communes. Thus the mayor in Vallemoz (Haute Saône) was dismissed for refusing to provide gendarmes with the names of workers in a small factory who seemed responsible for "seditious shouts"; his counterpart in Marciac (Gers) tolerated an alleged "socialist club" and passed around a petition against the drink tax.[86] The deputy mayor of Corneilla del Vercol in the Pyrénées-Orientales lost his position when he urged people of the commune to disobey the prefect's warning not to dance in the town square in a region where dancing was fraught with political significance.[87] Yet the replacement of one mayor by another was in itself no guarantee of compliance. Some municipal councils elected another person of similar views to be mayor. The minister of the interior dissolved 276 municipal councils between April 1849 and March 1851.[88]

In rural communes, teachers were often interpreters of electoral *professions de foi*, readers of official proclamations, and instant political sages. In all, the repression eliminated about 1,200 "dangerous" schoolteachers. In the Gers, authorities terminated 42 of 333 teachers during these years, 26 for political offenses ("socialist propaganda," "demagogic deviation," "seditious talk," and so on).[89] The Falloux Law (March 1850), still debated in France in 1994, allowed Catholic clergy to open secondary schools and permitted them to serve on education committees. One of the practical consequences was that villages now could turn operation of their schools over to the clergy.

Certainly the threat of being dismissed was sufficient to end the democratic ardor of many teachers, particularly after the Falloux Law formalized the inspection process. Between September 1, 1850, and April 1, 1851, 353,628 letters were exchanged between rectors, averaging almost 4,000 for each rector, about 23 per day. The historian Jules Michelet, of course, was the most notable political victim in French academic life during the years of this republic.[90]

The purge of national guard units, reconstituted after the February revolution, also struck at the freedoms of 1848. The government promulgated at least 286 acts of dissolution, ranging from a single company to the entire guard in 20 to 30 communes within a single *département*. Examples included the "hostile reception" provided the prince-president on tour in 1850 (Joigny, Châtellerault, and Pont-à-Mousson), the illegal distribution of weapons (Barbaste, Lot-et-Garonne), parading through town with a "seditious" flag and then holding a banquet (La Charité), refusing to help close a club (Lodève), and so on.[91] In the Hérault, only that of St. Pons, "which has always shown itself to be a friend of order," survived.[92]

The left nonetheless possessed organizational resources rooted in some of the routines of daily life. These, too, brought the repression of banquets planned to celebrate republican anniversaries, informal electoral meetings, and even cafe sociability. Carnival, particularly in the Midi, was easily transformed into political allegory with costumes identifying the enemies of the Montagnard community. On Ash Wednesday in 1850, people in Mauzé in the Deux-Sèvres demonstrated their anger at the demise of the freedoms won in 1848: "under the pretext of a burying carnival," the *procureur* wrote, "a long procession passed twice through the bourg: a certain . . . apprentice joiner, nineteen years of age, coiffed in a red cap, wearing a white robe and a red vest, his right wrist held by a chain which fell to his feet, and holding a tricolored flag, thus represented Liberty enchained." Two carts led a crowd singing "Le Chant des vignerons" through the streets.[93] Authorities moved against politicized charivari and other "seditious" demonstrations, including funerals, singing, chanting, placards, political graffiti, any use of the word "social"; and against other Montagnard symbols such as red ties and belts, Phrygian caps, and so on. Symbols of the French Revolution itself, including the "*Marseillaise*" and even the number "93," if publicly displayed, were illegal. The government banned demonstrations for the republic, as well as those directed against unpopular officials, and even large funerals for deceased Montagnards.[94]

One of the consequences of the repression was that the Montagnard leadership became more "popular," as middle-class leaders abandoned the political struggle. But if the repression succeeded in breaking apart the radical apparatus in much of France, it drove the *démoc-soc* movements underground. The members of the secret societies were, for the most part, artisans and peasants. Members swore an oath of allegiance to defend the "democratic and social Republic." Arrested in a village in the Puisaye in the Yonne, a 33-year-old mason, Prudent Saison, described his initiation in the rites and symbols of the Nouvelle Montagne:

I admit that I took part in the secret societies. I was initiated at the end of last October [1851] in the warren of de Boutin by Louis Laguin, called Jolly, animal-trader, and Simon Majeuan, cultivator, both of Deffant. It was Languin who won me over. I was on a bit of a spree. They told me that if I should die, they would take care of my wife. They blindfolded me and made me swear to defend the democratic and social republic. I heard the clatter of weapons, such as rifles and pistols, as they moved about. When the blindfold was removed, I was alone. They had fled. I believe that they gave me, as a password, "the hour," to which one had to reply, "has sounded"; and to another question, one had to respond "Mountain."[95]

The government had become gradually aware of the secret societies, particularly in the Midi, for the most part in late 1850. They accentuated the repression—and the determination of the Montagnards as well—and led to prosecutors announcing the existence of various "plots" in the Midi against the state. These included the extended network of secret correspondence of Alphonse Gent, a former representative of the Vaucluse in the Chamber of Deputies who had moved to Lyon that year. Arresting Gent, authorities announced the "discovery" of the "Plot of Lyon," based on the assumption that France's second city was about to rise up again, and obtained a number of convictions of *démoc-socs* before military courts by virtue of the state of siege.[96] The heavy-handed repression, which included use of the army, led to serious incidents in the Drôme, the Ardèche, and the Cher in the fall that the government characterized as revolts, there too implementing the state of siege.

Although the constitution limited the presidency to one term, Louis Napoleon had no intention of stepping aside after the Chamber of Deputies rejected a proposal to allow him to serve a second term if reelected. On December 2, 1851, the anniversary of the battle of Austerlitz and of the coronation of Napoleon Bonaparte as emperor, Parisians awoke to read an official poster that announced the dissolution of the National Assembly.

A small uprising broke out in eastern Paris and troops broke up demonstrations in several other major cities. But, in all, more than 100,000 people in eighteen *départements* took arms in defense of the republic. Resistance was strongest in the Midi, particularly the Basses-Alpes, Var, Hérault, and Pyrénées-Orientales. Insurgents in the Basses-Alpes captured the subprefecture of Forcalquier. Two gendarmes were killed in Bédarieux, another in the river town of Clamécy. These deaths allowed the future emperor to propagate the myth that the dangerous classes had risen up in a furious bloodletting which justified the destruction of the republic. In many areas, the ragged forces of artisans and peasants armed with rusty rifles and pitchforks were quickly and easily dispersed by troops before they got very far. Military courts tried over 26,000 democratic-socialists and almost half that many went into exile. Victor Hugo was among those forced to flee France; his bitingly critical brochure "Napoléon le petit" reached the coast of Brittany by floating ashore from boats in wooden barrels.

Ted W. Margadant's convincing analysis of the resistance to the coup contributes to our understanding not only of what was the largest national insurrection in nineteenth- or twentieth-century French history, but also of the relationship between economic development and politicization.[97] The extension of small-scale and often rural manufacturing linked to expanding markets in *bourgs* accounted for much of France's economic growth during the Restoration and the July Monarchy. It was precisely these proto-industrial networks that drew ordinary people into political life. With the exception of Paris, France's cities remained quiet, despite attempts to organize resistance in several places, because of the government's military preparedness, again in sharp contrast to July 1830 and February 1848.[98]

The coup d'état, completing the repression of the Montagnards, marked a crushing victory for state centralization. Louis Napoleon Bonaparte laid claim to the restoration of a sham universal manhood suffrage. It consisted of two appeals to the people in the form of plebiscites and subsequent elections for the Corps Législatif in which official government-sponsored candidates were given every advantage. Napoleon III further honed the apparatus of the centralized state; prefects, not local *notables*, now could dispense an unprecedented degree of patronage (such as determining towns through which a new railway would pass).[99] The authoritarian empire restricted the freedoms that had been achieved in 1848, weakening republicanism and socialism for more than a decade.

≺ III ≻

The Last Revolution, 1870–71

Another coalition of opposition to the existing regime emerged in the 1860s. Napoleon III's decision to "crown the edifice with liberty" by initiating the "liberal empire" in 1859 aided the political opposition that weakened, and eventually was to overthrow, the Second Empire. The 1868 law legalizing public assembly facilitated opposition. Many of the public meetings in Paris took place in the *hangars* and dance halls of the periphery, where workers stood up to denounce the government. These public meetings served as veritable parliaments of the people; those who attended listened to impassioned speeches and debated republicanism, socialism, and anarchism.[100] Republicans and socialists mobilized against the empire, particularly in the big cities, which had never rallied to Napoleon III and which helped elect five republicans to the Corps Législatif as early as 1857. In 1865, some of the regime's opponents had demanded the decentralization of government in their "Nancy program"; many legitimists, too, were dissatisfied with Bonapartist centralization. The republican Belleville program of 1869 included disendowment and disestablishment of the Church, complete freedom of press and of assembly and association, and free elementary education. Strikes spread early in 1870. Denis Poulot, a former foreman who had become *patron* of a small workshop, complained bitterly about working-class insubordination to employers.[101]

But if a growing number of people did not expect the empire to survive, its collapse was precipitated by another of Napoleon III's foreign policy debacles. On July 19, 1870, the emperor, goaded by the empress and Parisian crowds, declared war on Prussia. But the French armies were overrun by strong, well-drilled Prussian troops and Napoleon III was captured at Sedan on August 31. In Paris, insurgents ran through virtually empty streets to proclaim the republic at the hôtel de ville on September 4. On September 23, the Prussian army laid siege to Paris.

After four months of resistance and hunger, Paris finally capitulated on January 29, 1871. With the siege over, wealthy Parisians returned from the safety of the countryside. But for ordinary people in the capital, hard times continued as landlords insisted that back rents be paid immediately and the National Assembly abolished pay for service in the national guard. The government angered ordinary Parisians by refusing to allow municipal elections. In February, provinces returned a monarchist majority to the National Assembly. Finally, early in March, the provisional government established its headquarters at Versailles. This seemed to many republicans and socialists to be sheer monarchist provocation.

The Commune itself began, very early on the morning of March 18, 1871, on Montmartre. Alerted by women early at the market, a crowd resisted attempts by troops sent there and to Belleville to seize the national guard artillery pieces in order to begin to disarm the city. As in July 1830 and February 1848, government military preparations were inadequate. The crowd put the generals Clément Thomas and C. M. Lecomte against the wall and executed them. Long before, in February 1848, Thiers had advised the last Orleanist government to withdraw its troops to outside the capital and then besiege the city. Now, having been elected head of the provisional government by the Assembly, he ordered his army, its number increased by prisoners of war released by Bismarck, to move out of and then surround the capital. That some troops had fraternized with the crowd contributed to the decision to withdraw the army from the capital.[102]

Parisians soon controlled the neighborhoods and the mairies of the north and northeast, as well as in the thirteenth, fourteenth, and fifteenth arrondissements.[103] Elections on March 26 led to the formation of a government of the Commune. A second siege of Paris began, this one a civil war. Army officers worked to assure the morale of the troops, so that there would be no repeat of the incidents of "fraternization" on March 18. On April 1 a Communard *sortie* in the direction of Versailles failed disastrously. The next day, the army undertook hostilities against Paris, losing a few troops to fear-induced desertion and shooting five prisoners.[104]

Surrounded by armies commanded from Versailles, the Commune set out to defend Paris. The central committee of the national guard took over as a provisional government. Although its members considered its very existence a blow for freedom, not all agreed on what freedom meant. The leaders of the Commune held a variety of political views. Jacobins and radical socialists were inspired by the memory of the French Revolution. Some moderate republicans wanted Paris to become again the capital of an anticlerical republic, but one which accorded more rights to municipalities. Several thousand *Blanquistes* believed that revolution in France could only be achieved by a small cell of determined men seizing power, but they offered no specific program. Anarchist followers of Pierre-Joseph Proudhon hoped that an independent Paris organized by producers would provide a model by which the state would be destroyed, while *Blanquistes* accused them of having been in league with the empire. Proudhonists had played a leading role in the *chambres syndicales* that had increased their activities over the past few years, emboldened, in part, by the legalization of strikes in 1864.

Within the limits of "free" Paris, revolutionary clubs continued to spring up in working-class districts. These were something of a continuation of the public meeting movement. With the guns of the provisional government bombarding the capital, the Communards debated ideological issues while organizing the defense of Paris. All sides agreed on resolutely anticlerical policies, replacing priests with republican teachers, insisting that school be secular and offer science, humanities, and trade.[105] While not proposing projects that would deny the rights of private property (although *chambres syndicales* and cooperatives were allowed to take over factories not in use in order to start production), and permitting the Bank of France to continue operations, the Commune enacted a number of significant social reforms. Léo Frankel, Marx's friend, responded to the appeal of a "women's union": "The Commune is not simply the administrative municipal authority, but above all the affirmation of sovereign power . . . as a means toward realizing the very aim of the revolution, namely the emancipation of labor." The Communards then took the notion of popular sovereignty a step forward in the quest for freedom.

With their situation increasingly desperate, it is remarkable how much the Communards accomplished in a short time. The Versailles government of Thiers worked almost frantically to prevent in the provinces diffusion of news of the Commune's moderate "Declaration to the French People" of April 19, which privileged municipal liberties. "Paris once again works and suffers for all of France," the declaration began. "The political unity, such as Paris wishes it, is the voluntary association of all local initiatives, the free and spontaneous concourse of all individual energies for the common aim, the well-being, the liberty and the security of all."[106]

The Commune also reflected the influence of associationism as it had developed since the early 1830s. Forty-three workers' cooperatives formed, at least on paper. Specific reforms included the creation of a labor exchange and an education commission. The social reforms initiated by both were impressive, given divisions within Communards and the urgency of war-time conditions. The Commune abolished night baking—long a grievance of bakers—and ended the *livret*, established nurseries for working mothers, and acknowledged the rights of workers' organizations to receive preference when the municipality contracted work. A strongly feminist movement developed among some women workers, including some who in mid-May proposed an organizational plan for cooperatives. The Russian émigré Elizabeth Dimetrieff founded the Union for the Defense of Paris and Aid to the Wounded, which had links to the International, and the feminist Louise Michel emerged as a Communard leader.

But with the countryside hostile or at least indifferent to the Commune, 1870–71 reflects some discontinuities. There was nothing like the mass mobilization of 1848–51, a fact perhaps best explained by the wrenching, complex circumstances of war and sudden defeat, and the desire for peace at almost any price. The provinces provided the Communards with no assistance; rather, conservative regions sent volunteers to fight for the Versailles forces. *Notables* still held sway in many regions. Bonapartism still existed here and there, most notoriously in the southwest center. In one Charentais village, strong attachment to the empire in a time of rumor and near panic as French armies fell back, combined with hostility to nobles and anti-republicanism, exacerbated by memory of the unpopular 45 centimes tax of 1848, led to the gory murder of a young noble on market day, generating rumors of cannibalism.[107]

Small uprisings occurred in Lyon, Marseille, Limoges, Narbonne, Saint-Etienne, and Le Creusot.[108] To a certain extent, then, the revolution of 1870–71, like its immediate predecessor, spread from Paris into the provinces, but not into the countryside. Mobilization in a number of provincial cities reflected local economic, social, and political structures, a combination of middle-class dissatisfaction with Bonapartist centralization, republican enthusiasm, and socialist mobilization. Louis Greenberg's contention that Commune-like movements in provincial cities were the result of essentially middle-class opposition to Bonapartist centralization is not incompatible with the classic left-wing interpretation that the Paris Commune contained a large degree of working-class socialist sentiment.[109]

Paris alone held on. Families from the proletarian northeastern districts ventured into the fancy western neighborhoods, now half deserted as their wealthy occupants had once again left Paris for safer places. For a time, the Commune became "the festival of the oppressed." On Gustave Courbet's recommendation the Commune ordered the Vendôme column, topped by a statue of Napoleon I, pulled down.

But the war against the "free Commune" was unmatched in the nineteenth century for its savagery. Specifically targeting working-class neighborhoods, the repression reflected the determination of the provisional government to destroy socialists and anarchists who espoused their own definitions of freedom.

After the capture of Fort Issy on May 22 troops poured into Paris through the western gates, which had been left virtually undefended.[110] Montmartre fell the next day and soldiers pushed into central Paris. The Versailles troops used some of the boulevards created—with such repression in mind—by Haussmann to approach the centers of popular resistance in the recently annexed inner suburbs. By the night of May 24, they held all of western Paris; remaining residents of the *beaux quartiers* greeted troops with wine, kisses, and money. The volunteers of the Seine began to slaughter prisoners at Montmartre. As fires broke out in central Paris, sparking rapidly spreading rumors that *les petroleuses*—female incendiaries—intended to burn Paris to the ground, Communards were rounded up and shot in groups of 150 at the mur des Fédérés in Père Lachaise Cemetery.[111] Communard atrocities were minor in comparison.

By the evening of the 26th, the Communards—approximately 20,000 participated in the fighting—had fallen back on the northeast. Troops surrounded Belleville. After fierce fighting, the last barricades fell two days later at the *mairie* of the twentieth arrondissement, as fighting continued among the tombstones of Père Lachaise. For a quarter of an hour, a single *fédéré* defended the last Communard barricade, on the rue Ramponneau.[112]

Perhaps as many as 25,000 people died at the hands of the army and the provisional government in the capital where in the opinion of one magistrate "everyone is guilty."[113] Because Paris largely remained a city of artisans and skilled workers, with small-scale production and craft industries dominating its economy, the average insurgent was young, born in the provinces, and a worker, with semi-skilled workers more represented than during the *journées* of 1848.[114]

The Commune was also in part a struggle on behalf of the prosperous western neighborhoods and the commercial center against the popular quarters of the east and the periphery.[115] Jacques Rougerie has described the Commune as the "vengeance of those expelled by Haussmannization."[116] Ordinary people from the proletarian quarters of the north and northeast came into Paris, wandering through the *beaux quartiers*. They inverted the role of the bourgeois dandy as *flâneur* during the heyday of the imperial capital, visiting neighborhoods most had never had occasion to see and were now free—though not for long—to visit.

To the "forces of order," some Parisians seemed more guilty than others. Belleville suffered disproportionately from the fury of the repression.[117] "I do not know," a contemporary noted of the Parisian upper classes, "which of these two evils terrified them most; they hated the foreigner but they feared the Bellevois much more."[118] The victims of summary executions were tossed into common graves which soldiers forced passers-by to dig. On the rue de Tourtille, "a officer shot ten or twelve Communards with his pistol . . . a concièrge on the rue de Belleville denounced all of the renters of his building. The outraged officer shot all of the renters, but he also shot the concièrge for good measure."[119]

The "moral" conquest of free Paris followed. Thiers wrote the new archbishop, whose predecessor had been executed by the Communards, and asked him to take responsibility for building a new basilica on Montmartre, "a public act of contrition and reparation . . . will stand amongst us as a protest against other monuments and works of art erected for the glorification of vice and impiety."[120] A *rapporteur* for the Congrès général des comités catholiques de France applauded the proposed emplacement "sur le lieu du crime. En même temps, elle repoussera les dangers du présent, elle servira de lécon pour l'avenir."[121] A chapel was dedicated to "Jésus-Ouvrier," standing where the Communard leader Eugène Varlin was put up against a wall and shot.[122]

There has been no revolution in Paris since, unless the *revolution manquée* of 1968 is counted. The economic and social transformation engendered by Haussmannization not only continued to accentuate the dichotomy between the more prosperous western quarters and the east, but accentuated the proletarianization of the periphery and the embourgeoisement of the center, particularly the western neighborhoods. To some the events suggested the futility of armed rebellion against modern armies. Future *journées* would be those of the right, disturbances at the time of the Dreyfus affair, at the time of the canonization of Jeanne d'Arc after World War 1, and on February 4, 1936. These also were not successful.

The Commune sharpened political divisions in France. For the left, it seemed to be a glimpse of the future proletarian revolution that would overthrow bourgeois society. It offered a frightening glimpse of plebeian insurrection to conservatives, who resolved to oppose movements for social and political change with armed force.

≺ IV ≻

The Achievement of the Republic

The nineteenth-century revolutions helped shape the relationship between French citizens and the state, implanting democratic freedoms and secular ideals. Public opinion swept away the post-Commune government of the so-called "moral order," what amounted to a "monarchist republic." With the establishment of a republic with strong support across the social spectrum, the French Revolution came "into port." [123] In 1880, France became the only republic among the major European powers.

The nine-year period that followed the fall of the Commune, crucial in the emergence of modern France, was thus a peaceful denouement to the nineteenth-century revolutions. Early in June 1871, the Assembly repealed the law of exile, permitting the return of the royal families. But the refusal of the comte de Chambord, the legitimist pretender to the throne, to accept the tricolor flag ended, for all intents and purposes, the possibility of a Bourbon restoration. Thiers himself now supported a conservative republic ("The régime that divides us least"), based on the evolution of his Orleanist faith in parliamentary government. The monarchists, however, did not give up so easily. In May 1873, they forced the angry resignation of Thiers. They selected General Patrice de MacMahon, hero of the Crimean War, to be president. MacMahon selected the Orleanist duc de Broglie as premier.

France thus became a republic with monarchist institutions, a representative government without sovereignty of the people. Following passage by one vote in January 1875 of the Wallon amendment, France had a president elected for a term of seven years by absolute majority vote of an aristocratic Senate, which itself was elected by indirect election. The Senate was thus intended to provide a monarchist counterweight to the Assembly. The electoral system of single-member constituencies by which the Chamber of Deputies was to be elected, too, worked to the advantage of monarchists, by giving an advantage to local *notables* in elections in which no candidate won a clear majority on the first ballot. This was a likely scenario because republican unity could not be assured.

The goal of General MacMahon's attempted coup d'état of May 16, 1877, was to assert stronger executive authority in order to counter the political power of the Chamber of Deputies and prepare the way for a monarchist restoration. The *coup de seize mai* should be seen in the context of the election of 330 republicans and only 155 monarchists to the Chamber of Deputies in 1876. As the electoral campaign revealed, clericalism remained a deeply divisive political issue in France, capable of mobilizing republican support when the government of the "moral order" sought to revive the Restoration alliance of altar and throne. Since the July revolution of 1830, France had had no state religion.[124] Even in areas where during the Second Republic *démoc-soc* politics had been infused with the theme of "Jésus le Montagnard," few on the left or even the center wanted the Church to retain a political role in France. The clergy, after all, had blessed Louis Napoleon's 1851 coup d'état. MacMahon's attempt to strengthen executive government and prepare a monarchist restoration called into question the place of the Church in French society and politics. Workers and peasants in the Limousin, Bourbonnais, and several other regions feared that the revival of clerical influence might ultimately lead to the reimposition of tithes. Confronted by the possibility of monarchical clericalism amid a revival of missionary Catholicism and pilgrimages to Lourdes and La Salette, the majority of the French population rallied to the republic during the 1870s.

Defying republican success in the 1876 elections, MacMahon refused to name Gambetta, a former Jacobin now distancing himself from the more radical old *quarante-huitards*, to be first minister. On May 16 he asked the moderate premier Jules Simon to resign, naming a monarchist in his place. When the Chamber refused to vote its approval, MacMahon dissolved it. In the subsequent electoral campaign, the monarchist president sought to capitalize on clerical influence. Despite ecclesiastical interference, French electors returned another, though smaller, republican majority to the Chamber. The results forced MacMahon to name a strongly republican premier. In 1879, partial elections for the Senate left monarchists in a

minority in the upper house created to reflect their interests. Mac-
Mahon resigned, and with him went all chances for a monarchical
restoration.[125] The republicans elected as president Jules Grévy, a
staunch republican who had been elected to the Constituent Assembly in 1848.

The Third Republic would also be nationalist (despite a later
strong wave of anti-militarism), particularly because of the loss of
Alsace and much of Lorraine. But, rejecting Bonapartism, it would
not have a strong executive authority. Grévy, the new president, had
in 1848 proposed the abolition of the position. The memory of Louis
Napoleon Bonaparte's destruction of the Second Republic also explains the intensity of suspicion of Caesarism.

The dialectic of radicalization and state repression brought a republic whose relatively weak executive authority in the wake of the
coup de seize mai belied the strength of the centralized state. During
the monarchist republic, Orleanists and republicans had agreed that
the president should have the right to name members of the council
of state: "the two camps perfectly expressed the French consensus on
administrative centralization which had persisted through the century."[126] In the words of Charles Tilly, "a previously revolutionary
state had consolidated its power to a degree matched by few other
European countries."[127]

In 1879, the year in which the constitution was revised to reflect
the republican reality, the *"Marseillaise"* became the French national anthem. A year later July 14 officially became the national festival. Also in 1880, the Communards were amnestied and busts of
Marianne wearing a Phrygian cap appeared on town squares. That
same year a law made it easier to open cafes and cabarets, in contrast
to policies of MacMahon's government, which had undertaken a
massive repression of cafes deemed seditious.

Winning the support of moderates by disassociating democracy
and revolution, the Third Republic nonetheless was founded on the
principal freedoms demanded by nineteenth-century revolutionaries,
including those enumerated in the republican Belleville program of
1869, "a key reference of radical republicanism."[128] Although women
would not have the right to vote until after World War 2, universal
manhood suffrage ended the rule of *notables*. By the law of July 19,
1881, the Chamber of Deputies guaranteed freedom of the press,
with the right of printed reply. Laws passed the next year and sub-

sumed in more legislation two years later gave municipal councils the right to elect mayors, with the notable exception of Paris, which did not have a mayor until 1977. Trade unions became legal in 1884. The freedom of association, too, was guaranteed, but only in 1901 once the problem of the religious *congrégations* had been resolved.

The Chamber of Deputies also moved quickly to pass secularizing legislation. Divorce became legal, though difficult to obtain, particularly for women. Sunday work no longer was forbidden. Article VII of the 1880 schools law forbade teaching to be carried out by congregations not authorized in France. In 1881 the Chamber of Deputies made public primary schooling compulsory and free of charge. Three years later, the Chamber ended public prayers at the start of its session. The formal separation of church and state came in 1905.

Although Gambetta and Ferry insisted on the "restorative and integrative virtues of the Republic" that they hoped would make class conflict unnecessary, many workers and most socialists remained outside its appeal.[129] Despite the amnesty of Communards in 1880, large segments of the working class remained alienated from the republic. If much of what the democratic-socialists of 1848–51 had demanded had been gained with the Third Republic, for Guesdists, Allemanists, and syndicalists, descendants of the left-wing Communards, the struggle for new rights and freedoms would go on. Yet by World War 1, socialists had become contenders for political power within the context of the republic. In 1914, they would march to the front in defense of France. The nineteenth-century dialectic of radicalization and repression gained democratic freedoms while at the same time reinforcing the power of the state, an intriguing paradox still more apparent in daily life in France than in any other western nation.

The Paradoxes of Italy's Nineteenth-Century Political Culture

RAYMOND GREW

ITALIAN SOCIETY IN THE nineteenth century produced a demanding sense of what the public sphere should be like and a widespread conviction that reality was scandalously different. The nature of the political culture that produced such expectations and disappointments is the central concern of this chapter, which, while looking at the interplay of liberty and revolution, barely treats nationalism, the obvious focus of the Risorgimento; gives little independent attention to the Catholic church, an autonomous participant in and outspoken opponent of most of the trends of the period; and slights peasant concerns, pressing social issues, burgeoning capitalism, a growing labor movement, and regional differences, much as national politics did.[1] That such omissions are conceivable is in itself significant, for Italy formed a public sphere with weak ties to Italian institutions and social structure.

≪ I ≫

Revolutions

Revolution in nineteenth-century Italy was a continuing possibility, a common memory individually experienced and diversely interpreted, like remarkable weather, something unpredictable that might recur. There were a lot of revolutions to keep track of, perhaps a score between 1799 and 1860, although the number would be far higher if one counted separately every time local leaders used force to compel the lowering of a hated flag in some town square. The number of revolutions involved in the founding of the Cispadane and Cisapline republics in the 1790s (like the question of how much autonomy they ever had) can be endlessly debated, but a case can be made for there having been revolutions at least in Bologna, Ferrara, and Modena. Over the next few years, until Napoleon turned away from republican forms, political changes that French officials engineered in northern, central, and southern Italy often had some of the trappings of revolution.

The governments restored at the Congress of Vienna were shaken by revolutions in Naples in 1820, in Piedmont in 1821, and in Modena, Parma, and the Papal States in 1831; by important Mazzinian attempts at revolution in 1831 and 1834; and by revolutions in Sicily, Tuscany, Piedmont, Rome, Milan, and Venice in 1848 and 1849 (when cities often experienced more than one revolution). In 1859 there was certainly something like a revolution in the states of Parma, Modena, and Tuscany, and in the Romagna, involving independent revolts in several of the major cities of each province; and the uprisings in Sicily and those encouraged by Piedmont in central Italy in 1860 made possible the creation of the Kingdom of Italy. These figures pale, of course, before the seven thousand revolutions Guiseppe Ferrari identified in Italian history from the Communes to the Reformation.[2] In any case most of Italy's political leaders in the nineteenth century had experienced, some many times, the contingencies and accidents, the misinformation, the miraculous successes and the dashed hopes of revolution. By the 1860s, if there were not many dedicated revolutionaries in Italy, there were not many leaders immune to the idea that a revolution was possible.

Even the revolutions that took place under French aegis had built on a local base of democratic support, and they had won significant sympathy from moderates as regimes stimulated by the French example and prodded by the presence of French officials demonstrated that revolutionary institutions could work effectively. Thereafter, despite Metternich's determination to prevent it, revolution in Italy could be presented as a practical means for effecting change. There was also always the possibility that it might explode out of the patterns of violence among peasants (in Basilicata, Sicily, and Lombardy); build from brigandage in the north, in the south, and on Sicily and Sardinia; or expand from the well-organized networks of smuggling along each of Italy's many mountainous borders.[3] Simmering discontent and these patterns of violence all had some structural connection to the repressive policies of the established regimes, and it was

easy to imagine that at any moment social outrage, anti-state attitudes, and illegal practices could become attached to a more general
political program, could in effect be mobilized for revolution. At various times in many Italian regions revolution became an obsession.[4]

While remaining a perpetual possibility, revolution in Italy was
subtly redefined in practice. The revolutions that accompanied the
arrival of French armies were truncated versions of the revolution in
France, without the Terror or civil war, the organized factions, or systematic conflict with the Church. Italian radicals would later construct from this experience a rather mild and ambiguous picture of
what future revolutions would be like. They knew some blood would
have to flow but thought primarily of patriotic martyrs who would
expose the vulnerability of the restoration regimes and stimulate
the masses to lift their heads. Events reinforced that picture, for the
weakness of those restoration governments was demonstrated again
and again. Some Italian revolutionaries espoused social programs radical enough to be called socialist,[5] but most such programs remained
imprecise about just whose property was threatened, where lines of
social conflict would be drawn, or how extensive violence might
have to be. The very unattractiveness of governments like the one
in Naples eased consciences about clandestine activity and allowed
men who were pillars of respectability otherwise to countenance
plots against the state.

Taken together, the extended Italian discussions distinguished
revolution from what it was not. Revolution, first of all, was no mere
coup d'etat. Radicals and moderates alike heaped contempt on conspiracies, like the one in Modena in 1831 that involved shadowy figures conniving with people in the inner circles of government and
perhaps the duke himself. Throughout his career, Giuseppe Mazzini
had to battle charges that he relied on plots, conspiracies, and assas-
sinations. Those charges were harmful not merely because they
made him seem morally repugnant and devious but because they
contradicted his claim to represent the popular will, which was his
greatest strength, and thus undermined his program.

Nor, in Italian usage, could just any uprising be called a revolution.
Revolution begins, Mazzini said, where insurrection ends.[6] Shapeless
protests, however violent, and revolts that were quickly repressed
were called *moti*, uprisings or riots; and that general distinction,

common to most European languages, was especially important in Italy. Revolutions were victorious, and equally important, were understood to effect changes that furthered the march of historical progress. In 1796 conservative forces in Lucca triumphed over the local Jacobin revolutionaries until the latter got French support,[7] but that was not called revolution. Neither was the political uprising in the Veneto in 1797 of angry peasants and landowners opposed to taxes and French offenses to religion.[8] The plebes demonstrated against the constitution of 1799 in Genoa; filled the squares of Florence in the Viva Maria! demonstrations; and in Naples, after having been mobilized by Cardinal Ruffo, proceeded to beat and murder and burn in the process of overturning the revolutionary government. These eruptions were probably not the pious opposition to atheistic republics that conservatives claimed them to be nor the spontaneous expression of popular sentiment that many historians have assumed that they were.[9] Nevertheless, the identification of them as conservative kept even those who claimed that such collective violence taught important lessons from recognizing them as revolutions.

Beyond the requirement of significant popular participation, at least some brief success, and a generally progressive political direction, the circumstances that constituted revolution, like the conditions that could lead to it, were hard to specify. Southern radicals driven into exile from 1821 to 1860, while frustrated to see how little revolutionary agitation they left behind,[10] agreed that unrest, popular anger, and open violence were not enough to constitute revolution although they differed over what else was needed. Mazzini's conspiracies were less plots to capture power than plans to demonstrate to the people their potential power and thus to stimulate revolution. The tragedy in the quixotic expeditions to the Kingdom of Naples of the Bandiera brothers in 1844 and Carlo Pisacane in 1857 lay not in their capture and execution by the forces of order but in the silence that followed. "Material revolutions are achieved," Pisacane had written, "when the driving idea behind them [l'idea motrice] is already popular."[11]

Garibaldi's successes, on the other hand, while they involved real military skill, resulted from his ability through personal popularity to meld armed force and peasant anger into revolution. After unification had been achieved, Garibaldi's name and image remained—

like the chance to cheer him or the memory of having done so or the simple act of naming a son after him—a kind of celebration of the myth of revolution.[12] In Italy revolution came to mean the participation of ordinary people in the sudden transformation of public life. That participation did not have to be massive or consistent, nor the political transformation extensive, provided that immediate changes were thought to set Italy on the course of historical progress toward greater freedom. Risorgimento nationalism thus accepted shouting crowds and patriotic banners as popular participation and the expulsion of foreign rulers as a political transformation equivalent to revolution. Indeed, the widespread belief in the inevitability of progress and that history moved in a clear direction[13] made it possible to treat progress itself as the equivalent of revolution. The institutional continuity which this view of revolution permitted would not have surprised Tocqueville, who would also, however, have noted the absence of anything analogous to a religious reformation, which he thought an essential element of the French Revolution, and who would have found it curious (as did generations of Italian thinkers) that Italy's revolutions so little fitted the great French model.[14]

If across the peninsula prominent Italians abandoned reformism and created instead a "straightforwardly revolutionary political culture,"[15] that was in large part because a transformation of the political culture was what revolution was thought to be about. The revolutions of 1848 were the expression and the greatest achievement of this belief, much as Garibaldi's expedition to Sicily in 1860 fulfilled the myth that spontaneous uprisings could make a revolution (even if that was not quite what happened in either period). The defeat of the Sicilian revolution of 1848 by Bourbon armies fortuitously obscured its ambiguous base and the risk of social war it had briefly revealed.[16] Both in conception and in the way events unfolded, revolution as Italians thought about it was limited. In 1851, Pisacane, who was truly dedicated to revolution, could write to Carlo Cattaneo, who was far more conscious of the dangers of social revolution, that "I fully agree with you that in Italy there is no revolutionary idea or guiding principle, aside from the general desire to change for the better."[17] Although there were real interests at stake and real conflicts over power in many Risorgimento clashes, there was little consistent sense of who the enemy was beyond Austrian forces and individual reactionaries.[18] Class conflict was clearest in the general indifference to peasant concerns and therefore in the issues not raised and groups not mobilized.

At the beginning of the century, the French presence had spared Italians from having to capture power while reducing the opportunity for revolutionaries to bicker among themselves (though allowing them in retrospect to attribute their disappointments and failures to the role of foreigners). Subsequently, most revolutionaries tried in their propaganda and in their brief moments of power to avoid offending Catholic sentiment so that, like the provisional government in Genoa in 1797, they could reassure "citizens [who are] misled and seduced" and "calm any doubt: the Religion of [our] Fathers will be maintained in all its purity."[19] Anticlericalism was not central to Italy's revolutionary movements, and many leading Catholic intellectuals took part in the new governments created in 1848 and propagandized before and after for national unity.[20]

So circumscribed, revolution got a remarkably good press. Democrats, of course, remained committed to a more unfettered conception of revolution;[21] but the dominant understanding allowed moderates also to write admiringly of revolution, as in Michele Amari's account of the Sicilian Vespers and Carlo Botta's epic on the American revolution. There were of course many opponents of revolution in general and of each specific Italian uprising. All the classic arguments of figures like De Maistre and Chateaubriand were well known and frequently if partially used, but there was no anti-revolutionary intellectual tradition in Italy outside those in the Catholic tradition who followed the editors of *Civiltà Cattolica* (and published relatively little outside its pages). Thus, although the effectiveness of the Spanish guerrilla against Napoleon was understood everywhere as proof of the strength of popular opposition to revolution and to the French invaders, in Italy the major use of the Spanish example was to demonstrate the contribution partisan warfare could make to revolution.[22] In the course of the Risorgimento hundreds of Italians wrote works on the history of Italy as well as historical accounts of their own times. By liberals and Catholics and democrats, sometimes heavily documented and sometimes highly personal, these accounts shared one remarkable quality. Almost none was politically reactionary in cast, even after the disappointments of 1848.[23] The division between democrats and moderates, a major element of the Risorgimento, may have been fatal then;[24] but afterward a patriotic aura encouraged both groups to take some pride in having participated. The lesson of 1848 was not that revolution led to civil war but that revolution alone was not enough to make change permanent.

This affection for a delimited sort of revolution was so entrenched that it became a lasting part of Italy's intellectual tradition. Although hardly a radical, Benedetto Croce gave revolution a central place in his discussion of the formation of Italy's political culture, combining a regional and national patriotism in his account of Masaniello's revolt in Naples in 1647 and more remarkably still in his treatment of the Neapolitan revolution of 1799. After acknowledging all that was superficial and foolish about that venture, he could not resist a larger and yet more personal point:

When I think of those Calabrians and Abruzzians, Basilicatans and Apullians, and Neapolitans of Naples, who raised burning political problems in the republican papers of the Cisalpine [republic] and in pamphlets and broadsides, who joined the Italian legions then being formed, who accepted positions with the French or the new democratic governments, and when I read the documents of the relations and friendships that then tied them to the Lombards and Piedmontese and Ligurians and Venetians, I say to myself:— Here is the birth of modern Italy, of the new Italy, of our Italy.[25]

In this sort of reading, the importance of revolution was largely symbolic, an attitude common throughout the nineteenth century. And if revolutions mattered for their symbolic meaning rather than the destruction of enemies or the lasting capture of power, then symbols could easily be taken for signs of revolution. So shouts in the opera house, demonstrations in the piazza, and broadsides covertly passed from hand to hand were treated (on all sides) as part of a larger revolutionary process only sporadically visible. The revolution of 1848 in Milan was great theater, which began quite literally in theaters. Stendahl had been struck by their popularity there and the importance of La Scala as a place of public meeting. Theaters, encouraged by an Austrian government that apparently hoped cultural conviviality might substitute for politics, proved hard to discipline; and the government grew fearful that they threatened morals and fostered patriotism. When in January 1848 the government barred bouquets tied with tricolor ribbons, the theaters emptied; when official attendance was made mandatory, the audience came in mourning. Shouted slogans and patriotic anthems became the performance, which spilled out into parades beneath lighted windows. Flags and cockades appeared everywhere. "The Milanese," the perplexed Austrian ambassador reported, "know how to adopt in superlative measure the arms of demonstration."[26]

Soon a crowd invaded the Palazzo del Governo. Imperial symbols were ripped from their standards, furniture smashed and glass broken, shots fired. Two guards were killed, and barricades went up. When the Austrian army found it wiser to retreat, the Five Days of Milan, which had begun as theater, became the very model of popular triumph.[27] Genoa's participation in the revolutionary excitement of 1848 was marked by the appearance on stage of 48 dancers wrapped in the tricolor and singing Mameli's "Fratelli d'Italia,"[28] which a generation later would become Italy's national anthem. There were comparable scenes in Venice, Verona,[29] and across the north. In 1859 a rising tide of similar demonstrations conducted with less risk of revolutionary violence and simpler political goals would drive the old regimes out of Tuscany, Modena, Parma, and the Romagna.[30] By 1860 such demonstrations, now an established form, were reduced to a Cavourian contrivance used to justify his sending in regular troops.[31]

The process of national unification codified this latitudinarian understanding of revolution, placing a patriotic gloss on past risings and demonstrations, making heroes of old leaders and allowing many who had joined (or maybe merely applauded) some demonstration to recall it as part of their revolutionary past. Revolution in retrospect became respectable in a tradition that was wonderfully catholic. It incorporated childhood memories of being taken to see liberty trees that had been planted twenty years earlier; recollections of parental table talk in which liberty, constitution, and independence were common shibboleths;[32] descriptions recalling meetings of Carbonari and Freemasons, Saint Simonian socialists, and membership in Young Italy or even the Italian National Society—all memories associated with a warm if diluted sense of revolution.

By 1859 and 1860 this sense of revolution added significance to the plebescites that were, of course, a clever device for deflecting Napoleon III's objections to Piedmontese expansion but also part of the new kingdom's claim to legitimacy. Those plebescites were representations of the revolution that Italy got, a ritualized revolution in which the masses, accompanied by banners proclaiming their unanimity and music expressing communal joy, marched in good order (often led by their social superiors) to vote for Italian unification.

If the very term Risorgimento had the advantage in the nineteenth century of implying an inevitable cultural renewal rather than the violence of political revolution, it has had the subsequent effect of encouraging Italians to believe (and often regret) that Italy never had a true revolution. As early as 1796 there was concern that Italy had not enjoyed a spontaneous revolution, a concern assuaged by likening the French presence in Lombardy to Louis XVI's call for a meeting of the Estates General.[33] On the eve of the revolution of 1848, Ferrari worried that in Italy insurrections had triumphed too easily.[34] That concern lasted, for it has been the most consistent and one of the most effective criticisms of modern Italy, the basis for many analyses of its social continuity and political limitations.[35] An incidental effect of such changes has been to reinforce a cultural affection for revolution. The idea that Italy's was a merely "passive" and therefore flawed or fraudulent revolution—which was part of Cuoco's famous contemporary criticism of the Neapolitan revolution of 1799, to be repeated a century later in Gobetti's influential analysis of liberal Italy's missing revolution (*la revoluzione mancata*)— was central to Gramsci's interpretation of Italian history, too.[36] The failure to build from a popular base was the "historic error of the ruling class."[37] Historians have made much of the myths of the Risorgimento, but for modern Italy the myth of the missing revolution may be more important still.[38]

Paradoxically, a land in which politics seemed to revolve around the possibility that revolution might occur and in which for 60 years revolutions were in fact frequent, then developed a national political culture preoccupied with the absence of revolution. For moderates that absence was a fragile accomplishment to be protected. From a more radical perspective, that incompleteness was a haunting failure. None of the revolutions in Italy in 1799 and throughout the Napoleonic period, in 1820–21, in 1830–31, in 1848–49, and in 1859–60 had held uncontested power for long; none attained the autonomy and inertial energy that might have resulted in systematic internal conflict and bloody purges. Italy's revolutions, in short, did not leave the deep and painful social scars so often part of a revolutionary heritage. Revolution could be remembered for its initial promise and momentary enthusiasm, for the transformation promised but not achieved. In fact, practical concerns had shaped Italy's revolutions, which were always constrained, by the French presence at the end of the eighteenth century, cooperation with monarchy in the 1820s and 1830s, nationalist goals and war with Austria in 1848, and the prominence of Piedmont in 1859–60. By 1860 revolution was reduced to fairly contrived demonstrations that legitimated unification under Piedmont.

In a further paradox, this experience over two generations nourished a grander conception of revolution, vaguer and more abstract yet in its way much more far-reaching. Once all the real revolutions were over, it was this imagined one—remarkably like the one Mazzini dreamed of (and, in its survival as a myth, his ultimate triumph), a spontaneous welling up of all the best in human nature that could create from its own energy a new society of free cooperation—that became a vibrant element of Italian political culture, a yardstick that could only measure failure.

≺ II ≻

Constitutions

With the French Revolution, the word constitution acquired a kind of mythic force throughout Europe; but it had a particular resonance in Italy where nineteenth-century constitutions were associated with the liberties of medieval communes; the historical and patriotic perspective of Muratori; the romantic figure of Paoli popularized by Rousseau; and the eighteenth-century projects for constitutions in Corsica, Tuscany, and Lombardy, which were written by prominent Italians and widely discussed across the peninsula.[39] From Sicily to Fruili, every region of Italy could point to some parliamentary experience in its past.[40] Italians thought a lot about constitutions. They wrote about the sort that would be most suitable for a famous competition in Milan in 1796–97; they wrote books about them;[41] and they wrote so many constitutions in the nineteenth century that to list them risks exaggerating their importance. Many of them were from the first largely symbolic, many were hastily written, many were imitations (often under considerable political pressure) of constitutions written elsewhere.

Nevertheless, this experience was significant. There was notable progaganda in all those announcements that a constitution might be promulgated, in the denunciation of past "debasement" with which constitutions on the French model began and in their resounding declaration that a new era had begun. Nowhere in Europe was the adjective democratic used more widely or positively.[42] An extensive process of education took place in those assemblies called shortly after the armies of the French republic arrived and in the public discussions stimulated by all this activity. In Genoa, the revolution and the constitution it led to were for some time more independent of French influence than most,[43] but the parallel ventures in Milan and Emilia also had genuine local roots and enthusiastic participants. Although Bonaparte's intervention in the Cispadane constitution was heavy handed, the delegates who gathered to write it held 38 sessions before Napoleon decided the talk had gone on long enough.[44]

From the constitution composed in Bologna in 1796 to the ninth *Statuto Costituzionale* of the Kingdom of Italy in 1810, thirteen constitutions were written in northern Italy (if we count as only one the 1805 constitution of the Kingdom of Italy and the nine amended versions that had followed it by 1810), which were preoccupied with titles and land and hardly constitutions at all. Even the 1805 constitution itself began with a kind of apology for all that it could not promise, a reminder of how much more had once been expected.[45] Still, about half of these thirteen constitutions were created with some serious deliberation. One hundred delegates met in Modena in 1797 to approve the Cispadane constitution, which was quickly written by a committee of eight using the French model and then discussed for more than a month by the delegates. The writing of the Cisapline constitution was even more directly supervised by Napoleon,[46] and its revision in 1800 was the work of Melzi and Talleyrand, but the 454 delegates assembled in Lyon reworked the draft presented them to strengthen its protection of liberty.[47] As a kind of training, Italian participation in the work of writing those French-sponsored constitutions was intellectually and socially significant.[48]

Three more constitutions were written in Naples and Sicily between 1808 and 1815. The Neapolitan constitution of 1799, which Cuoco criticized for its enlightenment abstractions, in fact strayed farther than most from the French model and involved a good deal of local engagement in its actual formulation.[49] The Sicilian constitution of 1812 reflected the presence of the British navy in its provisions for a House of Commons and a House of Peers and was not the product of a constituent assembly, but it was the subject of months of discussion while the Sicilian parliament debated its more than 500 articles. The nineteenth-century claim that after 1816 every Sicilian cobbler knew his legal rights and resented any infringement of them, however exaggerated, is in itself evidence that constitutions had an importance that extended beyond their legal authority or longevity,[50] and Croce was confident that constitutional sentiment in the Kingdom of the Two Sicilies rose steadily in the years following Murat.[51]

The constitutions proclaimed in Naples in 1820 and in Piedmont in 1821 were barely more than translations of the Spanish constitution of 1812, general promises more than plans to reorganize power.[52] Nor could the revolt against papal rule in 1831 accomplish much more in its two months, although the delegates who gathered in Bologna to adopt a constitution had been elected at public meetings held in 23 cities and towns; and they knowledgeably tried to resolve the ambiguities of papal rule by providing for a strict separation of powers.

After 1830, Italian governments were increasingly willing to accept some form of elite consultation; and that was seen on all sides as a first step to some more systematic and extensive representation.[53] That sense of inevitability, and the widespread belief that progress demanded constitutions, flowered in 1848. By then constitutions meant much more than mere revival of some consultative body or assemblies of old regime orders.[54] Ferdinand II explained his decision to grant a constitution in the Two Sicilies as a result of "having understood the wish of our beloved subjects to have the guarantees and institutions appropriate to their present state of development" and in the prologue declared his desire "to establish in this Realm a Constitution corresponding to the current state of civil society [conformi all'attuale incivilimento]."[55] Pius IX declared that "Inasmuch as our neighbors have judged their peoples mature [enough] to receive the benefit of representation not merely consultative but deliberative, We do not wish to have less esteem for our people."[56] The regency in Parma similarly cited the "norms of Italian governments" as a reason for needing a constitution and "enjoying the consumate advantages of representative government."[57] When Ricasoli, as Gonfaloniere, petitioned the grand duke of Tuscany for a constitution, he combined a sense of where universal progress must lead with an appeal to local patriotism, "[c]onsidering that the Tuscans' very ancient civilization and experience of liberty cannot make this people less worthy of the institutions that have been conceded by their Kings to the people of the Two Sicilies and the States of Sardinia."[58] The commission that the duke of Modena appointed in 1848 explained to him that a constitution was "the perfection of social order" and would "reconcile exercise of the public franchise with public tranquility and security."[59] Even Florestan I of Monaco saw himself hastening to join the "regeneration" that marked "a new era" by granting a constitution.[60]

Constitutionalism in Italy had been naturalized, and governments of every sort knew (as did the grand duke of Tuscany when he named Gino Capponi) just whom to turn to when it was time to make constitutional government work.[61] An important change, the proclamation of a constitution could nevertheless be presented as a part of a continuing discourse. Thus the revolutions of 1848 rapidly produced ten more constitutional projects.[62] The one of these that lasted, to become the constitution of united Italy, Piedmont's was perhaps the most imitative of the lot, an adaptation of the French and Belgian constitutions of 1830 and like them a gift from the king.

In Italy, then, throughout the nineteenth century constitutions were widely admired as essential to liberty and progress. Even in the counter-revolutionary atmosphere of 1814, the municipal council of Milan, glad enough to get rid of Napoleonic domination, had sent a delegation to Paris to tell the victorious Allies what they hoped for: enlarged territory, a monarchical or hereditary government, and independence but also a "liberal constitution."[63] There were of course many in Italy then and later who did not want a constitution of any sort. It is all the more remarkable, therefore, that such opposition, though often entrenched and thoroughly reactionary, had relatively little resonance. The appeal of anti-constitutional attitudes, strengthened by close association with the Catholic church, was at the same time diminished by awareness that the Church, like foreign powers, had its own interests to defend. There was enormous enthusiasm, however, when Gioberti suggested that the papacy and an Italian state were compatible, thereby contributing to "that constitutional ideology that Italy finds irresistible."[64]

In some respects the governments restored in 1815 had contributed to the cause of constitutionalism in Italy. Their rejection of even the most limited charter added to the symbolic significance of constitutions, while their preservation of Napoleonic administrative structures simplified the constitutional argument. The ideas justifying restoration authoritarianism were, like the restoration itself, as blatantly imported or imposed as anything stemming from the French Revolution; but the need to restructure governments (outside the Papal State) was now a less salient issue, and that made it easier to focus on constitutions as a purely political matter having to do with the rule of law and public participation in government. When the restoration regimes quickly abandoned the constitutions squeezed from them in 1821, 1830, and 1848, however, their cynicism helped to connect constitutional aspirations to national unification.

Whether viewed as a concession painfully wrung from established governments or an open-ended promise for the future, constitutions represented a familiar step in no sense foreign or alien. Cultural traditions supported that view. Italy had more universities than any other nation, and law was the principal subject of university study. Chairs of constitutional law were established in Bologna, Pavia, and Ferrara in 1797–98,[65] and there were plenty of prominent figures in and out of governments who believed themselves capable of drawing up or interpreting constitutions.[66] Prominent throughout the nineteenth century, lawyers maintained the continuity of (and strong insistence on) legalistic procedures, in the process privileging lawyers and the urban professional class.[67]

The Italian constitutions of the nineteenth century, including those of 1848, can of course be seen as the effort of a social class to legitimate its claim to represent all the people. Democrats were rarely allowed the constituent assembly they believed essential. In 1848 only Sicily and the Roman republic enjoyed that luxury; and the Piedmontese parliament, in its reply to the first speech from the throne under the new constitution, joined the leaders of Milan, Tuscany, and Rome in calling for a constituent assembly. But it was not held then nor in 1859–61 when the demand again arose.[68] Italy's imitative constitutional arrangements[69] lacked any formal popular basis, a fact that, more than any missing revolution, haunted the politics of united Italy. Figures like Stefano Jacini and Sidney Sonnino would continue until the end of the century to seek a way by means of constitutional adjustments to connect governing institutions to the society they were supposed to rule without risking a transfer of power to peasants.[70] Moreover, most of Italy's constitutions were in themselves somewhat incomplete, statements of general principles combined with some specific instructions as to how government could function. They left much else that mattered to be worked out in practice, content merely to provide a sketch of a modern state.[71] A kind of unstated compromise, these constitutions were acceptable because of widespread confidence that the mere existence of constitutional practice would unleash a political and social process from which all other changes would follow.[72] Most of these constitutions, after all, were drafted in emergencies, under the threat of war or in the presence of foreign armies; but their authors also needed to avoid making enemies and to achieve majorities by leaving a good deal unsaid.

The general principles were nevertheless admirable. The Neapolitan constitution of 1798 was unusually philosophical in declaring that "every man has the right . . . to better himself" and "to exercise all his moral and physical faculties,"[73] and the more democratic constitutions revealed their high aspirations. The Sicilian constitution of 1848 found that "Sovereignty resides in the university of Sicilian citizens";[74] and the Roman republic proclaimed that its institutions would "promote the improvement of the moral and material conditions of all citizens."[75] Although not especially venturesome, most of Italy's constitutions guaranteed that power would not be exercised arbitrarily, established that there were public rights to be recognized, and declared certain obligations and restrictions essential for civil life. Respectful of property and favorable to Catholicism while allowing freedom of worship, these constitutions declared political liberty a desirable and achievable goal (and the adoption of a constitution in itself essential to liberty). The similarity in these formal statements suggests a kind of consensus on the expectations and general norms of freedom.[76]

For Croce, "the concept of constitutional liberty" became truly Italian when it was no longer merely a protective, defensive device but a sign of and the means to achieve "the highest moral conscience and national independence and grandeur."[77] It would be hard to say just when that occurred, but throughout the nineteenth century bitter experience made the broader and moral meaning of constitutions more important than their specific provisions. Such idealism intertwined with a practical realism that fostered skepticism and left indeterminate which elements of established authority would be undermined or what interests might dominate constitutional practice. Those disappointed by the outcome would have further reason for imagining a more satisfactory revolution.

With similar realism, the admiring discourse about constitutions and constitutional law acknowledged the limited capacity of written constitutions to resist external force or internal disorder. As early as 1821 an Italian in exile in Paris published a book with a subtitle that described this central dilemma of the Risorgimento: "The Need in Italy to Accommodate Power with Liberty."[78] Power lay outside Italy; and although there were multiple models of constitutions to choose from, each had shown how little the printed page could really guarantee. Well aware of the differences in the French constitutions of 1791, 1793, and 1795,[79] Italians did not probe their subtleties; and Italian Jacobins would never really recapture the enthusiasm with which they had greeted the constitutions of 1798–99. The subversion of political liberty under Napoleonic rule had emptied the Imperial constitutions of lasting appeal, while the Sicilian constitution of 1812, with its awkward imitation of Britain's unwritten constitution, had few claims as a model for the future. More promising, the lengthy and very democratic Spanish constitution of 1812 remained untested; and its light-hearted adoption in Naples and Piedmont in 1821 resulted more from the desire for some constitution than a commitment to this one,[80] offered in haste "as a symbol of hope and faith."[81]

As those experiments were swept away and visions of a federation under papal leadership faded, essentially two models remained: the cautious French constitution of 1814 (which was both tactically and practically attractive) and that of some kind of republic, which most democrats continued to favor (if given a stronger executive than in the Spanish example). Experience had made it increasingly difficult, however, to believe that either could transform society. Mazzini spent his life envisioning a different and better kind of society, but he had little interest in writing constitutions. Even the constitution of the Roman republic in 1849, which specified very clearly the sanctity of property and individual rights, was rather vague about most other procedures. Believing in a society of harmony and brotherhood, Mazzini gave little thought to techniques for resolving conflicts. For democrats, a constitution meant establishment of a new order. For moderates, a constitution's first obligation was simply to assure stability. That and responsiveness to public opinion mattered more than the breadth of suffrage or which officials were directly elected. Italy's elites had more reasons than most to know that the effect of laws, and even constitutions, could be changed without formal amendment.

Reformers nevertheless knew the practical importance of administrative procedures, and the way elections were conducted. Many a figure of the Risorgimento would have agreed with Gramsci that constitutions lead to laws and laws to regulations and that a nation's real juridical and political structure is revealed in its regulations.[82] Constitutions in this experienced, practical sense were important primarily for establishing the principle of representative government and the machinery of responsible rule. Form mattered less. The influential philosopher and priest Antonio Rosmini published his elaborate treatise on a constitution for Italy with the reassuring claim that, because the laws "on which civil society" is based remain the same, his constitutional project could be made suitable to a monarchy or a republic by changing the name of the office at the top.[83]

Experience had taught that constitutions thrived on local ties more than logical structure, and conservative intellectuals were keenly aware of all that had not been accomplished by cameralism, Leopoldine reform, Jacobinism, Napoleonic institutions, and consultative assemblies. Conservativism's influence on Italian constitutional history lay in the rejection of excessive optimism. Cautious figures, like G. D. Romagnosi, Cesare Balbo, or Pellegrino Rossi, therefore favored constitutions that did not specify too much. From the beginning, Italian constitutions were notably discreet. The Bolognese constitution of 1796 recognized corporations or guilds without quite indicating what that meant. Nearly all provided for religious liberty, but none meddled in the organization of the Church nor attacked Church property. While property was protected, issues of greater social equality or welfare were generally avoided. Style as much as specific provisions revealed underlying political attitudes. Guarded and convoluted language was a sign of monarchical ambivalence, directness the mark of optimism and confidence, as in the Roman constitution of 1849.

If the constitutions written in Italy expressed a general commitment to civil liberty[84] and indicated, through telling silence, a readiness for tolerance and compromise, they nevertheless tended to be surprisingly detailed in two respects: their often hasty blueprints of how to make a government function and their affectionate description of political community. Many of these constitutions listed cabinet and subordinate offices, giving them quaint and evocative names, specifying the duties of each official, working out their lines of communication, and fixing the size of committees and the frequency of their meetings. This sort of detail, responding to the needs of the moment, lessened the quality of constitutions as magisterial and permanent guides. Deviations from these prescriptions would soon become so sensible that objections on the grounds of constitutionality would inevitably seem trivial.

When this founding attention to administrative detail was not part of the constitution, the alternative was to organize the state by decree. The penal and civil codes of united Italy were issued by decree; and those decrees, an electoral law, and provisions for the administration of public instruction, charity, public health, public works, and the judiciary were all determined in just over two months[85]—a pale and distant echo of the constituent assembly once so widely anticipated. The historical prominence of bureaucracy in Italy, in addition to its historic roots, was thus written into the handling of constitutional matters.[86]

At this time, a Rousseauian concern for political community showed forth in the wonderfully detailed prescriptions for electoral rites. The precise definition of electoral districts, included in many constitutions throughout the century, instructed citizens about their new role by assuring them that each neighborhood had its place on the larger electoral map, a concrete manifestation of the general principles constitutions presented.[87] The Bologna republic of 1796 specified that the secretary and three assistants of each parish's electoral committee ought to know how to read and write but thoughtfully waived the requirement for everyone but the secretary in parishes where too few men were literate.[88] The Genoese constitution described how illiterate voters could name their choice orally.[89] The 1820 constitution of the Two Sicilies called for a mass of the Holy Spirit in parish churches before the voting and a Te Deum afterward. The Tuscan constitution of 1848, in addition to the detailed identification of each electoral district, devoted 50 articles to the electoral assemblies in which voting would take place, describing the way to identify voters, the manner of electing presiding officers, the hour at which voting for representatives should then take place. Illiterates, the constitution explained, could ask a trusted friend to write their ballot, and it specified an elaborate system for having the ballots pass through several hands as they were opened and counted in public, giving presiding officers the responsibility to prevent disorder, and forbidding voters from carrying firearms.[90]

Electoral turnout was often very high,[91] for voting was more important as a social rite than for decision making. As such it could be adapted by a variety of regimes. In its later years, Napoleonic rule tried representation by occupational groups as a way to have participation without disagreement (an experiment that deserves more analysis than it has received). While hardly a careful inquiry into what citizens really wanted, the plebescites of 1859 and 1860 were more than a legalistic façade and a means for silencing Napoleon III, whose own regime rested on plebescites. Their ceremonial quality was their principal point, the mechanism by which they conveyed legitimacy. The electoral campaigns that followed were conducted almost as if the suffrage had not been drastically restricted, with election manifestoes and the voting itself a civic ritual more prominent than questions of who was permitted to vote or how candidates had been selected.

Constitutions, in short, were educational devices, establishing the practices of freedom, describing how government could quickly be made to work, and teaching a people about the civic sphere.[92] The famous competition in 1796 for the best essay on "What form of Free Government Best Accords with the Happiness of Italy" was part of a project for public instruction,[93] and the constitutions of 1796–99 were published in large editions and accompanied by a propaganda campaign that included republican catechisms, pamphlets of dialogues and maxims, and the formation of constitutional clubs that included women and young people.[94] On a reduced scale, similar publicity and public discussion accompanied most nineteenth-century constitutions. The losers in the history of the Risorgimento were those who opposed any constitution at all, and they did not make much of a public case. If the excited optimism about constitutions at the beginning of the century gradually subsided, the idea that a constitution was essential to a decent society was so broadly shared that the inability of the restoration regimes to accommodate that

belief was a principal source of their weakness. National unification brought arguments about whether the Piedmontese constitution should be kept, amended, or replaced with the work of a constituent assembly; but no one doubted that a formal, written constitution was essential.

Paradoxically, these all but universal constitutional convictions
were accompanied by explicit skepticism, sustained by long experience, as to how much of social or political life constitutional provisions could affect. Indeed, confidence that a constitution could make
all the difference was probably more widespread when constitutions
were understood to be a product of revolution than after they were
considered to be a pillar of order. In practice the Piedmontese constitution was generally honored in united Italy's slow evolution toward democratic suffrage, but Italian political experience taught that
institutions, interests, and patronage did more than constitutions
could to determine how power was exercised. The sense that communal education was part of a constitution's very purpose, once an
expression of revolutionary optimism, was sustained by a pessimis-
tic recognition that constitutional provisions in themselves could
make only a limited difference.

≺ III ≻

Civic Life

Italian thought in the nineteenth century was permeated with the
principle of nationality.[95] Indeed the fortuitous confusion of language
between a free nation and freedom from authoritarian and foreign
rule lessened the need for deeper explorations of the meaning of freedom (although the rhetoric denouncing vile servitude and oppression, inciting Italians to break their chains, was a powerful, general
indoctrination). The devotion to freedom was sincere and central;[96]
no one imagined nationhood without constitutional guarantees of
liberty, and there was almost universal agreement as to the minimum list of freedoms to be provided. With that much settled, all
sides agreed that the nation required more.

Mazzini, and many other Italian nationalists, insisted that the nation existed most fundamentally not in territory or language but in
consciousness. It was created by history and education but explicitly

not by race or soil, and its locus was civic life. Thus the nation was in the piazza, in the cafes and among the people passing by; in the arguments and more formal harangues, the monuments and ceremonies that attached the past to the issues of the moment, the figures currently in power to local public life.[97] The nature of civic culture is an especially important theme in Italy's intellectual history from humanism to Norberto Bobbio, not merely as an abstraction but as a way of describing how society functions.[98]

Writing in 1796, Carlo Botta had declared that a good constitution fostered a society in which rich and poor mixed in balls, theaters, and festivals;[99] but Italian commentators more often agreed that creating an Italian civic life was a more formidable challenge. Leopardi complained that Italians had no sense of society, and the charge would be often repeated.[100] One hundred fifty years later, an Italian looking back would explain that "Italy's liberal institutions . . . had to function in a generally conservative country of uncomplying individualists in whom illiteracy, poverty, and submission had effaced any capacity for consistent cooperation in public life."[101] The problem was how to go about creating a civic sense. If Cavourian liberals stopped short of Mazzinian emphasis on national mission, most leading Italians were remarkably close to Mazzini's assumption that a nation implied a shared civic culture; and the ambiguity of language—in which the word *comune* evokes communes, communal, common, and shared—was invaluable when Mazzini wrote that a nation means a thought, law, end, and principle that are *comune*.[102] As Italians understood it, civic life was first of all urban; and its quality would depend on *"civiltà,"*[103] civil development, civilization, progress— terms repeated in those preambles to the constitutions of 1848.

Italy offered impressive foundations on which to build. When Italians wrote a constitution or met to deliberate, there were always handsome spaces in which to meet, places redolent with history, power, authority, propriety, and high culture. Their rhetoric echoed not in some tennis court but from the palaces, town halls, theaters, and court chambers that were monuments to the civic pride of medieval communes, Renaissance universality, baroque authority, and enlightenment rationality. Sensitive to that, Michelet found in Italy "the only people who had a civil architecture in diverse epochs where other nations knew only religious architecture" and confidently defined the locus of Italian "genius": "It is not at all the natural world of the family, of the tribe, it is the artificial world of the city."[104] Freedom and civic virtue always had available a legitimating past open to many interpretations. Civic ceremonies in public spaces were important events in which familiar faces expressed community and familiar rites connected the local and immediate to the national and historical.[105] If they encouraged patriotism, and they surely did, they also stimulated irony, for the grandeur of handsome façades and historic piazzas inevitably contrasted with the disorder of civic reality. Piazzas themselves remained ambiguous spaces, stages for unpredictable events where the lines were rarely sharp between contained ritual and collective action and where observers, participants, and plotters were not easy to tell apart.[106]

Those constitutional descriptions of *comizi elettorali* offered a picture of civic life as mutual instruction, beginning with local participation. Connected to the constitution and contained by ritual, these electoral meetings of neighbors would be a lesson in civics.[107] Civic life should also reflect a community built on shared values and a common confidence in the future. Thus the secret societies, the Carbonari and their successors, which protected themselves from the police with oaths of silence and rituals of loyalty, represented the revolutionary ideal of what the public sphere should become. Men passionately loyal to a great cause and to each other would form associations, and they in turn would link with each other until they encompassed the entire nation. The sense of networks extending beyond the horizon, fundamental to the democratic secret societies,[108] fed the expectation that civic life should be harmonious. When Gramsci wrote about the distinction between the Church as a "community of the faithful" (with, he said, a democratic function) and the Church as a clerical organization, he was immediately led to think about the distinction between the state and civil society, as a shared belief.[109]

The unification of Italy had been made to seem a civic activity,[110] and there was a great flowering of civic life just before and after unification. Often stimulated by competition between moderates and democrats, all sorts of activities were involved, from founding newspapers and new kinds of organizations (such as the Liberi Comizi, the Nazione Armata, and the Società Nazionale Italiana) to circulating petitions, organizing demonstrations, raising money, gathering volunteers to fight with Piedmont and Garibaldi, preparing for plebiscites, and campaigning in elections. After unification, a vigorous associational life combined civic education with assertion of elite leadership, but national civic life was more bounded than in the great moments of the Risorgimento. The shift of power to a national center and a narrow suffrage sapped the energy from those gatherings, parades, and demonstrations that had allowed some part for everyone.

In the north some associations made serious efforts to reach into the countryside, but in Italy civic life was understood to be urban, an important limitation which reflected the importance of Italy's small towns as well as its cities. Peasants often lived in towns and walked to their fields; and, north and south, they filled tiny piazzas on market days and festivals. In that sense they were observers and occasionally participants in civic life, but they had little connection to its institutions. Landowners often lived in towns and were frequently prominent in civic life; but the forms, regulations, and negotiated interests operative there only sporadically and indirectly extended into the countryside and to the relations of landlord and tenant or day laborer. Thus in Italy the separation between civic life and countryside was both greater and better marked than in most societies. Peasants saw enough to confirm resentment and distrust but rarely touched the levers of politics.

Although the victorious moderates expected civic life to become calmer and more disciplined, they did not conceive of society as a mere collection of individuals and considered elections less as a mediation among competing interests and personalities than as an opportunity for the public to recognize its natural leaders, choosing from among the local elite those of greatest probity and culture. "Representative government must be a means by which select and honest talents acquire in public affairs the authority due them and not a way for the lazy, the inept, the wicked aspiring to raise themselves" to do so by associating with those naturally above them.[111] That outlook made united Italy's narrow suffrage quite acceptable for those content to let "liberty be fossilized in loyalty to the Statuto."[112] Yet when elections became more democratic, progressives would complain of the lack of culture among the deputies;[113] suffrage remained a problem for all the days of the liberal monarchy[114] despite a long tradition of setting all sorts of specific standards for good citizenship (the Sicilian constitution of 1812 had banned men whose children were not vaccinated from running for office). The self-interest of the historic right in denouncing partisanship was apparent to all, but it spoke for most of the nation in its denunciations of factions and parties.[115] A generation would pass after unification before parties would be reluctantly accepted as legitimate ways of organizing the civic sphere.[116] In the meantime, a narrow electorate sustained an often isolated elite. The practice of *trasformismo*—by which from 1876 to World War I majorities were built by relying on the deputies' selfish and local interests to overcome more principled differences—had been admired as patriotic compromise before it was recognized as institutional corruption.[117] The democrats of the Risorgimento were the ones who acknowledged being professional politicians, although they reached a broader public as journalists than as parliamentary representatives.[118]

The changing participation of women was another important sign of the narrowing of civic life. Surprisingly, there has been little study of the role of women or concepts of gender in the process of national unification, although the passionately committed *donne* of the Risorgimento became a fixture of patriotic lore.[119] Mazzini was explicit:

Half the human family, that half from which we seek inspiration and comfort and to which we confide our children, is by a curious inconsistency held to be inferior from the civil, political, and social point of view, and is excluded from the unity of the human family.[120]

Much of his voluminous correspondence was addressed to women and, like his strong ties to English and American activists such as Jessie White Mario and Margaret Fuller, deserves a new look. Some aristocratic ladies were in fact political leaders, like Princess Belgioioso and Marchesa Pallavicino. Hundreds of women wrapped bandages, sewed banners, and joined various women's auxiliaries, transforming established middle-class activities into public roles. Anita Garibaldi symbolized the female revolutionary, and her death from a bullet wound was quickly made into one of the romantic moments of the Risorgimento, a favorite topic of prints. The exotic heroism of the South American woman on horseback, her martyrdom, and the sentimental portrayal of the loyal helpmate were powerful symbols; and the feminist movement of the 1880s would build on these memories.[121] But the increased formal participation of women outside piazza and salon that might have followed from the Risorgimento, on the whole did not.

The narrow electorate, the exclusion of women, and the absence of parties did not destroy civic life, but its most vital, local core was left only loosely connected to the state, a fundamental weakness that showed most clearly in the south. The differences in civic life of north and south were as great as the differences in their economies. Participation in the public sphere was more open to new groups in the north, more dominated by traditional elites in the south. In the north elites strengthened their positions by participating simultaneously in local associated life and in national politics, a linkage however indirect. There, the new state relied on national officials with strong connections to local elites, although strains soon developed and social change gradually undermined the position of some local notables. Southern elites, who owed their position to landed wealth, a system of clientage, and family position, instead negotiated with the state, meeting some of its immediate needs by relying on their clients but limiting the state's influence on local affairs while maintaining their own dominance. Adding one more layer to an old system, political bossism further integrated corruption as an essential lubricant of national politics.[122]

To nationalists who had imagined in detail the practices of a vital civic life, the weakness of the state looked like the failure of national will that they had long feared. In 1848 Romagnosi had warned that, "The I, the family, and one's own *paese* are three levels of human affection in society. The fatherland, in the sense of a nation, is a term that evokes a phantasm that scarcely touches the imagination."[123] It was thus easy to see communal vitality as a fatal flaw rather than a potential strength (and an argument against a federal system).[124] Even under a centralized state, where prefects were often symbols of the power the government meant to have but did not,[125] towns remained the vital centers of social and political life; but the uncertain linkages with national politics weakened both. It was, after all, easier (north and south) to ignore the state than to influence it.

Italian intellectuals and professionals continued to imagine a national society that would be an enlargement of their little civic worlds in which the members of the elite all knew each other through their clubs and public activities. As they found themselves instead only indeterminately connected to local economic or national political power, they relied on official titles and ceremonies that invoked the status system (and pomp) of the old regime to display their importance. The respect for authority and legitimacy that many saw as characteristic of Italy was also a substitute for the more direct participation that might have generated more focused civic spirit and spurred demands for social justice.[126] The political elites' ties to the landed aristocracy, stronger in Piedmont, Tuscany, and the Romagna, were spottier, still more personal and less dependable, elsewhere. The well-to-do could·vote, but the practicing Catholics among them were instructed not to take part in national elections;[127] yet the Church, with the strongest national network and largely hostile to the new political order, remained a central part of civic life. Elections and elected deputies were thus constricted conduits of political values. Associational life, for all its vigor, was more local than national, its relationship to national policy indirect, likely to represent local factions more effectively than a broad civic coalition and only indirectly engaged with national policy. Entrepreneurs, patriotic associations, and at times even workers' movements could make themselves felt in Rome but more as pressure groups than institutionally legitimate participants in public life.

In practice, society functioned by a heavy reliance on proceduralism in parliamentary debates, administration, and law courts. This emphasis on legal forms came easily to a political world dominated by lawyers and elites formed in Italian universities, an earnest cloak for a lasting insecurity about the legitimacy of the political system.[128] The social tendency was to assume mutual distrust and to rely on elaborate procedures to contain its effects. While recognizing the state, Italy's leaders viewed the law and legal tradition as anterior and more fundamental.[129] Bureaucratic viscosity served as social cement.

The proper relationship between society and state remained unresolved. That complex issue[130] proved especially troubling in a state where civic life was older than the nation and where one of the goals of politics was, in the name of freedom, to broaden and elevate civic life. When, at the end of the century, Bertrando Spaventa philosophized about an ethical state, he recapitulated themes that had run through nineteenth-century political discourse, a discourse that continued to sustain standards so abstractly admirable they could only make ordinary politics an embarrassment. Catholics and Mazzinians agreed, for all their differences about what education and civic responsibility implied, that the state should take an active part in the formation of a civic sense. For Mazzini, that was at the heart of the difference between a real society and a laissez-faire collection of individuals. Mazzini had believed that

the present problem, the problem that must concern us, is faith in sure principles and beliefs, [in order] to make men better, to unite them, to turn them from the insensate egoism that devours them, [otherwise] all is useless [and] whatever form of government you have, the same inequality and the same wretchedness will recur in a different form.[131]

Despite disagreement as to what those principles were, the leaders of Italy's liberal monarchy tended to concur that a healthy polity required that the state be by precept and in practice a source of instruction in civic duty.

Paradoxically, then, some of the greatest strengths of the public sphere in Italy—multiple forms of participation, a high degree of political consciousness, the practice of toleration and compromise— tended to present themselves and to be interpreted as manifestations of the inadequacy of civic life and of the weakness of Italian institutions, subject to the intrusions of patron and party. Personal freedom in Italian society, one of its significant achievements, was sustained by elaborate social codes; but when these behaviors were extended to official actions, the result was mixed. Individuals and groups enjoyed the liberty of considerable tactical choice in dealing with the state. On the other hand, the inconsistent application of public rules was quickly identified as a characteristic cultural and moral defect. Italians displayed their civic sense most commonly in the concern that corruption was all but universal.

≺ IV ≻

Political Culture

The argument that Italy developed a distinctive political culture cannot ignore the work of a generation of social scientists who characterized that culture as one of suspiciousness, particularism, and parochialism, even though these views have recently been subject to considerable criticism.[132] The distrust in Italian public culture was aimed especially at institutions. The revolutionary demand that public institutions be free of private interests, while widely accepted in Italy, ran counter to experience; and reality produced a kind of revulsion as public institutions across the peninsula were in fact used by private interests—economic, foreign, and familial. There were immediate and historical reasons to distrust those groups with privileged access to political power, but the sense of disquiet was increased by the absence in Italian political culture of clear boundaries between the private and public spheres.[133] Revolutions promised to cleanse these institutions, and constitutions were intended to constrain their behavior, but neither could prevent their succumbing in the future to interests independent of those that were, officially at least, the state's.

Italian culture places a very high value on the importance of social life lived in the piazza, as a place for meeting and endless talk in the shadow of power,[134] and for public display of respectability asserted as *bella figura*. Such customs contributed to the lasting appeal of revolution's promise to make society like a family writ large, where brotherhood would reduce conflict and provide security. In Italian political culture the public sphere was not represented as some neutral arena[135] but as a source of community. The complicated contrast between this ideal and ordinary life reinforced the sense that public life had gone awry and led to accusations that the Catholic church, Freemasons, political parties, or labor unions used their liberty to compete with each other and weaken society.

To many contemporaries (and subsequent social scientists) these divisions expressed dangerous parochial loyalties, understandably strong in a polity struggling for national unification and a society that valued face-to-face relations. If local loyalties seemed to threaten the formation of a national political culture, however, the insistence on consensus was more divisive. The fluorescence of associational life during and after the Risorgimento did link local elites to national politics; and these local organizations flattered the new order by imitating the constitutional and bureaucratic ways of the liberal state.[136] But the ideologies prominent in Italian public culture—Catholicism, French revolutionary Jacobinism, liberalism, and later socialism—all claimed a kind of universality. Italian nationalism itself stressed its place in European civilization from Rome and Christianity, to medieval trade and Renaissance culture. Mazzinian nationalism criticized the French Revolution and Austrian rule for their offenses to international fraternity, not for being French or German.[137] In Italy, devotion to parish or piazza or party was rapidly attached to larger issues and wider spheres; it was these larger aspirations that diminished an uninspiring national government. The localism that for two centuries has so troubled commentators, Italian and foreign, was a measure less of the strength of competing regional cultures than of the weakness of Italian national politics.

The expectation that a vital political culture would produce consensus was reinforced by the strength, despite localism, of a more general national culture. When Italians wrote about their distinctive regional cultures, each with its own characteristics and millennial history, they highlighted local figures who had become internationally recognized, intellectuals whose accomplishments reflected well on the region. The cultural achievements that mattered most had universal meaning, were part of the intellectual formation of all educated Italians, and composed a national high culture. Only the style was regional.[138] Folk traditions and popular culture received relatively scant attention. Compared to much of the rest of Europe, there was little romanticization of peasants as an alternative source of national values, little tendency to find in peasant life an alternative to urban culture or indigenous qualities that defined *Italianità*. Even in Tuscany, where some early nineteenth-century writers expressed admiration for the rhythm of rural life and the social order it embodied, interest was more anthropological than ideological; and the landowners of the *Accademia dei Georgofili* were far more interested in agricultural improvement than peasant culture.[139] However sympathetic they might be, most of Italy's intellectual and political leaders, radical or conservative, did not much admire the peasant world; and even those concerned to close the gap between popular and high culture showed little inclination to build on any *tradizioni volgari*.

If throughout the Risorgimento many writers advocated a literature more open and less arcane, the model was Manzoni, who put ordinary people at the center of his great novel and rewrote his call to the nation in elegant Italian. Ippolito Nievo, a young writer who conspired against Austria in the Veneto, fought with Garibaldi in Sicily, and truly cared about the peasants, believed deeply that literature must have a social purpose; but even for him that lay in the connection between literature and civil life. He cited Dante and Manzoni as examples of writers who knew how to mediate the *popolare* and the *civile*.[140] Although there were Italian intellectuals who had peasant origins, there were not peasant intellectuals.[141] When Gramsci objected to the culture's habit of giving the cultivated classes sole credit for making the Risorgimento, he did so principally on the grounds that Italy's elites deserved no special praise because it was their historic role to lead. Conservative members of these *classi colte* would have agreed.[142] Gramsci's very concept of cultural hegemony was a reflection of Italian experience;[143] good democrat though he was, Gramsci saw combatting folklore as one of the necessary purposes of schooling.[144]

The sense of the nation, of liberty, and of political culture remained closely connected to these traditions of high culture. Nineteenth-century reformers of every sort insisted on the importance of education as essential to civic life. Articles which filled journals like Vieusseux's *Antologia* or Cattaneo's *Politecnico* with discussions of educational systems praised the economic and personal benefits that education would bring but cared above all about the good citizens that civic education would create. The assumption that a whole nation would come to share a common political culture, just as the educated all knew Dante, shines through the nationalist writings, revolutionary programs, constitutions, newspapers, and speeches of the nineteenth century. Through public ceremonies in public spaces, piazzas and theaters, the people were to be educated to a sense of communal purpose—an explicit goal in the Neapolitan constitution of 1799, which wanted theaters, national festivals, and public schools to provide civic training.[145]

The consensus that did emerge about the liberties that good government must guarantee was as cultural as it was political, although constructed from revolutionary rhetoric and more circumspectly repeated in the solemnity of constitutions. Failure to achieve these freedoms universally or to hold them inviolate prompted analysis of Italy's moral and historical inadequacies. After representative government, equality before the law was perhaps the principle most universally cited, used to argue both for greater social equality and for the protection of property (and therefore inequality). Milan's municipal council in 1848 specified universal (male) suffrage, a free press, a constituent assembly, and a national guard as essential before it turned to a rather legalistic discussion of the terms for union with Piedmont.[146] Most revolutions and most constitutions paid homage to a free press and free speech, although with a certain guardedness. Presented as universally desirable, they were usually not treated as absolute rights; and there were often some qualifications, especially with regard to religion. Liberty was understood to require the right of association, sometimes with specified restrictions. Rarely was there much effort to determine in advance the degree to which the right of association would or would not constrain a government's power to act against conspiracies, subversion, political organization, labor organization, or simple agitation. Still, it was widely understood that freedom had practical and immediate meanings, including the abolition of feudal obligations, the inviolability of the home, and the legitimacy of multiple public voices.

The centrality of law in this picture of liberty deserves emphasis. The effect was socially conservative. An independent judiciary was a universal goal intended to prevent arbitrary exercise of state power; but this was also associated with a civil police force, a standard reform demanded in the name of liberty, which reflected the preoccupation with order.[147] The emphasis on due process was a lawyerly one that rested not so much on individual rights as on a proceduralism in which law protected liberty indirectly by maintaining continuity and therefore predictability. The judicial process was understood less as an arena of contestation than as the application of generally prescribed rules. Liberty lay in the assurance that the law would be equally—but also wisely—applied, honoring principle but effecting compromise. Even while insisting that the health of society depended on the traditions of a moral culture rather than particular political forms, wise and cultivated men like Luigi Luzzatti (activist, reformer, professor, and founder of associations) relied on strong institutions as well as civic virtue. Liberty, he proclaimed, does not grab center stage but is outshown by the light of the works it accomplishes, not the "ostentation of external display" or grand speeches but the "strong organization of effective institutions."[148]

Political liberty so conceived is consonant with liberalism but not inherently liberal. The liberal concept of a neutral state, for example, was never wholly embraced by Catholics, monarchists, or progressives, although espoused by Cavour. If united Italy seemed a triumph of liberalism, that was only partly a reflection of the constitutional procedures and economic policies associated with Piedmont and very much an effect of the pressure of events, which eliminated alternatives. Political discussion in Italy in the years between 1850 and 1870—although often heated and complexly divided over issues of state making, social reform, and international relations—was fortuitously narrowed by the dominance of nationalist goals and the events of 1848–49. The rhetoric of freedom could be used by those concerned primarily with removing foreign rule and eliminating disorder. The range of serious political debate fell for the most part between conservatives loyal to representative government and radicals whose memories of peasant politics encouraged ambivalence about untrammeled democracy and explicit doubts about universal suffrage.[149] Constricted in this way, political discussion necessarily fell within the liberal spectrum, but that was less a victory for liberal theory than the result of excluding peasants and artisans, Catholics, reactionaries, and early socialists. These groups (plus landowners but rarely peasants) were active instead at the local, civic level where the associational and political life of towns enjoyed a variety and vitality national politics lacked. The demand for liberty was separated from the issue of democracy not simply because the liberals were not democrats but because Mazzinians did not see liberty as a goal separable from social issues and Catholics were uncomfortable discussing either.

Catholics and Freemasons, conservatives and radicals, elitists and egalitarians, landowners and labor leaders, southerners and northerners—like newspapers and intellectuals of every stripe—expected to flourish and to make themselves heard in Italian public life. Yet toleration, which to many seemed mere skepticism,[150] won rather weak institutional and ideological commitment, leaving each faction likely to feel unprotected and inclined to attribute its freedom not so much to a liberal state and a tolerant society as to its own institutional strength and political skill. Italy had developed a tolerant political culture in which the limited theoretical admiration for tolerance left participants merely "resigned to compromises."[151]

The famous criticisms of Italian national life presented themselves as external, courageously outspoken, and unusual but were, whatever their merits, intrinsic to Italian political culture. On the eve of Fascism, Piètro Gobetti, who wrote so influentially about Italy's missing revolution, lamented that since the Risorgimento Italy had not known how to create "the great myths around which the thought of a nation is organized over the course of history"; and he noted the harm done by tendentious memories of an idealistic but impractical Mazzini and a cynical but effective Cavour.[152] The criti-

cism (and the expectation that independent thinkers would agree
with it) was as characteristic of Italian culture as the conditions criticized, and it was one-sided, for it was at least equally true that the
myths were too great. This insistence that national life was tragi-
cally flawed sapped cautious reforms and modest accomplishments
of their power to dignify politics or win public allegiance. It invited
instead more utopian calls for some fundamental transformation;
and intellectuals, politicians, and academics (then and since) promulgated competing definitions of what was first required: civic virtue, greater democracy, land reform, the unmitigated rule of law,
national pride, or modernization. Although for each of the disabilities attributed to Italy, one could point to other European nations
in which injustice, stratification, regionalism, systemic political ineptitude, economic stagnation, or even corruption was as grave or
graver, Italian political culture understood such failings as distinctive and endemic.

Similarly, pride in the extensive social, economic, and political
changes taking place during the nineteenth century was lessened by
the tendency of Italy's high culture to assess the contemporary world
in terms of ancient Rome, Dante, Machiavelli, and Manzoni. That
made change less threatening and legitimated traditional (hegemonic)
culture, but it also left Italy's political culture singularly vulnerable to
the complaint from tired conservatives and frustrated radicals alike
that nothing ever really changed. In a political culture that admired
unity (cultural and national), a vigorous public life looked like failure.

A political culture does not cause social problems or conflicts,
but it does shape the way they are understood and dealt with; and
these paradoxes of the public sphere do not define some Italian national character. They are not valid for all time, and they are not a
necessary or logical outcome of thought or political practice. They
represent, rather, a pattern woven from the experiences of the century that began in 1799. Through repetition some elements of that
pattern were so effectively built upon that they became intrinsic to
political culture. Risorgimento nationalism sought a lively public
sphere in a liberal and revolutionary tradition, but power often lay
elsewhere, behind institutional facades, beneath organized interests,
buried in family status. The pressure on Italian affairs from Austria,
France, international alliances, or the Vatican was not much affected

by activity in the public sphere, except in moments of crisis. With unification, limited suffrage added a further public marker of social stratification, and the political system reinforced clientelism more than participation. Thus a civic life, which in its very vitality continued to reflect fissures in social structure and to disseminate conflicting ideas, contributed to a political culture that sustained stability but tested institutional weakness and made chaos seem imminent, adapted to change while regretting stasis, and expressed a sense of community—ideological and geographic—through division and conflict, thereby advertising the continuing contrast between promise and reality.

The German States and the
European Revolution

JAMES J. SHEEHAN

HISTORIANS EMPLOY THE TERM *revolution* in two quite different ways: first, to refer to a particular set of events that effects sudden, violent changes in the political and social system; second, to describe long-term processes that produce structural changes in politics, society, or culture.[1] The classic theorists of revolution have usually assumed that there is a significant connection between these two sorts of revolution, that radical, episodic changes express, advance, and accelerate deeply-rooted changes in structure. The most intellectually powerful and historically significant statement of this view is, of course, by Karl Marx, whose theory of history was based on a belief in slow, inexorable social transformations that eventually produce violent transfers of political power from one ruling class to the next. Great revolutions were rare, Marx maintained, but they were necessary transitions from one historical era to another. Although only a minority of historians accept the details of Marx's historical vision, many more share his conviction that revolutionary events are the necessary confirmation of revolutionary processes. In some ways, this volume rests upon this assumption.

Perhaps it is worthwhile to register some modest skepticism about the proposition that revolutionary processes must be confirmed by revolutionary episodes. In the first place, it is worth noting that this alleged connection between the two meanings of revolution is usually based—either explicitly or implicitly—on the French example, or rather on a particular interpretation of the French example. But even if the great revolution of 1789 has the place in the development of modern France to which generations of historians have assigned it, there is no reason to take French developments as the norm. Although, as many of the chapters in this book make clear, the French revolutionary tradition had great historical influence in Europe and beyond, it was replicated nowhere else. It certainly does not represent the normal path of historical change from which all deviations are in some sense pathological. When we look carefully at revolutionary episodes throughout Europe and America we find them to be extraordinarily diverse. The eighteenth century revolutions in France and America, for instance, certainly have some interesting similarities, but neither their origins nor their outcomes suggest that they are necessarily part of the same historical processes. Indeed there are good reasons to doubt that the events in America were a revolution at all. Second, in any particular revolutionary episode, the precise relationship between events and process often turns out to be extremely difficult to establish. This is not to say that revolutions are accidents, events without long-term causes and connections; obviously, revolutions, like all historical phenomena, are shaped and limited by the historical world around them. But revolutions, perhaps more than most phenomena, are also shaped by the contingent conjunction of particular personalities, chance encounters, and unpredictable events. This is why they always turn out differently than their friends and enemies expect.

These reflections seem particularly fitting at the beginning of the chapter devoted to Germany in a book on revolutions. Germany, after all, is usually considered a land without revolution: Hans-Ulrich Wehler, for example, opens his magisterial *Deutsche Gesellschaftsgeschichte* with the lapidary remark, "In the beginning, there was no revolution," thereby calling our attention to an absence that is powerfully present in recent German historiography.[2] Because Germany lacked a successful revolution, historians have often argued, it followed a different historical path from that of western Europe. Because there was no German equivalent to 1688, 1776, or 1789—because no German monarch mounted a scaffold for violating the constitution and no German parliament ever successfully established itself as the source of national sovereignty—Germany never developed powerful participatory institutions. Instead German history is haunted by the specter of failed revolutions—of 1848–49, when the opposition failed to create a liberal nation state; and of 1918–19, when workers failed to establish a socialist republic. In German historiography, the same kind of teleological vision that makes the French revolution of 1789 or the Russian revolution of

1917 seem inevitable, makes the absence or failure of revolution seem like the source of unavoidable catastrophe.

In Germany, the forces for change appear to come either from above—from forceful leaders like Frederick II, Bismarck, or Hitler— or from outside—from conquerors like the French in 1806, the Entente powers in 1918, or the allies in 1945. As Ralf Dahrendorf argued in one of the most influential expressions of this point of view, Germany was a "faulted nation," in which traditional institutions and values persisted. Although anything but a Marxist, Dahrendorf shared Marx's belief that authentic historical change had to have a revolutionary component. Therefore, only when the destructive combination of National Socialism, World War 2, and the postwar occupation provided a belated, surrogate revolution was the historical debris of the old regime finally cleared away and the potential for a liberal society created.[3]

There is an important kernel of truth in these views of the German past: unlike England, the United States, and France, a popular revolution does not seem to be the source of modern Germany's political development. But in trying to understand the role of revolution and the meaning of freedom in the German states, it would be a mistake to see only absence and failure. Germany may have lacked a single episode of apparent revolutionary success, but the German states surely participated in those great revolutionary processes that began to transform European politics and society in the second half of the eighteenth century. And as in the rest of Europe, the impact of these changes on the German scene was determined by historical preconditions and particular events. In this respect, it is by no means clear that Germany belongs in a class by itself, more unlike France or England or the United States than any one of these nations was unlike the others. Looked at in terms of their individual histories, each nation has followed its own path to the modern world, just as each was part of larger historical movements.[4]

It is also a mistake to underestimate the participatory forces at work in German history. To be sure, German opposition movements were never victorious and no doubt were always weakened by the lack of a revolutionary legacy and its energizing myths. But Germans were neither the inert objects of revolutions from above nor the passive victims of outside intervention. In the public sphere of discussion and debate, in representative institutions, and in direct confrontations with their governments, Germans sought to express their views, defend their interests, assume responsibility for their futures. They attempted, in other words, to make their own history. But, in Marx's famous phrase, while people make their own history, "they do not make it under circumstances chosen by themselves, but under circumstances directly found, given and transmitted from the past.[5]" Germans' attempts to make history and the circumstances that shaped and limited these attempts are the subjects of this chapter.

≺ I ≻

The Old Regime and the German Revolution

When Alexis de Tocqueville called Frederick the Great "a precursor, one might almost say a promoter of Revolution," he obviously had in mind not the great events of 1789 but the deeply-rooted historical process of which these events seemed to be no more than a dramatic episode. In this larger revolutionary process, the Prussian king and the Parisian regicides were unwillingly allied, the Prussian Legal Code and the Declaration of the Rights of Man improbably alike. Despite their differences in motives and intentions, Tocqueville believed, the autocratic revolution from above and the popular revolution from below both represented "a vast highly centralized power which attracted to itself and wielded into an organic whole all the elements of authority and influence that hitherto had been dispersed among a crowd of lesser, uncoordinated powers." Both kinds of revolution grew within the body of the Old Regime, were nourished by its endemic weaknesses, and eventually led to its demise.[6]

Tocqueville was surely correct to emphasize the tension between autocratic leaders like Frederick and the "lesser, uncoordinated" institutions of traditional Europe. In Frederick's Prussia, the struggle between the ruler and these institutions had been going on since the seventeenth century, when the Hohenzollern began to demand the right to raise money in order to pay for the expensive business of being a prince—maintaining a standing army, building palaces, supporting a court. From these fiscal demands developed the early structures of the Prussian state: administrators, tax collectors, and judicial officials, who were, in theory at least, the obedient servants of the

Crown. Originally recruited from the traditional aristocracy and from the ranks of university-trained commoners, these officials gradually developed a sense of corporate self-interest and identity. By the last decades of the eighteenth century, Prussian bureaucrats had been able to create a network of rules that they could use to defend their political authority and institutional autonomy. From "royal servants" they had become "servants of the state," the personification of the state's higher interests, which they claimed to represent not only in opposition to their old rivals in the nobility, but also against the arbitrary power of the monarch himself.[7]

As Tocqueville recognized and as generations of German historians have affirmed, the development of bureaucratic institutions in Prussia and in other German states had profound consequences for the nature of political life. Perhaps we can best summarize these consequences by looking at the changing meaning of two key concepts, *Bürger* and *Freiheit*, the German words for citizen and freedom. In the old regime, a *Bürger* was the resident of a city who possessed a set of rights and responsibilities—to participate in municipal affairs, to own certain kinds of property, and to conduct some kinds of business—which set him apart from outsiders, as well as from the less powerful and privileged inhabitants of the city itself. In other words, the value of *Bürgerschaft* in no small measure depended on the fact that it was possessed by some people and not by others. The same thing was true of freedom in traditional society: *Freiheiten* belonged to certain groups and conveyed particular rights and privileges—to carry on a trade, to work a body of land, to share a common pasture, or to gather wood or hunt in a forest. Once again, the value of these freedoms depended on their particularity; they were of no use if everyone had them.

In the political and legal vocabulary of the bureaucratic states, these keywords gradually took on new meanings. *Citizen*, which some Germans now began to refer to as a *Staatsbürger*, came to mean not only a member of a restricted social group, but also someone who was directly under the control and protection of the state, subject to the state's laws, responsible for its financial support, liable for service in its armies, obliged to attend its schools. Similarly, *freedom*, which began to be used in the singular rather than plural form, now came to mean not only special privileges but also universal rights—the freedom to settle anywhere one wished, to marry when and whomever one wanted, to run a business, and to buy and sell land. In sum, these new ideas of citizenship and freedom challenged the special categories and particular privileges that provided the foundation of the traditional social order; in their place, they held out the promise of a single, integrated political community of which everyone would be an equal member, subject to the same laws, serving the same state, governed by the same corps of officials.[8]

It was, of course, much easier to change the language of legal codes and administrative documents than the everyday realities of German social and political life. We should not, therefore, judge the impact of bureaucratic institutions on the basis of their own aspirations and declared intentions. Until well into the nineteenth century, these new concepts of citizenship and freedom had little meaning for most Germans, especially those still caught in some form of dependent relationship on the land. Tocqueville's comment that the Prussian Legal Code was "a modern head" attached to a "thoroughly Gothic body" might apply to even the most highly-developed bureaucratic states, in which the power of the central authority was qualified by the persistence of local rights and special privileges. Everywhere the administrative apparatus was small, its power contested, its ability to control events in the hinterland limited by poor communications, institutional inefficiency, and personal incompetence. Nowhere were *Staatsbürger* more than a small minority of the population.[9]

It is also important not to view German state-building solely in terms of the Prussian experience, the best known but by no means the most characteristic case. In the imperial cities, most ecclesiastical principalities, and many other smaller states, traditional institutions retained their autonomy much longer than they could in Prussia. Moreover, in some states, such as Württemberg, complicated compromises were worked out between the ambitions of the prince, the power of the upper bureaucracy, and the persisting influence of traditional representative bodies.[10]

Finally, and for our purposes most important, bureaucratic state-building did not take place in a social vacuum. Just as the Russian autocrats described in chapter 9 activated as well as repressed social forces, so German officials helped to set into motion a variety of movements in their society. Perhaps the most striking example of this process comes from the Mark Brandenburg, the traditional heartland of the Prussian monarchy, which is often seen as the *locus classicus* of German authoritarianism. As William Hagen has recently shown, throughout the last third of the eighteenth century social life in the Prussian countryside was disrupted by a series of court cases, strikes, and popular protests through which peasants expressed their opposition to their landlords' efforts to raise rents and increase their labor services. So intense was this conflict that in July 1787 King Frederick William II felt compelled to issue a decree admonishing the "lower orders" not to abuse the legal system with their "unbridled passion for litigation" and warning estate owners not to abuse their rights and harass their subjects. Clearly to some residents of rural Prussia, the growth of the state's legal apparatus presented new opportunities for action as well as new instruments of subordination.[11]

The litigious Brandenburg peasantry was just one of many social groups activated by political developments in eighteenth-century Germany. Throughout German-speaking central Europe, men—as well as a small group of women—formed organizations in which they could discuss contemporary issues. These organizations were ubiquitous and diverse. Practically every German city had its Masonic Lodge or other secret society, its reading circles and patriotic societies, its clubs and associations. Some of these were purely social, others were devoted to cultural pursuits, a few tried to influence decision makers directly. Their membership included businessmen and professors, officials and pastors, sometimes army officers and courtiers. All were nourished by the publications that spread throughout Germany in the course of the century—the books written by the first generations of great German poets and philosophers, as well as an expanding web of periodicals, newspapers, and pamphlets. Seen together, these organizations were the foundation of a German public, a sphere of discussion, debate, and personal connections that joined people from different regions and social strata. It was on this public, Immanuel Kant wrote in 1784, that the future of enlightenment in Germany depended.[12]

Historians have often viewed the institutions sustaining this public as "surrogates" or "compensation" for the lack of "real" political opportunities in eighteenth-century Germany. German history is full of such alleged compensations, just as it is full of unfortunate absences—both symptoms of Germany's assumed deviation from the western norm. In fact, it might be better to regard the emergence of the German public on its own terms, as a distinctly German expression of growing political engagement and increasing participatory energy. To be sure, the public was not like a modern political movement; nor was it interested in those constitutional questions that would dominate nineteenth-century political discourse. Its members were more interested in how political power should be used than in how it was distributed. Nevertheless, the German public was concerned with a range of issues of contemporary importance, from the condition of the peasantry to the social role of the aristocracy, from the emancipation of the Jews to the relationship between church and state. How might the public have evolved? Is there a chance that Kant was right to think that, in the long run, the free development of public debate would have reformed German institutions? We will, of course, never know. But one thing is clear: German political life had begun well before the revolution in France transformed European politics.

The vitality of the German public was apparent in its response to the revolutions, first in the American colonies, then in France. While only a few Germans fully understood what was at stake in the American war for independence, most sensed that the colonists' struggle signaled the beginning of changes that would affect everyone. They were, therefore, filled with enthusiasm for what one writer called the land "where sweet equality dwells and where the nobility's brood, old Europe's plague, does not mar simple virtue." At first, the German response to the revolution in France was no less positive. Friedrich Gentz, a junior Prussian official who would eventually become one of the revolution's most obdurate enemies, initially regarded it as "the hope and consolation for so many of those ancient ills from which mankind has suffered." When the revolution became more radical and its foreign policy more aggressive, most, if by no means all, of its former admirers turned against it. At the same time, the various governments took action against potentially subversive elements; periodicals were closed, censorship tightened, alleged conspirators arrested.[13]

The news from France also triggered social unrest. In a few western cities, journeymen struck against their masters, while in Mainz, a group of German Jacobins declared their solidarity with the French. There were also brief outbreaks of rural violence throughout central Europe. The most important of these was in Saxony, where ten thousand peasants appealed to the elector for help against the rapacity of their landlords. But none of these rebellions amounted to much. Urban agitation was easily repressed. The Mainz Jacobins turned out to be few in number and uncertain in purpose. Even in Saxony, a judicial blend of armed force and tactical concession restored order after a brief period. Nowhere in German Europe was there any real danger of a successful revolution.[14]

It should not surprise us that there was no French revolution in the German states. In the first place, the historical situations were vastly different: German Europe lacked a center in which a struggle for power could have had implications for the entire state; the German middle strata were smaller than the French, more diverse, less politically sophisticated, more closely tied to the states; popular movements were scattered, easier to isolate and then repress. It is also important to remember that there was no French revolution in most of Europe, not even in England, the most "advanced" European state. In fact, there would never again be a revolution quite like the one that began in 1789. Its primacy guaranteed its uniqueness: thereafter, people would always know—or think they knew—what revolutions looked like, what they meant, how they might turn out. Obviously this was not so in 1789, when first the king, then the moderates, then the radicals, and finally the supporters of Napoleon got what they least expected. The would-be heirs of the revolution, however much they might try to emulate their heroes, would never be able to recapture their apparently limitless capacity for surprise.[15]

Most Germans experienced the revolution not as a matter of intellectual interest or a source of social unrest, but rather as a series of military defeats and political disruptions. The era between 1789 and 1815, like the Thirty Years War of the seventeenth century and the world wars of the twentieth, was filled with reciprocally-reinforcing crises of both the domestic and international order. The revolution in France resulted in a series of wars, which in turn "revolutionized the revolution" at home and intensified its influence abroad. For most of this period, Germans were on the losing side, defeated first by the revolutionary forces that occupied and then annexed the Rhineland, then by the armies of Napoleon, who used his victories to reorganize German Europe. By the time the emperor was finally defeated, more than half of the German population had changed rulers at least once.

Vast quantities of blood were spilled and treasure squandered during this period. Ancient institutions disappeared, chief among them the Holy Roman Empire, which was dissolved in 1806 after having failed to protect its members from their enemies at home and abroad. The empire took with it most of those polities that had depended on it for their existence: the imperial nobility, all but a handful of free cities, the ecclesiastical principalities, and numerous other small sovereignties. The great German powers, Prussia and the Habsburg monarchy, survived their battles with Napoleon, but both were diminished in size and eventually forced into an alliance with the French. By 1809, Napoleon had only allies or victims in German Europe.

Individual Germans responded to French hegemony in many different ways. The majority, one suspects, regarded the French and their agents as just one more set of masters, who demanded what masters always did: money for their upkeep, young men for their armies, and obedience to their laws. Some Germans enthusiastically supported the new regimes, exploited the new economic opportunities they provided, eagerly served in the new governments, loudly cheered the victories of the man whom Hegel called "the world spirit on horseback." But there was a considerable amount of hostility toward the French as well. Some of it came from that familiar hatred of foreigners which often seems to be a timeless element in human society. Such hatreds were most common among those with something to lose: craftsmen who could not compete with French firms, householders who chafed under the need to provide quarters for French troops, priests and their congregations who objected to French religious policies, aristocrats who feared the loss of their privileges. Occasionally these hatreds would lead to violence, more often they were expressed in the smoldering resentment and quiet acts of noncompliance with which people so often confront those who have defeated them.[16]

When they viewed these anti-French feelings through the lens of their own patriotic enthusiasms, later historians frequently saw in them the origins of German nationalism. It is certainly true that under the pressure of defeat and humiliation, some intellectuals began to argue that Germans needed a nation-state to establish and defend their identity as a people. In the final stage of the battle against Napoleon, which began with his defeat in Russia in 1812, these voices became more insistent and found more willing listeners, especially among young people eager for adventure and statesmen anxious to undermine the position of Napoleon's remaining German allies. But we should not overestimate the consistency or the popularity of these early nationalist thinkers. Most of the opposition to Napoleon came from traditional animosities, not national enthusiasms. And in the end, he was defeated by regular armies in the service of sovereign states, whose leaders repressed nationalist propaganda as soon as it was expedient to do so. As we will see in the next section, German nationalism did not become an important force until it was joined to ideas and institutions of the political opposition in the 1830s and 1840s.[17]

The most important result of the revolutionary era in Germany was not the origins of nationalism but the final triumph of the bureaucratic state over "the lesser, uncoordinated powers" of the old regime. These powers had been the chief casualties of Napoleon's reorganization. Their lands and wealth had passed to a group of middle-sized polities, which the emperor established as buffers between France and her potential enemies to the east: these included satellite states such as the kingdom of Westphalia, ruled by one of Napoleon's large family, and greatly-enlarged independent states, such as Baden, Bavaria, and Württemberg. All of these states faced two closely-connected problems: first, the need to integrate the large and extraordinarily diverse territories they had so greedily accepted, and second, the need to satisfy their imperial patron's apparently insatiable demand for resources. Except in Württemberg, where King Frederick played an important role, the power in all of these new states passed into the hands of seasoned bureaucrats, who seized the opportunity to put into practice their ideas about political and social reform. The same sort of men came to power after Prussia's humiliating defeat by Napoleon in 1806; here too the dangers and opportunities of the revolutionary era seemed to clear the way for a new era of reform.

In all of these states, reform involved a strengthening of the bureaucratic apparatus itself. This meant, first of all, clarifying lines of responsibility within the ministry and between central and local authorities. But it also meant new regulations that increased the bureaucracy's power over the recruitment, promotion, and conduct of its own members and thereby protected them from outside interference, even by the monarch. Reform also involved some measure of social emancipation: the removal of traditional restrictions on mobility, property, and labor, the liberation of peasants from forced labor and of Jews from many, but not all, of the restraints on their social and economic freedom. One motive for these emancipatory measures was practical: it was simply impossible to absorb into the new states all the myriad of rights and privileges that had obtained in traditional society. But equally important was the belief, shared by most reformers, that emancipation would encourage the productive powers in society and thereby promote economic growth and social progress. Bureaucratic reform and social emancipation were different sides of the same revolutionary process; both cleared away that complex web of institutions which had once restrained, privileged, and protected the members of corporate society, thus leaving each individual potentially free and practically subordinated to the state. In Germany, freedom and state citizenship, *Freiheit* and *Staatsbürgerschaft*, were inseparably intertwined.[18]

The victory of the bureaucratic states was confirmed by the political settlement of 1815, which insured that most of Napoleon's Germany survived its creator. Despite vigorous lobbying by representatives of the traditional nobility and ecclesiastical authorities, the major powers at the Congress of Vienna made no effort to recreate the patchwork of small states, imperial cities, ecclesiastical principalities, and semi-sovereign aristocratic lands that had ordered German life for centuries. Instead, Napoleon's former allies in the south and west retained the lands they had been given; Prussia, which claimed a major role in the "liberation" of Germany from the French, acquired part of Saxony as well as the Rhineland and Westphalia. Although unnoticed at the time, the economic vitality and natural resources of these western areas would provide the basis for Prussia's rise to preeminence after 1850.

The political settlement of 1815 was confirmed by a Confederation of German States, whose representatives met at Frankfurt under Austrian leadership. The Confederation fell short of what some patriots had wanted; it was a federation of states rather than a federal state. It did, however, represent an internationally guaranteed source of order in central Europe; its institutions helped to balance the interests of the various German states, protect the weak from the strong, and provide the means of settling disputes. As part of the larger concert of nations that emerged in 1815, the Confederation contributed to the decades of peace that followed a quarter century of war and revolution. But for all its virtues as a source of international order, the Confederation was unable to win the loyalties of most politically active Germans. Metternich, its chief architect and advocate, used the Confederation to encourage and coordinate censorship and repression among the states. As an instrument of reaction, the Confederation encouraged progressive Germans to think about alternative ways of organizing national politics.[19]

≺ II ≻

The Origins of Participatory Politics, 1815–1848

In the famous memorandum he prepared during the summer of 1807, the leading Prussian reformer Karl von Hardenberg proclaimed his desire to make "a revolution in a positive sense, one leading to the ennoblement of mankind, to be made not through violent impulses from below or outside, but through the wisdom of the government . . . Democratic principles in a monarchical government—this seems to me to be the appropriate form for the spirit of our age." This represents a succinct summary of the bureaucratic reformers' central goal: a revolution directed from above, which would give them access to the forces that had made revolutionary France apparently so irresistible, but without undermining the authority of the monarch or his officials. But what exactly would this revolution look like? In what ways would it be democratic? For Hardenberg and for most of his counterparts in the other states, "democracy" meant the achievement of "freedom" through the removal of traditional restraints. Only secondarily did it mean the right to participate in public affairs, to have a share in deciding what "the wisdom of government" might be. Like the other reformers, Hardenberg acted with a small group of likeminded officials, who utilized the crisis situation to impose their will, often against the efforts of traditional elites.[20]

Although the participatory elements in policy making during the reform era were insignificant, most reformers recognized that political participation of some sort belonged to what Hardenberg called "the spirit of our age." Hardenberg himself had made some fitful efforts to build a political base for his program and he continued to work—in vain—for a constitution with representative institutions for Prussia. In the new states of the south and west, where the problems of political integration and state finances were especially for-

midable, representation seemed an unavoidable part of state building. The Bavarian constitution of 1818, for example, established a
bicameral legislature, with an upper house composed of hereditary,
ex-officio, or appointed members, and a chamber of deputies elected
indirectly by five categories of voters. In practice, the Bavarian parliament, like the similar bodies established in Baden and Württemberg,
was clearly subordinated to the monarch. Moreover, the rules governing its election and proceedings were designed to limit its ability to
represent or mobilize public opinion. Nevertheless, like the French
Chamber, these parliaments did have authority over the budget and
some sorts of legislation, as well as the power to hold the ministry
responsible for unconstitutional actions. And perhaps more important, the very existence of these bodies affirmed the principle that
political legitimacy was inseparable from constitutionally-defined
representative institutions.[21]

The question facing German governments in the years immediately after the Congress of Vienna was how far this principle would
spread. The answer would be determined by what happened in Berlin. King Frederick William III, under pressure from Hardenberg and
his colleagues, had reluctantly promised his people a constitution as
part of the reform program introduced after 1806. If he fulfilled this
promise, constitutional government would become the norm, at least
for German territories outside the Habsburg monarchy. But Frederick William's commitment to a constitution had always been shaky;
once Napoleon was safely defeated, the political opposition to reform
grew and the king's own doubts intensified. In 1819, Prince Metternich manipulated fears of revolutionary conspiracy to persuade the
Prussian king to abandon the promised constitution and support a
coordinated campaign against political radicalism. This decision had
great long-term significance: not only was the reform movement in
Prussia effectively halted and the progress of constitutionalism limited to the middle-sized states of the south and west, but the German
Confederation became permanently identified with a policy of reaction and repression.

The reactionaries' victory in 1819 did not stop the growth of political participation, but it did define the institutional realm in which
participation could take place. This realm was, first of all, extraordinarily diverse. In addition to state parliaments in Bavaria, Baden,
Württemberg, and a few other medium-sized states, there were cor-

porate *Stände* in states like the Mecklenburgs and in the free cities of Hamburg, Bremen, Lübeck, and Frankfurt; there were provincial *Stände* in Prussia and in parts of the Habsburg monarchy, and of course a broad array of local representative institutions in hundreds of cities and towns. The rules governing the election and power of these representative institutions varied greatly, as did their vitality and effectiveness. In some places, state or local parliaments became centers of political activism; in others they remained the exclusive property of old elites.[22]

As significant as the diversity of German participatory politics was its fragmentation. Poor communications, especially before the development of an adequate railroad network, inhibited travel and personal contacts. At the same time, political repression, limitations on political organization, and censorship made it difficult to create the kinds of institutions in which people from different areas could learn to act together, identify their leaders, and clarify their views. The strongest ties reaching across local institutions and experience were cultural: national organizations of scholars, national newspapers and periodicals, national associations for the promotion of art and literature. These cultural connections, whose roots were in the eighteenth-century public, had a powerful impact on the style and character of German political discourse—its penchant for abstraction, its strong moral tone, and the persistent role of intellectuals among its national leadership.

By the early 1820s, some of the most active members of the German political public thought of themselves as "liberals," a term first used in Spain and then taken over by progressive people everywhere in Europe. To be a liberal was, first of all, to be in favor of change, progress, movement; indeed liberals thought of themselves as the "party of movement," the political expression of social, economic, and cultural progress. As one young liberal put it: "We are the times." In addition to this self-identification with progress, liberals were united by what they opposed: tyranny and injustice (but not the constitutionally defined power of the state), ignorance and superstition (but not authentic religious belief), unearned privilege (but not the rewards of hard work and superior education), censorship and repression (but not the defense of law and order).[23]

Behind their common opposition to the forces inhibiting progress, liberals were deeply divided on a wide range of issues. Consider, for example, liberal attitudes about the central issue of economic and social freedom. Of course, all liberals favored freedom as an abstract goal, but they differed greatly about its meaning and application. Some believed that the state should play no role in social life, others looked to it for protection against what they considered unfair and harmful competition. Some liberals favored free trade, others did not. Some opposed the guilds, a few thought they might serve a useful purpose. Some wanted complete religious freedom, others were convinced that people had to be protected from the unhealthy influence of the clergy. Or take the question of citizenship, the other key category in the vocabulary of modern politics. Liberals were all committed to citizenship as an abstract goal, but differed about its practical implications. Every liberal, for instance, believed in legal equality; virtually no liberal thought this should apply to women as well as men. Every liberal assumed that citizens should have the right to participate in public affairs, but very few wanted this right extended to all males, not to mention all adults. Active citizenship, they believed, required independence—and liberals characteristically had great difficulty determining who was and was not independent. In the German states, as in the rest of Europe, liberals claimed to speak for the people, the *Volk*, without being able to define what this word should mean.[24]

In German Europe the problem of defining "the people" had a national dimension as well. German nationalism had many different sources: the cultural awareness prevalent in the eighteenth century, the anti-French sentiments awakened during the revolutionary era, the radical student groups that arose after 1815, and the feeling of national identity sparked by conflicts along German Europe's complex ethnic frontiers. But only when it was linked to liberal goals and values could nationalism become a political movement, "seeking or exercising state power and justifying such action with national arguments."[25] On national questions, as on the rest of their program, liberals were divided. Some wanted a reformed federation, others a unified national state. Some—usually Protestants and northerners—wanted Prussian leadership; most Catholics did not want to exclude Austria because it would turn them into a minority. As long as they shared a common opposition to Metternich's Confederation, these differences could remain latent. They would emerge, as we will see, as soon as the liberals faced the practical question of what kind of Germany they wanted to create.

The political community that liberals imagined was national, but the one in which they lived and worked was usually local—the city council, a social club, a charitable organization. The prime movers in this political world were, as we should expect, local notables—lawyers, professors, publishers, tradesmen and merchants, and, in many places, civil servants. The prominence of officials among its leaders was one of the distinctive characteristics of German liberalism and another sign of the powerful but ambiguous role of the state in public life. While the liberals' leadership tended to come from men with education and property, what Germans call the elites of *Bildung* and *Besitz*, their support extended much more widely and deeply in German society, including small landholders, minor officials, craftsmen, school teachers, and various others from the *Mittelstand*. In its social composition, as in everything else about the liberal movement, we sense deep divisions, which were concealed or contained by the institutional fragmentation and repressive pressures of early nineteenth-century public life.[26]

Liberalism was the most prominent political movement in the first half of the nineteenth century, in part because liberals produced the largest amount of written material, which not only captured contemporary attention but also insured their historiographical centrality. But in addition to those who were engaged in various kinds of liberal political activity, there were many more Germans who participated in public life through traditional forms of collective action—riots to protest food shortages, demonstrations against local businessmen who seemed to be responsible for rising prices or falling wages, attacks on unpopular landowners or employers. Characteristically, popular violence was apt to occur along the lines that divided the community or separated it from outsiders. Hard times and new rules could easily bring trouble, as during the volatile years right after 1815, when Jews were attacked by opponents of the emancipatory laws that had been part of reform in many states. Any incident—a disagreement about a bill, a drunken quarrel, an unintended slight—might spark clashes between students and townspeople, masters and apprentices, journeymen from different trades. Festivals, carnivals, and other ceremonial occasions could become political demonstra-

tions or expressions of social conflict. Similarly, a variety of traditional social institutions—guilds, journeymen's associations, and the
like—could be turned to political purposes. Although carried on in
different forums and based on different rules, these forms of collective action represented attempts to express values and influence
events. They were, therefore, different from, but no less "political"
than, the liberals' speeches, clubs, and treatises.[27]

The impact of the French revolution of 1830 demonstrated that
German participatory politics had entered a new era. Unlike the situation in 1789, when the popular echo of French events had been faint
and uncertain, the fall of the Bourbons produced an immediate and
vigorous response. Once again, we are struck by the variety of events:
riots, demonstrations, violent clashes between angry crowds and
soldiers, parliamentary debates, mass petitions, and electoral campaigns. The waves of agitation lasted for more than two years, culminating in a broadly-based movement for political reform in the Bavarian Palatinate which was only put down through a massive show of
military force. By then many Germans had come to believe that they
too were no longer free from the dangers of revolution: "The beast
of the Apocalypse," wrote Prince Johann of Saxony in June 1832,
"which until now only touched our dear Germany indirectly, has
suddenly risen up [among us], its skin inscribed with blasphemies."[28]

Like their attitudes towards democracy in general, liberals' relationship to the revolution of 1830 was a mixture of antipathy and col-
lusion. On the one hand, most liberals feared violence and hated what
Karl von Rotteck called "the mob's personal passions, crude energy,
irrationality, and larcenous desires." On the other hand, liberals were
prepared to use these passions, energies, and desires for their own
ends. In some states, therefore, local leaders took advantage of popular unrest to extract concessions from frightened rulers. As a result,
several smaller German states—Brunswick, Hesse-Kassel, Hanover,
and Saxony—acquired constitutions. Although many of these constitutional agreements were broken as soon as rulers felt secure again,
they did foreshadow that same alignment of political and social forces
that would transform German public life in 1848.[29]

In the 1830s religious issues also began to take on a new political
significance. In part, the origins of these issues reached back to the
division of western Christendom in the sixteenth century. But as in
so many other aspects of German life, the revolutionary era gave re-

ligious division a different shape and a new meaning. The secularization of religious territories and the disappearance of hundreds of
small states and principalities broke the clear connection between
dynasty and confession established in the sixteenth century; there
were now large Catholic minorities in Protestant states like Prussia
and Baden, and a significant Protestant minority in Catholic Bavaria.
When these states tried to regulate religious issues or mobilize religious values, a series of conflicts erupted, sometimes between Protestants and Catholics, sometimes between religious and secular authorities. Coexisting and sometimes intersecting with these
antagonisms were a series of conflicts within the major confessions,
usually over matters of doctrine and church authority: during the
1840s, the "German Catholic" movement and the Protestant *Licht-
freunde* both mobilized supporters behind a program of theological
and institutional reform. For our purposes, the most important thing
to note about all of these conflicts is how easily they could be politicized by being linked to demands for state action on behalf of a particular group or interest. In Germany, therefore, as in the rest of Europe, religious loyalties and religious conflicts did not diminish in
the nineteenth century: on the contrary, religion became a political
issue, which drew on deeply-rooted social and cultural commit-
ments with lasting consequences for public life.[30]

During the 1840s the intensity and variety of political participation were increased by a growing sense of social crisis throughout
central Europe. In many ways, this crisis was just another expression
of a common structural problem in traditional society. Whenever the
population grew too quickly, there were more people than places—
more graduates than government jobs, more farmers than available
land, more journeymen than master's positions. And as usual, these
demographic pressures produced more beggars, paupers, and brigands, whose increasing prominence threatened the well-off members
of society and made those on the margins wonder if they might be
the next to lose their place. In retrospect, of course, we can see that
in the 1840s the German economy was entering a period of substantial growth, marked by the dramatic expansion of railroads and various other sectors. But in the short run, even these developments
seemed to make matters worse by intensifying the competition for
certain kinds of labor, capital, and goods. Moreover, these expanding

sectors of the economy were not immune to strikes, lockouts, and other forms of social conflict.[31]

The social crisis of the forties may have been unusually severe: perhaps population growth was faster and social dislocation more extensive than in earlier crises; perhaps there really were more beggars and thieves, more destitution and hunger, more food riots and labor unrest. But it was certainly true that now more people were aware that something was seriously wrong, not only in their own community but in the larger social world. No social crisis had ever been so widely discussed, vividly described, and intensively analyzed by poets and novelists, journalists and academics, civil servants and clergymen. In this way, the crisis of the forties reflected as well as intensified the growth of political awareness in the German lands.[32]

With this awareness of social crisis went the realization that the authorities lacked the ability, and perhaps the will, to do something about it. Governments could, to be sure, take measures to avoid mass starvation; there was no German equivalent to the Irish famine. But most of those who turned to their states for protection, support, or encouragement—peasants worried about keeping their land, craftsmen anxious about their trades, businessmen eager for secure markets—usually came away frustrated and dissatisfied. It was not even clear that states could defend the social order from attack. No government had much police power at its disposal; cities characteristically employed a few watchmen, most rural areas were patrolled by a handful of gendarmes. This meant that whenever there was serious trouble, it was usually necessary to call out the troops, often with tragic results. This is what happened, for example, in the early summer of 1844, when a group of weavers in Silesia attacked the homes of merchants who were exploiting them. By the time the army arrived, the crowd was large, boisterous, and overly confident of its own power. The soldiers were either frightened or provoked into opening fire; before the day was over, eleven people had been killed, many more wounded. The provincial governor of Silesia was surely not alone in viewing these events as part of a "universal assault of the poor against the rich."[33]

The governments' repeated inability to master the social crisis undermined their legitimacy and intensified the desire for change. In social clubs like *Ressource* in Breslau, in city councils throughout

Prussia, and in the parliaments of the southern and western states, Germans talked about the need for reform. Sometimes these calls for reform were soft-spoken and respectful, as was the privately-printed plea for constitutional government delivered to Prussia's King Frederick William IV in 1840 by Theodor von Schön, a senior civil servant. Sometimes they were more strident and insistent, like the pamphlet written by Johann Jacoby, a young Jewish physician, which caused a sensation when it appeared in 1841. And while most political action remained local, men like Jacoby quickly achieved national prominence as their ideas were spread and discussed through the political public. Slowly and still informally, leaders of the opposition began to establish contacts with one another that reached beyond single states and isolated communities.[34]

Under the pressure of events, divisions began to appear in the opposition. Most liberals continued to want to work within the system, to reform the Confederation, expand the competencies of existing institutions, establish constitutional government where it did not exist. Gradual change, new leaders, better laws—these were the best ways of insuring progress and avoiding chaos. But for those on the opposition's left wing gradualism was not enough. They lacked the liberals' patience, confidence in the existing order's ability to change—and fear of excessive change from below. Younger, poorer, less well-established, these radicals were willing to use democratic means to achieve democratic ends, to mobilize the masses in order to create a state based upon the Volk. For a minority, radicalism involved some form of socialism; the majority remained radical democrats who drew their inspiration from the traditions of French republicanism.[35]

In 1846 and 1847, both the social and the political situations deteriorated. Crop failures, including potato blight, pushed up the price of food and caused locally-severe shortages. At the same time, a downturn in the trade cycle cut demand for goods, increased unemployment, and forced many marginal concerns into bankruptcy. In the first months of 1847, riots occurred in Berlin, Hamburg, and other German cities, when angry crowds protested high prices by attacking bakeries and storehouses. At the same time, symptoms of political weakness were everywhere. The opposition won stunning electoral victories in Baden in 1846, and in Hesse-Darmstadt in 1847. In Bavaria, King Ludwig's infatuation with the beautiful but expensive

Lola Montez had created a full-blown scandal, which led to the resignation of the ministry. In the summer of 1847, the Swiss cantons fought a brief but bitter civil war in which the liberal Protestants defeated conservative Catholics. And, perhaps most important of all, the joint session of Prussia's provincial parliaments, called by the king in April 1847 to mobilize support for new financial measures, ended five months later in bitter disappointment for both government and opposition. That same fall, the radical and moderate wings of the opposition held meetings to define programs and consider strategies for the changes they believed to be essential.[36]

Into this atmosphere of anxiety and expectation came the news that, once again, the people of Paris had risen against their king.

⋜ III ⋟

The Revolutions of 1848–49

The very scope and scale of the revolution of 1848 make it seem like a force of nature: after the first successful revolt in Sicily in January, unrest spread throughout much of the Continent, engulfing hundreds of communities between the Russian frontier and the Channel; ministries fell, monarchs fled their capitals, landlords and officials bowed to the will of angry crowds. As we have seen, the revolution came at the end of a decade of unrest, in the midst of a severe economic depression, and within months of a series of political crises. Was it inevitable? Perhaps not. In retrospect, we can see that things had begun to stabilize around the turn of the year 1847–48. A successful harvest had made food cheaper and more plentiful. In some areas, popular discontent seems to have been waning. But many contemporaries remained convinced that something was going to happen, that the earth would shake, the volcano erupt, the epidemic suddenly appear. In the end, it may have been these contemporary convictions of inevitability that are most important, because they inspired those who wanted change and demoralized those who opposed it. A revolution may not have been inevitable in 1848, but the fact that many people expected, feared, or welcomed one certainly made it difficult to avoid.[37]

However difficult it might have been to avoid serious unrest, the course of the revolution that spread across Europe was certainly not predetermined. Had the authorities in the major capitals—Paris, Vienna, Berlin—acted with more resolve, they could at least have delayed the revolutionaries' victories and thereby produced a different outcome. Moreover, we should never lose sight of the enormous variety of the revolution, which differed greatly in various cities, towns, and villages. In a sense, of course, all these outbreaks of popular action were connected; revolutions are contagious. But unlike epidemics, revolutions do not have the same etiology and course as they spread from place to place. What spreads is the impetus to act, to protest against existing injustices and seek a better future. But the character of people's actions, like the nature of their discontents and their visions of the future, differs widely. As long as the revolutionaries share a common enemy, these differences can be hidden; as soon as that enemy recedes, the differences emerge and help to shape the revolution's future.

From the start, the revolution of 1848 was what Mack Walker called a "revolution of conflicting expectations." As soon as the news from Paris reached Germany, there were political demonstrations, mass meetings, and social unrest, first in the southwest, then spreading swiftly throughout the German lands. Workers, artisans, peasants, students, civil servants, businessmen were all involved, sometimes peacefully, sometimes in a violent confrontation with authorities. In the capital cities of the states, every monarch eventually gave in to the moderates' demands and appointed a reformist government. In Vienna and Berlin, this was preceded by the familiar sequence of the insurrectionary drama: barricades, street fighting, and revolutionary martyrdom. Elsewhere reform came without bloodshed, as rulers recognized they had no choice but to yield to the moderates or risk having to face more dangerous foes. Except for Bavaria's hapless King Ludwig, who was compelled to abdicate in favor of his son, no German monarch lost his throne. Nowhere was the institution of monarchy and all its attendant sources of authority in serious jeopardy. Two things helped to produce the moderate outcomes that characterized the revolution's first stage: the swiftness with which the governments accepted reform and the absence of outside intervention; the first precluded the radicalizing effect of a long struggle for power, the second, of a foreign war.[38]

But while the moderates formed ministries and began making plans for political reform, the revolution went on. In fact, the amount of violence seems to have increased after the moderates' victory; between April 1 and June 1, the *Augsburger Allgemeine Zeitung* reported 53 violent incidents as opposed to 42 during the preceding three months. In the countryside, peasants demanding an end to seigneurial dues and services continued to seize records, threaten landlords, and occasionally burn down manor houses. Villagers invaded forests and defied previous restrictions on wood gathering; elsewhere, they reclaimed and redistributed the common lands. In the cities, old animosities—over taxes, food prices, the conduct of troops—quickly surfaced. Craftsmen attacked the machines that they feared would rob them of their livelihoods; apprentices demanded better treatment from their masters, outworkers higher prices for their labor. Among those expressing their discontents and defending their interests, industrial workers—the proletariat whom Marx and Engels had viewed as the one true revolutionary class—were usually greatly underrepresented.[39]

The persistence of popular protests heightened the divisions within the political opposition. Moderates, frightened by disorder and largely satisfied with the regimes established in March, wanted slow, gradual reform within the protective structures of the existing order. The alternative was to yield power to the mob, whose destructive potential had been burned into historical memory by the Jacobin terror of 1793–94. Radicals, however, saw the situation quite differently. To them, the persistence of social unrest seemed to promise the possibility of more fundamental changes in which they, as the true spokesmen for the Volk, could claim the power that had been denied them for so long. In many areas, therefore, radicals began to establish organizations to mobilize and direct popular energies. In Saxony, for example, the left wing of the opposition abandoned its partnership with the moderates and founded Fatherland Associations, in which only "progressive, determined men" were welcome. Radicals were also active in the Palatinate, where veterans of the reform movement of 1830–32 set up democratic associations throughout the province. But the sharpest and most violent break between moderates and radicals came in Baden, where in April radicals launched an armed rebellion against the liberal government. They were swiftly repressed.

The impetus for the Baden uprising had been the radicals' failure to control the preparation of national elections that had begun when the so-called Pre-parliament gathered in Frankfurt on March 31. This body, composed of political notables from throughout German Europe, decided on what we can now see as a characteristic compromise. On the one hand, they called for national elections to select a constituent assembly that would prepare a new order for Germany. But on the other, they recognized the continued power of the states and acknowledged that the governments of these states were, for the moment at least, the only legitimate sources of authority. Like those who joined the reform ministries, the moderate majority at the Preparliament wanted to make a revolution with, not against, the established order.

According to the suffrage regulations agreed upon at the Preparliament, all "mature, independent citizens" could vote—there seemed no reason to stipulate that they meant "male" citizens since almost everybody took this for granted. The various states interpreted "independent" in different ways, sometimes to include virtually all males, sometimes only those with a certain amount of property. Furthermore, most states used an indirect system of voting, which gave the final choice of candidates to a group of electors. Given the brevity of the campaign, the lack of well-developed political organizations, and the inexperience of the electorate, it is not surprising that most of the successful candidates were national celebrities or, more often, local notables, men prominent enough to be known and trusted by their voters, with the resources necessary to devote an unspecified length of time to public life. The National Assembly, therefore, was dominated by the same elites of education and property who had been active in public life since the eighteenth century: civil servants (by far the largest single group), professors and teachers, lawyers, businessmen, landowners, and a handful of writers, journalists, and others. The political outcome of the elections reflected the variety of opinion and alignment which we saw as characteristic of pre-revolutionary politics. In a region like the Palatinate, which had a long radical tradition, men with strong democratic views were elected; in the Prussian Rhineland, clerical influence was important; and in a few districts conservatives predominated. Overall, however, notables who were identified with the moderate opposition were most likely to be chosen.[40]

On May 18 the newly-elected delegates held their first meeting, in the Paulskirche, in Frankfurt, where most of them would remain until the final vote on the constitution ten months later. The record of their debates is among the nineteenth century's most remarkable political documents, not only because of the range of issues discussed and the variety of opinions expressed, but also because it so vividly shows the problems of transforming theory into practice. Within a relatively short period of time, the members of the Assembly had to learn how to turn principles and values into statements about fundamental rights and political institutions, as well as how to draft legislation, build coalitions, and effect compromise. Despite what is often said about their garrulousness and naiveté, the men at Frankfurt learned these lessons with remarkable speed and success. They failed less because they could not do what they set out to do, than because by the time they had finished their work, it had become irrelevant.[41]

The difficulties the delegates faced swiftly became apparent when they began debating the question of "basic rights," which were to serve as the foundation for the new constitutional order. They had little problem agreeing on the freedom of speech and assembly, and on individuals' rights to form organizations and be free from unauthorized search and arbitrary arrest. Nor did they have trouble establishing civil equality, which included the abolition of the nobility's special privileges and the end of restrictions on religious groups, including the Jews. When they turned to the problem of church and state, however, the delegates ran into serious disagreements. What did freedom of religion mean? To radicals, it meant state-imposed limits on the church's power to persuade and coerce its members. To Catholics, it meant the church's right to manage its own affairs. The moderate solution, which guaranteed church autonomy but acknowledged the state's ultimate authority, pleased neither camp.

A similar set of conflicts emerged over the question of citizenship and economic freedom. Were individuals free to live where they wished and practice whatever trade they chose? Or were communities and guilds free to limit their membership and preserve their autonomy? Disagreement on these matters reflected disagreements about the meaning of freedom and citizenship, those key terms in the evolution of modern politics. The instincts and experience of most Frankfurt delegates inclined them towards equality and universality rather than limited rights and corporate autonomy, but hundreds of petitions from towns and guilds suggested that a majority of Germans thought otherwise. On these critical issues, therefore, the Assembly was unable to come to a satisfactory conclusion.

The parliamentarians eventually left many questions about basic rights open or tried to cover their disagreements with general statements. On the central constitution question facing them, however, delay or evasion was impossible. Here the painful transition from theory to practice would have to be made.

In 1848–49, as so often in German history, national and domestic issues were inseparably intertwined; the men at Frankfurt had to decide both what the new Germany should look like and how it should be governed. The national issue turned out to be more difficult than most people expected. For one thing, it was by no means clear how to establish national boundaries, between Germans and Poles in the east or Germans and Danes in Schleswig-Holstein. Most people believed in national self-determination—but who should prevail when Polish or Danish national self-determination threatened German national interests? Even more perplexing was the question of Austria, a German polity firmly set in a multinational empire. Many delegates, especially Catholics and southerners, did not want to exclude Austria, which would produce both a Protestant majority and Prussian preeminence. For just those reasons, Protestants and Prussians favored what came to be known as the *kleindeutsch* solution, that is, a Germany without Austria.

Early in 1849, the Assembly was deadlocked; the pro-Prussian party's proposal of a monarchical state without Austria was defeated by a coalition of radicals, conservatives, and Catholics, none of whom had enough support for an alternative. Early in March the Austrian government made clear that it would not participate in a German nation under any circumstances, which left some kind of a *Kleindeutschland* as the only option. Its supporters managed to gather a majority by compromising with the left on constitutional issues, which included diminished monarchical authority and a democratically-elected national parliament. At the end of March, a narrow majority elected Prussia's king Frederick William IV German emperor. Early in April, a delegation traveled to Berlin to offer him the crown. The National Assembly had done its work.

From start to finish, the Assembly was dependent on the power of the states. As we have seen, the Pre-parliament had acknowledged states' authority and had enlisted it to administer the May elections. Although at the beginning of its deliberations the Assembly had created an executive organ, it was without power to do any of the things a government must be able to do—collect taxes, administer justice, raise an army. In September 1848, the consequences of this weakness were painfully revealed, first, by the Assembly's inability to control Prussian policy in Schleswig-Holstein, and second, by the need to call in troops to keep order in the city of Frankfurt itself. The restoration of monarchical power and the formation of conservative governments, first in Vienna, then in Berlin, further alienated the Assembly from the sources of power and set the stage for their final disappointment, which came when King Frederick William categorically refused their offer of a German crown, dissolved the Prussian parliament, and threatened to use force against the Frankfurt Assembly.

The parliamentarians' assumption that they could count on the support of the states came from their conviction that they spoke for the Volk. But in the summer and fall of 1848 this conviction was also revealed to be shaky as many Germans turned away from, and in some cases against, the Frankfurt Assembly. There was an extraordinary democratic revolution in Germany throughout 1848 and the first half of 1849; millions of Germans joined political organizations, protested and demonstrated, signed petitions and attended meetings. In comparison to the pre-revolutionary period, popular politics was more intense, articulate, and organized. And yet, as in the years before 1848, German politics remained diverse, fragmented, and without an institutional center or national focus.[42]

A great deal of popular energy continued to be applied to social and economic issues. Craftsmen, workers, and other occupational groups formed organizations to express their interests. Often these organizations were themselves divided and sometimes split: in the summer of 1848, for example, a national association of craftsmen met in Frankfurt and called for limitations on the rights of journeymen, who promptly established their own organization. Religious issues also had a powerful resonance among ordinary men and women. The Catholic Pius Association for Religious Freedom, founded in Mainz in March 1848, had 400 local branches by October; they bombarded the Frankfurt Assembly with 1142 petitions, containing over a quarter of million signatures. In October 1848, Catholics established the German Catholic Association to coordinate their activities on a national level. Although these various economic and religious special interest groups had political significance, they tended to cut across and therefore to weaken those political movements that depended on popular support.[43]

All of the major political movements, from the conservative defenders of throne and altar to the radical advocates of republicanism, made some effort to mobilize a popular constituency. By far the most successful of these campaigns was carried out by the democratic left wing of the political opposition, whose efforts were spurred by their democratic values and aspirations, as well as their lack of access to other sources of power. The democrats established a dense network of clubs and associations throughout the German states, which they tried to coordinate and direct through national organizations. The core of their support came from the urban middle strata—professionals, craftsmen, shopkeepers—but they also reached out to workers, to peasants, and in a few areas to women, who made their first active appearance on the political stage during the revolution.[44]

The democrats were also the most active participants in the broadly-based protest movements that greeted Frederick William's rejection of the Frankfurt constitution. Throughout Germany, the king's decision was greeted by angry speeches, demonstrations, and some armed resistance. As would be the case in France two years later, the most vigorous protests occurred outside the political centers. Berlin and Vienna remained relatively quiet, whereas in Saxony, the Palatinate, and Baden, democratic groups seized power, defeated the local authorities, and set up revolutionary regimes. But while they fought tenaciously and with considerable popular support, these regimes were no match for the Prussian army, which moved against them with speed and resolution. The Saxon revolution lasted a few days, the regimes in Baden and the Palatinate a few weeks. By the time the last revolutionary garrison at Rastatt had surrendered on July 23, all of Germany had been pacified.[45]

The particular pathos of the German revolution of 1848 comes from the contrast between its early, almost effortless triumph and its total defeat just sixteen months later. The two were causally connected. The revolution's easy initial successes postponed rather than settled the decisive struggle for power upon which the outcome of every revolution ultimately depends. When this decisive struggle came, first in Austria and Prussia during the fall of 1848, then in Saxony, the Rhineland, and Baden during the spring and early summer of 1849, the revolutionaries were divided and easy to isolate, while their enemies had recovered their will and capacity to act and had been able to mobilize allies at home and abroad. Against the formidable military power that could then be arrayed, the revolutionaries had no real chance for success.

≺ IV ≻

Revolutions and German History

Probably the most famous epitaph for the demise of revolutionary hopes in 1849 was Friedrich Engels's bitter comment that "from now on, political liberalism, the rule of the bourgeoisie, is forever impossible in Germany." Engels realized that, contrary to what he and Marx had hoped and expected, the German bourgeoisie had failed to play their assigned revolutionary role. Instead of taking over the state as their French counterparts had done in 1789, and thus preparing the ground for a proletariat revolution, the German bourgeoisie had betrayed their potential allies and insured reaction's triumph. They would not get another chance. Many other historians, even when they do not accept the details of Marx and Engels's analysis, come to similar conclusions about the revolution's meaning. To be sure, non-Marxists usually do not explain the revolution's defeat in terms of class interests and betrayal; they are more inclined to portray the revolutionaries as politically inept or as the tragic victims of historical circumstances. Nevertheless, they agree with Marx and Engels that the revolution's failure in 1848 represented an opportunity lost forever: for nationalist historians, the opportunity to forge a unified nation; for liberals, the opportunity to create a truly progressive Germany. Marxists, nationalists, and liberals agree that, whatever its cause and character, the failure of the revolution opened the way for a "revolution from above," which—depending on their chronological and ideological vantage point—they saw as the source of either the glories of the Bismarckian *Reichsgründung* or the miseries of twentieth-century German politics.[46]

There is no doubt about it: the revolution of 1848 did *not* result in the "rule of the bourgeoisie" (whatever that might be), or in the

creation of a national state, or in the foundation of a democratic political order. But what *did* happen? How are we to fit the revolution
into the course of German history?

Perhaps the place to begin is by noting the self-evident but essential fact that revolutions are political phenomena. They may have
social and cultural causes and consequences, but, as Charles Tilly
has recently reminded us, "the character, locus, and outcome of revolutionary situations varies systematically with the organization of
states and systems of states." To understand the historical meaning
of the German revolution of 1848, therefore, we must consider its
significance for the organization and the system of states.[47]

On the surface of things, the revolution's impact on the system of
states seemed minimal: unlike 1789, it did not directly lead to an
international crisis; unlike 1917, it did not directly result from one.
In fact, the European order in 1850 appeared to be much the same as
it was before the revolution. Nevertheless, the revolution affected
the system of states in at least two important ways. First, the fall of
the French monarchy and the creation of the Second Empire removed
France from the ranks of the status-quo states and thus significantly
undermined the great power consensus upon which the settlement
of 1815 had depended. Second, and of more direct concern to us, the
German Confederation that was restored in 1850 was substantially
weakened by the events of 1848–49, especially the mobilization of
public opinion in favor of a unified nation state and the intensifica-
tion of the Prussian-Austrian rivalry. After 1850, the restored conservative governments of the middle-sized states clung to the Confederation as the best defense of their own sovereignty, but even they
recognized the need for federal reform. Seen within the long-term
development of the European order, therefore, the revolution appears
as a transition between the relatively stable and peaceful years after
1815 and the turbulent era between the Crimean conflict of 1854 and
the Prussian victory over France in 1870.

The revolution also produced important changes in the internal
organization of states. Although the moderates were ultimately defeated, some of their most important accomplishments remained.
For instance, the residues of the seigneurial system virtually disappeared from most of central Europe. Equally important, Prussia retained the constitution granted by Frederick William IV in December 1848. Even in its revised, less progressive form, this constitution

profoundly altered Prussian political life and, by isolating Austria, helped establish the basis for Prussian preeminence in the German state system.

In addition to rural reform and the Prussian constitution, the revolution had other important effects on the organization of German states. Most obviously, the experience of revolution encouraged governments to acquire more effective means of regulating and controlling their populations. In several states, the police force was reformed and expanded so that it was no longer necessary to count on the army to maintain order. In Berlin, for example, a new chief of police, Carl von Hinckeldey, created a uniformed, semi-military organization to keep order and regulate social life, as well as a corps of undercover agents to combat subversion. At the same time, greater discipline and conformity were imposed on state administrations, which slowly increased in both size and responsibility. States were, of course, still a long way from having the massive bureaucratic apparatus with which we are all too familiar, but as early as 1863, the economist Adolf Wagner could formulate a law tracing the inevitable expansion of the bureaucracy's role in social and economic affairs. In the long history of German state building, the revolution has a definite role to play.[48]

Initially, the growth of the state's power seemed to inhibit the development of participatory politics. During the early 1850s, fear, disappointment, and repression combined to cast a pall on public life. But this did not last long. By the end of the 1850s, political activity resumed everywhere, elections were contested with renewed vigor, new political periodicals began to appear, and a variety of participatory organizations were founded. Many of these activities built upon the personal ties and institutional connections Germans had gained in 1848 and 1849. Indeed, the speed and vigor with which German participatory politics recovered during the "new era" are impossible to imagine without the legacy of the revolution.

The most obvious heirs of this legacy were the liberals, who quickly became the most dynamic political force throughout German Europe. Many of liberalism's leaders first came to prominence during the revolution, which gave them the kind of national forum and experience that had been missing before 1848. The democratic left recovered more slowly and less completely; it had borne the full weight of repression in 1849, which had sent many of its leaders into

exile. Nevertheless, democratic traditions lived on, either in a separate organization like the *Volkspartei* in Württemberg, or on the left
wing of liberal parties like the Prussian Progressives. Contrary to
what is sometimes argued, the revolution did not drive liberals and
democrats from public life, nor did they all suddenly become "real-
istic" supporters of the state. From the late 1850s to the early 1880s,
liberalism remained the most successful political movement, not
only in most local and state governments, but on the national level
as well. It is a mistake, therefore, to connect liberalism's decline at
the end of the century to its temporary defeat in 1849.[49]

The revolution was also important for the development of the
other political movements that emerged after 1850. Perhaps too much
has been made of the revolutionary origins of Social Democracy; as
Jonathan Sperber has recently shown, in 1848 German workers were
most likely to be politically active when they were least class conscious. Nevertheless, many future leaders of German Socialism, including Ferdinand Lassalle, began their political careers on the radical wing of the revolutionary opposition. On the other end of the
political spectrum, German conservatives acquired their first painful
lessons in participatory politics when they tried to mobilize opposition to the revolution. The leading conservative newspaper, the
Kreuzzeitung, was founded in Berlin in 1848. Finally, political Catholicism, which emerged as an independent force with extraordinary suddenness in the 1860s, surely drew upon the organizational
talent and experience that had made the Pius Associations such a
formidable presence in 1848–49.[50]

In most histories of Germany, the influence of the revolution on
the growth of participatory politics has been overshadowed by the
giant figure of Otto von Bismarck, who became minister president of
Prussia in September 1862. From the start of his career, Bismarck
liked to contrast his own policies with those of the failed revolution.
"The great questions of the day," he told the budget committee of
the Prussian parliament on September 30, "will not be settled by
speeches and majority decisions—that was the great mistake of 1848
and 1849—but by blood and iron." In a sense, the revolution's failure
was sealed by Bismarck's triumphs—over the liberal majority in the
Prussian parliament, as well as over his international antagonists. He
never let his domestic rivals forget that he, not they, had created the
united Germany which the men at Frankfurt had sought in vain.[51]

Nothing is to be gained by ignoring the obvious: the German nation was created by a combination of Bismarck's diplomatic skills and the military power of the Prussian army. But we should not take an overly restrictive view of his "revolution from above." After all, Bismarck would never have been appointed minister president without a political crisis created "from below" when the Prussian parliament refused to vote for the government's military reforms. Furthermore, despite his disparaging remarks about "speeches and majority decisions," Bismarck himself was constantly aware of the importance of public opinion and participatory politics, with which he had an intense if frequently antagonistic relationship. Finally and most important, one result of the Bismarckian revolution was a dramatic expansion of participatory politics, made possible by the creation of a democratically-elected national parliament. Just as "revolutions from below" often produce a centralization of power from above—this certainly happened after 1789 and 1917—so "revolutions from above" often stimulate the mobilization of power from below.[52]

The absence of a "successful" revolution, a revolution like the great French upheaval of 1789, did not force Germany on a separate historical path. As in the rest of Europe, German political life combined forces "from above" and "from below" and was shaped by both bureaucratic and participatory institutions. And in Germany, as everywhere else, the relative weight and interaction of these institutions had a distinctive pattern, created by historical experience, social and economic conditions, and cultural values. Seen from this perspective, what set Germany apart from most other European states was less the power of its bureaucracy than the coexistence of bureaucratic power and substantial participatory institutions. This coexistence was at the center of Bismarckian Germany's political existence, the source of some of its strengths and many of its weaknesses. To trace the evolution of this political system, and to do justice to its achievements as well as to its failings, would take us far beyond our present task. One thing, however, should be clear: the development of German politics cannot be reduced to a clear contrast between "the revolution from above" and "the revolution from below." The relationship of the German states to the European revolution was always more complicated than that.

Lawful Revolutions and the Many Meanings of Freedom in the Habsburg Monarchy

ISTVÁN DEÁK

THE CONCEPTS OF FREEDOM and revolution had a host of different meanings for the dozen or so nationalities that constituted the Habsburg monarchy; but for all of them, these terms held out a great promise: the fulfillment of long-cherished political aspirations. At the same time, the words contained the threat of still more ominous oppression by rival nations: during the revolutions of 1848–49, people in the monarchy who felt their newly-won freedoms endangered by their neighbors within the realm outnumbered those who felt endangered by Habsburg power. Clearly, this augured well for the dynasty inasmuch as among all those who had raised the banner of revolution in the spring of 1848, only the Hungarians were willing to sustain their actions to the bitter end. On April 14, 1849, their national assembly proclaimed the dethronement of the House of Austria. Within a few months, however, Hungary's struggle for independence was defeated by the combined armies of Austria and Russia.

While the revolutions failed, and the Habsburg army won the day, what emerged from the conflict was a changed central Europe.[1] In the 1850s, modernization began in earnest. True, individual citizens, the several provinces, and the many nationalities of the monarchy enjoyed even less freedom for a time than they had under the old regime; but by the 1860s, such notions as liberty, active participation in politics, cultural and material progress had become integral components of public discourse. In turn, growing prosperity, the spread of literacy, and the universality of individual freedoms had the effect of hastening the recoupling of liberal with nationalist ideas. After 1867, when the Habsburg monarchy was divided into Austrian and Hungarian halves, nearly all the political groups in the realm attempted to impose what they viewed as their own progressive national values on the ethnic minorities. Only arch-conservatives and Marxist social democrats insisted on internationalism and ethnic impartiality.

It should be clear from these brief introductory remarks that, in order to understand developments in mid-nineteenth century central Europe, we must attempt to see them through the eyes both of a beleaguered but temporarily successful ruling house and of a diverse group of dynamic, aggressive, and self-confident reformers and revolutionaries who had lost the immediate conflict but were gradually gaining ground.

≺ I ≻

Uneven Developments

The Habsburg patrimony had been pieced together chiefly through marriage contracts, although military conquest and political maneuvering had played an important role as well.[2] The entire geographical complex, extending in the eighteenth century from what is today central Romania and western Ukraine to the Swiss border and northern Italy, and in addition a few enclaves in southern and western Germany as well as present-day Belgium, did not even have a name. These were simply the feudal holdings of the Habsburg family or House of Austria, linked together *indivisibiliter ac inseparabiliter* by the so-called Pragmatic Sanctions. The latter had been negotiated between 1719 and 1723, both among the Habsburgs themselves and between Emperor Charles VI and each one of his major possessions.

The Habsburgs fervently desired to hold their patrimony together; nonetheless, in the 75 years between Maria Theresa's accession to the thrones of Hungary and Bohemia in 1740 and the end of the Napoleonic wars, the dynasty lost all of its western European possessions while gaining substantial territory in eastern Europe, in northern Italy, and along the Adriatic coast.[3] Meanwhile too, the Habsburgs renounced the theoretically elective but virtually hereditary title of Holy Roman Emperor and set themselves up as hereditary emperors of Austria. In the course of the next 60-odd years, between 1815 and 1878, the Austrian emperors were excluded from the affairs of Germany and lost most of northern Italy. On the other hand, they acquired the city republic of Cracow and occupied the Ottoman

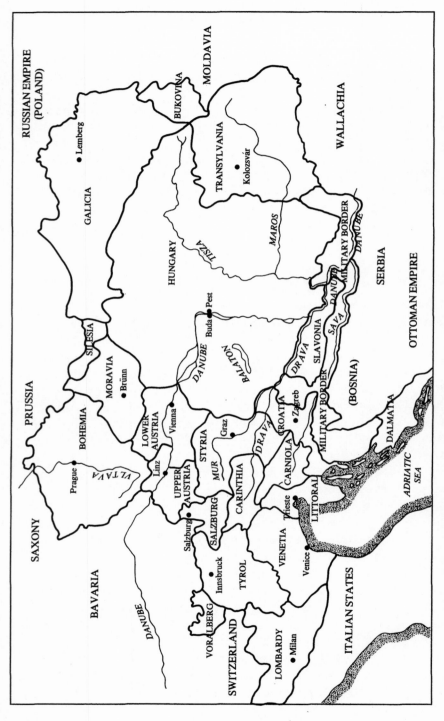

The Habsburg Monarchy in 1848. From István Deák, *Beyond Nationalism: A Social and Political History of the Habsburg Officer Corps, 1848–1918* (New York: Oxford University Press, 1990).

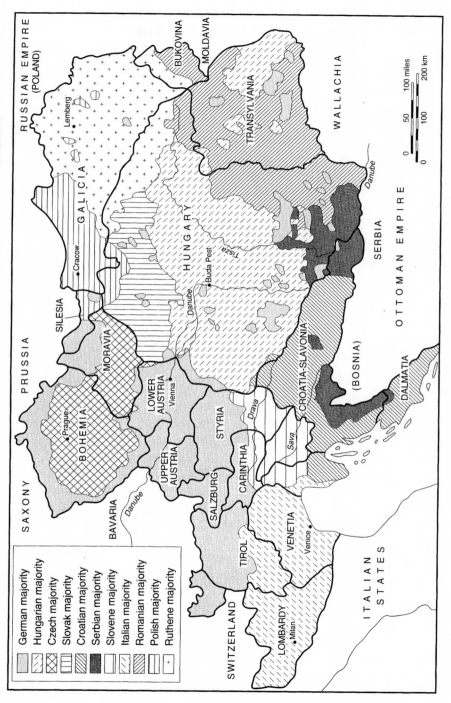

Nationalities of the Habsburg Monarchy in 1848

Legend:
- German majority
- Hungarian majority
- Czech majority
- Slovak majority
- Croatian majority
- Serbian majority
- Slovene majority
- Italian majority
- Romanian majority
- Polish majority
- Ruthene majority

RUSSIAN EMPIRE (POLAND)

BUKOVINA

MOLDAVIA

WALLACHIA

OTTOMAN EMPIRE

SERBIA

TRANSYLVANIA

GALICIA

Lemberg

Cracow

HUNGARY

Tisza

Buda Pest

Danube

Danube

SILESIA

PRUSSIA

SAXONY

MORAVIA

BOHEMIA

Prague

LOWER AUSTRIA

Vienna

UPPER AUSTRIA

BAVARIA

Danube

STYRIA

SALZBURG

CARINTHIA

Drava

Sava

CROATIA-SLAVONIA

(BOSNIA)

DALMATIA

TIROL

VENETIA

Venice

LOMBARDY

Milan

SWITZERLAND

ITALIAN STATES

100 miles

50

100

200 km

0

provinces of Bosnia and Hercegovina. In that later period, too, they abandoned their comprehensive title of emperors of Austria and became instead, in 1867, emperors of the "Kingdoms and Lands Represented in the Imperial Parliament (Reichsrat)" and kings of the "Lands of the Hungarian Holy Crown," or, as the Hungarians later renamed their country, the "Hungarian Empire." For the sake of convenience, the two places were unofficially referred to as Austria-Hungary. With the loss of so many western and central European provinces and the gain of kingdoms and lands to the east of Vienna, the territory of the Habsburg monarchy shifted markedly eastward in the nineteenth century, a development with a profound influence on its politics, society, and economy.

The myriad Habsburg possessions were variously governed. Each had, at least in theory, its own diet and its own laws and customs. Even such a super-centralizer and revolutionary modernizer as Emperor Joseph II (Holy Roman Emperor, 1765–90; ruler of his family possessions, 1780–90) issued his ordinances separately for nearly every province in his realm, and what was valid for one part of the monarchy was only exceptionally valid for all. With a great deal of oversimplification it is possible to distinguish between four types of Habsburg possessions. In the first group were the so-called Hereditary Provinces (corresponding very roughly to today's Austrian Republic) and Lands of the Czech Crown, where a centrally trained and salaried bureaucracy governed and where, beginning in the mid-eighteenth century, taxes and recruits were collected on the basis of fixed quotas extracted from weakened provincial diets. In the second group, consisting of the Lands of the Hungarian Holy Crown, the Austrian Netherlands (effectively lost to the family in 1793), and the Tyrol, government was in the hands of administrators elected from among the local elite, and taxes and recruits were collected as the interests of the local notables dictated. Other parts of the realm, such as Galicia, Lombardy, and Venetia, lay somewhere between the two extremes. Finally, the so-called Military Border, which occupied the southern parts of Croatia-Slavonia, Hungary, and Transylvania, was governed, barracks-fashion, directly from Vienna.

In brief, more than half of the Habsburg possessions enjoyed an autonomy that made a mockery of the Habsburgs' authoritarian ambitions, and the two serious attempts to put an end to this anomalous state of affairs, under Joseph II in the 1780s and under Francis Joseph in the 1850s, nearly wrecked the entire edifice. What saved the monarchy each time was a drastic return to decentralization and the reaffirmation of the more important local autonomies. At last, in 1867, the monarchy was divided into two equal parts, each with its own autonomous subdivision: Polish-governed Galicia, in Austria; and the Kingdom of Croatia-Slavonia, which was attached to Hungary.[4]

≺ II ≻

Emperor and Nobles

At least until 1848, but in many ways until the collapse of the Habsburg monarchy and even thereafter, political, social, and economic power lay in the hands of the nobility. The trouble for the historian is, that in the Habsburg lands noble status was practically undefinable and unidentifiable. In the eyes of the Habsburgs, only those to whom the House of Austria had bestowed a noble predicate for their services to the Crown were nobles, although the dynasty was rather profligate in handing out hereditary noble titles to, for example, all army officers who had served the emperor for 30 (later 40) years. In Hungary, Poland, Croatia, Transylvania, and other eastern lands, however, noble status was seen as deriving from the nation's ancient, tribal history. In those places, a noble was simply a free man, one who was not an immigrant colonist, a city burgher, a Jew, or a serf. Thus while in Bohemia only one out of every 828 males was a nobleman, in Hungary the proportion was one in 20.[5] The nobility in the eastern half enjoyed an almost unbelievable number of rights and privileges, such as freedom from taxation on their directly owned lands, freedom from military service, freedom from arbitrary arrest, an exclusive right to private landownership, the right to hold office in the local and the national administrations, and the active as well as passive vote. Yet many of these nobles were poorer than the simplest of Vienna artisans or some of the unfree peasants in their own district.

In theory, all nobles were equal; in reality there existed a vast and complex hierarchy dominated by the great landowning magnates or aristocrats, whose fate, if they were Catholics, was closely tied to that of the Habsburgs. This high aristocracy owned most of the land in the eastern half of the Hereditary Provinces and in Bohemia, Galicia, Croatia, and Hungary; and it occupied many of the highest posts in the Court, the diplomatic service, and the army. Local administration, however, was in the hands, in the west, of trained imperial functionaries, and in the east, of modestly wealthy, untitled noble landowners, who functioned as judges and administrators. The political activity of the rest of the nobility, that is, the vast majority, was limited largely to efforts to protect its privileges.

The principle of noble participation in the political process had been affirmed at the time when the respective diets offered the crown of their land to the Habsburgs. The offer was made in the hope of obtaining the military and financial protection of the mightiest family on earth. In the course of time, the power of the ancient, local nobility had been weakened or even broken, as in Bohemia after the Battle of the White Mountain in 1620, but the old elites were soon replaced by a new Habsburg aristocracy. The latter in turn could never resolve the dilemma of remaining loyal to the Habsburgs, their original benefactors and ultimate protectors, while simultaneously pursuing their family interests in the province or provinces in which they held property. It is indeed fascinating to follow the passage of such archetypical Habsburg Catholic creations as the Schwarzenbergs, Lobkowitzes, Sternbergs, Aehrenthals, Fürstenbergs, or Thuns through various changing identities, from a Habsburg or Old Austrian patriotism to a provincial "Bohemian" loyalty, and then to a Czech and even Czechoslovak nationality. Often such families split into a poorer branch, whose members served the Habsburgs as salaried high-level officials and officers, and another, wealthier branch, for whom state service consisted of a part-time diversion as an ambassador or cavalry officer. The latter group could, of course, more easily afford the luxury of appearing as Czech or other non-Habsburg patriots.[6]

That during the revolutions of 1848–49 much of the Habsburg nobility was still cosmopolitan, at least in style, is typified by the case of the wealthy aristocrat Count Lajos Batthyány, prime minister of revolutionary Hungary from March to September 1848. After the war between Austria and Hungary, in which he had not participated, he was unjustly accused of treason as well as other crimes, sentenced to death by an Austrian military tribunal, and executed on October 6, 1849. When facing the firing squad, Batthyány refused to have his eyes covered and personally gave orders to the elite military unit to shoot. He uttered his command in three languages, French, German, and Hungarian: "Allez, Jäger, éljen a haza!" (Go ahead, Rangers, long live fatherland!). No less remarkably, some of the former Habsburg officers who were executed by the Austrians after the war for having fought, as generals, in the Hungarian army, died protesting that they had only done their duty in defense of king and fatherland. By the latter, they incontestably meant not Hungary alone but the entire Habsburg realm.[7]

The Habsburgs in turn could never decide whether they wished for more or less participation in public affairs by the nobility who were both indispensable and dangerous to the Crown. Aristocrats helped to govern, and they shared the ruler's interest in wishing to prevent a social revolution; but they stood in the way of an immediate, direct relationship between the throne and the commoners; they tended to disguise their material interests behind the pretense of defending provincial rights and liberties; and beginning in the early decades of the nineteenth century, they could no longer be trusted as determined opponents of destructive nationalism. Thus the Habsburgs hesitated.

Maria Theresa, for instance, attempted to domesticate the landed nobility by creating schools for its cadet members in Vienna, and by insisting that the high nobility take up residence in the capital, at least during the winter season. By creating a number of central governmental institutions, by enlarging the army and the bureaucracy, and by severely regulating the relationship between noble landowners and peasants, she weakened the power of the nobles, which meant simultaneously reducing the autonomy of the individual lands. Maria Theresa also expanded the practice of putting commoners into command positions, less so in the army than in the administration. But she also preserved most of the privileges of the nobility.[8]

≺ III ≻

A Revolutionary Emperor and His Radical Opponents

Joseph II, who had been emperor and co-regent since 1765, gained full control over the patrimony at the death of his mother in 1780. With him began the famous new era of a revolution from above, in part certainly to prevent revolution from below. Joseph promoted even more vigorously the establishment of an immediate, direct relationship between the state and all its subjects; he attempted to convert both clerics and nobles into civil servants; he tried to abolish both corporate privilege and restrictions on such specific groups as the Jews; and in general, he wished to govern his possessions in a rational, enlightened manner. Such things seemed necessary both for the survival and the vigorous military expansion of the state.

The Josephinian experiments brought contradictory results. There was a sudden expansion of a free press that proved often scurrilous and was increasingly felt to be subversive. Free speech was accordingly converted into strictly controlled and restricted, but still progressive speech. In the Hereditary Provinces, for instance, the drastic relaxation of censorship in 1781 yielded to ever more severe censorship measures beginning in 1784. In 1790, the press became freer again, but new, restrictive steps were taken a year later.[9]

The forcible introduction of German as the official language of communication within the entire realm as well as other centralizing measures brought about the revolt of the Hungarian, Belgian, and north Italian estates until Joseph II was defeated. At the end of his life he revoked many of his important ordinances, but much of what he created still exists today: a well-trained and caring bureaucracy that often represents the best educated elements in the country but is characterized by self-satisfied punctiliousness. Or a press that is militant toward those of different persuasion but unctiously submissive to authority. Or a public that can never decide whether it ought or ought not to be part of the political process. The peculiar relationship between the central European churches and the state is equally a legacy of Joseph II, who despite his piety strictly regulated every move of the priests and ruthlessly fought the secular power of the Catholic church. Finally, the overwhelming presence of the state in the media, the education, and the economy clearly reflects the Theresan and Josephinian traditions in even such a democratic country as today's Austrian republic.[10]

Discouraged by the partial failure of his brother and by the turbulent French and Polish events, Leopold II (1790–92) made his compromises with the estates of his realm, but not without first using his political police to incite the peasants against the rebellious landowners so as to coax the latter into a policy of compromises. The success of some provincial estates again increased public participation in the political process. It was now, however, mostly reforming and radical members of the Hungarian, Polish, and other nobilities, rather than the plebian journalists of Joseph II's Vienna, who agitated for human rights. This was, indeed, a most remarkable feature of the political convulsions racking central Europe in the late eighteenth century: following in the footsteps of the emperor, but in opposition to him, local elites, or the most radical element among them, embraced the ideologies of the Enlightenment, of Rousseau, even of the Jacobin revolutionaries. The aim was to combat a modernizing central power. With the change of rulers in 1792, and the radicalization of the French Revolution, the ruling house reverted to a policy of repression. In the mid-1790s a number of Jacobin radicals were executed: some of them had served Joseph II and Leopold II as secret policemen and imperial propagandists.[11]

The French Terror and Napoleonic wars created a sense of emergency among the social elites, and because the wars also brought prosperity to many landowners, the dynasty did not lack elite support in those difficult years. As for the lower classes, there is no evidence of anti-monarchical feelings among them. The great peasant revolts of the 1770s and 1780s, in Bohemia, Transylvania, and elsewhere, were directed against the landowners and against officials thought to be in the pay of the landowners, not against the mythical figure of the emperor. The Transylvanian peasant upheaval of 1784 was precipitated when benefits and privileges that allegedly had been given to others by a reforming emperor were late in arriving in this outlying and backward province. For this, the local nobles and the authorities seemed to be responsible. The bloody revolt of the peasant leaders Nicolae Horea and Ion Cloşca was finally suppressed by imperial troops dispatched against those who had been devastating noble and cameral estates in the name of the emperor.[12]

During the Napoleonic wars there were no open signs of lower class discontent, and the Austrian troops, nearly all of them forcibly inducted, behaved neither better nor worse than soldiers of other dynastic armies. The one popular revolt that occurred at that time, under the Tyrolean innkeeper Andreas Hofer, was directed, in 1809, not against the authorities but against the French and Bavarian occupiers. The patriotic enthusiasm of the Tyrolean peasants caused considerable embarrassment to Emperor Francis (Holy Roman Emperor,

1792–1806; emperor of Austria, 1804–35), who suspected, correctly, that patriotism of whatever motivation was more dangerous to the House of Austria than were enemy armies. Hence the famous story about some courtiers praising Andreas Hofer to Emperor Francis for being a great patriot. "Ah,—the emperor replied—but is he a patriot for me?" After the conclusion of an armistice with Napoleon in July 1809, Austrian troops left Hofer and the Tyroleans to the mercy of the French.[13]

≺ IV ≻

Many Nationalisms

It is impossible to say when national movements began in the monarchy, or at what point the scholarly efforts of linguists and writers to modernize a vernacular can be said to have become political. No doubt, there were enormous differences in this respect among the several ethnic groups.[14] In the German- and Italian-speaking provinces the city population used the same language as the country population, which facilitated the spread of national consciousness. In the rest of the monarchy, the cities were almost invariably alien, in language, religion, and culture, to the countryside: German and Jewish in Polish and Ukrainian Galicia; German and Jewish in the Czech lands; German, Hungarian, and Jewish in the Slovak regions of northern Hungary; German, Hungarian, Jewish, and Armenian in Transylvania where the majority of the population spoke Romanian, to cite a few.

Those planning to raise national consciousness had to decide first in what language and within which groups they wished to create such novel feelings. Every vernacular spoken in the monarchy, including German, needed modernizing, but it made a great difference whether a classical literature already existed in that language. The Hungarian, Czech, and Polish literary languages could look back to many centuries of written practice and great works of literature. The question was, therefore, how to force these languages upon the local authorities who preferred to use German and Latin, and also how to make the literary language understood by people speaking myriad dialects. Without the great educational reforms begun under Maria Theresa, such efforts would surely have been in vain. Still, it took about a hundred years for a linguistic-national movement to create a sense of, often very confused, national identity in its target group. If literacy is a *sine qua non* of nationalism, then it is worth recalling that in the mid-nineteenth century the majority of the monarchy's adult population did not know how to read and write.[15]

Things were even more difficult in the case of languages spoken by such peoples who lacked a traditional social elite, or whose native nobility had long been driven out of the country or had been assimilated by other groups. Among the Serbs, Croats, Ruthenes (Ukrainians), Slovaks, and Slovenes, the early debates among patriotic intellectuals concerned less the rejuvenation of the language itself than the question of which dialect should be rejuvenated and then superimposed, as a literary language, over several dialects.[16]

All national movements underwent the same three stages of development from the scholarly work of linguists and folklorists through the political nationalism of the educated classes to the nationalism of the masses.[17] But some groups had barely reached the first stage by mid-nineteenth century: it has been said that when the Czech nationalist leaders met in the spring of 1848 in a public bath in Prague to discuss the dawn of freedom, one of those present remarked that if the roof caved in suddenly, that would mean the end of Czech nationalism.[18] Or let us remember Marx and Engels, who called František Palacký, the founder of the Czech national movement, "a learned German run mad, who even now cannot speak the Tschechian language correctly and without foreign accent."[19] In truth, Palacký had written his monumental Czech history in German.

Other nationalisms, such as the Hungarian, could already claim a measure of popular following. Hungarian nationalism had demonstrable medieval origins and Hungarian patriots yielded to none in the vehemence of their convictions. Yet as late as 1848, the word Hungarian was still often used in the form of *Populus Hungaricus* or *Natio Hungarica*, meaning the nobility of the land without any consideration of ethnicity. True, the word had also come to denote the modern Hungarian nation encompassing every inhabitant of the country without regard to class or language; or those who spoke the Hungarian language and were thus ethnic Hungarians; or, finally, those who were of the Hungarian "race," which meant excluding such Hungarian speakers as, for instance, the Jews from the body of the nation. When, in the 1840s, the German colonists in Transylvania, called the Saxons, protested against their expected inclusion into the Hungarian state and thus the loss of their privileges as a historical *Natio*, the Hungarian liberal nationalist writer Baron Miklós Wesselényi indignantly rejected their claim by arguing that only the progressive Hungarian constitution guaranteed their liberties as a nationality and as individuals.[20]

The Hungarian, or Croatian, or Polish, or Czech romantic national movements of the pre-March period won enough followers to create an urgent demand for the building of national theaters, the creation of patriotic clubs and academies of sciences, the writing of national dramas and epopees, and the publication of patriotic papers in sometimes as many as five thousand copies. In Hungary, younger nobles and *bürgerliche* intellectuals, especially women, were among the most avid readers of literary and political journals often disguised as fashion magazines. These publications transformed and modernized the Hungarian language: Lajos Kossuth's greatest service to the nation was probably not his politics, but his creation of a modern, democratic political vocabulary and style. In 1844 the Hungarian Diet made Hungarian the "diplomatic" language of the country, that is the language of official commmunications. Thereafter, only the Croatian deputies to the Hungarian Diet continued to speak in Latin.

All this would seem to demonstrate the rather rapid spread of nationalist sentiments; yet, when in 1846 progressive Polish nobles raised the flag of revolt in Galicia and called on the peasants to rally behind the national cause, the result was a catastrophe for the insurrectionists. They had promised sweeping reforms to the peasants and attempted to incite them to kill the Austrian officials. Instead, the Polish and Ukrainian serfs massacred over a thousand noblemen. The peasant uprising was spontaneous, and it preceded the Polish noble revolution by a few days. A German journalist asked a group of Galician peasants who were leading bound Polish insurrectionists toward the city in order to hand them over to the Austrian authorities: "Aren't you Poles?" "No, we are not Poles,"—the peasants replied—"we are imperial Austrians." "Who then are the Poles?" "Ah, the Poles! They are the gentlemen, the stewards, the scribes, the scholars; we, on the other hand, are peasants, imperial peasants."[21]

Rather than identifying themselves by nationality, many people still named—and then only when asked—the province or town in which they had been born or in which they happened to live. Peasants tended to identify themselves by their social status under the noble landowner and by their confessional community. As late as the second half of the nineteenth century, a significant proportion of military recruits in Austria-Hungary reported that they were from "here."[22]

≺ V ≻

Protest Movements Before 1848

Despite various incidences of local violence, there is little evidence that the mood before 1848 was revolutionary.[23] Only a few groups, such as the Polish Democratic Society, the Italian Carbonari, and Young Italy, can be identified as aiming at the violent overthrow of the Habsburg monarchy, and the power, popularity, and historic significance of these groups within the Habsburg monarchy was quite limited.

Much more influential were the many non-revolutionary reform movements which, rather than wanting to abolish the monarchy, hoped to reshape it in their own image. In other words, they were the enemies of Habsburg autocracy but not of Habsburg rule. Most conspicuous among these movements were the Lower Austrian Reading Circle, the Czech activists around František Palacký and František Rieger, and the Hungarian liberals led by Ferenc Deák, Baron József Eötvös, and Louis Kossuth. Unlike the radicals who fought for national independence and for a democratic or perhaps even egalitarian society, the reformers strove for constitutional government, peasant emancipation, confessional equality, an extended but still limited suffrage, freedom of the press, the abolition of anachronistic regulations impeding the free flow of labor, goods, and money, and, of course, national autonomy. All this, however, was to be preferably within the framework of the Habsburg monarchy and under the rule of the emperor-king.

Freedom meant different things to each reforming group. For the Hungarian liberals, the most important achievement would have been to end "the tyranny of the alien camarilla" in the Vienna Court and to transfer the monarchial center from Vienna to Budapest, the newly designated capital of the Hungarian kingdom. For the Czechs, liberty and reform meant the recognition of Czech sovereignty within the monarchy and the transfer of the monarchy's center to Prague. Finally, the German reformers considered it indispensable for the emperor to become—or become again—a genuine German prince, and for the other peoples of the monarchy to accept the benevolent guidance of the educated and politically progressive German element.

In order to understand the events of 1848, it is essential to differentiate here between three groups or types of nationalities. Those in the first group, the Germans, Hungarians, Poles, Italians, and Croats, had never lacked the presence of a native landed nobility. The existence of such a well-established elite, forming a political class, allowed for the creation of ideologically opposed political clubs or parties even before 1848. In the second category were the Slovenes, Slovaks, and Ruthenes or Ukrainians, whose native nobility had been part of the noble estate of a larger territorial unit, and who consequently could not claim a long tradition of political sovereignty. The small, new elites of these nationalities, made up mostly of priests and other professionals, were generally content to form a single political movement with the goal of attaining the recognition of their nation. The third category might be characterized as "in between." It included the Czechs, Serbs, and Romanians, whose political leaders could boast a long history of national greatness, but whose landed elite was only beginning, around that time, to rediscover its "ethnic roots." The events of 1848 would bring something to all these people, but obviously it would be a very different thing for different groups.[24]

Against all these activities the forces of the old order had very little defense. The Metternich regime operated a fairly extended network of police spies, but it did not possess a police force capable of maintaining order; nor was the army trained to deal with civil disturbances. The press was heavily censored, but the Court could barely make its views known in the few newspapers it tolerated. The Hungarian press, livelier than elsewhere in the monarchy, was on the whole critical of the Vienna government. Educated people regularly read books and newspapers smuggled in from abroad. Because tax collection in large parts of the monarchy was still handled by the noble landowners, revenues at the center never met expectations; the state was always heavily in debt, and it is no great exaggeration to say that, before 1848, the Habsburg state was less in the hands of its government than in those of its foreign creditors.[25]

The Habsburg monarchy was a police state, but it held few political prisoners. In Austria, these were mainly Italian and Polish revolutionaries. In Hungary, the first act of the revolution was to free the country's two political prisoners: Mihály Táncsics, a Hungarian radical of peasant origin, and Eftimiu Murgu, a Romanian nationalist.

≺ VI ≻

Peaceful and Not-so Peaceful Revolutions

In 1848–49 political, social, and ethnic conflicts emerged simultaneously with the dilemma of multiple national unifications. We must remember that one of the main goals of the political activists in 1848 was national unification: that of German-Austria with the other German lands; that of Hungary with Transylvania and parts of the Military Border; that of the Galician Poles with Prussian and Russian Poland; that of the Serbs in Hungary and the Military Border with the Serbian Principality in the Ottoman Empire, and so on.

Most of the western half of the monarchy had been part of the German Bund or League before 1848. In the view of the German nationalists, these provinces had therefore to become an integral part of a future, unified Germany. Similarly, the Austrian provinces of Lombardy and Venetia had once been Italian states, and in the opinion of Italian patriots they were destined to provide the foundation of a unified Italy. But certain provinces within the German League, such as the Tyrol and the Adriatic Littoral with Trieste, contained substantial Italian minorities or even an Italian majority. This provided for an immediate clash of interests between German and Italian nationalists.

In the Lands of the Hungarian Holy Crown the main questions were how to reunite the country with Transylvania, which had become a separate province during the Turkish wars in the sixteenth century; how to return the center of political power from Vienna to Budapest; and how to secure what the Hungarian leaders considered the country's ancient but recently violated constitutional liberties. Some of the fundamental points of the Hungarian argument were that, just as in England, Hungarian parliamentarism and constitutionalism could be traced back to the thirteenth century, and that such hallowed institutions had been abused by Maria Theresa and, even more, by her son Joseph II. Among other things, Joseph had refused to have himself crowned king of Hungary so as to avoid obeisance to the constitution. Thus the Hungarian political movement, undoubtedly the most dynamic of all, had an historical, restorationist character from the very start.

The events of 1848–49 were to move in many different directions, depending on the history and legal status of the province and on the diverse rights and privileges possessed or not possessed by its inhabitants. The Lands of the Hungarian Holy Crown and Galicia can be best described as oligarchies in which the power of the great magnates was nevertheless mitigated by the freedoms of a lesser nobility comprising as much as 10 percent of the total population. The Tyrol and Voralberg, at the other end of the political spectrum, resembled Switzerland in their mixing of patrician power with peasant democracy.

Well before 1848, it became clear to all politically thoughtful persons in the monarchy that a reorganization of that archaic state complex would be necessary. The question was whether the reorganization should be drawn up along historic, ethnic, or economic lines. This dilemma caused friction not only among the self-appointed leaders of the diverse national groups but also within each nationality, although the general tendency was to combine the ethnic, historic, and economic arguments in order to claim a maximum amount of territory.

In Milan and Venice, the revolutionary events began with violent clashes between the Habsburg military and the Italian civilians. Within a few days, these turned into an outright war between Austria and the king of Piedmont, who exploited the revolt of the Milanese against their Habsburg overlords for his own ends. Whether the Piedmontese and the northern Italian irredentists enjoyed the full support of the population in Austrian Italy remains a matter of historical controversy.

In Vienna, student demonstrations became violent after the suburban industrial proletariat, pursuing its own economic goals, joined in the fray, and the imperial military commanders panicked. From then on, violence alternated with periods of quiet as Great German nationalists, pro-Habsburg liberals, radical democratic students, and famished workers vied for power. Finally, Field Marshal Prince Alfred Windisch-Graetz put an end to it all by storming the city at the end of October.

In all other parts of the monarchy, the revolutions took place without bloodshed; in fact, in Hungary the revolution was celebrated as a return to normalcy following a long period of extra-constitutional rule. Not that the country was lacking in mass demonstrations and threats of violence, but the Diet and its long-established liberal leaders knew how to control the mob and how to conjure up the threat of a peasant jacquerie in order to gain concessions from the Court and the landed nobility. Using more than the usual amount of blackmail, the Hungarian political leadership achieved all the goals it had fought for in the preceding half a century.

Finally, it is worthy of note that urban areas in Austria proper, northern Italy, and Bohemia played a crucial role in the events of 1848 while the politically active city inhabitants in Hungary found themselves systematically shunted aside by the revolutionary leadership. Further to the east and south, the few cities that existed played even less of a role in the unfolding events.

The intricate intertwining of social, political, and national concerns led to a situation in which literally no one, certainly not feeble-minded Emperor-King Ferdinand (1835–48) or even his advisers, could follow the flow of events or distinguish clearly between friend and foe. Nearly all the competing forces, for example, claimed loyalty to the emperor-king, arguing that they alone were upholding the principle of legitimacy.

Following an initial period of euphoria and interclass as well as interethnic brotherhood, conflicts arose between Czechs and Germans, Hungarians and Croats, Hungarians and Serbs, western and eastern Christians, landowners and peasants, masters and journeymen.

Early in the summer of 1848, the Hungarian Count Majláth exclaimed that "the King of Hungary declared war on the King of Croatia, while the Emperor of Austria remained neutral; yet all three monarchs were one and the same person." In other words, in 1848–49, the state had lost the ability to assure the Pax Austriaca it had successfully exercised since the end of the Hungarian Rákóczi Rebellion in the early eighteenth century. Majláth's statement also pointed up the importance of legitimacy and dynastic loyalty for those engaged in a civil war. The case of Colonel Baron Friedrich Blomberg illustrates how, in 1848, people were motivated by conflicting ideals and goals embracing nationalism, regionalism, the defense of corporate "national" privilege, and class and caste interest.[26]

In the summer of 1848, Colonel Blomberg of the Habsburg army, himself of German Austrian descent, was in charge of one of Emperor-King Ferdinand's Polish Uhlan (lancer) cavalry regiments, which was stationed in the Banat, a prosperous region of southern Hungary inhabited by a mixed population of privileged German and Bulgarian colonists, Hungarians, Orthodox and Catholic Serbs, Romanians, Slovaks, and others. In June of that year, Serbs in the region had rebelled against the newly constituted Hungarian government. What the Serbs wanted, besides not wishing to live under direct Hungarian rule, was rather unclear, but then this was the case with every revolutionary group in the region in 1848. Among the small number of politically conscious Serbs, some dreamed of a Great Serbian state encompassing brother Serbs from Hungary, Croatia, and the territories still nominally or effectively under Ottoman rule south of the Danube. Others thought in terms of a federation or union of all South Slav peoples. The Serbian Border Guards of the Habsburg army feared a Hungarian take-over of the lands held by their regiments and the consequent loss of their modest privileges as the emperor's military serfs. Other Serbs had different desires, depending upon whose land they inhabited.

We should note at this point that, whereas the Hungarian government, which had been set up in March 1848, has been seen ever since as "revolutionary," it was in fact quite legitimate. Its establishment had been sanctioned by the king; Habsburg soldiers stationed in Hungary, and thus also Colonel Blomberg, had been made to swear loyalty to King Ferdinand and the Royal Hungarian Government just a few weeks before the outbreak of this specific conflict.

Upon receiving news of the Serbian attack in his region, Blomberg turned to his corps commander, a native Croat, for instructions. As a Habsburg general, the corps commander disliked the new Budapest government, which, in his opinion, consisted of "a bunch of scribblers and lawyers." Still, true to the oath he had recently taken to the king of Hungary, he ordered Colonel Blomberg to combat the rebel Serbs, who were mostly soldiers from Habsburg Border Guard regiments. Even more in favor of combatting the rebels was the local Hungarian government commissioner, a landowning nobleman who happened to be a Serb. Blomberg did defeat the Serbs, but when the leader of the rebels, a Habsburg army colonel of Austro-German nationality, begged his friend Blomberg to think of his duty to the emperor rather than his duty to the king (the two were one and the same person, of course), Blomberg ordered his Poles out of the region. He thereby left his German co-nationals, who happened to be loyal to Hungary, to the fury of the Serbs.

Much disturbed, Blomberg wrote to the Austrian minister of war, General Count Theodor Baillet de la Tour: "Have pity on us, recall us from this place of uncertainty. We can no longer bear this terrible dilemma." But Blomberg was not recalled, because, as he was subsequently reminded by the Austrian minister, his regiment had been placed under Hungarian authority. Instead, Blomberg was ordered "to consult his conscience." The area formerly under his protection was occupied by the Serbs, with accompanying brutality and plunder, but it was liberated twice by the Hungarians, first under the command of a former Habsburg officer of Serbian nationality and then under the Polish revolutionary General Józef Bem, who in 1848 had entered Hungarian service.

≺ VII ≻

Towards an Austrian Constitution?

Despite their manifold antagonisms, the revolutionaries of 1848 held on to identical symbols and many of the same aims. Their flag was the tricolor, whether the black, red, and gold of the Great German liberals; or the red, white, and green of the Hungarians; or the blue, yellow, and red of the Romanian nationalists. Their goal was freedom, both individual and collective, in which the collectivity was clearly defined as a nation and not an estate or a class. That the two freedoms, the individual and the national, would clash, as would, of course, the many divergent national programs, was the devastating surprise of the 1848 revolutions.

All the constitutions adopted or proposed in 1848 were based on the principles of popular sovereignty and the rights of man. Even though the franchise laws of 1848 contained a great deal of variation, they were all either liberal or democratic and radical. In Austria, the so-called Pillersdorf Constitution, reluctantly promulgated by the

Court on April 25, 1848, provided for a two-chamber Reichstag with political power equally divided between emperor and parliament. The suffrage law, announced on May 11, gave all power in the upper house, or Senate, to the large landowners, and it provided for indirect elections to the lower house. Workers paid by the day or the week, domestic servants, and persons in receipt of public assistance were excluded from the primary franchise. This led to violent protests in Vienna, with the result that, on May 16, an imperial rescript promised a unicameral parliament and no property qualifications for the primary vote. The elections were, however, still to be indirect, with the primary electors choosing a smaller number of secondary electors, who then chose the members of the Reichstag.[27]

It was under this radical formula that elections were held in June-July 1848. They brought to the Reichstag a most colorful assemblage, made up, among others, of Czech intellectuals picked by the Czech political leadership; scores of fairly well-to-do Galician peasants who in the Reichstag invariably took the counsel of fellow deputies from Galicia who were landowning nobles; some Italians, Poles, and Romanians as well as a great number of Germans, who ranged from Tyrolean ultra-clericals to Vienna radical socialists. There were no industrial workers, and middle-class intellectuals provided the largest group.[28] The dilemma of later Austrian parliamentary politics was foreshadowed by this Reichstag, in which the German deputies were divided along ideological lines, whereas the representatives of most other nationalities were there simply on behalf of their nationality.

In October 1848, this divided assembly moved to Kremsier in Bohemia to escape the turbulence of revolutionary Vienna and to write a constitution. The draft that the parliament finally adopted, early in March 1849, was the outcome of many months of toil and many compromises. Although never promulgated, it served as a model for all later constitutional drafts. The deputies had proceeded from the principle that all sovereignty derived from the people; therefore, the government was to be responsible to the people's representatives. However, when the ministers of young Emperor Francis Joseph protested against what they called an assault on monarchial rights, the deputies changed the draft to read that the government was to be responsible both to the monarch and to parliament.

The nervousness of the new emperor's advisers regarding his prerogatives was quite understandable in view of how he had come to power. On December 2, 1848, in a political move of doubtful legality, Prime Minister Prince Felix Schwarzenberg and the monarchy's leading generals had caused Emperor-King Ferdinand to abdicate in favor of his nephew, Francis Joseph (1848–1916), who was then eighteen years old. Among the many reasons leading to this decision was the desire to rid the state of a monarch who had signed away too much of his own power. It was even argued in Court that the new ruler would be less bound by the solemn promises made by its predecessor.[29] Small wonder, then, that the revolutionary Hungarian national assembly proclaimed Ferdinand's abdication unconstitutional and Francis Joseph a usurper.

The draft Kremsier Constitution left foreign policy and war in the hands of the monarch; it authorized him to dissolve the Reichstag but with the obligation of convoking a new one within three months; it also gave the emperor veto power over legislation but provided for the Reichstag's ability to overrule the veto. The draft constitution abolished the titles of nobility, established the principle of equality before the law, and guaranteed all civil freedoms. Furthermore, the Kremsier plan deprived Roman Catholicism of its dominant status, and it stated—a little vaguely, to be sure—the equality of ethnic and linguistic rights.

Ethnic and linguistic questions as well as the administrative reorganization of the monarchy were the most difficult issues to settle. In a development foreshadowing what was to happen after 1918, representatives of the major nationalities, such as the Germans and the Czechs, insisted on preserving the old historico-political boundaries within the monarchy, which would have given them territories larger than those merely inhabited by their own co-nationals. Representatives of the smaller nationalities, such as the Slovenes and Ruthenes, advocated national self-determination and the setting up of ethnic frontiers. Furthermore, whereas the Germans favored a strong central government, the Poles and Czechs were in favor of a federal solution. At the end, the Reichstag temporarily accepted the existing internal frontiers. In addition, there were to be two houses of parliament: an upper house representing the several provinces of the monarchy, which was to be based on indirect elections; and a lower house, elected directly by voters at least 24 years old and paying a minimum tax rate of five florins (equal to about two contemporary dollars). All in all, the solution was somewhat more favorable to the German Austrians than to the others.[30]

The date for proclaiming the Kremsier Constitution was set for March 15, but by then members of the government, especially Minister of Interior Count Philipp Stadion and Minister of Justice Alexander Bach, had finished preparing their own version of a constitution, which was proclaimed on March 4. In fact, no sooner was this so-called Octroyed (oktroyierte) or Stadion Constitution proclaimed than the Kremsier assembly was dissolved by imperial order: the radical deputies barely escaped arrest by the military authorities.

If put into effect, the Kremsier Constitution would have turned Austria into one of the most advanced democracies in Europe. Its greatest shortcoming was its lack of clarity regarding administrative centralization and ethnic rights. The Stadion Constitution itself was no less liberal on the rights of citizens; moreover, it too made the ministers responsible, although it was not made clear to whom. What it established firmly was the principle of a single central authority, and it made clear that the many provinces, including Hungary, together were to form a uniformly governed, indissoluble whole. There was to be only one coronation, one citizenship, one legal system, one central parliament, and a single customs union. In the bicameral parliament the upper house was to be composed of delegates from the provincial parliaments or Landtage, and the lower house was to be elected by voters paying a slightly higher income tax than what was foreseen by the Kremsier constitutional draft. The monarch was to exercise legislative power together with the parliament; he was to have an absolute veto over legislation; he could dissolve the Reichstag at any time, and in case of an emergency, he could govern by decree. Finally, the Stadion Constitution provided for a sort of grassroots democracy by offering autonomy to towns and other communities to the detriment of provincial and ethnic rights.[31]

If put into effect, the Stadion Constitution would have brought the greatest benefits to the smaller, more helpless nationalities and probably also to the lower social classes. However, that constitution was not implemented either, and within two years Francis Joseph established a highy centralized, absolutistic regime. In the several later Austrian constitutions or constitutional projects there appeared some of the essential features of both the Kremsier and the Stadion constitutions. After 1867, Austria became a democracy in which parliament was, however, often unable to operate because of ethnic controversies and anti-Semitic hysteria, while the emperor protected civil rights and religious as well as ethnic equality with the help of a cabinet of functionaries and emergency decrees.

≺ VIII ≻

Reforming the Hungarian Constitution

The arduous efforts of the Kremsier assembly had no echo in Hungary, for the liberal leaders there had already rejuvenated the country's ancient, unwritten constitution in the so-called April Laws of 1848. These laws were meant to bring revolutionary change to Hungary while simultaneously guaranteeing the continued dominant position of the landed gentry.

Sanctioned by Emperor-King Ferdinand, the April Laws abolished all noble and corporate privileges, and they gave the franchise to all men with some property or another source of secure income as well as to all educated men. But they also guaranteed continued franchise to all those who had had the vote before, which meant that no matter how destitute or uneducated, the nobles preserved their ancient political rights. All in all, the new franchise raised the proportion of qualified voters from one fourth to one third of the adult male population: a very high proportion for the period and in Hungary itself not to be surpassed until after World War 1. Hungary was again to have a bicameral parliament; in practice, however, the upper house, made up of great aristocrats and representatives of the country's major institutions, gradually faded into insignificance during the revolution.[32]

National elections under the new Hungarian franchise took place in June-July 1848, but in certain areas, especially in the south, where the Serbs were in rebellion against the Hungarian government, elections could not be held. The ballot was open, as had been the tradition in Hungary, and there were neither more nor less of the usual illegalities and abuses. In Hungary, parliamentarism had had a long tradition, and so had political corruption. Compared with the earlier elections, however, there was now only one party, that of the new national government, although many opposing candidates ran in the name of the same party. Outsiders were not easily tolerated: the radical, plebian poet Sándor (Alexander) Petőfi, for instance, was roundly defeated in scandalous circumstances, having been almost killed by his drunken opponents.

The composition of the lower house brought no surprises. Seventy-five percent of the deputies were noble landowners; the rest were qualified as *bürgerliche*, even though most of the latter also had noble predicates. All in all, this was an assembly of the untitled nobility, as all previous parliaments had been and as all assemblies in the next several decades would be. There were perhaps three peasants among the 414 deputies, and the ethnic minorities (who constituted an absolute majority of the population in Hungary) were only barely represented.[33]

The events in Hungary, which I prefer to call a lawful revolution, eliminated the most fervent servants of the Habsburgs from the Hungarian political scene; and by weakening the upper house of parliament, they further increased the political power of the untitled nobility. These men dominated both the National Assembly and the National Defense Committee, which was set up in September 1848 to govern the country. Modeled after the French Revolution's Comité de Salut Public, the National Defense Committee, too, was formed from members of the National Assembly. Its head and the virtual dictator of the country until April 1849 was Lajos Kossuth, yet his and the Committee's powers were held to be purely temporary. On April 14, 1849, when it seemed that the Austrians had been finally defeated, the assembly proclaimed Kossuth governor-president of Hungary; he in turn appointed a new, constitutional ministry. Thereafter, both president and cabinet were dependent on the National Assembly. Dissolved before the surrender of the main Hungarian army to the Russians on August 13, 1849, the Hungarian parliament was restored to life in 1860 and remained a formidable political force all through the existence of Austria-Hungary. Its social composition changed, however, from one with a majority of landed nobles to one dominated by functionaries and professionals, who were variously déclassé nobles or of lower-class origin. The political ideals and lifestyle of this new class, however, closely resembled that of the historic gentry.

Kossuth himself was one of the earliest examples of such a déclassé nobleman. Landless and poverty-stricken, he had to earn his living as a journalist and politician. As such, he felt a great deal of contempt for the landed aristocracy and even for the gentry, and yet he did everything in his power to preserve the dominant position of the nobility and to strengthen the county administration that was their stronghold. The main reason for this seemingly contradictory attitude was Kossuth's fear that the political decline of the nobility would lead to the triumph of Hungary's non-Hungarian majority.

Whether the triumph of Kossuth and friends should be considered an aristocratic reaction or a democratic revolution depends on what aspect of the events we wish to examine. By assuring its survival in a modern world, the nobility made it nearly impossible for genuine democracy to develop in Hungary; and by legislating the supremacy of the Hungarian language in the multinational Hungarian state, it prevented a peaceful resolution of the nationality question—assuming that a peaceful resolution of that question would have been possible. Still, by emancipating the peasantry and by introducing scores of enlightened reforms, the revolutionary leadership opened the way to rapid modernization.

Finally, it must be said that, even though the national question caused the revolutionaries to fight one another all across the monarchy, the opposing groups showed remarkable similarity in their behavior, depending on their ideology. Thus it is possible to distinguish the practitioners of radical politics, moderate politics, and conservative politics from one another, irrespective of whether those groups served or opposed the emperor. Radical democrats, whether German, Hungarian, Serbian, or Romanian, began the revolution sincerely enthusiastic about the fraternity of nations and the great European community of freedom, but because of their firmly held belief that only their own national cause truly served the cause of universal freedom, they ended up being the most intolerant of other nations' aspirations. Thus, for example, the extreme hostility of Marx and Engels to the national aspirations of the Czechs, whom both men saw as a reactionary nation deserving extinction, reflected a common attitude among left-wing German and German-Austrian intellectuals.[34] Such moderate politicians as the German-Austrian prime minister Baron J. F. Wessenberg, the Czech Palacký or the Hungarian Count István Széchenyi, on the other hand, were much more ready to make compromises in the nationality question, while conservatives generally rejected the idea of nationality in favor of peace in the region and the continuation of their socially dominant positions.

≺ IX ≻

How Many Revolutionaries?

The initial political demonstrations in Milan, Venice, Vienna, and Budapest each attracted tens of thousands of participants. The armed citizens in Milan completely overwhelmed the few thousand soldiers of Field Marshal Radetzky, who evacuated the city on March 22, 1848.

Because there was really no such thing as a police force in Vienna, imperial-royal grenadiers, most of whom happened to be Hungarians, tried to maintain order in the city on March 13–14, and while so doing shot to death three men and a woman. Thereafter, the military succumbed to the demonstrators and withdrew from the capital. On the night of March 15, a crowd, rather optimistically estimated at 100,000, celebrated the arrival of Lajos Kossuth and his fellow-Hungarian "Argonauts" in Vienna.

In Budapest, on the afternoon of March 15, the poet Petőfi addressed some 10,000 spectators in front of the National Museum; a few hours later, an estimated 20,000 people crossed the Danube on a pontoon bridge from Pest to Buda in order to force the supreme royal authority, the Vice-Regal Council, to accept the revolutionary demands. The presence of 20,000 demonstrators in a city of 150,000 (assuming that the contemporary estimates were reliable), was truly remarkable: against them the imperial-royal garrison of 7,000, made up mostly of unreliable Italian recruits, proved powerless. Indeed, the Vice-Regal Council surrendered without a murmur. Yet within a few days, the revolutionary Committee of Public Safety was taken over by moderate burghers and the envoys of the Hungarian Diet in Pressburg: Petőfi and his radical fellow-poets and writers became a powerless opposition.[35]

The hard-core demonstrators everywhere were university students, young intellectuals, and artisans, especially apprentices and journeymen; in the initial, happy phase of the events there were many ordinary burghers. The German-speaking inhabitants of Budapest rallied to Petőfi, whose poems and Twelve Demands, presented in Hungarian, they may or may not have completely understood. In Vienna alone did industrial and railroad workers from the suburbs represent a completely novel political element.[36]

A few weeks after the March events, anti-Jewish pogroms broke out in Pressburg and a number of other western Hungarian cities; the mob was made up almost exclusively of German-speaking journeymen and apprentices. The new Hungarian government and its hastily created militia proved powerless, and to the government's great humiliation, regular troops had to be called in to restore order.[37]

Despite manifold fears and rumors, in no place did the peasantry descend on the cities to plunder and kill. But there were many incidents in the countryside in which peasants attacked manor houses and local cadaster bureaus, mostly in search of reputed documents which would prove their ancient right to this and that piece of property. These attacks had been precipitated by the news of emancipation, and again regular troops had to be dispatched to restore order.

The worst excesses occurred in southern Hungary and Transylvania, where hundreds of landowners were killed and thousands had to flee for their lives. In Transylvania, the rebelling peasants were almost without exception Romanian-speakers and the landowners Hungarians. It is hard to tell whether social or ethnic discontent motivated the peasants, but certainly the Hungarian authorities chose to see the excesses as expressions of national hatred. The culprits, therefore, had to be the Romanian and Serbian clerics and political leaders. Over the next year and a half, civil war raged on in these regions. In Transylvania it pitted units of the new Hungarian National Army, Hungarian militia, volunteers from the privileged Székely (Hungarian) peasant *Natio*, and the landowners' own armed servants against Romanian peasants. In the conflict, "Saxon" German burghers and wealthy peasants sided with the mostly dirt-poor Romanians, as did local units of the old Habsburg army as well as the Russian troops who had been sent to Transylvania to help the Austrians as early as January 1849. In southern Hungary, the Hungarian authorities and landowners were assisted by Hungarian and Romanian peasants as well as by German and Bulgarian settlers against the Serbian Border Guards and peasants as well as some units of the old Habsburg army. In this region, called the Banat, every village fought its ethnic war.

On May 15–17, 1848, some 40,000 Romanians—or so it was re-

ported at the time—demanded national autonomy and peasant emancipation at the so-called Blaj (Balázsfalva) congress in Transylvania.
It is estimated that one million Romanians lived in Transylvania at
that time. On May 13, 8,000 Serbs met at Karlowitz (Karlóca, Kar-
lovci) to create the Vojvodina, an autonomous Serbian province. This
is a somewhat unimpressive figure in view of the half a million or
so Serbs who lived in the region. The social and political programs
adopted by the Blaj and Karlowitz congresses were quite radical, yet
we must recall that both Romanians and Serbs supported the Habsburg counterrevolution against the Hungarian revolution.[38]

In Vienna, the so-called second revolution began with a clash, on
October 6, 1848, between the imperial troops and the Viennese radicals as well as with the lynching of Minister of War Count Baillet de
la Tour, whom the mob wrongly suspected of supporting the "reactionary" Croats against the "progressive" Hungarians. Subsequently,
the former Habsburg lieutenant Wenzel Cäsar Messenhauser and the
Polish general József Bem commanded a volunteer force of 25,000
against overhelming imperial forces. The latter were made up mostly
of Croatian Border Guards and Czech draftees, but also of peasant
volunteers, both Czech and German, from Bohemia and Moravia.
The second Vienna revolution ended on October 31, when Field Marshal Windisch-Graetz's armies stormed the city. Nothing better demonstrates the contempt of imperial officers for bourgeois values and
national sentiments than the fact that, following the fall of the city,
they opened up the country's capital to three days of looting. The
Border Guards played a leading part in those events, behaving as if
they were in occupied enemy territory.[39]

Earlier in Hungary, about 30,000 Croats under the Habsburg general Baron Josip Jelačič had clashed with about the same number of
Hungarians, led by the Habsburg general János Móga. Troops on
both sides consisted of imperial-royal regulars (the Croatian Border
Guards counted as regulars), newly recruited National Guards, and
armed peasants. Many of the regulars were neither Croats nor Hungarians; thus the guns on both sides were manned by Czech soldiers
from the same Fifth Imperial-Royal Artillery Regiment of Prague.
This was simply because some units of this regiment were serving in
Hungary and other units in Croatia under Jelačič. We do not know
why soldiers from the same regiment were willing to fire at each
other. Nationalism could not have been the cause, as the gunners

were Czechs in the midst of a Hungarian-Croatian conflict. We must also dismiss the possibility of a social conflict, for both sides proclaimed the emancipation of the peasants and claimed to be reformers. Most likely, the Czech soldiers did not even understand what the whole thing was about, and following the orders of their officers, fired their guns as if on a military exercise. It was important for the outcome of the revolution, however, that the Czech gunners on the Hungarian side aimed better than the Czech gunners on the Croatian side.[40]

By early spring 1849, Kossuth had managed to create an army of about 170,000 men, which almost succeeded in wiping out the Austrians. There were thousands of volunteers in this army, but the bulk was made up of conscripts. The commanding officers of the Hungarian national army, or *honvéd*, were mostly imperial-royal regulars; perhaps half the Hungarian generals were not Hungarians by origin; and several generals of Hungarian background did not speak Hungarian. A few of these officers were demonstrably motivated by ideological convictions; the great majority, however, had just happened to be serving in Hungary or in a Hungarian regiment when the war broke out. Promotion and pay were much better in the *honvéd* than in the Austrian army. Still, there were at least as many Hungarian professional officers in the Habsburg army facing the Hungarians as there were professional officers in Kossuth's Hungarian army. In 1848 the Hungarian army of Kossuth received many volunteers, but in the summer of 1849 the army of his main opponent, the Austrian general Baron Ludwig Haynau, did not lack volunteers either. In fact, Haynau, the "Hyena of Brescia," who was known for his cruelty to Italian civilian rebels, was affectionately viewed by his troops as a dashing and caring leader.[41]

One half of the 16,000 Italian soldiers of Field Marshal Radetzky deserted in the early weeks of the north Italian conflict, but his Hungarian and Croatian units fought "shoulder to shoulder" with the German-speaking and Czech-speaking soldiers against the Piedmontese army and the Italian revolutionaries. This motley army won the war.[42]

To interpret all of this clearly is on its face impossible. Did one half of Radetzky's Italian soldiers desert because of Italian patriotic propaganda, or because these soldiers, most of whom originated from Lombardy and Venetia, found it easier than others to hide? Did Jelačič's Croats invade Hungary in September 1848 because they had been ordered to do so, or because the campaign promised rich booty which was the traditional reward of the hard-fighting Border Guards, or because they were Croatian patriots? Did the Hungarian peasants rally against Jelačič because they feared for their family and property or because they were defending the fatherland? If the latter, then how to explain that the peasant National Guards and other volunteers went home or ran away from the battlefield during the early campaigns against the Austrians? This was the main reason why the war had to be fought with trained conscripts. But, of course, not all National Guards ran away, and some of the peasant militia later became brave soldiers in the regular *honvéd* army.

In the case of Italy, the historian Alan Sked convincingly emphasizes the great effect that Italian patriotic agitation had on Italian soldiers of the Habsburg army stationed in northern Italy.[43] Yet my own research on the Austrian military campaign in northern Italy in 1859, that is eleven years later, seems to indicate that desertion from the Habsburg army was mainly a question of opportunity. Thus, more Lombard troops than Venetian troops escaped from the ranks in 1859 for the simple reason that the war was being fought in Lombardy. Hungarian troops in 1859 may have wished to obey the call of the exiled Lajos Kossuth to desert, but many were held back by the rumor that the French troops of Napoleon III were killing Hungarian prisoners. In reality, the French were not interested in massacring the Hungarian prisoners; they were more concerned with the Croats, whom they suspected of not giving quarter to French prisoners of war. If they killed surrendering Hungarians, it was only by mistake, for the French did not know that both Croats and Hungarians in the army of Francis Joseph wore characteristic "Hungarian" tight trousers.[44] Back in 1848–49, a non-Italian soldier of Radetzky may have thought twice before deserting because of the cruelties perpetrated by Italian patriots on prisoners of war, for example the massacre of wounded Austrians in the Brescia hospitals.[45]

The revolutionary ardor of even the most fervent patriots was frequently in doubt. Kossuth often complained about the Hungarian county administrators who, while Field Marshal Windisch-Graetz's troops were not there, swore never to surrender to the "hordes of reactionary Austrian bandits," yet as soon as the latter arrived, quietly handed over the money and the recruits they had collected for Kos-

suth's army.[46] Considering that the Hungarian revolutionary government and army long maintained the fiction of serving their legitimate king, the departure of one Hungarian royal commissioner and
the arrival of another, both in the baggage train of opposing armies,
could easily confuse the politically uneducated. And truly, the drastic change in friend and foe (often wearing identical uniforms) must
have passed unnoticed by many a peasant conscript.

All in all then, relatively few participated voluntarily in the revolutionary events and the wars, but many participated in obedience to
traditional authority, no matter in which political direction that authority led them.

≺ X ≻

Epilogue and Conclusion

By October 1848 the Habsburg army had recovered its self-confidence
and strength and, with a few violent measures, restored law and order
in large parts of the monarchy. Having disposed of the Piedmontese
threat as well, it now had only the Hungarian problem to face. For a
while, the Hungarians were more successful in conscripting soldiers
than were the Austrians; and in the spring of 1849, while war with
Piedmont flared up briefly in northern Italy, the Hungarians enjoyed
material and numerical superiority over the Habsburgs. Unfortunately for the Hungarians, however, all other nationalities and social
strata except for some of the Polish gentry, the Italian intelligentsia,
and many Germans and Slovaks in Hungary supported the Habsburg
army in its struggle against Kossuth's Hungary. Hence, after the second war against Piedmont had been successfully concluded, the victory of the Habsburg army in Hungary was only a question of time.

One wonders, however, how much these events had to do with
revolution. The revolutionary phase in the Habsburg lands may well
have ended in October 1848; what came later was a war between the
Hungarian national government and other parts of the monarchy.
The Hungarians lost the war, but they soon recovered their strength,
and in 1867 they created a partnership of equals with the German-
speaking political elite. They then put into effect a liberal nationalist program in Hungary that proved both a blessing to some and an
abomination to those who were not part of the Magyar elite.

The revolutions in central Europe had been unprepared; there existed no conspiratorial centers. Yet once civil disturbances began, mostly over poverty, hunger, and the threatened collapse of the Austrian currency, there were enough ideologically committed young intellectuals to inspire thousands of ordinary citizens. Together they mounted demonstrations which almost eliminated the old regime.

The events of 1848 had, from the beginning, a national and social character: ethnic and social issues were closely intertwined. The support given to the revolution by middle class elements, workers, and peasants was hesitant and fleeting. Therefore, all the revolutionary movements collapsed in short order, except for the Hungarian lawful revolution. The latter upheaval pitted two state powers against one another. The majority of the monarchy's politically conscious inhabitants (who made up only a small minority of the total), made clear in 1848–49 that they preferred Habsburg supranationalism to nationalism and civil war.

Perhaps with the exception of northern Italy, there was never again a revolution in the Habsburg monarchy until the collapse of the state following military defeat in the fall of 1918. Almost all in the monarchy favored a peaceful process; the exiled Kossuth was totally unsuccessful in trying to whip up a revolution in Hungary during the international crises of 1859 and 1866.

The monarchy that emerged from the wars and revolutions of 1848–49 has often been described as neo-absolutist. In reality, the term is valid only for the period 1849–60, when the military and then the bureaucracy ran the country under the control of young Emperor Francis Joseph and his advisers. After the defeat at Solferino in 1859 in the war against France and Sardinia, the monarchy gradually veered toward a constitutional system.

Neo-absolutism differed from the old in that the authorities showed far less respect for the traditional estate liberties and historical inner boundaries than they had in the so-called absolutist age under Chancellor Metternich. In a veritable revolutionary move, Hungary was divided into a number of large provinces whose boundaries were not defined by history but by bureaucratic practicality. The ethnic principle of the 1848 revolutionaries was replaced by the consciously enforced supranationality of imperial rule. Peasant emancipation adopted by revolutionary assemblies was not only not revoked but promulgated by imperial decree and put into effect with considerable enthusiasm. Finally, great efforts were made to lure French and other Western capital into the country: it is in the 1850s that the creation of private banks, industrialization, and railroad-building began in earnest.[47]

The guiding principle of all this was the old enlightened or Josephinian one. Its main elements were reliance on a well trained bureaucracy and officers' caste; a profound suspicion toward the often rebellious and fractious nobility from whom, nevertheless, the bulk of the higher ranking officials and officers were recruited; a lingering faith in the "good and loyal (bieder)" peasantry; and concurrent hostility to intellectuals and urban elements in general. The neo-absolutists counted on the Catholic church as a spiritual source of public order, yet they also moved to take moral and political control over the citizens out of the hands of church authorities. The neo-absolutist age, also called the Bach period after Minister of Interior Baron Alexander Bach, was marked by often efficient measures aimed at increasing the authority of the emperor, the wealth of the state, and the satisfaction of its loyal citizens. The foreign political goal, or rather dream, was the unification of Germany under Habsburg leadership.[48]

The neo-absolutistic experiment did not outlast the military defeat of the monarchy in 1859, but the liberal politicians who now took over inherited a state and society very different from what they had been before 1848.

Beginning in the 1860s, Western technology and Western ideas led to a golden age of material progress and political as well as religious emancipation in central Europe. However, in the western half of the monarchy, faith in free trade and free thought did not last much longer than in other parts of Europe. In the 1880s and 1890s, mass politics, demagogic anti-Semitism, clerical anti-liberalism, and Marxist socialist agitation created a completely new political situation. Faced with radicalized politics and power-hungry nationalist politicians, Francis Joseph tried, as a last resort, to assume the role of the people's emperor. Hoping to drown nationalist agitation in a flood of social controversy, he and his bureaucratic advisers introduced, in 1907, universal, secret male suffrage. The Austrian parliamentary elections that followed brought the hoped-for success to the Social Democrats and Christian Socials, two class-based parties with a coherent social program. Yet parliament still remained unworkable, and in the Austrian half of the monarchy the emperor was forced to govern more or less by decree until the collapse of the dynasty in 1918.

Liberal parliamentary politics remained in effect much longer in Budapest than in Vienna. This meant the oppression (a very relative term in view of what happened later in the twentieth century) of the ethnic minorities, the exclusion of the lower classes from politics, and a vigorous parliamentary life exercised by the political elite. All the greater the crash, then, when World War I appeared to prove wrong everything that Kossuth, Deák, and other liberals had believed in.

Despite the anti-liberal and anti-bourgeois agitation, basic human rights and fundemantal freedoms were respected in the Habsburg Monarchy until 1914. Ironically, however, the best defenders of these freedoms were not the radical nationalist heirs of the 1848 liberal nationalists. Instead, the rule of law and freedom of speech were upheld by Emperor-King Francis Joseph, once a mortal enemy of all free-thinkers, and now perhaps the last genuine liberal in his country. He had had trouble learning to be a constitutional ruler, but once his rather slow and methodical mind had absorbed the message, and once he had come to the conclusion that liberal politics alone could be trusted to prolong the rule of his house, he applied the Austrian and Hungarian constitutions with great consistency. In so doing, he resisted the clamor of some of his military advisers that he set up a military dictatorship, at least in unruly Bohemia and Hungary. He also ignored the advice of civilian politicians that he change the dualistic system to a trialistic system, granting equal sovereignty to one or another Slavic-inhabited province; or that he introduce anti-Semitic measures; or that he dissolve parliament and reestablish absolute rule. Yet the emperor-king was able to cope with the pressure of mass politics only until 1914.[49] During that crisis, his own dynastic sensitivities and the new Social Darwinist ideology of the civilian and military leadership led him to declare war on Serbia. The Great War doomed not only his family and monarchy but liberal politics as well. The nationalistic, xenophobic, and anti-Semitic politics of the interwar years were a direct consequence of the democratization and radicalization that had begun in the monarchy well before 1914.

Revolution and the Theater of Public Life in Imperial Russia

LAURA ENGELSTEIN

THE RUSSIAN EMPIRE remained an absolutist state until it collapsed in February 1917. Twelve years earlier, the revolution of 1905 had compelled the tsar to grant the rudiments of modern political life: a parliament and the promise of limited civil rights. But the regime retained its administrative prerogatives; and the exercise of imperial rule, though repeatedly challenged, was never seriously impaired.[1] Indeed, the use of extrajudicial, administrative methods of political repression reached its apex in the years after 1905.[2] Yet for all their staying power, the tsars had been haunted for almost a century and a half by the specter of revolution. The "long nineteenth century," punctuated by the Decembrist rebellion of 1825, began with a massive popular uprising in 1773–74 and ended with the revolution of 1905. This chapter traces the relationship between the forces of order and the forces of change—social, intellectual, and institutional—in the course of these 130 years. It will leave unresolved the question of Russia's fate in the aftermath of the first of its twentieth-century revolutions, suggesting that the final outcome was not yet written in stone.[3]

The story of revolution and potential revolution in nineteenth-century Russia can best be told in three registers. First, it involves an activist state that exemplified arbitrary rule in two dimensions: by ignoring all rules and consistently defying expectation, and by regularly changing the rules it constantly broke. Second, it involves the efforts of educated people outside the apparatus of the state to challenge its claims to legitimacy and either modify its operations or bring it crashing to the ground. Some tried to mobilize the force of popular discontent for political ends, but many spent at least as much effort in converse with officialdom and their cultural peers. The story of intellectual resistance to absolutism cannot be restricted to the role of radicals. It was vastly more widespread and diverse, and without the receptive audience of an alienated professional and privileged class the radicals would not have loomed as large on the political landscape. Third, the story involves a long tradition of popular resistance and revolt, which sometimes emerged in the form of serious disturbances but more often simmered below an ominous surface compliance.

Until the end of the nineteenth century, the major challenge to the political complacency of the regime was enacted not in the village or the factory but on the stage of public opinion, as a dialogue among the privileged few. Despite the efforts of intelligentsia activists beginning in the 1870s to build a popular movement, their systematic contacts with the common folk were limited. By the 1890s they had indeed developed a small following of politically educated workers, but these did not represent the laboring mass. When in the course of that decade textile workers launched a wave of giant strikes, this was not the result of direct political intervention. Likewise, in 1905, radicals helped shape working-class protests once these had begun, but their influence was always tenuous. In terms of bringing the crisis of 1905 to a head, they were more important as ideological gadflies among the disaffected elite, pushing frustrated moderates toward ever more daring gestures of political defiance. The radicals did not stand outside the bounds of the emerging public sphere in which educated Russians struggled against their political disenfranchisement. Whatever one may think of the ultimate consequences of October 1917, the revolutionary challenge that preceded it was not the work of social riff-raff, intellectual fanatics, or criminal misfits, but of respected men with connections in the halls of power and a rich cultural capital. Their allies were less respected, often younger and more impatient, but not isolated from the whole. Nor was 1905 a playground on which the influence of educated leaders— moderate or extreme—held absolute sway; traditions of popular mobilization shaped the contours of collective behavior more decisively than any brand of ideological intrusion.

≺ I ≻

Cossacks and Gentlemen

The story of revolutionary agitation and upheaval in tsarist Russia begins in the eighteenth century. All the essential elements are in place by the time Alexander I comes to the throne in 1801: a politics of radical rupture and cultural innovation implemented by the state; the institutional basis of public opinion, which turns the official ideology of enlightenment against the principles embodied in serfdom and autocratic rule; and the violence of popular rebellion.

The policies of Peter the Great exemplified the primary contradiction of Russian absolutism: the inculcation of Western principles, including the institution of the law, using the unlimited powers of a coercive state. Catherine raised this contradiction to an acute degree by assuming the mantle of enlightened despot. Having colluded in the murder of her husband, the empress advertised her devotion to the rule of law, while never abandoning her belief in absolute power.[4] She fostered public discussion by authorizing the first private printing presses, encouraging the publication of satirical journals, and inviting her subjects to communicate their suggestions for legal reform.[5] She did not, however, allow any challenge to imperial authority, refusing to institutionalize the legal principles proclaimed in her famous Instruction of 1767, revoking the right to private publishing when it suited her whim, confiscating manuscripts that displeased her, and sending intellectually obstreperous subjects to prison for appropriating the values she herself proclaimed.

The greatest challenge to Catherine's rule came, however, not from the cultural elite but from her lowliest subjects, inhabitants of the imperial frontier inspired by a crafty veteran of military service, the Cossack Emelian Pugachev. A clever propagandist as well as charismatic chief, Pugachev led his followers in a bloody assault on the persons and property of the landed class, which lasted from 1773 to 1774 and culminated in a prolonged struggle with the imperial armed forces. The rebellion united the discontents of a motley following, angered by the regime's violation of traditional norms and incursions on particular freedoms: Cossacks, defending their autonomy; serfs and factory workers, fleeing bondage and exploitation; religious sectarians and dissenting priests, guarding outlawed practices; miners and foundry workers; misfits and vagrants (army deserters, escaped convicts, bandits); and members of non-Russian tribal communities.

Styling himself the true tsar Peter III, Pugachev issued numerous decrees and missives couched in the language and form of imperial authority. Surrounded by a mimetic court, complete with rituals and courtiers named after Catherine's favorites, the rebel captain disciplined his followers with the same penalties inflicted by the state, including hanging and threats of torture. Pugachev and his men exhibited an extreme degree of ferocity in attacking their enemies, their property and cultural assets: factories were destroyed; towns, monasteries, and churches stripped and smashed; estates set to the torch, contents as well as structures obliterated. Members of the nobility met gruesome deaths at the rebels' hands, usually in summary fashion. Sometimes, in his capacity as "monarch," Pugachev held court and imposed sentences upon them.[6]

Pugachev had confronted Catherine not only with the use of armed force (learned in service in the imperial army) but also with purloined signs of authority: the name of a dead tsar, the symbols of imperial office, the rituals of formal justice. Catherine replied in kind, with military might, judicial authority, and the ritualized language of retribution. In the end, Pugachev's followers renounced their allegiance, and he was betrayed by fellow Cossacks. Captured and interrogated, he was placed in an iron cage and taken to Moscow, where the public could marvel at his shame.[7]

Catherine now had to please two audiences with vastly different expectations: an imagined European public of modern views; and a Russian one, which anticipated the pleasure of revenge. With an eye on Western opinion, the empress insisted on a proper trial. Though Pugachev's followers met truly grisly deaths, and nobles wished to spare the leader no possible torment, Catherine instructed the judges to exercise moderation, so as not to offend her own "love of humanity" or earn the country a reputation for "barbarity."[8] On January 10, 1775, on a square below the Kremlin, Pugachev was therefore decapitated before being cut apart. The corpse must be left on display, wrote the official in charge of the proceedings, "in order to impress the restless mob," enraged by "the well-known ferocity and inhumanity of the miscreant and his henchmen."[9] The crowd must also watch the culprit die. Those who gathered to witness the execution saw the rebel cross himself and bow. Before the axe severed the head from his body, he spoke his final words: "Farewell, Christian folk; forgive me for all my offenses before you; farewell, Christian folk."[10]

The execution was the third since the death penalty had purportedly been abolished in 1753. Despite her scruples, Catherine thus seemed to have acted in contradiction not only to her self-proclaimed enlightened principles but also to the law of the land.[11] Yet the decision was consistent with the views expressed in the bible of enlightened jurisprudence, Cesare Beccaria's *Essay on Crimes and Punishments* (1764), which had influenced the empress's own Instruction. Though Beccaria denounced the use of torture and the death sentence, he believed that corporal punishment was appropriate for certain crimes and considered death the proper response to rebellion.[12] Subsequently, in 1824, the State Council decided the decrees of 1753 and 1754 had not intended to eliminate the death penalty altogether, and certainly not in cases involving attacks on the sovereign or the state; rather they favored the substitution of exile or corporal punishment.[13] The death penalty was valued not only for its practical effects (eliminating the culprit) but for its psychological and symbolic power.[14] It remained in the tsarist criminal code until 1917, though restricted to crimes against the state and quarantine violations. At the same time, and increasingly after 1881, the death penalty was inflicted on civilians convicted of a wider range of crimes by the military courts, which were governed by separate statutes.[15]

The confrontations between sovereign and rebel reveal a persistent confusion, on both sides, between the literal and the symbolic registers. In the case of errant intellectuals, Catherine punished cultural expression as though it were physical insubordination. Alexander Radishchev became a criminal for having written a text critical of the monarch. Catherine is said to have called him "a rebel, worse than Pugachev."[16] Though the seditious author was condemned to death, the empress was hampered by the niceties of the law in imposing the sentence. In addition to the decrees of 1753 and 1754, there was the 1785 Charter of the Nobility, which exempted members of the class from corporal punishment. In view of these limitations, Catherine commuted Radishchev's sentence to ten years' exile in eastern Siberia and stripped him of his rank, honors, rights, and privileges. Treated harshly while in prison and interrogated at great length, Radishchev did not undergo a public trial; his fate was decided behind closed doors by high judicial officials.[17] On the way to Siberia, he was kept in fetters, a mark of humiliation, but no crowd registered his shame.

Radishchev's subsequent fate mirrored the changing politics of succeeding reigns and showed how much the intellectual preoccupations of rulers and their critics were intertwined. The early years of the nineteenth century were a period of high-minded rhetoric and projects of institutional reform. Under Alexander I, enlightenment was the language of legitimacy as well as of opposition. Four days after coming to the throne in 1801, Alexander restored Radishchev to his rank and honors (he had been released from exile by Paul, who delighted in undoing his mother's legacy). The former exile was soon appointed to an imperial commission charged with revision of the laws. He dreamed of establishing a legal system in Russia comparable to the English one he so admired, but his hope proved vain. In 1802 Radishchev took his own life, in a calculated gesture of protest against the tsar who had set him free but disappointed his faith in the promise of enlightenment from above.[18]

Like Radishchev, many of the guards officers who staged the Decembrist uprising of 1825 were aristocrats close to the throne who embraced the principles of the Enlightenment. In the aftermath of Alexander I's death, when the order of succession was yet unclear (the heir had secretly renounced his claim, while the next in line, the future Nicholas I, did not immediately assume the throne), the officers attempted to prevent the transfer of power by mounting an armed insurrection on St. Petersburg's Senate Square and organizing armed resistance in the south. Their goal was to replace the absolutist monarchy with a different kind of political regime. Their venture into organized opposition thus represented a transition between old and new styles of political intervention. On the one hand, they followed in the tradition of the palace coup, in which highly placed courtiers meddled in the process of succession, either by physically dispatching the legitimate heir or promoting one contender over another. Like the tsaricides who did away with Peter III and later Paul, the Decembrists were privileged men who took it upon themselves to affect the question of who should hold supreme power. On the other hand, in challenging the legitimacy of autocratic rule, the conspirators also represented something new. While Alexander had been flirting with the idea of a constitution and the rule of law, authorizing projects of reform (though strictly behind closed doors), the Decembrists too worked on plans for change. They joined Masonic lodges and formed their own secret committees, in which they dreamed of transforming the principles of enlightened governance into the outline of a renovated state.[19]

They did not, however, work entirely in private. Their goal was not only to achieve practical victory but also to make a moral impression on the society in which they moved. Even before they took to the streets with their ill-fated final performance, they enacted their disaffection in the ballrooms and salons of the capital. As Iurii Lotman has so brilliantly observed, they used the cultural idiom of their own aristocratic world to fashion a language of rebellion and even a new social type, in opposition to, but also in dialogue with, the representatives of power. Exploiting the ritualized structure of their social milieu, they inverted its meanings, attending balls in order ostentatiously not to dance, staging feasts in order not to drink to excess. They imbued every word and gesture with moral significance and were highly sensitive to the impression they produced.[20]

If the rebels' behavior reflected their sensitivity to the importance of public opinion, the opening act of their final drama had disappointing results. The popular audience, composed of the troops who might have rallied to their cause, did not respond as hoped, and Nicholas had seized the heroic lead, establishing the legitimacy of his rule by using force against the adversary.[21] The second act of the Decembrist drama had no audience at all but occurred as a private performance, enacted and witnessed by the principals alone; there was no public trial. Brought from their gloomy cells one by one, the culprits were questioned by Nicholas in person. A commission was appointed to ferret out the particulars of the plot.[22] The evidence and charges were heard by a specially appointed court, which met only to endorse the commission's findings. The defendants first learned of the proceedings when the results were announced. Half the original 579 men brought to trial were acquitted; of the 121 identified as ringleaders, five were sentenced to be quartered, 31 to beheading, and the rest to exile and hard labor. Nicholas commuted the sentences to hanging for the five (including the poet Ryleev) and hard labor for the 31. The pretense of a trial was apparently designed to impress the world with Russia's respect for lawful procedure.[23]

The third act of the Decembrist drama involved execution, exile, and posthumous myth. The hangings were carried out at three in the morning before a small audience. The five men were first stripped of their military honors in a ceremony of symbolic degradation, including the breaking of swords. The bodies were neither mutilated nor displayed but buried in secret. Alexander Herzen recalls in his memoirs that the public was nevertheless shocked by the sentences of death.[24] These were not, after all, bloodthirsty brigands from the imperial frontier, but one's own friends and peers.

Unlike Radishchev, the executed Decembrists did not control the circumstances of their demise. They did not turn their final moments into one last chance to speak through calculated gestures. Rather, the survivors spoke to their fellow countrymen through the pathos of the journey into exile. Their dignity, their continued loyalty to the cause (advertised through the circulation of letters and news), the self-sacrifice of their wives in following them into captivity—this mythic afterlife in the wake of "civic death" completed the narrative of heroic self-dramatization.[25]

In common to the language and gestures of all three acts of resistance—Pugachev, Radishchev, and the Decembrists—was the deployment of official rhetoric and ceremony for subversive ends. Whether Pugachev's "true" tsar and his mimetic court, Radishchev's invocation of the dialogue of enlightened monarch and loyal interlocutor, or the guards officers' secret societies, constitutional dreams, and military heroics—all used the idiom of political legitimacy to challenge the claims of the absolutist state. For most of the intellectual and cultural elite, the Decembrist revolt severed the connection between court ideology and public values. The contrast was not, however, absolute. Nicholas continued to tinker with the problem of eliminating serfdom (in secret, just as Alexander had done); and some of the institutional reforms, such as codification of the laws, begun but abandoned in the preceding reign, were accomplished in the reign that despised Western influences and the rule of law.[26] But Nicholas broke with the posture of enlightenment and Westernization, which had dominated the court at the start of the century and remained the idiom of much of educated society (though in educated circles, as well as at court, conservatism found a newly influential voice). Intolerant of any unauthorized form of expression, Nicholas made free thinking a crime—the natural extension of Catherine's response to Radishchev, though in his case ideologically more consistent.

The legal context shaped not only the consequences of revolt but its very definition. The Criminal Code of 1845 (which remained in effect until 1917) defined "crimes against the state" in broad terms, to cover three kinds of actions: physical assault on the person of the tsar (or members of the imperial household); mass uprising; and propaganda hostile to the sovereign or government or inciting to rebellion. In each case, it was also unlawful to attempt or even intend to engage in such action; to form an association with any of these goals; to participate, aid and abet, or even know about such activity without reporting to the police. The death penalty attached to any involvement in attempts on the person of the tsar or members of the imperial household, as well as to any role in promoting insurrection. Any form of expression injurious to the regime was also penalized: from "bold speech" critical of the government, to the production and/or dissemination of insulting or disrespectful texts and images, as well as damage to likenesses of the sovereign. Initiative in planning and carrying out attacks on the government was punished on a par with any form of participation in such affairs or the failure to report them.[27]

These laws drew on precedents dating back to the seventeenth century, which treated with equal severity the mere intent to rebel, preparation for revolt, and attempts to put the plans into action. The early decrees also prohibited associations promoting such goals, communicating these purposes to others, or failing to report them to the authorities. The 1845 code perpetuated this legacy by defining subversive intention in the broadest possible terms and uniformly applying the death penalty to the full range of subversive acts. Russia was not, of course, the only nation to punish attempts at insurrection with death, but European codes exempted cases in which plans were never carried out or in which conspirators were foiled in the early stages of preparation. Late nineteenth-century Russian legal reformers believed the death penalty was appropriate in the case of attempted insurrection, successful or not, but criticized the existing code for failing to distinguish between more or less direct threats to the established order and among degrees of criminal responsibility. The abuse of ultimate sanctions, they argued, encouraged extremism among critics of the regime, who were bound to suffer in the greatest measure for the least involvement in the most tenuously subversive acts.[28]

Not only was it thus easy to fall afoul of the law, but the law was not always deployed as the favored instrument of repression; administrative reprisals were more common still. Peter Chaadaev was declared insane and put under police and medical supervision for having published the first of his "Philosophical Letters," in 1836. Alexander Herzen was sent into administrative exile on several occasions, which he describes as a series of petty humiliations. As these examples show, the reign of Nicholas was a period largely of intellectual, not practical, opposition. Only one "conspiracy" against the established order—the socialist discussion group led by Michael Petrashevskii—was uncovered by the vigilant police, and even it never translated talk into action.

The one active challenge Nicholas confronted after 1825 had nothing to do with the psychological and philosophical turmoil of the Russian elites or with the anger of the Russian masses, but stemmed from the nationalist resentments of the Poles. The Polish uprising of 1830 originated in the political discontents and romantic longings of army officers, who, like their Russian counterparts, and in the same years, formed secret societies and dreamed of national liberation. They demanded full implementation of the Polish constitution recognized by Russia in 1815 and return of the formerly Polish provinces that had been incorporated directly into the Russian part of the empire.[29] The Polish rebels did not share the Decembrists' vision of social and constitutional change and were not involved in their plans, but contact with the Decembrists led to the arrest and trial of a few Polish officers, who thereby achieved the status of national martyrs. The symbolic link between the two movements was underscored in January 1831, when the rebellious Diet commemorated the Decembrists' execution six years before and unseated Nicholas as king of Poland.[30]

The events of November 1830 were sparked by a group of younger officers galvanized to action by the example of revolution in Belgium and France, by the news that Nicholas was preparing to send Lithuanian and Polish troops to help suppress it, and by the rumor that Grand Duke Constantine, the tsar's brother in charge of Poland, was preparing to arrest the conspirators before they had a chance to proceed with their plans. No less inept than the Decembrists when it came to practical steps, the rebels bungled the beginning of the coup. Having attacked the grand duke's residence, they failed to seize him, and they found no senior officers who would agree to assume command. The awkward start escalated into a serious challenge, however, when the lower classes of Warsaw rallied to the rebels' cause and when moderate leaders, and eventually the Diet itself, lent their support to the struggle against Russia. Constantine's refusal to apply armed force at the very beginning permitted the movement to build up steam. Apparently troubled by legal considerations, the grand duke believed that Poland's status as a separate political unit limited Russia's right to impose itself on Polish affairs.[31]

Though Nicholas, too, allowed himself to be governed in some regards by the provisions of the Polish constitution, he took immediate steps to crush the insurrection. Refusing to consider the appeals of Polish moderates, the tsar sent troops to restore order. Despite considerable ineptitude on the part of Polish commanders, it nevertheless took the Russians nine months to bring the Poles to their knees.[32] The major reason for the Polish defeat was the impossibility of resisting Russian military force without the backing of western powers, which refused to intervene on Poland's behalf. The fight for national independence could not be won on the battlefield. In ideological terms the Polish elite was divided between the conservative to moderate majority, which rejected any program of social reform, and a small number of radicals who were the only ones to gain a popular following, and that only in the towns. The peasantry as a whole viewed the war with Russia as a conflict between landlords and tsar and resented being called upon to fight. In the amputated eastern provinces, many Lithuanian peasants supported the Polish cause but most Ukrainian peasants were anti-Polish.[33] In the aftermath, many prominent figures emigrated; the officers and implicated civilians who remained behind were tried and sentenced to severe penalties, though none were put to death. Poland lost the limited autonomy it had enjoyed since 1815: the rights granted in the constitution were suspended, the independent army, Diet, and universities abolished.[34] The Polish nationalist feeling and the resentment of Russian domination were reinforced by defeat.

If one thinks of the Polish events as an echo of the Decembrist debacle, Nicholas can be said to have gotten satisfaction once again

by asserting military preeminence and using the judiciary to teach a
political lesson. Combating the revolutions of 1848 and their domestic consequences proved a more complex undertaking. Nature and
politics seemed to conspire in that year: a bad harvest led to famine,
followed by a cholera epidemic, and drought encouraged widespread
fires, while the threat of revolution swept ever eastward across the
European continent. After seditious leaflets of foreign origin appeared
in Poland and the Baltic and western provinces in March 1848, Nicholas announced his readiness to defend Holy Russia against the revolutionary peril and sent troops into the region. A year later he sent
forces into Hungary to support Hapsburg rule. From the start, the
regime had feared unrest would erupt in Russia itself. Officials warned
against the spread of "communist" ideas. Censorship was extended to
a ludicrous degree, leading a contemporary to complain that the tsar
was waging a "Holy War against scholarship and knowledge." It was
in this context that the members of Petrashevskii's socialist discussion group (including Fedor Dostoevskii) were arrested and condemned to death in 1849. So oppressive was the campaign against free
expression that even moderates exulted in 1855, when the "thirty-
year tyranny" of Nicholas's reign finally ended.[35]

≺ II ≻

Reform and Rebellion

With the death of Nicholas I and the Crimean defeat, an important
shift occurred in the relationship between Russia's three dynamic
elements—activist state, educated society, and restive populace. In
some obvious ways Nicholas had repudiated the principles of his predecessor's reign: where Alexander I, until his last years, had kept
alive the prospect of enlightened governance, Nicholas made conservatism his official creed and military discipline his civic model.
Alexander had raised hopes of reform; Nicholas had dashed them. Yet
there were striking similarities as well. Both contemplated, behind
the closed doors of secret committees, the modification of serfdom.
Before 1812 Alexander had fostered rumors of constitutional change,
but in the end neither monarch did anything to weaken the autocracy's power.

By contrast, Alexander II initiated a process of reform that not only resulted in real social and institutional change, but for the first time opened the door to public participation in political affairs. The making of peasant emancipation and the "Great Reforms" involved the joint activity of progressive bureaucrats, who had nurtured hopes for change in the inhospitable climate of the preceding reign, and representatives of the nobility. To facilitate their task the state allowed the circulation, within limited bounds, of opinion and the airing of conflicting ideas (the famous "artificial *glasnost'*"). The regime was thus more energetic (unsettling rather than merely intrusive) and more tolerant than it had been for over 30 years.

The second element, located in the educated elite, flourished under the new dispensation. From highly placed personages, prominent landowners, and staid university professors, to disgruntled former students, professional journalists, and radical aristocrat émigrés: all engaged in what might be considered a national conversation. Debate and civic activity were facilitated by a number of institutional changes. The relaxation of censorship permitted the formation of professional journals and associations that widened the range of discourse on public affairs. The organs of local self-government known as zemstvos, introduced in 1864, became the focus of hitherto unthinkable civic activity, providing a context in which respected public figures could press for a broader mandate, for the introduction of constitutional change, for a legitimate role in national life. The elected delegates progressed, with ever increasing disaffection, from respectful petitions to the tsar in the 1860s, to gatherings of angry notables in the 1890s, to the awkward alliance of socially modest but morally intense paid professionals and their well-born but increasingly frustrated gentry employers on the eve of 1905.

If zemstvo activism had a long fuse, which eventually helped spark the outbreak of revolution, the immediate impact of the judicial reforms, also implemented in 1864, was more dramatic. With new rules of procedure, an independent bar, legally protected judges, trial by jury, public access, and published proceedings, the new courtrooms offered a rare opportunity for tolerated free speech. For defendants, their lawyers, sometimes even the judges, and certainly for the public at large, they served as a substitute for political life. While establishment liberals welcomed the changes in their own terms, as a step toward constitutional government and the rule of law, hot-headed members of the younger generation used the platform pro-

vided by the regime as a stage on which to dramatize their opposition
to moderation and compromise of any sort.

The terms of emancipation, announced on February 19, 1861,
ended peasant bondage but left the former serfs with meager allot-
ments of land, heavy financial burdens, and continuing civic liabili-
ties. In the wake of the disappointing decree, the young radicals had
set their hopes on provoking a popular revolution, but they had less
success delivering their message of liberation in the village than before the courts. The third element in the revolutionary equation—
the nation at large—was fitfully restive throughout those years but
generally unresponsive to the issues that moved the privileged few.
The reign of Nicholas I experienced continuing peasant disturbances,
which increased with the rumors of impending liberation. During
the Crimean War peasants enlisted in the hope of gaining freedom
in return; afterwards thousands moved to the Crimea, expecting to
settle there as free men. The authorities had been frightened by a
peasant rebellion in Austrian Galicia in 1846 and anticipated the
worst in 1861.[36] Once the decision had been made, authorities feared
the good news would itself generate unrest.

Indeed a spate of disorders followed the announcement of the
terms of emancipation, which gravely disappointed peasant hopes,
but violence was rare. In the most famous incident, villagers in the
hamlet of Bezdna insisted they had found "true freedom" in the
emancipation decree and had divined the tsar's real motives behind
the misguided claims of his agents in the field. Anton Petrov, a semi-
literate peasant, "discovered" the word freedom in the official text.
Neighbors who heard his message and refused to believe he was
wrong were dispersed by gunshot and a number were killed. Petrov
was seized and shot. The survivors professed the loyalty of their intentions.[37] But the Bezdna incident, strikingly symbolic though it
was, was notable for its isolation.

The most serious challenge to the regime in the 1860s did not
stem from tensions within Russian society but from the frustrated
aspirations of Polish nationalists. Russia's defeat in the Crimean War
and the death of Nicholas I had raised Polish hopes of a new dispensation. But Alexander II, though conciliatory, was firm. Ready to tol-
erate a wider range of cultural activity than Nicholas had been, the
tsar appointed officials sympathetic to Polish interests but refused to
weaken Russian control over Polish life. As early as June 1860 Polish

students and returned émigrés, inspired by the Italian Risorgimento, first mounted public demonstrations in the streets of Warsaw; by February 1861 Russian troops were being called in to disperse them. As in 1830, Polish moderates tried to elicit concessions from the imperial authorities; their efforts this time were crowned with a certain success. But the radicals once again pursued a more aggressive course. Demonstrations in spring and summer 1861 stirred public enthusiasm but were suppressed by Russian troops. By fall the tsar had declared military rule. Churches and synagogues closed in protest.

In the end, Russian policy helped consolidate a united national front of radicals and moderates. In August 1862, when Constantine arrived in Warsaw to assume the post of viceroy, an attempt was made on his life. In response, Constantine and Alexander Wielopolski, then head of the Polish government, ordered the perpetrators publicly hanged. In the wake of this ill-considered attempt at symbolic intimidation, Polish leaders buried their differences in obdurate resistance to Russian might. Despite these divisions and the movement's inability to elicit support from peasants in significant parts of the kingdom and eastern provinces, the insult to national pride and the desire for autonomy kept the cause alive.

In September 1862 the leadership constituted itself Poland's national government and on January 22, 1863, announced a state of insurrection. It declared equal rights for all Polish citizens regardless of religion or ethnic descent and offered the peasants land and freedom. In April the tsar made a conciliatory offer, including amnesty for any who surrendered arms. Meanwhile, England and France supported Polish demands for restoration of the 1815 constitution and return of Lithuania and Ruthenia to the Polish kingdom. But the Poles refused the tsar's offer, and the Western powers failed to intervene. Popular backing for the Polish cause remained uneven; Russia ultimately secured peasant support by instituting agrarian reforms favorable to peasant interests. The Poles continued to differ among themselves over the purposes of the insurrection, and they failed to gain the sympathy of Russian liberals, most of whom saw the struggle as one not of political principle but of power politics, a conflict between states. Ultimately, the Poles were defeated by force of arms and the last of their commanders hanged on a square in Warsaw. In the aftermath, Russia confiscated gentry estates, eliminated the qualified autonomy granted by the constitution of 1815 (already partly eroded after 1830), and introduced a policy of cultural and administrative Russification.[38]

The Polish rebellion was serious: it challenged the integrity of the empire and resulted in a prolonged military confrontation, yet it was by definition a limited threat. More disturbing, because more pervasive and harder to defeat, was the development of cultural and political disaffection among the Russian elite. University students were quick to respond to the freedoms promised by the new era. Their activism represents a classic example of the energy generated between the contradictory poles of tsarist policy. Admission had been expanded after 1855 to include young men of humble background; diversity and relative freedom of speech on university grounds promoted fervent intellectual debate, which in turn led the authorities to restrict the students' liberties and their scholarships. Restrictions on what had so recently been conferred provoked more meetings and discussion, and in 1861 the indignant young men finally poured into the streets in St. Petersburg's first public demonstration. The authorities at first tolerated the protests, but soon lost patience and closed the universities.

The young people who caused this trouble constituted a new generation in cultural as well as biological terms. Its members were generally less exalted in family origin than the highly cultivated, socially prestigious men of the 1830s and 1840s who had nourished critical ideas in the shelter of private salons. The newcomers were often ill-mannered, aggrieved, and prone to ideological grandiosity. They repudiated established ideas and social forms and the absolutes of religion and beauty in the name of a worldly social good; devoted to Reason, Science, and Materialism, they subordinated art to practical purposes, yet set their hearts on the utopian dream of universal happiness. The generation of the 1860s was the first to be dubbed "the intelligentsia," in the sense of denoting a particular cast of mind and intensity of moral commitment, attributes denounced by critics such as Fedor Dostoevskii as the seeds of a great Moral Evil.

Sociology certainly separated the figures of the 1830s and 1840s from their successors. Well-bred, sure of his importance, the wealthy Alexander Herzen chafed under the petty humiliations supplied by the administrative regime. A proud individualist, he disdained the vulgar laissez-faire individualism of the bourgeois life he encountered

in Europe after 1847. Nicholas Chernyshevskii and his peers, by contrast, were obliged to improvise a sense of social worth and com-
pensated with overweening intellectual assurance for agonies of personal anxiety. Yet a sociological ground shift cannot account for the
persistence of the project of self-fashioning that spans the generations—from the Eugene Onegins and Decembrists of the 1820s, to
Herzen and Nicholas Ogarev adopting the model of Romantic friendship and later the sentimental free thinking of George Sand, to the
mock Bazarovs of the 1860s.[39]

The self-styled new men and women of the 1860s chose Chernyshevskii's novel *What Is to Be Done?* as their guide. Vissarion Be-
linskii had told them literature was a social enterprise; texts were to
describe the world, reveal its defects, and propose remedies. In fact,
its effects were not only social but personal. *What Is to Be Done?*
provided the younger generation with the model for a distinctive cultural style, affecting the shape of haircuts, the terms of romance, as
well as political ideas. So convinced were contemporaries (not the
radicals alone) of the power of literature that the establishment liberal Boris Chicherin blamed Chernyshevskii for "inject[ing] the revolutionary poison into our life." The authorities were just as literal-
minded. In 1862 Chernyshevskii was arrested on charges of having
written a radical proclamation and instigating public disturbances.
Despite the complete absence of proof, he was convicted.[40] The novel
was published in 1863, by an oversight of the censor, while Chernyshevskii was in prison.

The novel provided a cast of characters on which to model one's
behavior—the selfless, though self-assertive woman; the gentle, self-
abnegating man; and the ruthless, self-disciplined revolutionary. The
author also became a hero in his own right. Chernyshevskii's conduct at his civil execution and his subsequent dignity in exile produced a saintly aura around his person.[41] The execution also provided
an opportunity for public participation in the drama of political martyrdom. The deprivation of juridical rights and social status, known
as "civil death" (grazhdanskaia smert'), was marked by a public ceremony. The purpose of the performance was to induce contrition in
the condemned and leave an "edifying" impression on the crowd.[42]
Symptoms of such edification were demonstrated in May 1862, when
one of Chernyshevskii's followers was sentenced to exile for distributing a subversive pamphlet. In the words of a witness, spectators

"expressed the bestial desire that [the culprit's] head be cut off, that he be flogged with the knout or at least tied to the column with his head down, as he had dared to go against the Tsar."[43]

Things were different in Chernyshevskii's case. Early in the morning on May 19, 1864, a well-dressed group assembled in the heavy rain on St. Petersburg's Mytninskaia Square.[44] As the sentence was read, Chernyshevskii stood hatless, in prisoner's garb, as was the custom, his crime inscribed on a board hung round his neck. He paid little attention to the proceedings and showed no remorse—for a "crime" he had in any case not committed. The executioner lowered him to his knees and broke a sword over his head, then chained him to the pillory for the required ten minutes of silence. After the ceremony, the crowd thronged the carriage bearing the prisoner away. Admirers threw flowers in his direction and followed in his tracks. One started the cry, "So long [proshchai], Chernyshevskii!!" Others yelled the more poignant, "Til the next time! [do svidaniia]." Even after the police tried to hurry the convoy along, people continued in pursuit, crying out and waving kerchiefs and caps.[45]

Thus did heroes become criminals and criminals heroes. The public no longer consisted of local inhabitants drawn by curiosity to the site of easy moral drama, ready to throw the unfortunate miscreant a few spare kopecks for Christ's sake.[46] The public in May 1864 was a select group determined to frustrate official intentions. And unlike Pugachev, who in traditional fashion begged forgiveness of the crowd, or those among the Decembrists and the Petrashevtsy who repented of their ways,[47] Chernyshevskii rejected the terms of his condemnation. His demonstrative indifference to the process of public humiliation, as well as his followers' celebratory response, defeated the edifying purpose of the event.

The history of these rituals shows that the symbolic repertory of absolutism, on which they so heavily relied, had begun to lose its hold. In 1864, the judicial reform commission complained that public executions had ceased to function as serious political theater, becoming instead "a frivolous spectacle" (prazdnoe zrelishche).[48] One could chain Pugachev and expect the ladies to faint and the crowd to howl, but spectator and perpetrator were no longer what they once had been. Even after 1864, crowds were sometimes indifferent or even hostile to the fate of condemned revolutionaries, but the results were no longer predictable.[49] What had been, in Pugachev's time, "terrifying and meaningful," was now often "a sad and vulgar comedy"[50]—or worse, an occasion for ritualized inversions. The reversal of signification that occurred between 1864 and 1881 under the pressure of the radical assault led to the abolition of public executions and the removal of political cases from the (semi-open) civilian to the closed military courts.[51] Legal procedure and publicity both suffered a defeat, but the defeat was the regime's as well. Not only had the modern features of the reformed judicial system veered out of control, but the archaic elements of traditional discipline had also gone off course.

≺ III ≻

Populists on Trial

What began in the aftermath of 1861 as a scattershot series of disturbances and demonstrations soon gave rise to an organized movement of opposition among the disenchanted "children" of the 1860s. The Populists (Narodniki), as they were called, tried to undermine the autocratic regime and instigate revolution in three different ways: by encouraging the peasantry to rise up against the old order; by promoting the moral value of popular liberation among educated society; and by using violence to attack and kill members of the regime, most importantly the tsar himself. Uniting the movement's disparate groups and varied strategies was a belief in the moral superiority of the peasantry and its collective way of life, a hostility to modern forms of social organization, and an exalted spirit of self-sacrifice. The story of the Populist epoch is one of diversity and disagreement; and also, as in the case of the Decembrists, of public posturing and mythmaking.

The earliest formal organization to emerge after 1861 called itself Land and Liberty—Nicholas Ogarev's answer to the rhetorical question, "What do the people want?" The activities and outlook of this organization were modest. Having opened a bookshop and library to educate Russian society, its members were arrested for corresponding with Herzen in London and the group soon dissolved. At the same time, others rejected the painstaking work of cultural uplift. In 1862 the first "Russian Jacobins," as Franco Venturi calls them, launched the manifesto, "Young Russia," which called for violent revolution, to be followed by a dictatorship of the revolutionary party during the transition to a democratic, federative, collectivist popular regime. Members of Land and Liberty objected to such impatience, insisting their job was not to make a revolution for the people but to assist them once they rebelled on their own and, moreover, to moderate the violence the rebels were sure to inflict on the privileged classes.[52] This disagreement embodied a tension that was to divide Populism throughout its existence: whether to act in the name of the people, if necessary without their participation, or limit oneself to helping them actualize their own presumably rebellious desires; whether to destroy the architecture of privilege and scorn its occupants or find allies among the progressive elite; whether to encourage violence or avoid it.

Until 1866 exhortations to violence had been merely rhetorical. In that year Dmitrii Karakozov attempted to assassinate the tsar. With no clear vision of what was supposed to ensue, Karakozov failed to win the support of his friends in the group led by Nicholas Ishutin and proceeded on his own. Having shot and missed, he was arrested along with the others. Karakozov was tried and hanged; Ishutin, who denounced the act, was reprieved on the scaffold and died in prison. The deed served only to alienate liberal sympathies and push the government toward greater intolerance of radical ideas. The crowd at Karakozov's execution—several thousand strong—did not greet him as a hero.[53]

Even among radical youth, his gesture was unpopular. The various groups that formed in the last years of the 1860s preferred to work among the people rather than take potshots at the regime. Karakozov's act did, however, spark the imagination of a man even more obsessed, and certainly more ruthless, than himself: the infamous Sergei Nechaev. Nechaev was a charismatic "man of the people," who wanted nothing so much as to escape his common roots. Having impressed the leading lights of Populist ideology, Nechaev collaborated with Peter Tkachev and Michael Bakunin in defining the figure of the dedicated revolutionary. This type was an outlaw operating beyond the pale of civil society, one who had "broken every tie with the civil order, with the educated world and all laws, conventions and generally accepted conditions, and with the ethics of this world."[54] Bakunin believed this voluntary outlaw, dedicated to total destruction, would make common cause with the romantic criminals of popular legend, the revolutionary brigand, in the style of the now mythic Pugachev.[55]

Despite their collaboration, Bakunin and Nechaev were separated by an important difference: the anarchist Bakunin dreamed of spontaneous destruction, while Nechaev envisioned the overthrow of the existing order as the work of a conspiratorial core. It was not this distinction, however, that finally drove them apart, but the uninhibited ruthlessness of Nechaev's methods. After a spell in Europe hobnobbing with radical émigrés of the older generation, Nechaev slipped back into Russia where he created an organization with alleged ties to the international revolutionary movement. Suspecting an associate of disloyalty, Nechaev had persuaded other members of his small dedicated band to collaborate in the young man's murder. The deed was swiftly uncovered; Nechaev's followers were arrested and tried; Nechaev himself was extradicted from Switzerland, whence he had fled, tried in 1873, and sent to prison, where he died of scurvy in 1882.[56] His civil execution was held at dawn on January 25, 1873. The few people gathered at the scaffold heard him shout: "Down with the tsar! Long live freedom! Long live the free Russian people [narod]!"[57] The crowd showed no sympathy but, according to the police report, responded to this outburst with the cry: "For this he should be shot!"[58] Even Bakunin repudiated the man he had earlier hailed as a "young fanatic."[59]

In the aftermath of Karakozov's failure and Nechaev's ignominious end, both violence and personal heroism fell into disrepute. The young people who dreamed of social justice now stressed the ethical basis of their endeavor, dedicating themselves to the "people's cause" in a spirit of almost religious fervor. While there was no single Populist ideology, the attitudes reflected in the movement of the early 1870s converged around a set of generally shared assumptions. These spokesmen of agrarian socialism represented themselves as agents of the people's good. The young men and women who abandoned comfortable family lives to toil in the villages in the summer of 1874 urgently tried to speak to the people but generally insisted they wanted the people to speak for themselves. Feeling morally obliged to repay the luxury of social privilege they enjoyed, the radicals launched their pilgrimages to the rural heartland in the spirit of collective self-sacrifice. They denounced political institutions as instruments of oppression, scorned constitutional distinctions as an indulgence of interest only to the elite, and believed their movement would swell from below to institute a paradise of social equality. Some favored peaceful "propaganda" (the followers of Peter Lavrov), others provocation (the Bakuninite "rebels") as a means to start the peasants off, but in either case the movement would be massive and democratic.

Because the Populists took as their ideal the collective organization of peasant life and denounced the individualism, social hierarchy, and economic exploitation of Western capitalism, they hoped to forestall further erosion of traditional peasant ways. In the spirit of Alexander Herzen, they counted Russia's "backwardness" a moral blessing.[60] Thus speed was of the essence. It was not only the rigidity and intolerance of the regime that threatened their enterprise but its (however limited) readiness for change. Insofar as the autocracy promoted economic modernization, it contributed to the demise of old social forms; insofar as it modified its own structure to allow limited public participation in administrative and legal affairs, it opened the door to the further development of the principles of individual rights and freedom of expression. While the regime feared the destabilizing potential of such changes, the radicals worried that increased national wealth and extended political liberties would produce a stable social order based on civic inequality and economic exploitation much harder to challenge than the oppressive, slow-moving system currently in place.

Initially, therefore, the Populists rejected the value of political change and focused instead on mobilizing broad social forces against the regime, not in order to achieve liberty in a formal sense but to promote social justice by direct action. The second Land and Liberty organization, established in 1876, concentrated on propagandizing the peasants, while also making contacts among St. Petersburg workers. But, as in the first encounters of 1874, the activists were disappointed with the people's response. By the end of the 1870s, the Populists had recognized the need to address the political context in which they operated. Their relationship to the political system took two forms: first, making use of existing institutions to promote their ideas and gain a following in educated society; and second, trying literally to destroy the political regime. Sometimes the two approaches merged, as in the case of terrorists brought to trial for acts of violence against the state, who then used the courtroom as an opportunity to address the public and the scaffold as a stage on which to enact the heroism of ultimate self-sacrifice and dramatize the villainy of the established order.

The striking contradictions of the post-reform monarchy were underscored by these political trials. For the generation that came of age after the judicial reforms, the legal system presented both a threat and an opportunity. The new courtrooms constituted a protected zone of free speech, in which subversive ideas not only found utterance but reached the widest possible audience. The 1864 statutes had introduced trial by jury for serious criminal cases but made an exception for crimes against the state, which were to be heard in special chambers. Correct procedure was nevertheless to be observed, and except in cases of seditious speech, trials were open to the public.[61] Despite its general suspicion of both law and public life, the regime was at first convinced this system could work in its favor. Officials apparently believed that exposure to the radicals' ideas would educate respectable society to their dangers and deprive the revolutionaries of the allure of mystery.[62]

The first trials immediately made clear, however, that the impact on public opinion was just the opposite. The confrontations with authority were at least as significant in making the Populists into a public force as their contacts with the people they hoped to arouse. From the government's point of view, the first problem was the relative autonomy of the reformed judiciary. In the trial of Nechaev's followers (1871) the judges, and even the prosecutors, strictly observed the rules of proper procedure. The accused were treated with respect, and the verdict was restrained; half the group were acquitted. The second problem was the unpredictability of the effect. The trial drew an eager and varied audience, ranging from officials to ordinary people, but composed mostly of students. Far from discrediting the defendants, their speeches made a vivid impression on the public. The right-wing press condemned the outcome, but others hailed the accused for their moral fortitude or praised the result as a triumph of legal principle.[63]

The authorities were dismayed at the outcome but could not argue that the rules had been ignored. The tsar considered the verdict scandalous and asked the minister of justice to protest, but there was no legal basis for doing so. Legal principle, however, could not prevail in an autocratic state. Two elements of the original procedure were soon altered: preliminary investigations were removed from the purview of judicial authorities and transferred to that of the police; and political cases were shifted from the regular courts and assigned to a special arm of the Senate, which had the option of sitting behind closed doors. From now on, published accounts of trial proceedings were truncated, and the right of appeal was curtailed.[64] The pitfalls of the political trial, which seemed to have vindicated rather than discredited the accused, were avoided in the case of Nechaev himself, who in 1873 was charged as a common criminal, for premeditated murder, not as a political offender. The jury returned a verdict of hard labor, which the tsar increased to life in prison.[65]

Even with these adjustments, the radicals still succeeded in using the courtroom to propagate their ideas and appeal to public sympathies. Their moral impact was greatest in the two cases in which the defendants were charged not with violence but with conducting propaganda or participating in an illegal association—the Trial of the 50 (March 1877) and the Trial of the 193 (October 1877 to January 1878). Eager to perform well, the prisoners rehearsed their speeches under the indifferent eye of the prison guards. In court they appeared as paragons of moral rectitude and champions of free thought, confronting the absolutist state with a posture of absolute virtue.[66]

The defendants in the "monster trial" of the 193 made the most of the courtroom setting. Protesting the tight controls on public access, the accused demanded their right to an open hearing.[67] The audience of officials and policemen hardly constituted "the public," complained Ippolit Myshkin: "To call this public access [publichnost'] is to make a mockery of one of the basic principles of the new judicial process." He insisted on the right to explain his beliefs "to all members of society not just a few bureaucrats."[68] When Myshkin was allowed to address the court, he complained he was not permitted to speak freely (net publichnosti, net glasnosti). "Here one cannot speak the truth," he railed. "Every honest word is stifled . . . [T]his is no court but a hollow comedy."[69] Ironic language for people who scoffed at the law and seized every occasion to stage political theater of their own.

What was amazing about this trial was not in fact the limited public access, but the respect for due process that prevailed, despite the theatrics of the accused and the literal disorder in the courtroom.

When the senators suggested transferring the case to a military court, Nikolai Tagantsev, the eminent legal scholar, persuaded them to continue. Although the court in the end affirmed the existence of a "criminal association," the verdict was mild. The senators emphasized the mitigating circumstances of the crimes and asked the tsar for leniency. But the minister of justice urged him instead to overturn the ruling, which Alexander did, increasing the severity of the sentences.[70] Even so, the tsar's caprice missed the mark: among those released were Sofia Perovskaia and Alexander Zheliabov, both later involved in Alexander's assassination. Of the 193 accused, only 64 were convicted. Over 100 innocent people had thus languished in prison, subject to harsh conditions and physical mistreatment, for three years awaiting trial. The defendants emerged from the ordeal with a new sense of collective identity, as victims of official malfeasance and the object of public sympathy.[71]

Under such circumstances, the sense of "justice" (both fairness and fair play) manifested by the principals in the trials (court personnel, lawyers, and jurymen) did not necessarily lead them to observe the content or formalities of the law. The trial in March 1878 of Vera Zasulich was the most famous instance in which the verdict constituted a moral but not a strictly legal decision. The day after the end of the Trial of the 193, Zasulich shot and wounded, but failed to kill, the municipal governor of St. Petersburg, Fedor Trepov, who had ordered the flogging of a political prisoner for refusing to remove his cap in the official's presence. The flogging had been approved by the minister of justice; the victim later died. Zasulich did not deny her deed, which occurred in front of witnesses. She was apprehended on the spot. Like Nechaev, Zasulich was tried not for a crime against the state but as a common criminal, for attempted murder. In her case, however, the strategy misfired.

Still eager for the prestige associated with formal justice and intent on depriving the terrorists of the aura of heroic devotion to a cause, the ministry of justice decided to risk an open trial by jury.[72] The St. Petersburg circuit court, presided over by Anatolii Koni, displayed remarkable independence, observed due process, and opened its doors to the public and the press. The argument centered on who had acted with greater contempt for the law, Trepov by beating the student in his custody (unlawfully inflicting corporal punishment on a gentleman) or Zasulich by shooting Trepov ("taking the law into her own hands" [samoupravstvo], the prosecutor said).[73] The jury, composed of educated city dwellers and lowly functionaries, was so impressed with the morality of her cause, that it minimized the obvious fact of the shooting.[74] The acquittal provoked a public demonstration of rejoicing, as Zasulich was whisked away by the crowd. Too late, the tsar tried to have Zasulich rearrested (she escaped) and would have liked to dismiss the court in its entirety. In an interesting example of the limits of law and lawlessness in the honeymoon years of legal reform, the tsar was apparently hampered from doing so by the elaborate procedure demanded (by law) for the dismissal of judges. The Senate nevertheless annulled the court's ruling.[75]

As the authorities continued to interfere with proper procedure, their tenuous claim to lawfulness was further eroded. The revolutionaries were cast in the role of defending justice, not in the sense of fairness (social justice or morality), but in the sense of rights and protections. When Ivan Koval'skii was sentenced to death by a military court in July 1878 for armed resistance to arrest, an army officer complained: "In Russia there is no law. Koval'skii was tried in public [glasno], but his fate was sealed behind the scenes [bezglasno]."[76] When General Nicholas Mezentsev, head of the Third Section, was shot by Koval'skii's friends two days after his execution, the moral balance did not shift in the regime's favor.[77] A crucial attribute of "justice," in the minds both of the accused and of the public, was access—*glasnost'*. What was morally and politically reprehensible was what occurred behind closed doors.

The political trials had become tribunals, in which the defendants played dramatic roles in a spell-binding theater of ideas. The gravity of their offenses got lost in the pathos of endangered justice. Despite their contradictory views of the institution that brought them together, judges and lawyers became the radicals' allies in a struggle with the administration and the Crown. Soviet historians used to say that "bourgeois justice" (primarily in the person of high-minded defense attorneys) was morally enhanced by its association with the revolutionary cause, but one can more reasonably argue that the revolutionary enterprise was ennobled by the dignity of justice, which championed the rule of law even on behalf of the lawless.

The attorneys were to a man defenders of legality, not partisans of revolution. They were often distinguished members of the profession. In the words of Vladimir Spasovich, they were "the knights of the living, free . . . word."[78] They spoke not only in defense of their clients' rights but in defense of their own freedom to speak. The authorities acknowledged their power by limiting their ability to use it. In 1872, the ministry of justice advised the senators to prevent attorneys from "develop[ing] arguments contrary to the law," and in 1882 the minister of war instructed the military courts to prohibit defense attorneys from using "inappropriate criticism, metaphors, allegories, and other oratorical devices."[79]

The defendants praised their defenders: one of the accused at the Trial of the 193 said the lawyers not only helped the group's legal cause but "to a significant degree enhanced the trial's political meaning and its influence on public opinion."[80] Attorneys typically stressed their clients' moral purity (women stood as icons in this regard: Sofia Bardina, Zasulich, Perovskaia).[81] Even in the case of the tsaricides, lawyers blamed the government for driving the conspirators to extremes.[82] They challenged the very definition of criminality: Peter Aleksandrov, who had prosecuted the followers of Nechaev in 1871, argued in defense of Zasulich in 1878: "What was yesterday considered a political crime, today or tomorrow will become a highly regarded feat of civic prowess. Political crimes often represent values that have not sufficiently matured, for which the time is not yet ripe." One radical said of Aleksandrov: "He did not so much defend Zasulich as indict the entire [political] system."[83]

The authorities seemed to share this view: a police officer complained that the speeches for the defense, "besides the influence they exert on the unfortunate outcome of the trials, engender intellectual ferment and dissatisfaction and by undermining the foundation of government authority, more than anything else breed support for agitation."[84] Until 1881, trial accounts were published in the newspapers, which provided detailed (if incomplete) accounts with the appeal of serial thrillers. A few journals ran into trouble with the censor for openly supporting the defendants and their cause. Sympathizers hectographed accounts of the trials which circulated among the public. The radicals also made deliberate appeals to moderate opinion, emphasizing the issue of political freedom, guaranteed, of course, by proper legal procedure, as central to the interests of Russian society at large. After 1881, however, both authorized and underground accounts virtually disppeared.[85]

Who was serving whom? as Lenin might have asked. The Populists believed the professionals were promoting the cause of revolution by depicting them as self-sacrificing idealists, victims rather than perpetrators of violence and lawlessness. The lawyers saw the situation in reverse. During the Trial of the 50, Spasovich remarked to one of the accused: "Do you know that nevertheless you are working not for social revolution, which is still far away. You are doing no more than clear the path for us 'bourgeois-liberals,' as you call us. We will make use of your efforts and your sacrifices." Indeed, the experience of the trials provoked a strong mood of support for the principles of legality. Translations of Beccaria's treatise appeared in 1878 and 1879. Establishment liberals issued appeals for constitutional protections and the rule of law, which were published abroad and smuggled back into Russia.[86]

The courtrooms thus provided an arena for the exercise of public opinion, for a form of participation in civic affairs that was at the same time a protest against the limits of that possibility. This was as true for the audience as for the principals. People slipped into the courtrooms (2,000 at Zasulich's trial). Crowds gathered at executions: 80,000 for Alexander Solov'ev in 1879, 100,000 for the tsaricides in April 1881.[87] The regime had banked on the malleability of the audience: the "simple folk" (prostoliudie), whose emotions could be plied by well-staged spectacles of suffering. It had not counted on a "public," whose reactions to edifying displays could not be controlled.[88]

The government's disdain for correct procedure only encouraged the mimetic tendencies among the Populists. The sequence of arrests, resistance, trials, and executions, coming upon the radicals' failure to inspire rebellion among the folk, enhanced their preference for terror. Land and Liberty vowed to "disorganize the state," to exploit the appeal to well-meaning liberals for revolutionary purposes. In March 1879 an attempt was made to assassinate Alexander Drentel'n, who had replaced the late Mezentsev as head of the Third Section. In April, with the organization's tacit approval, Alexander Solov'ev took a shot at the tsar; he was hanged a month later. In August Land and Liberty made Alexander's assassination its top priority.[89] At this point the tension between partisans of social revolution and of terror finally broke the organization apart. Those who stuck with the "orthodox" approach of revolution from below left to form a group called Black Repartition, which was soon decimated by arrests. Those committed to terror dubbed themselves the People's Will, or the People's Freedom (Narodnaia volia). It was they who plotted and carried out the assassination of Alexander II on March 1, 1881. Their case was the last of the period's big political trials and their execution the last to be staged before a crowd.

≺ IV ≻

Workers and Social Democrats

The triumph of terror was also its undoing. The people did not respond with favor to the assassination of the tsar. The regime moved political trials to the military courts, curtailed publicity, and conducted subsequent executions within prison walls. In August 1881, exceptional legislation, known as the "Regulations on Measures for the Protection of State Security and Public Tranquility," imposed an emergency regime, in some cases amounting to martial law, that allowed the administrative apparatus to ignore the procedural restraints enacted in 1864. Introduced as a temporary measure, these laws were not consistently invoked, but they remained in force until 1917.[90]

Thanks to this legislation and to other changes in legal procedure, the courtroom ceased to function as a forum for the expression of political ideas and the occasion for moralistic self-dramatization. As the regime curtailed the institutional gains of the 1860s, terror diminished and opposition took new forms: Marxist Social Democrats offered an ideological and organizational alternative to Populism, and polite society began to mobilize in support of the liberal cause. Factory workers embarked on massive strikes to improve economic conditions.[91] As the high drama of early Populism faded, deep processes of social and cultural transformation were at work that altered the disposition of political forces. When the long-desired climax came in 1905 it was not the movement early radicals had dreamed of. Modernity, not tradition, proved the key to political transformation, just as tsarist officials had feared.

Yet it was tsarist policy that set the stage for the process of change. The stimulation of economic development emerged from the same calculation that lay behind emancipation and the Great Reforms: Russia must modernize to retain its stature on the international scene. The social consequences of this policy initiative could not, however, be controlled by the old legal instruments and administrative techniques. Cities grew and the industrial work force expanded. More peasants than ever before sold their labor in rural hiring markets, engaged in crafts and cottage production, and left home for seasonal factory employment. Meanwhile, the lives of villagers left behind were altered by contact with printed material, manufactured goods, new styles of clothing, and the tall tales of boastful friends. Factories appeared in the countryside as well as in urban centers; a large proportion of manufacture occurred in rural settings. Yet, even surrounded by fields and muddy roads, work in a nearby textile mill was different from spinning in one's hut or milking the cows.[92]

The process of social transformation and extended cultural opportunity initiated in 1861 affected the privileged as well as the common folk. With the expansion of higher education, the professions grew in size and developed an organizational context. Despite tight controls over public association, the trained elite formed its own groups, societies, and journals. Science, progress, enlightenment were the dominant values of the 1860s and 1870s. Economists and physicians studied Russia's changing social landscape and devised ways in which scientific knowledge might promote the national and popular welfare.[93] The young "nihilists" and rationalist utilitarian critics of the 1860s merely reflected the spirit of the times in their scientific fervor and enthusiasm for spreading the light. Although they warned of the dangers of modernity, the Populists, too, participated in the enterprise of enlightenment. In addition to bringing knowledge to the village, early Populists also founded study circles for workers. They sometimes claimed they sought only to profit from the workers' village ties and persisted in believing that factory laborers retained their country values, but in fact it was easier to communicate with people who had left the rural context behind (if not necessarily forever).[94]

In the wake of the Great Reforms, establishment professionals turned to the study of social problems: economists, labor specialists, ethnographers, and physicians produced information useful to the formation of social policy and participated in programs of social improvement. Far from confronting each other across an abyss, the radical devotee and the state servitor occupied points on a continuum.[95] At the same time, the Populist ethos was considerably wider and more pervasive than the number of its heroic protagonists in the

1870s would suggest. A set of attitudes associated with Populism permeated the thinking of wide strata of educated society. Many socially engaged professionals shared the Populists' idealized vision of the common folk.

The diffuse Populism of the 1880s also differed from the hard core in its attachment to the liberal ideals of civil rights, individualism, and the rule of law. Many marked by its spirit managed to combine this outlook with the kind of paternalism that motivated tsarist social policy. The case of factory legislation, for example, shows how official and oppositional values converged: these laws were designed by bureaucrats as much to fulfill the traditional obligations of the custodial state, as to ward off the "proletarianization" of the industrial labor force. In protecting workers from the exploitation of the profit-seeking boss, the regulations expressed a distaste for capitalist mores that persisted within the government, despite the promotion of industry and enterprise by forward-looking officials.[96] It was a distaste Populists, both hard and soft, typically shared.

Despite these congruences, in political terms professionals were hostile to the administrative state, and their hostility grew as the century progressed. They themselves did not want to be subject to state control; if social discipline were to be exercised, they wanted to administer it themselves. They wanted the right to form associations, hold meetings, raise questions, print articles, and determine policy. They wanted a civil society in which to exercise the authority generated by knowledge, cultural standing, and scientific expertise. So resistant, however, was the regime to sharing its mandate with the social and cultural elite, that the beneficiaries of the state's half-hearted measures of reform found the ambivalence more than they could bear.

The roots of liberal constitutionalism go back to the 1860s, when provincial gentry pressured the tsar to widen the opportunities for public involvement in government.[97] The terror campaign of the 1870s and the administrative reprisals it provoked elicited a renewed burst of activism in respectable circles. Believing terror and repression were two sides of the same coin, some zemstvo delegates called on the revolutionaries to abandon violence and join in the movement for reform (the offer was refused) and on the regime to create the preconditions for normal civic life.[98] The tsar took a step toward accommodating such initiatives in 1880, when he appointed the conciliatory Count Michael Loris-Melikov minister of internal affairs, but the potential for reform was once again extinguished on March 1, 1881.

The break was not, however, absolute. Alexander III may have wanted to undo major features of the judicial reforms, but even his powers were not unconstrained. In the first place, the process of industrial development could not be reversed. Russia's performance in the war against Turkey (1877–78) suffered from some of the same technological deficiencies apparent in the Crimean War. Economic traditionalism was not a policy option. In the second place, the progressive spirit that had animated the bureaucracy in Alexander II's day persisted into the 1880s. Members of the State Council did not always hide their disagreement with the new monarch's ideas.[99] In some cases ministries undertook projects of reform, such as plans to redraft the civil and criminal codes, that hardly matched the spirit of the new era.[100]

Not surprisingly the balance weighed in the monarch's favor: the restrictions on due process already introduced in the 1870s in response to the Populist trials remained on the books. The dominance of police over judicial authority was consolidated, as we have seen, in August 1881, when political trials were shifted from the regular to the military courts and local officials acquired extraordinary repressive powers; in 1889 the elected justices of the peace were replaced by the so-called land captains appointed by the central administration; in 1890 the powers of the zemstvos were curtailed. Official tolerance for criticism reached an all-time low, and conservatives denounced the institutional legacy of the Great Reforms as politically subversive. Arrests and trials of radical activists continued at a vigorous pace, though not in open court, until their organizations were decimated.[101]

But dissatisfaction was mutual. Educated society blamed the devastating famine of 1891–92 on the government's economic policies. The impression arose that officials were incapable of dealing with the catastrophe they had unleashed. Local gentry, distinguished intellectuals (Leo Tolstoi most notably), rural physicians, and concerned city dwellers volunteered their help. It was in a similar spirit of civic patriotism that the Tver gentry addressed the new ruler upon his accession to the throne in 1894. They called for respect for the rule of law, including individual and civil rights, and in particular freedom of expression. Nicholas, in his famous reply, denounced the petition as an expression of dangerous and "senseless" dreams.

At the start of the last Romanov reign respectable society thus found itself caught between an administratively active but politically rigid regime that stubbornly denied it access to power and an ideologically impatient intelligentsia eager to destroy the basis for political stability and social cohesion. Although this intelligentsia did not set the revolutionary crisis in motion and never exercised anything resembling control over the popular forces that joined in the fray, it produced a language of politics and offered a map of the social terrain which governed the way participants understood their own actions and how commentators later described the events. It is therefore important to take note of the ideological watershed that occurred in the 1890s among the heirs to Populist radicalism.

Populism as a movement was shattered by political repression. Terror had neither brought down the autocracy nor slowed the capitalist tide. The "people" had not risen in revolt but was assuming a new social profile. Marxism appealed to Russian intellectuals in the 1890s because it accepted and explained the facts of economic and social change. Rather than deploring the advent of capitalism as the doom of popular liberation, Marxists hailed its arrival as a necessary step in the transition to a socialist future. But Marxism in its Western European version did not fit the Russian case. Russia was undeniably moving toward a capitalist system of production. Yet it was just as clear that the country remained predominantly agrarian and that absolutism had not given way to the bourgeois constitutionalism supposed to accompany the capitalist order and understood by Marx as the precondition for the emergence of truly democratic public institutions. Some Marxists therefore argued that in Russia the proletariat would play an even more essential role than in the West, providing the cutting edge not only for the ultimate socialist revolution, but also for the more immediate, so-called democratic one. Marxist theory thus assimilated the Russian case to a universal paradigm, while making allowance for its peculiarities. Instead of insisting that revolutionaries fight the tide of progress, as the Populists had done, Marxists offered the hope that history might be on their side.[102]

Marxism also provided the framework for a radical culture that drew on Populist precedent while marking a distinctive turn. Competing for influence, Marxists took pains to distance themselves from

their forerunners, stressing their acceptance of capitalist development and the workers' key role in the revolutionary cause. In turning
toward the proletariat and renouncing terror, they were in fact continuing the recent shift in the Populists' own orientation. Although
more strictly defined, Marxism also resembled Populism in providing a range of intellectual (and tactical) options for political activists
hostile to the tsarist regime. Some Marxists, like Lavrov, emphasized grass-roots work and propaganda; others, echoing Bakunin, proclaimed their faith in the masses' elemental rebelliousness; still others, in the spirit of Tkachev, stressed party leadership and the role of
violence.

Although no single version of Marxism at first prevailed, the
idea of orthodoxy itself exercised a powerful authority, replacing
the aura of moral prowess with which the Populist heroes had in-
vested themselves. Deliberately exacerbating theoretical differences,
Lenin imposed ideological standards that served disciplinary ends.
The Bolshevik-Menshevik split that crystallized in 1903 exemplifies
the manufactured incompatibility that helped him seize the organizational upper hand. The split also reflected the tension between the
revolutionary voluntarism of Marx's political thinking and the evo-
lutionary implications of his historical analysis. Mensheviks emphasized the need to build a mass following, to stress democratic process
within the party, to work together with opposition liberals in overturning absolutism to make way for a bourgeois-democratic regime.
No less convinced that the winds of history were blowing their way,
the Bolsheviks nevertheless stressed the need to manage one's sails
and move in advance of the stream. Revolution would never emerge
from below; it must be launched by a disciplined conspiratorial
party.[103] But not even Lenin abandoned the ideal of the revolutionary
mass movement. He envisaged a party that would not replace but
lead the proletariat in its designated historical role, even if the workers were not entirely clear where they were headed.

What indeed had the people been doing since emancipation that
kept the intelligentsia's revolutionary hopes alive? What, in particular, had the proletarian newcomers contributed to the potential for a
popular movement?

Peasant unrest fluctuated with the hardships of the agrarian economy. It also responded to policy changes and public events: the Crimean War, emancipation, the assassination of Alexander II. The forms

of rebellion and the values to which they were attached were largely traditional, however. As we have seen, the peasants of Bezdna resisted the terms of liberation by appealing to the authority of the tsar. The same tactic (or belief) characterized other examples of peasant defiance in the 1870s, leading the Populists to admit their best hope was not to challenge the people's resilient monarchism but to "put the revolutionary party in the place that the mythical Tsar now holds in the eyes of our citizens."[104]

Far from embracing the Populists as substitutes for the monarch's divine authority, however, the people expressed their indignation at Alexander's death in a form more compatible with the values of autocracy than the ideals of its intellectual critics. The anti-Jewish pogrom, a common form of popular violence in the post-emancipation period, emerged with renewed vigor after 1881. At once a vestige of archaic attitudes and a reflection of social change, pogroms originated not in the villages but in the towns. They were set in motion by workers of various sorts—those somewhat detached from their communities (migrants and the unemployed) but also those perfectly well integrated (artisans, craftsmen, factory hands, railwaymen).[105] For all their ugliness, moreover, pogroms had their own "moral economy," if one can extend E. P. Thompson's limited sense of the term to cover demonic forms of community action.[106] They revealed a logic, a recognizable choreography, a sense of grievance, and a coherent vision of the world as a place of traditional values violated by invidious outsiders connected with commercial gain (the Jews). Tolerated or sometimes encouraged by local authorities, the pogroms were not instigated from outside. If tsars and ministers shared the mythology behind the disorders, they condemned the riots themselves, fearing the target would shift from the Jews to the upper classes and the regime itself as the ultimate sources of popular misery. The Populists, for their part, deplored the mythology but celebrated the events as harbingers of larger, more systematic unrest.

If sometimes folk attitudes were clearly unacceptable, at other times rebellion presented radical leaders with a confusing mix of conduct and views. Populists were often mortified, and more often frustrated, by the actual belief systems they encountered in the villages. They were considerably more successful in their interchanges with workers, who had access to urban life and its cultural opportunities; but if departure from the countryside made laborers more receptive to new ideas, the experience of change did not necessarily bring enlightenment. The pogroms, after all, were not initiated by the most remote, traditional peasants, but by workers or part-time peasants with a wider exposure to the world.

Shifting from peasants to workers as the target of political mobilization did not resolve the ambiguities of social definition or cultural outlook. In trying to establish an ideological link with their putative constituency, Marxists focused much of their debates on the question of whether Russian workers constituted a class (the proletariat) in the classic sense of the term, and what kind of consciousness these workers (proletariat or not) could be said to have developed. Recognizing that Russian workers were not uniformly or deeply urbanized (their families remained in the villages; they retained ties to the land, went home for the holidays) and many were virtual peasants still (textile operatives being the prime example), Social Democrats struggled with the same problem of "backwardness" the Populists had confronted in reverse. This proletariat (in the loose sense of the term) had not only to perform both the democratic and the socialist revolutions but to do so with a fractured sociological and cultural profile. How could a social formation lacking a proper class constitution (varied relations to the means of production, uncertain connection to city life, deep ties to patriarchal custom) produce "class consciousness" let alone "revolutionary class consciousness"?[107] Insofar as such half-baked proletarians did in the end generate widespread disorders, was their activism a product of their modern half or of their incomplete modernity?[108]

In fact, most activists neglected such theoretical niceties and behaved as though workers could learn the basic lessons of socialism from the experience of factory labor, economic exploitation, and political oppression, regardless of the anomalies of their cultural situation. It was after all clear that common people, from peasants to workers, no matter how raw, were capable of concerted mass action. Early protests by serfs attached to factories, wage bargaining in the rural labor markets, and, most dramatically, the spontaneous textile strikes of the 1870s and 1890s proved the point.[109] Radicals therefore concentrated on producing a stratum of educated workers, exposed to culture in general and to socialist ideas in particular, which would bring ideological direction to the rebellious but unstable mass. Candidates for such a politicized labor elite emerged in the last decades of the century as a result of the expansion of industrial production, the increased demand for literate, skilled workers, and the workers' own thirst for self-improvement. But although ambitious working-men and radical activists came into frequent contact, these "advanced" men were not necessarily more amenable to intelligentsia interests than their "backward" brethren, though for different reasons.[110] Some wanted culture, not revolution. Others wanted revolution, but on their own terms. In either case, they were not passive objects of political manipulation.

From the intelligentsia point of view, workers remained unreliable, both practically and ideologically. In terms of action, some were more likely to mobilize than others; some were resistant, some receptive to formal organization. Many joined collective protests only under the threat or impact of violence by their fellows. In terms of values and aspirations, workers responded to a variety of appeals. In the attempt to undercut the attraction of socialist ideas and forestall labor protest, the regime had done its best to promote the workers' economic interests and thus present itself, in paternalistic guise, as champion of the popular good against the exploitation of greedy bosses. Officially sponsored factory legislation limited hours and conditions of employment and defined certain rights and standards of conduct in the workplace. At the turn of the century, the police undertook the even bolder step of forming authorized labor associations, hoping in like fashion to defuse the radical appeal by satisfying so-called economic grievances.[111]

This tactic conformed to Lenin's fear that the urge for self-betterment which lay behind popular unrest could be satisfied within the bounds of the status quo, or some modified version of it, without challenging the existing social hierarchy or the political framework of autocracy. Yet both factory laws and police unions demonstrated the complexity of the popular response. On the one hand, workers welcomed the opportunity to improve their circumstances and willingly joined the unions. As Mark Steinberg has argued in the case of the printers, the most highly educated of skilled workers, and in 1905 at the forefront of labor militancy, their outlook on the world was fully compatible with the conventional paternalism of their employers.[112] In both cases, on the other hand, conservative expectations were foiled. By introducing the notion of "the worker" as a unifying rubric, marked by the possession of a special booklet and qualifying for special rules and specified treatment, the factory laws encouraged a sense of social coherence that transcended the many differences among actual workers. The experiment in police unionism proved even more dangerous. To demonstrate their authenticity, these unions organized and financed strikes that sometimes got out of hand. Factory owners protested that political loyalty was being purchased at their economic expense. Officials themselves finally realized they had helped promote exactly the kind of collective action they deplored. Once the crisis of 1905 exploded, workers who had previously been involved in police unions proved unusually susceptible to radical appeals and exceptionally likely to join or form new organizations.

Russian workers were a diverse lot (not even to mention their geographic and ethnic variations). Buffeted by changing social and economic circumstances and by competing value systems, some made deliberate choices, some vacillated between extremes. Some acquired the cultural attributes of a working-class elite, which might incline them either to accommodation or to a career of professional revolt. If they were ideologically fickle, workers also learned from experience, and experience seemed to dispose them to revolutionary ideals. But not always, and not exclusively. If we saddle ourselves with the notion of class consciousness, we are bound to seek a consistent outlook tied to economic and social circumstances. But some of the very same workers who went on strike and rallied to socialist slogans were capable on occasion of attacking Jews and bristling at offense to the tsar.[113] Lynching a plant manager may seem less objectionable than killing a Jew, because the manager exercises direct power over his subordinates, whereas the Jews, particularly the impoverished victims of violence, were as vulnerable as their assailants, if not more so. But who is to say the Jewish threat was any less "real" to the peasant or railwayman steeped in anti-Semitic fears and prompted by right-wing agitation than the manager's abuse of authority to the worker on his shift? If we discount the power of symbols then no ideology makes sense. And, after all, the absurdities of anti-Semitism were rife in educated circles; why should the common folk be immune?[114]

Peasants, too, were capable of a range of collective behavior. In addition to the pogroms, which reemerged in waves of increasing virulence in 1903 and again in 1905, and to the widespread violence in the countryside during the revolutionary years, a capacity for self-discipline also emerged. In the general social mobilization of 1905, some peasants organized meetings on the model of the traditional village assemblies, where they debated the ideas of schoolteachers, zemstvo employees, and activists from the cities, and elected delegates to congresses and a national "peasant union."[115] In their capacity as soldiers and sailors, peasants mutinied in massive numbers, sometimes to the accompaniment of political slogans, sometimes not. John Bushnell has argued that peasant-soldiers disobeyed when they felt authority to be endangered; as soon as superiors recovered their confidence, order returned. In short, like the perpetrators of pogroms who struck when authority slackened after the murder of Alexander II, the mutineers did not defy authority but took advantage of its breach.[116]

≺ V ≻

Society Against the State

However uncertain the political awareness of workers and peasants, the revolution of 1905, when it finally came, presented a massive challenge to the principles embodied in the autocratic regime. Not only did it unite the disparate constituents of Russian society in a movement for fundamental change in relations of power and deference, whether enacted on the factory floor or on the governing boards of city councils. It also linked the articulate political goals of the educated elite to the visceral unhappiness of the popular masses, combining classic elements of peasant revolt with patterns of behavior, organizational forms, and political ideology generated by the modern sector of Russian life. Set off in January 1905, when troops opened fire on a procession of respectful workers petitioning the tsar, the revolution reached a bloody climax in December of that year, when politicized workers, now militant and armed, confronted government troops over the rooftops of a Moscow factory district. Persisting into 1906, in a profusion of violence on both sides, the revolution finally gave way to the routine of newly instituted electoral politics, a concession wrested from the reluctant regime only under the pressure of violent confrontation.

If the revolution was "popular" in the sense of all-encompassing, it was not popular in its origins. Initiative in bringing opposition to a head came from the privileged, not the downtrodden. While intelligentsia radicals had been laboring to build a popular base, critics of autocracy among the gentry and professional classes built a political movement centered on their own civic claims. Just as the regime's contempt for its own legal institutions prompted law-abiding attorneys to defend the honor of their radical clientele, so restrictions on the legitimate activities of trained professionals and notables (limits on the professional autonomy of physicians, interference in the activities of zemstvo delegates) generated widespread discontent among groups with no sympathy for revolutionary methods or goals.[117] Educated men and women who found their ordinary affairs imbued with political meaning soon progressed to the formation of associations with overtly political goals.

In the same period radical activity also took more solid, though still illegal, organizational form. In 1898 the Social Democrats established themselves as a national party. In 1901 Populism reemerged in the shape of the Socialist Revolutionary Party, which championed the rights of the "laboring masses," peasant and worker alike, and revived the tradition of political terror. Assassins removed the minister of education in 1901 and successive ministers of internal affairs in 1902 and 1904.[118] Disobedience among university students reflected the rising level of public impatience. Staging massive demonstrations, which led to massive arrests; defying academic authorities and the police; boycotting classes—students acted without their elders' inhibitions. When the ministry of education threatened the miscreants with military conscription, the educated public took their side.[119] These were, after all, their own children. What also helped maintain a sense of common cause among the disparate strands of disaffected opinion was the government's unwillingness to tell them apart: in official eyes radicals and reformers were equally suspect. It was no less illegal to meet in a private apartment to discuss civic affairs than to establish a revolutionary party. Laws banning strikes and labor unions likewise made it hard for workers to ignore the political consequences of economic self-defense.

In the end the regime so narrowed the compass of legitimate public action that confrontation was almost inevitable. The revolution, when it finally exploded in January 1905, began as an outgrowth of strikes in St. Petersburg metal factories that had been organized by a government-sponsored labor association. On what became known as

Bloody Sunday, a procession of workers led by the Orthodox priest Father Gapon made its way toward the Winter Palace with a petition for the tsar. Originally recruited by the police, Gapon had built a mass organization, without abandoning the classic rhetoric of traditional popular protest. Imploring justice from the throne, as peasants for generations had done, Gapon's followers were stopped by gunfire before they reached their goal. The shooting at Bezdna had not affected the ancient compact between faithful folk and benevolent ruler. Now the magic no longer worked. The massacre was the signal for a general explosion of popular indignation: thousands of workers all over the empire walked off the job.[120]

The January strikes were not the work of agitators. But the readiness of laborers to take to the streets, and of course the general public response to the shooting, reflected the degree to which society as a whole felt the tsar's mandate had failed. After arousing initial enthusiasm, the war against Japan, begun in 1904, soon resulted in humiliating Russian losses that alienated public opinion. Peasants suffering from land hunger and heavy taxation had rioted in 1902–3, the same year that strikes peaked in the south and massive pogroms swept the southwest. However isolated the common villager may have been from national affairs (though clearly news reached far beyond the cities, through rumor and more recently, the press), the peasantry was not in fact insulated. As soldiers, peasants were called upon to contain civil disorders (to restrain pogroms, stop strikes, and ultimately to suppress the revolution); in 1904 they were mobilized to fight in Japan. Conscription itself provoked dismay and disorder. There was not a corner of the social landscape sheltered from the impact of structural change, free from doubt as to the legitimacy of the old social contract, unaffected by the willful and inconsistent policies of a fearful and repressive regime.

It was the comprehensive sweep of this disaffection that generated the political volatility, but also the creativity, of the revolutionary events. In urban communities, the breakdown of order brought disparate social groups into contact for the first time. Workers met students in university lecture halls. Printers met municipal employees on city squares. Neighborhoods formed councils (the *sovet*, a term which had not yet acquired its future political meaning), in which delegates from different factories joined to oversee local affairs. Each time the government summoned a committee to quiet the unrest, elections were held, representatives constituted; when the committee was dispersed, the constituency had learned a lesson in electoral process and acquired another layer of distrust for the regime.

What was notable about 1905 was not the continued existence of archaic patterns of popular revolt, its least surprising feature, but the extent to which the common folk engaged in novel forms of collective action and responded to the rhythms and aspirations of a cross-class social movement. Indeed, if one looks for the points at which political meaning and social participation crystallized, they are to be found at the intersection of class and cultural categories: where professional staff met gentry notables in zemstvo administration; where blue- and white-collar employees crossed paths in the transport, communications, or public service sector; where educated noncommissioned officers commanded urban garrisons; where skilled metalworkers plied their trade amidst the common labor force of giant mills; where recruits returned to the village or peasants returned from factory jobs.[121]

In this context, radical ideology provided symbolic cohesion where social reality was fragmented and diverse. It served as the lingua franca of the revolution. Russia had no true proletariat (if one existed anywhere), but rather a congeries of artisanal trades, skilled shop workers, manual laborers, machine operatives, service workers, and shop clerks. Among these the trained and literate provided the political lead, while the destitute and oppressed followed in their wake. There was no true bourgeoisie, but rather a disparate range of respectable types associated with the various aspects of modern economy and culture: entrepreneurs and industrialists, defensive about their social standing in a culture hostile to commercial life; professionals (doctors, lawyers); establishment intellectuals (professors, journalists); artists, writers, and performers; and the "petty bourgeois" fringe (office workers, teachers, librarians, bank clerks). Among these the capitalists did not stand out as a unified group interested in translating economic power into political rights.[122] And conversely, the "bourgeois" role was often filled by players from the premodern sector: notably gentry liberals immersed in provincial affairs.

Despite 1905's imperfect profile and precocious "proletarian" thrust, participants nevertheless understood it as the "bourgeois" revolution. While social claims energized the "masses," whose mobilization gave the political element the force it needed to prevail, constitutional demands provided the common denominator around which educated society could adhere. Yet the pathos of the revolution, like the moral drama of the Populist trials, stemmed not from the aspirations of the moderates, but from the heroic gestures of those on the social or ideological edge. The idea of socialism exerted a charismatic appeal that transcended sociological frontiers: liberals acknowledged the importance of the social question, as they struggled for basic political rights;[123] rallying to the proletarian flag, pharmacy clerks left their conciliatory employers alone in the shops, bemoaning the shattered bonds of patriarchal fellowship, struck with the incongruity of their assistants' claims.[124] Finally, the apocalyptic showdown in December 1905 between armed workers and tsarist forces intensified the "proletariat's" symbolic allure.

Yet the revolution did not topple the regime. Rather, the combined assault of society across the board—from city halls to peasant villages, battleships, railroad lines, post offices, armaments plants, and restaurants—forced the tsar to resume his role as political demiurge. The October Manifesto established a parliament and promised limited civil rights. Would the civil society that managed a fragile coherence in the course of 1905 survive the transition to institutional routine? Would the radicals who rallied their troops to the constitutional cause respect this solidarity or be driven by the lure of ideological extremes? Would the absolutist state encourage them in this direction, or would it permit the evolution of public life to proceed? Would it reevoke the massive disaffection that preceded 1905 by violating its own rules and maintaining the administrative ideal? Would the popular forces that fueled the mass movement in 1905 continue to expand and accumulate resentment, while keeping alive the memory of that astonishing moment when their power finally struck home? These questions were still unsettled in the wake of 1905.

＜＞

REFERENCE MATTER

Abbreviations

AAE	Archives des Affaires Étrangères, Paris
AHN	Archivo Histórico Nacional, Madrid
AHR	*American Historical Review*
AN	Archives Nationales, Paris
Annales	*Annales: économies, sociétés, civilisations*
CEH	*Central European History*
CHLA	Leslie Bethel, ed., *The Cambridge History of Latin America* 3 (Cambridge, 1985)
Col. de Ced.	Collección de Cédulas
EHR	*English Historical Review*
FHS	*French Historical Studies*
HZ	*Historische Zeitschrift*
JMH	*Journal of Modern History*
JSH	*Journal of Social History*
RH	*Russian History*
SHM	Servicio Histórico Militar, Madrid
SR	*Slavic Review*

≺ ≻

Notes

INTRODUCTION

1. Jacques Godechot, *The Taking of the Bastille: July 14th 1789* (London, 1970 trans.).

2. R. R. Palmer, *The Age of the Democratic Revolution 1: The Challenge* (Princeton, NJ, 1959), 306–17. For a more rounded and favorable view of Burke see Connor Cruise O'Brien, *The Great Melody: A Thematic Biography of Edmund Burke* (Chicago, 1992).

3. Among the surveys of the 1848 revolutions see Jonathan Sperber, *The European Revolutions, 1848–51* (New York, 1994); Peter Stearns, *1848: The Revolutionary Tide in Europe* (New York, 1974); Priscilla Robertson, *Revolutions of 1848: A Social History* (Princeton, NJ, 1952); and Francois Fejto, ed., *The Opening of an Era: 1848* (New York, 1973 trans.), which has the most encyclopedic geographic coverage.

4. See Stanley Mellon, *The Political Uses of History: A Study of Historians in the French Restoration* (Stanford, 1958); and E. J. Hobsbawm, *Echoes of the Marseillaise: Two Centuries Look Back on the French Revolution* (New Brunswick, NJ, 1990), chap. 1.

5. See especially F. Furet and M. Ozouf, eds., *A Critical Dictionary of the French Revolution* (Cambridge, MA, 1989 trans.), sec. 5: "Historians and Commentators"; also Alice Gérard, *La Révolution française: Mythes et interprétations* (Paris, 1970).

6. See Richard Cobb, *Reactions to the French Revolution* (Oxford, 1972), chaps. 1–2; Gwynne Lewis, *The Second Vendée: the Continuity of Counterrevolution in the Department of the Gard, 1789–1815* (Oxford, 1978); Jean-Clément Martin, *La Vendée et la France* (Paris, 1987), chaps. 8–9; Jonathan Skinner, "The Revolutionary and royalist traditions in southern village society: the Vaucluse Comtadin, 1789–1851," in A. Forrest and P. Jones, eds., *Reshaping France: Town, Country, and Region during the French Revolution* (Manchester, 1991).

7. See Isser Woloch, *The New Regime: Transformations of the French Civic Order, 1789–1820s* (New York, 1994).

8. See Robert Bezucha, *The Lyon Uprising of 1834: Social and Political Conflict in the Early July Monarchy* (Cambridge, MA, 1974).

9. Peter Amann, *Revolution and Mass Democracy: The Paris Club Movement in 1848* (Princeton, NJ, 1975).

10. This attitude is evoked in Louis Chevalier, *Classes laborieuses et classes dangereuses à Paris pendant la première moitié du XIXe siècle* (Paris, 1958).

11. See Ted Margadant, *French Peasants in Revolt: The Insurrection of 1851* (Princeton, NJ, 1979); John Merriman, *The Agony of the Republic: The Repression of the Left in Revolutionary France 1848–1851* (New Haven, CT, 1978); and Maurice Agulhon, *The Republic in the Village: The People of the Var from the French Revolution to the Second Republic* (Cambridge, 1982 trans.).

12. See Richard Herr, *The Eighteenth-Century Revolution in Spain* (Princeton, NJ, 1958), and compare Ernst Wangermann, *From Joseph II to the Jacobin Trials* (Oxford, 1959) on the Habsburg Monarchy.

13. See John Tone, *The Fatal Knot: The Guerrilla War in Navarre and the Defeat of Napoleon in Spain* (Chapel Hill, NC, 1995).

14. See especially D. A. Brading, *The First America: The Spanish Monarchy, Creole Patriots, and the Liberal State 1492–1867* (Cambridge, 1991), chaps. 24–27.

15. See John Lynch, *The Spanish American Revolutions, 1808–1826* (New York, 1986).

16. See R. R. Palmer, *The Age of the Democratic Revolution 2: The Struggle* (Princeton, NJ, 1964), chap. 10.

17. E. P. Thompson, *The Making of the English Working Class* (New York, 1966), 197–98.

18. See Margot Finn, *After Chartism: Class and Nation in English Radical Politics, 1848–1874* (Cambridge, 1993).

19. Reprinted in Palmer, *Age of the Democratic Revolution* 1:509–12.

20. See David Higgs, *Nobles in Nineteenth-Century France: The Practice of Inegalitarianism* (Baltimore, 1987).

21. Arno Mayer, *The Persistence of the Old Regime: Europe to the Great War* (New York, 1981), especially chaps. 2–3.

22. Daniel Klang, "Bavaria and the War of Liberation, 1813–1814," *FHS* 4 (Spring 1965): 22–41. The quotation is from 41.

23. Hans Rosenberg, *Bureaucracy, Aristocracy, and Autocracy: The Prussian Experience, 1660–1815* (Boston, 1958), 203. On Montgelas see Klang, "Bavaria and the War of Liberation."

24. On the liberals see James Sheehan, *German Liberalism in the Nineteenth Century* (Chicago, 1978), pts. 1–2; on the radicals see Jonathan Sperber, *Rhineland Radicals: The Democratic Movement and the Revolution of 1848–1849* (Princeton, NJ, 1991).

25. The harsh comments of Lewis Namier on the Parliament's handling of the nationality question are still worthy of consideration: *1848: The Revolution of the Intellectuals* (New York, 1964).

26. See especially R. John Rath, *The Viennese Revolution of 1848* (Austin, TX, 1957).

27. Karl Marx, "The Storming of Vienna, The Betrayal of Vienna," in id., *Revolution and Counter-Revolution*, ed. Eleanor Marx Aveling (New York, 1971 ed.), 67–68.

28. On all aspects of the Hungarian revolution see István Deák, *The Lawful Revolution: Louis Kossuth and the Hungarians 1848–1849* (New York, 1979).

CHAPTER 1

1. L. S. Mercier, *Le Nouveau Paris* (Paris, 1798), 6:160–62.

2. See A. B. Spitzer, "The Historical Problem of Generations," *AHR* 78 (1973): 1364–96; id., *Old Hatreds and Young Hopes: The French Carbonari Against the Bourbon Restoration* (Cambridge, MA, 1971).

3. As a political genre, the memoir existed in France since the Renaissance: see P. Nora, "Les Mémoires d'Etat," in id., ed., *Les Lieux de mémoire* 2, 2 (Paris, 1986): 355–400.

4. Quoted in G. Lukács, *The Historical Novel* (London, 1962 [1st Russian ed., 1938]), 56.

5. *The Collected Letters of Thomas and Jane Welsh Carlyle*, ed. C. R. Sanders (Durham, NC, 1977), 6:402. From a letter to John Stuart Mill, dated June 13, 1833.

6. Ibid., 446. From a letter to John Stuart Mill, dated Nov. 24, 1833.

7. H. S. Lindenberger, "The Literature in History: Büchner's Danton and the French Revolution," in id., *The History in Literature: On Value, Genre, Institutions* (New York, 1990), 109–29.

8. See L. Orr, *Headless History. Nineteenth-Century French Historiography of the Revolution* (Ithaca, NY, 1990); A. Rigney, *The Rhetoric of Historical Representation: Three Narrative Histories of the French Revolution* (Cambridge, MA, 1991).

9. According to images which had already consolidated in the first decade of Napoleonic rule: P. M. Lützeler, "Napoleon-Legenden von Hölderlin bis Chateaubriand (1798–1848)," in id., *Geschichte in der Literatur: Studien zu Werken von Lessing bis Hebbel* (München-Zürich, 1987), 264–99.

10. B. Ménager, *Les Napoléon du peuple* (Paris, 1988), 57–59.

11. Ibid., 24.

12. See Y. M. Bercé, *Le Roi caché. Sauveurs et imposteurs: mythes politiques populaires dans l'Europe moderne* (Paris, 1990).

13. J. Lucas-Dubreton, *Le Culte de Napoléon, 1815–1848* (Paris, 1959), 96 ff.

14. For a detailed account of the international circulation of the legend, see J. Dechamps, *Sur la légende de Napoléon* (Paris, 1931), esp. 65–82.

15. Cited in L. Droulia, "La Révolution française et l'hellénisme moderne," in M. Vovelle, ed., *L'Image de la Révolution française* (Oxford, 1989), 2:1437–45.

16. J. Tulard, *Napoleon: The Myth of the Saviour* (London, 1984 [1st French ed., 1977]), 346.

17. R. S. Alexander, *Bonapartism and Revolutionary Tradition in France. The Fédérés of 1815* (Cambridge, 1991).

18. A. Galante Garrone, *Filippo Buonarroti e i rivoluzionari dell'Ottocento, 1828–1837* (Turin, 1972).

19. P. Geyl, *Napoleon For and Against* (New Haven, CT, 1949 [1st Dutch ed., 1946]), 35; P. Geyl, "French Historians For and Against the Revolution," in id., *Encounters in History* (Cleveland, OH, 1961), 87–142.

20. See A. G. Mazour, *The First Russian Revolution. 1825: The Decembrist Movement* (Stanford, 1961 [1st ed., Berkeley, 1937]), 54–55.

21. J. M. Hartley, "Is Russia Part of Europe? Russian Perceptions of Europe in the Reign of Alexander I," *Cahiers du monde russe et soviétique* 23 (1992): 379–80.

22. E. Plimak and V. Khoros, "La Révolution française et la tradition révolutionnaire en Russie," in *La Révolution française et la Russie* (Moscow, 1989), 217–20.

23. L. Mascilli Migliorini, *Il mito dell'eroe. Italia e Francia nell'età della Restaurazione* (Naples, 1984), 19 ff.

24. P. M. Lützeler, "Revolution as a Theme in the Historical Novel of European Romanticism," in G. Hoffmeister, ed., *The French Revolution and the Age of Goethe* (Hildesheim-Zürich, 1989), 145–58.

25. Ibid., 149.

26. Later retitled as *Les Chouans*.

27. My argument relies on M. Lyons, "The Audience of Romanticism: Walter Scott in France, 1815–1851," *European History Quarterly* 14 (1984): 36–39.

28. See A. Gérard, "Burke et l'historiographie française du XIXe siècle," in *La storia della storiografia europea sulla Rivoluzione francese* (Rome, 1990), 2:85–86.

29. The best account remains the one by P. Bliard, *Les Conventionnels régicides* (Paris, 1913).

30. It has been argued that the romantic revolt against literary genres was, in itself, a reaction to the French Revolution: D. Punter, *The Romantic Unconscious. A Study in Narcissism and Patriarchy* (New York, 1990), 27.

31. M. Milner, *Le Diable dans la littérature française de Cazotte à Baudelaire* (Paris, 1960), 1:299–337.

32. C. Destay, *La Fille de Dieu, ou l'Héroïne des Pyrénées* (Paris, 1821), 93.

33. P. S. Ballanche, *L'homme sans nom* (Paris, 1828 [1st ed., 1819]), vii.

34. M. Milner, "Ballanche et la culpabilité révolutionnaire," in C. Croisille and J. Ehrard, eds., *La Légende de la Révolution* (Clermont-Ferrand, 1988), 353–62.

35. A. Manzoni, *La Rivoluzione francese del 1789 e la Rivoluzione italiana del 1859. Saggio comparativo* (Milano, 1889: posthumous publication of a manuscript which had been written between c. 1862 and 1871). See L. Mannori, "Manzoni e il fenomeno rivoluzionario. Miti e modelli della storiogra-

fia ottocentesca a confronto," *Quaderni fiorentini per la storia del pensiero giuridico moderno* 15 (1986): 7 – 106.

36. J. de Maistre, *Les Soirées de Saint-Pétersbourg, ou Entretiens sur le gouvernement temporel de la Providence* (Paris, 1924 [1st ed., 1821]), 21.

37. V. Hugo, *Les Misérables* (Bruxelles, 1862), 1:86 ff. See also J. Seebacher, "Evêques et conventionnels ou la critique en présence d'une lumière inconnue," *Europe* 40 (1962): 79–91.

38. Quoted in J. S. Allen, *Popular French Romanticism: Authors, Readers, and Books in the Nineteenth Century* (Syracuse, NY, 1981), 63.

39. S. Mellon, *The Political Uses of History. A Study of Historians in the French Restoration* (Stanford, 1958), 3.

40. A. Thiers, *Histoire de la Révolution française*, 10 vols. (Paris, 1823 – 27); F. A. Mignet, *Histoire de la Révolution française depuis 1789 jusqu'en 1814*, 2 vols. (Paris, 1824).

41. *Affaire des Mémoires de l'ex-Conventionnel Levasseur*, app. of R. Levasseur, *Mémoires*, 4 vols. (Paris, 1829–31), 4:313.

42. See Mellon, *Political Uses*, 32–34.

43. M. A. Baudot, *Notes historiques sur la Convention nationale, le Directoire, l'Empire et l'exil des votants* (Paris, 1893), 44.

44. B. Barère, *Mémoires*, 4 vols. (Paris, 1842–44).

45. T. S. Macaulay, *Miscellanous Works*, ed. Lady Trevelyan, 5 vols. (London, 1899), 3:490–93.

46. A. de Vigny, *Stello: A Session with Doctor Noir*, trans. I. Massey (Montreal, 1963), 77.

47. Auguste Blanqui's father, Jean-Dominique Blanqui, had been a deputy of the National Convention in 1792–95.

48. See R. Tumminelli, "Etienne Cabet," in B. Bongiovanni, L. Guerci, eds., *L'albero della Rivoluzione. Le interpretazioni della Rivoluzione francese* (Torino, 1989), 98; F. Kaplan, *Thomas Carlyle: A Biography* (Berkeley, 1993 [1st ed., Ithaca, NY, 1983]), 228–29.

49. H. Ben-Israel, *English Historians of the French Revolution* (Cambridge, 1968), 71 ff.

50. S. Luzzatto, *Mémoire de la Terreur. Vieux montagnards et jeunes républicains au XIXe siècle*, rev. ed. (Lyon, 1991 [1st Italian ed., 1988]), 141–78.

51. Vigny, *Stello*, 78. All quotations from Vigny in the following paragraph refer to this page.

52. For a detailed account of Vigny's readings in the domain of the revolutionary historiography, see P. Flottes, *La pensée politique et sociale de Vigny* (Paris, 1927), 103–21.

53. Which has been masterly portrayed by A. B. Spitzer, *The French Generation of 1820* (Princeton, NJ, 1987).

54. See R. Pozzi, "L'89 nella storiografia francese dell'Ottocento," in P. Viola, ed., *Mentalità e cultura politica nella svolta del 1789* (Napoli, 1987), 211.

55. See below, sec. 3.

56. Y. Knibiehler, *La naissance des sciences humaines: Mignet et l'histoire philosophique au XIXe siècle* (Paris, 1973), 164 ff.; E. J. Hobsbawm, *Echoes of the Marseillaise. Two Centuries Look Back on the French Revolution* (New Brunswick, NJ, 1990), 1–32.

57. See the seminal work of E. Berenson, *Populist Religion and Left-Wing Politics in France, 1830–1852* (Princeton, NJ, 1984); and J. B. Duroselle, "Buchez et la Révolution française," *Annales historiques de la Révolution française* 48 (1966): 77–107.

58. See A. Galante Garrone, "I sansimoniani e la storia della Rivoluzione francese," *Rivista storica italiana* 61 (1949): 251–78; P. Broué, "Un Saint-Simonien dans l'arène politique: Laurent de l'Ardèche (1848–1852)," *Cahiers d'histoire* 2 (1957): 59–79; B. H. Moss, "Saint-Simonians, Robespierre and the Making of the Parisian Working Class (1830–1834)," in Vovelle, ed., *L'image de la Révolution française* 2 : 1547–55.

59. R. B. Carlisle, *The Proffered Crown: Saint-Simonianism and the Doctrine of Hope* (Baltimore, 1987), 41–49.

60. G. G. Iggers, *The Cult of Authority. The Political Philosophy of the Saint-Simonians* (The Hague, 1958), 28.

61. See *The Doctrine of Saint-Simon. An Exposition*, ed. G. Iggers (Boston, 1958 [1st French ed. 1829]).

62. Uranelt de Leuze (pseud. Laurent de l'Ardèche), *Réfutation de l'Histoire de France de l'abbé de Montgaillard* (Paris, 1828), 283, 383, 435–37, 442.

63. The most complete study on the international diffusion of the Saint-Simonian ideas is the one by R. Fakkar, *Sociologie, socialisme et internationalisme prémarxistes. Contribution à l'étude de l'influence internationale de Saint-Simon et de ses disciples* (Neuchâtel, 1968).

64. See Sanders, ed., *Collected Letters of Carlyle* 6:302–3, 403, 446; R. K. P. Pankhurst, *The Saint-Simonians, Mill and Carlyle. A Preface to Modern Thought* (London, 1952), 84 ff.; J. D. Rosenberg, *Carlyle and the Burden of History* (Cambridge, MA, 1985), 76–90.

65. See the accurate analysis of H. Shine, *Carlyle and the Saint-Simonians. The Concept of Historical Periodicity* (Baltimore, 1941), 121 ff.

66. Quoted ibid., 143.

67. H. Heine, *Sämtliche Werke* 5 : 194.

68. See J. L. Sammons, "Heinrich Heine: The Revolution as Epic and Tragedy," in E. Bahr and T. P. Saine, eds., *The Internalized Revolution. German Reactions to the French Revolution, 1789–1989* (New York, 1992), 179–180.

69. I borrow my argument, almost literally, from G. G. Iggers, "Heine and the Saint-Simonians: A Re-Examination," *Comparative Literature* 10 (1958): 297. See also M. A. Clarke, *Heine et la monarchie de juillet. Etude critique sur les 'Französische Zustände,' suivie d'une étude sur le saint-simonisme chez Heine* (Paris, 1927), 242–271.

70. See M. Malia, *Alexander Herzen and the Birth of Russian Socialism, 1812–1855* (Cambridge, MA, 1961), 69–133. The most thorough ac-

count of Herzen's and his friend Nicolai Ogarev's apprenticeship of Saint-Simonianism has been given by M. Mervaud, *Socialisme et liberté. La pensée et l'action de Nicolas Ogarev, 1813–1877* (Paris, 1984), 79–88.

71. Quoted in F. Venturi, *Roots of Revolution. A History of the Populist and Socialist Movements in Nineteenth Century Russia* (New York, 1960 [1st Italian ed., 1952]), 10. Herzen's letter was dated July 19, 1833.

72. My discussion relies on Malia, *Alexander Herzen*, 125–26.

73. P. S. Ballanche, *Essai de palingénésie sociale*, 2 vols. (Paris, 1827–29).

74. See Malia, *Alexander Herzen*, 125–26. But see also E. Acton, *Alexandr Herzen and the Role of the Intellectual Revolutionary* (Cambridge, 1979), 14–15.

75. See J. Dresch, *Karl Gutzkow et la Jeune Allemagne* (Paris, 1904), 16 ff.; R. Boos, *Ansichten der Revolution. Paris-Berichte deutscher Schriftsteller nach der Juli-Revolution 1830: Heine, Börne, u. a.* (Cologne, 1977).

76. Quoted in A. Galante Garrone, "La Rivoluzione francese e il Risorgimento italiano," in F. Furet, ed., *L'eredità della Rivoluzione francese* (Rome, 1988), 186.

77. Quoted in Lindenberger, "Literature in History," 197.

78. See F. Furet, "The Tyranny of Revolutionary Memory," in B. Fort, ed., *Fictions of the French Revolution* (Evanston, IL, 1991), 157.

79. See F. A. Isambert, *De la Charbonnerie au saint-simonisme. Etude sur la jeunesse de Buchez* (Paris, 1966), esp. 44 ff.

80. See J. Droz, "Religious Aspects of the Revolutions of 1848 in Europe," in E. M. Acomb and M. L. Brown, eds., *French Society and Culture since the Old Regime* (New York, 1966), 137.

81. Berenson, *Populist Religion and Left-Wing Politics*, 36–73.

82. See M. David, *Le Printemps de la fraternité. Genèse et vicissitudes, 1830–1851* (Paris, 1992).

83. L. Gossman, "Michelet and the French Revolution," in J. A. W. Heffernan, ed., *Representing the French Revolution. Literature, Historiography, and Art* (Hanover, NH, 1992), 99.

84. See M. Moissonnier, "Les images de la République dans le monde et le mouvement ouvrier lyonnais au XIXe siècle," in *Le Dix-neuvième siècle et la Révolution française* (Paris, 1992), 173–89.

85. E. Cabet, *Histoire populaire de la Révolution française de 1789 à 1830, précédée d'une introduction contenant le précis de l'histoire des Français*, 4 vols. (Paris, 1839–40), 2: 104; see also M. Delon, "La Saint-Barthélemy et la Terreur chez Mme de Staël et les historiens de la Révolution au XIXe siècle," *Romantisme* 31 (1981): 49–62.

86. See P. Gerbod, "L'enseignement supérieur découvre la Révolution française au XIXe siècle," in Croisille and Ehrard, eds., *La Légende de la Révolution*, 597–604.

87. See R. Gosselin, *Les Almanachs républicains. Traditions révolutionnaires et culture politique des masses populaires de Paris, 1840–1851* (Paris, 1993), 70 ff.

88. M. Agulhon, "Politique, images et symboles dans la France post-révolutionnaire," in id., *Histoire vagabonde, 1, Ethnologie et politique dans la France contemporaine* (Paris, 1988), 283–318.

89. J. Burckhardt, *Letters*, ed. Alexander Dru (New York, 1955), 81. From a letter to Willibald Beyschlag, dated June 19, 1843.

90. The most thorough essay on young Marx's period in Paris has been written by J. Grandjonc, *Marx et les communistes allemands à Paris, 1844. Contributions à l'étude du marxisme* (Paris, 1974).

91. Cited in L. S. Kramer, *Threshold of a New World: Intellectuals and the Exile Experience in Paris, 1830–1848* (Ithaca, NY, 1988), 125.

92. See F. Furet, *Marx and the French Revolution* (Chicago, 1988 [1st French ed., 1986]), 26 ff.

93. J. Sperber, *Rhineland Radicals. The Democratic Movement and the Revolution of 1848–1849* (Princeton, NJ, 1991), 289–304.

94. See Kramer, *Threshold of a New World*, 207.

95. Quoted ibid.

96. E. Quinet, *Le Christianisme et la Révolution française* (Paris, 1845); J. Michelet, *Le Peuple* (Paris, 1846).

97. Burckhardt, *Letters*, 97. From a letter to Hermann Schauenberg, dated Feb. 28, 1846.

98. J. Talmon, *Political Messianism: The Romantic Phase* (London, 1960), 476–79.

99. Cited in W. Benjamin, *Das Passagen-Werk*, ed. R. Tiedemann (Frankfurt a. M., 1982), 1:363.

100. See D. Groh, "Cäsarismus, Napoleonismus, Bonapartismus, Führer, Chef, Imperialismus," in O. Brunner, W. Conze and R. Koselleck, eds., *Geschichtliche Grundbegriffe; historisches Lexikon zur politisch-sozialen Sprache in Deutschland* 1 (Stuttgart, 1972): 726–71. See also I. Cervelli, *Liberalismo e conservatorismo in Prussia, 1850–1858* (Bologna, 1983), 350 ff., 419 ff.

101. I am following here Lukács, *The Historical Novel*, 178.

102. P. Gay, *The Bourgeois Experience: Victoria to Freud*, 3, *The Cultivation of Hatred* (New York, 1993), 235–49.

103. The main examples being the historical works of Granier de Cassagnac and Edouard Fleury.

104. Good hints in A. De Francesco, "Democratici e socialisti in Francia dal 1830 al 1851," *Il pensiero. Rivista italiana di scienze politiche* 12 (1986): 459–94; T. W. Margadant, "French Rural Society in the Nineteenth Century: A Review Essay," *Agricultural History* 53 (1979): 644–51.

105. F. Furet, *La Gauche et la révolution. Edgar Quinet et la question du jacobinisme, 1865–1870* (Paris, 1986), 12.

106. Quoted in D. Guérin, *Proudhon, oui et non* (Paris, 1978), 27.

107. Particularly *L'Idée générale de la révolution au dix-neuvième siècle* (Paris, 1851) and *La Révolution sociale démontrée par le coup d'état* (Paris, 1852) had a lasting influence on both sides of the Rhine.

108. See G. Ferrari, *Scritti politici* (Turin, 1973), 877–78.

109. My discussion relies heavily on C. M. Lovett, *Giuseppe Ferrari and the Italian Revolution* (Chapel Hill, NC, 1979), 74–75.

110. See G. Ferrari, *L'Italia dopo il colpo di stato del 2 dicembre 1851* (Capolago, 1852).

111. For the encounter of and the collaboration between Herzen and Proudhon, see J. E. Zimmerman, *Mid-passage. Alexander Herzen and European Revolution, 1847–1852* (Pittsburgh, PA, 1989), 107–34.

112. See M. Mervaud, "Herzen et la Révolution française," *Revue des études slaves* 41 (1989): 169–87.

113. A. Herzen, *From the Other Shore and The Russian People and Socialism*, ed. I. Berlin (New York, 1956), 116–17.

114. Ibid., 94.

115. Quoted in Zimmerman, *Mid-passage*, 180. From a letter dated Sept. 13, 1850.

116. Quoted ibid., 140.

117. See F. Venturi, *Esuli russi in Piemonte dopo il '48* (Turin, 1959); F. Della Peruta, *I democratici e la rivoluzione italiana* (Milan, 1958).

118. See Venturi, *Roots of Revolution*, 90–128; C. Durandin, *Révolution à la française ou à la russe. Polonais, Roumains et Russes au XIXe siècle* (Paris, 1989), 250 ff.

119. See D. Groh, *Russland und das Selbstverständnis Europas; ein Betrag zur europäischen Geistesgeschichte* (Neuwied, 1961); B. Naarden, *Socialist Europe and Revolutionary Russia: Perception and Prejudice, 1848–1923* (Cambridge, 1992).

120. First published on *L'Avènement du peuple* in Aug.-Sept. 1851, reprinted as a brochure in 1852, and collected with other essays in J. Michelet, *Légendes démocratiques du Nord* (Paris, 1854).

121. Herzen, *The Russian People and Socialism*, 199.

122. See M. Mervaud, "Amitié et polémique: Herzen critique de Quinet," *Cahiers du monde russe et soviétique* 17 (1976): 58.

123. A. Momigliano, "Per un riesame dell'idea di cesarismo," in *Rivista storica italiana* 68 (1956): 220–29; W. Kaegi, "Jacob Burckhardt e gli inizi del cesarismo moderno," *Rivista storica italiana* 76 (1964): 150–71; A. Jenny, *Jean-Baptiste Charras und die politische Emigration nach dem Staatsreich Louis-Napoleon Bonapartes. Gestalten, Ideen und Werke französischer Flüchtlinge* (Basel-Stuttgart, 1969), 218–34.

124. See A. Herzen, *My Past and Thoughts* (New York, 1968), 3:1489–95.

125. Some hints are to be found in P. Mainardi, *Art and Politics of the Second Empire: The Universal Expositions of 1855 and 1867* (New Haven, CT, 1987).

126. According to the well-known distinction established by Benjamin, *Das Passagen-Werk*, passim. See also M. Jay, *Downcast Eyes. The Denigration of Vision in Twentieth-Century French Thought* (Berkeley, 1993), 120–47 (esp. 135).

127. See Lukács, *The Historical Novel*, 171–206.

128. The cultural significance of Old Regime style in nineteenth-century

furniture also deserves historians' attention: see L. Auslander, "After the Revolution: Recyling Ancien Régime Style in the Nineteenth Century," in B. T. Ragan and E. A. Williams, eds., *Re-creating Authority in Revolutionary France* (New Brunswick, NJ, 1992), 144–74.

129. See F. Orlando, *Gli oggetti desueti nelle immagini della letteratura. Rovine, reliquie, rarità, robaccia, luoghi inabitati e tesori nascosti* (Turin, 1993).

130. Ibid., 436 ff.

131. Who was then working at a novel with a Vendéen setting, *Cadio* (Paris, 1867).

132. See G. Flaubert and G. Sand, *The Correspondence*, trans. F. Steegmuller and B. Bray (New York, 1993), esp. the letters dated Oct. 8, 1867, Dec. 18–19, 1867, Sept. 19, 1868, Oct. 31, 1868.

133. "The publication of the *Histoire de la société française pendant la Révolution et sous le Directoire* opened the era of bibelot. One should not take this word in a pejorative sense: historical bibelots were once called relics" (R. de Gourmont, *Le Deuxième livre des masques* [Paris, 1924], 259).

134. G. Scaraffia, *Torri d'avorio. Interni di scrittori francesi nel XIX secolo* (Palermo, 1994), 206–21; L. Silverman, *Art Nouveau in Fin-de-Siècle France. Politics, Psychology, and Style* (Berkeley, 1989), 17–39 (esp. 30).

135. What follows in based on V. Gavrilitchev, "La Révolution française chez les publicistes démocrates révolutionnaires A. Herzen, V. Popov et D. Pissarev (de la fin des années 1850 aux années 1860)," in *La Révolution française et la Russie*, 370–77.

136. Publishing book reviews of foreign titles instead of original articles on domestic issues was Russian radicals' common device to deflect the attention of tsarist censorship.

137. My discussion relies on Plimak and Khoros, "La Révolution française et la tradition révolutionnaire en Russie," 235–37.

138. See J. P. Rioux, *Erckmann et Chatrian, ou le trait d'union* (Paris, 1990), 109–10; Lukács, *The Historical Novel*, 207–10.

139. See A. Gerschenkron, *Economic backwardness in Historical Perspective: A Book of Essays* (Cambridge, MA, 1962), 5–51.

140. A. Szabó, "La Révolution à la lumière d'une autre: *Nanon* de George Sand," in Bernard-Griffiths, ed., *Révolution française et romantismes européens*, 291–303; S. Petrey, *History in the Text: "Quatre-vingt-treize" and the French Revolution* (Amsterdam, 1980).

141. H. Taine, *Les Origines de la France contemporaine* (Paris, 1875–93), vol. 4, *Le Gouvernement révolutionnaire*, vii.

142. Ibid., vol. 2, *L'Anarchie*, 313.

143. A. Aulard, *Taine historien de la Révolution française* (Paris, 1908).

144. See R. Pozzi, *Hippolyte Taine. Scienze umane e politica nell'Ottocento* (Venezia, 1993), 287–89.

145. My own account is based on a well-informed and insightful article by B. Itenberg, "La société russe et l'oeuvre d'Hippolyte Taine sur la Révolution française," *La Révolution française et la Russie*, 127–40.

146. For their contacts in the populist milieux, see Venturi, *Roots of Revolution*, 455–56.

147. N. I. Kareev, *Les Paysans et la question paysanne en France dans le dernier quart du XVIIIe siècle* (Paris, 1899 [1st Russian ed., 1879]); I. V. Luchitsky, *La Petite propriété en France avant la Révolution et la vente des biens nationaux* (Paris, 1897). For Kareev's and Luchitsky's influence on the twentieth-century historiography on the French Revolution, see F. Venturi, *Historiens du XXe siècle* (Geneva, 1966), 11 ff.; G. Oliva, "Georges Lefebvre et les historiens russes de la Révolution," *Annales historiques de la Révolution française* 51 (1979): 399–410.

148. See Venturi, *Roots of Revolution*, 438.

149. Quoted in Itenberg, "La société russe et l'oeuvre d'Hippolyte Taine," 139.

150. Cited ibid., 138.

151. I am following here D. Shlapentokh, "The French Revolution in Russian Political Life: The Case of Interaction between History and Politics," *Revue des études slaves* 61 (1989): 132.

152. Cited ibid.

153. L. Engelstein, *The Keys to Happiness. Sex and the Search for Modernity in Fin-de-Siècle Russia* (Ithaca, NY, 1992), 130–44.

154. See C. Lombroso, R. Laschi, *Il delitto politico e le rivoluzioni in rapporto al diritto, all'antropologia criminale e alla scienza di governo* (Turin, 1890); C. Lombroso, "La delinquenza nella Rivoluzione francese," in *La vita italiana durante la Rivoluzione francese e l'Impero* (Milan, 1897). On the Continental influence of Lombroso's theories, see R. A. Nye, *Crime, Madness and Politics in Modern France. The Medical Concept of National Decline* (Princeton, NJ, 1984), 99ff.

155. See L. Mangoni, "Cesare Lombroso," in Bongiovanni and Guerci, eds., *L'albero della Rivoluzione*, 401–4.

156. Quoted in L. Mangoni, *Una crisi fine secolo. La cultura italiana e la Francia fra Otto e Novecento* (Turin, 1985), 99. For Taine's reading of the criminal and orgiastic debauchery of the alcoholic crowd in the French Revolution, see S. Barrows, *Distorting Mirrors. Visions of the Crowd in Late Nineteenth-Century France* (New Haven, CT, 1981), 78ff.

157. Quoted in Mangoni, *Una crisi fine secolo*, 102.

158. V. E. Orlando, *La riforma elettorale* (Milan, 1883).

159. See J. Van Ginneken, *Crowds, Psychology, and Politics, 1871–1899* (Cambridge, 1992), 52 ff. Van Ginneken underlines the fact that Sighele's quite neglected text precedes the much better known work of Gustave Le Bon, *La Psychologie des foules* (Paris, 1895).

160. See ibid., 67 ff.

161. See A. Gramsci, *Quaderni del carcere*, 4 vols. (Turin, 1975), 1:249.

162. P. Digeon, *La Crise allemande de la pensée française, 1870–1914* (Paris, 1959).

163. D. Lindenberg, *Le Marxisme introuvable* (Paris, 1975); D. Lindenberg and P. A. Meyer, *Lucien Herr. Le socialisme et son destin* (Paris, 1977).

164. C. S. Ingerflom, *Le Citoyen impossible: les racines russes du léninisme* (Paris, 1988).

165. See P. H. Hutton, *The Cult of Revolutionary Tradition. The Blanquists in French Politics, 1864–1893* (Berkeley, 1981).

166. See J. M. Mayeur, "La Révolution française est un bloc," *Commentaire* 45 (1989): 145–52; S. Luzzatto, *La "Marsigliese" stonata. La sinistra francese e il problema storico della guerra giusta, 1848–1948* (Bari, 1992).

167. See F. Furet, "Academic History of the French Revolution," in F. Furet and M. Ozouf, eds., *A Critical Dictionary of the French Revolution* (Cambridge, MA, 1989 [1st French ed., 1988]), 881–99.

168. See Luzzatto, *Mémoire de la Terreur*, 204–5.

CHAPTER 2

1. G. Desdevises du Dézert, *L'Espagne de la Ancien Régime: Les Institutions* (Paris, 1899), 50–86; Desdevises du Dézert, "Le régime foral en Espagne au XVIIIᵉ siècle," *Revue Historique* 62 (1896): 236–84. On the junta general of Vizcaya, Renato Barahona, *Vizcaya on the Eve of Carlism* (Reno, 1989), 13–19.

2. Helen Nader, *Liberty in Absolutist Spain: The Habsburg Sale of Towns, 1516–1700* (Baltimore, 1990).

3. Richard Herr, *Rural Change and Royal Finances in Spain at the End of the Old Regime* (Berkeley, 1989), 36–38, 53–56.

4. William J. Callahan, *Church, Politics, and Society in Spain, 1750–1874* (Cambridge, MA, 1984), chaps. 1, 2; Richard Herr, *The Eighteenth-Century Revolution in Spain* (Princeton, NJ, 1958), 11–36.

5. For the reign of Carlos IV as viewed here, see Richard Herr, "Good, Evil, and Spain's Rising against Napoleon," in R. Herr and H. T. Parker, eds., *Ideas in History* (Durham, NC, 1965), 157–81; Castro Bonel, "Manejos de Fernando VII contra sus padres y contra Godoy," *Boletín de la Universidad de Madrid* 2 (1930): 397–408, 493–503; 3 (1931): 93–102.

6. Herr, *Eighteenth-Century Revolution*, 173–80, 337–47, 405–10.

7. Juan Luis Castellano, *Las Cortes de Castilla y su Diputación (1621–1789)* (Madrid, 1990), 151–53, 200–252; Pere Molas Ribalta, "Las Cortes de Castilla y León en el siglo XVIII," in *Las Cortes de Castilla y León en la edad moderna* (3 vols., Valladolid, 1988–89), 143–69.

8. See Sarah Maza, "The Diamond Necklace Affair Revisited (1785–1786): The Case of the Missing Queen," in Lynn Hunt, ed., *Eroticism and the Body Politic* (Baltimore, 1991), 63–89.

9. Accounts differ on what took place in the next few days; see Francisco Martí Gilabert, *El motín de Aranjuez* (Pamplona, 1972). I use also the reports of Tournon to Napoleon, Burgos Mar. 16, 1808 (AN, AFᴵⱽ 1680, 9ᵉ dossier, pièce 8); François de Beauharnais to General Junot, Madrid Mar. 15, 1808 (AAE, Portugal, t. 127, fol. 59); Beauharnais to Champagny, Madrid Mar. 18, 1808 (AAE, Espagne, t. 673, fols. 361–62).

10. Beauharnais to Grand Duc de Berg, Mar. 21, 1808, AN AF^{IV} 1605A Plaque 1^1 pièce 57.

11. Edict of Arias Mon, Mar. 20, 1808, and Real Orden published by Council of Castile, Mar. 21, 1808, AHN, Col. de Ced., v. 30.

12. Beanharnais to Champagny, Mar. 25, 1808 (AAE, Espagne, t. 673, fols. 418–19).

13. Martí Gilabert, *Aranjuez*, 202–12; reports of Tournon to Napoleon, Burgos Mar. 19 and 24, 1808 (AN AF^{IV} 1680 9e dossier, pièces 9 and 10).

14. J. H. Elliott, "Revolution and Continuity in Early Modern Europe," *Past and Present* 42 (Feb. 1969): 35–56.

15. Laura Rodríguez, "The Spanish Riots of 1766" *Past and Present* 59 (May 1973): 117–46.

16. Henry to king of Prussia, Apr. 4, 1808 (AN AF^{IV} 1691, 2e dossier, pièce 66).

17. Beauharnais to Grand duc de Berg, Mar. 21, 1808 (AN AF^{IV} 1605A, Plaque 1^1, pièce 57); Baron Gregoire de Stroganoff to Comte de Stroganoff, Mar. 23/Apr. 4, 1808 (AN AF^{IV} 1694, 2e dossier, pièce 68). The French appear to have intercepted the correspondence of the Prussian and Russian ambassadors to Spain.

18. For events from the riot of Aranjuez through the Assembly of Bayonne, see Miguel Artola, *La España de Fernando VII* (*Historia de España*, ed. Ramón Menéndez Pidal, vol. 26, Madrid, 1968), 3–37, and Martí Gilabert, *Aranjuez*.

19. Artola, *Fernando VII*, 48–68, 309. See also R. Herr, "Nación política y pueblo en el levantamiento de España en la primavera de 1808," in L. M. Enciso Recio, ed., *Actas del Congreso Internacional El Dos de Mayo y sus precedentes* (Madrid, 1992), 231–41.

20. Herr, "Good, Evil, and Spain's Rising against Napoleon," 173.

21. Herr, "Nación política," 236 and nn. 26–28.

22. Artola, *Fernando VII*, 68.

23. Herr, "Nación política," n. 31. This interpretation of the creation of the juntas is different from the usual account, which sees them formed enthusiastically by their members. Anon. [Manuel José Quintana?], in the *Semanario patriótico*, no. 4, Sept. 22, 1808, calls the juntas "the first effect of" the efforts of the people (pueblo) against the French aggressors. This step was provoked by "the shouts and agitation of the most humble classes" and "was afterwards authorized by the higher classes (clases superiores)." This fits closely my analysis. See also the description of the crowds in Madrid by the Prussian ambassador, above. The Russian ambassador pointed to the effect of troublemakers in exciting the crowds in Madrid in April: "The government takes most efficient measures to calm the popular agitation and reestablish the order that several ill-intentioned persons such as can be found in every country try to disturb" (Baron Gregoire de Stroganoff to Comte de Stroganoff, Mar. 23/Apr. 4, 1808, AN AF^{IV} 1694, 2e dossier, pièce 68). We lack a study of these crowds similar to that for England and France in George Rudé, *The Crowd in History* (rev. ed., London, 1981).

24. Artola, *Fernando VII*, 50–51, 58–62.

25. The constitution can be found in *Constituciones de España 1808–1978* (Madrid, 1988), 15–37, and in English in Arnold R. Verduin, *Manual of Spanish Constitutions 1808–1931: Translation and Introductions* (Ypsilanti, MI, 1941).

26. See Artola, *Fernando VII*, 311–24.

27. Auto of Consejo Aug. 11, 1808, in circular of Aug. 12, 1808 (AHN, Col. de Ced. no. 1805).

28. *Manifiesto de los procedimientos del Consejo Real en los gravisimos sucesos ocurridos desde octubre del año próximo pasado* ([Madrid], 1808), 67, 76–77, 81, 87–88.

29. The swearing of recognition and obedience on Sept. 28, 1808, described in "Actas del Consejo de Estado," 1808 (2) AHN, Estado Libro 11. On the creation of the Central Junta, see Angel Martínez de Velasco, *La formación de la Junta Central* (Pamplona, 1972).

30. For example the worries of the junta of Granada, José Palanco Romero, "La Junta Suprema de Gobierno de Granada," *Revista del Centro de Estudios Históricos de Granada y su Reino* 1 (1911): 115.

31. Real Orden Nov. 22, 1808, in AHN Consejos, Sala de Alcaldes de Casa y Corte, Libro de Gobierno 1808, t. 1, fols. 1087–90.

32. Letter of junta of government of Lerida to Central Junta, Jan. 1, 1809; reply of Central Junta, Seville, Jan. 31, 1809, AHN, Estado, Leg. 31F, docs. 133, 134. Real decreto of Central Junta, Feb. 3, 1809, reaffirms a 1774 order giving local *justicias* authority in cases of popular disturbances (AHN, Estado Leg. 4A doc. 5).

33. María de la Encarnación Soriano, "El Padre Rico y el levantamaiento de Valencia," *Archivo ibero-americano*, 2ª época, 13 (1953): 271–72.

34. June 6, (1808); copy in France, Archives historiques du Ministère de la Guerre, Armées d'Espagne, Corr. C⁸7.

35. Pedro Quevedo y Quintano, *Respuesta dada a la Junta de Gobierno . . . con el motivo de haber sido nombrado Diputado para la Junta de Bayona* (Valencia, 1808), dated May 29, 1808 (SHM, Colección del Fraile, t. 27, fol. 224).

36. Miguel Artola, *Fernando VII*, 69.

37. "Instruccion de la Junta Suprema a sus Diputados a la Junta Central" (AHN Estado, Leg. 82A).

38. See Richard M. Morse, "The Heritage of Latin America," in Howard J. Wiarda, ed., *Politics and Social Change in Latin America: The Distinct Tradition* (Amherst, MA, 1974), 48–52. Although Suárez did not propound popular sovereignty, he argued that neither the king nor the people could alter the established pact unilaterally, but a people never lost its right to defend itself against a tyrant and could resist an illegitimate ruler with all the means at its disposal (see Vidal Abril Castelló, "Derecho-Estado-Rey: monarquía y democracia en Francisco Suárez," *Revista de Estudios Políticos* 210 [Nov.-Dec. 1976]: 129–88, esp. 142, 161–63).

39. Juan de Mariana, *Del rey*, quoted in Salvador de Madariaga, *The Rise of the Spanish American Empire* (New York, 1947), 213.

40. Junta suprema, oficio of Sept. 25, 1808, and order of Sept. 26, 1808 (AHN, Col. de Ced. no. 1810).

41. The concept of the junta as cortes was present in the call of the junta de Valencia for a junta central, July 16, 1808, in Manuel Fernández Martín, *Derecho parlamentario español*, 2 vols. (Madrid, 1885), 1:319.

42. "Reglamento para el govierno interior de la Junta Central," Cap. 3, art 1. The document says approved Oct. 22, 1809, but this is an error for 1808 (AHN, Estado, Leg. 1B).

43. Article 5 (AHN, Estado, Leg. 1P, doc. 7).

44. Hans Juretschke, "Concepto de las cortes a comienzos de la Guerra de Independencia," *Revista de la Universidad de Madrid* 4 (1955): 400–403.

45. "Reflexiones acerca de la *Carta sobre el modo de establecer un Consejo de Regencia con arreglo a nuestra constitucion*," *Semanario patriótico*, no. 4, Sept. 22, 1808.

46. Martínez de Velasco, *Formación de la Junta Central*, 207.

47. Miguel Artola, *Los orígenes de la España contemporánea* (2d ed., 2 vols. Madrid, 1975–76), 1:299, 303.

48. Many are published in ibid. 2:129–674, and in Universidad de Navarra, Seminario de Historia Moderna, *Cortes de Cádiz. Informes oficiales sobre Cortes* (3 vols., Pamplona, 1967–74).

49. Antonio Capmany, Informe of Oct. 17, 1809, in Artola, *Orígenes* 2:511–12.

50. Artola, *Orígenes* 1:319–27.

51. AHN, Estado, Leg. 111B, doc. 3.

52. José Palanco Romero, "Notas para un estudio de la Junta Suprema Central gubernativa. Tesis doctoral" ([Madrid, 1908?]), 115–21.

53. Artola, *Fernando VII*, 265–66.

54. Ibid., 411. The proposal of Calvo, AHN, Estado, Leg. 5D, doc. 38.

55. Reglamento para el Consejo de Regencia, AHN, Estado, Leg. 84A, doc. 13, art. 13.

56. I have seen many of these in the "Varios" collection of the Biblioteca Nacional, and the "Colección del Fraile" of the Servicio Histórico Militar. See the bibliography in Artola, *Orígenes* 2:11–109.

57. *Prevenciones que convendrá se tengan presentes en las varias provincias de España* (Jan. 1809? a folio sheet in Biblioteca Nacional, Varios, Fernando VII, Leg. 12 fol.).

58. JC to Council of Castile, Sept. 30, 1808, AHN Estado, Leg. 28A, doc. 2.

59. AHN Estado, Leg. 28C, docs. 149–51.

60. Representación of Lorenzo Calvo, Sept. 12, 1809, AHN, Estado, Leg. 22D, doc. 17.

61. See Artola, *Orígenes* 1:436–37.

62. Spain, *Diario de las Cortes* 1:1–3, Session of Sept. 24, 1810. This was the number listed as "suplentes"; however, another fourteen deputies not

called suplentes did not sign the constitution of 1812, indicating that they too were replaced. All but two (from junta of Aragon and province of Cuenca) of the regular deputies from peninsular Spain came from Galicia, Cataluña, Extremadura, Murcia, and Cadiz, meaning that almost all the deputies for the major part of Spain were suplentes at the outset. (Mallorca and Puerto Rico also each had one regular deputy.)

63. These are the figures given in Artola, *Orígenes* 1:463–64, presumably for the final count of deputies.

64. *Diario de las Cortes* 1:6, session of Sept. 24, 1810.

65. Speech of Diego Muñoz Torrero introducing the motion, ibid.

66. Letter quoted in A. Risco, "Las Cortes de Cádiz y el obispo de Orense," *Razon y Fe* 74 (1926): 526.

67. Gallego, Oct. 16, 1810, *Actas de las Cortes de Cádiz, Antología*, ed. Enrique Tierno Galván (Madrid, 1966), 20.

68. Muñoz Torrero, Oct. 17, 1810, ibid., 21–22.

69. *Decretos sobre la libertad de la imprenta y juntas censorias* (Mallorca, 1813).

70. "Discurso preliminar leido en las Córtes al presentar la Comision de Constitucion el proyecto de ella," Manuel Fernández Martín, *Derecho parlamentario español* 2:664–726.

71. See, e.g., the Cortes of 1789, Castellano, *Cortes de Castilla*, 226–29.

72. Art. 1. The text of the constitution of 1812 is in Fernández Martín, *Derecho parlamentario* 2:732–92, and in *Constituciones de España 1808–1978*, 39–102; and in English in Verduin, *Spanish Constitutions*.

73. Art. 2.

74. Art. 3.

75. Art. 248. The "Spanish territory" is defined in Art. 10.

76. Arts. 371, 172.

77. Arts. 8, 9.

78. Art. 6.

79. Fernández Martín, *Derecho parlamentario* 2:687.

80. Arts. 24 and 25. After 1830, illiterates would also be denied the vote, but the constitution declared that primary schools would be established in every *pueblo* (town and village) (Art. 366).

81. For an assessment of France's experience with national elections during the Revolution, see Isser Woloch, *The New Regime* (New York, 1994).

82. Arts. 91, 92. Fernández Martín, *Derecho parlamentario* 2:682.

83. Arts. 141–49.

84. Art. 226.

85. Art. 312.

86. Warren M. Diem, "Las fuentes de la Constitución de Cádiz," in María Isabel Arriazu et al., *Estudios sobre Cortes de Cádiz* (Pamplona, 1967), 351–486.

87. [Pedro Quevedo y Quintano], *Carta circular del Excmo. S. obispo de Orense, remitiendo á los parrocos y fieles de su diócesi exemplares de su*

representacion (Cádiz, 1812) and *Representacion del Exco. Sr. obispo de Orense, dirigida al supremo consejo de Regencia* (2d ed. Cádiz, 1812), both in SHM, Colección del Fraile. Artola, *Orígenes* 2:94, cites an edition of Madrid, 1812.

88. *Manifiesto del Obispo de Orense á la nacion española* (Coruña, 1813, 2d ed. Valencia, 1814).

89. Art. 12.

90. Antonio Puigblanch [pseud. Nataniel Jomtob], *La Inquisición sin máscara, ó disertacion en que se prueban hasta la evidencia los vicios de este tribunal, y la necesidad de que se suprima* (Cádiz, 1811).

91. Juan Antonio Llorente, *Anales de la Inquisicion de España* (2 vols., Madrid, 1812–13).

92. Juan Antonio Llorente, *Memoria histórica sobre qual ha sido la opinion nacional de España acerca del tribunal de la Inquisicion* (Madrid, 1812).

93. *Informe sobre el tribunal de la Inquisicion con el proyecto de decreto acerca de los tribunales protectores de la religion* (Cádiz, 1812).

94. See Francisco Martí Gilabert, *La abolición de la Inquisición en España* (Pamplona, 1975).

95. *Dictamen del doctor D. Antonio José Ruiz de Padrón, ministro calificador del Santo Oficio . . . sobre el tribunal de la Inquisición* (Cádiz, Coruña, Madrid, Mallorca, Mexico City, 1813, in Biblioteca Nacional, Madrid, Varios, Leg. 63, 4°, another Cádiz 1813 edition cited in Artola, *Orígenes* 2:93).

96. *Manifiesto de las Cortes á la Nacion Española, con el decreto sobre los tribunales protectores de la religion, que deben reenplazar al estingido santo-oficio* (Cádiz, 1813), dated Feb. 22, 1813.

97. I have found seven works specifically in defense of the Inquisition published in 1811 and eight in 1812, but only two opposed to it besides the above histories. These figures are misleading, however, because the periodicals took up the subject, so that it was being widely ventilated.

98. *Representacion que el Excmo. e Illmos. Sres. arzobispo de Santiago y obispos de Galicia . . . solicitando suspendiese la execucion de los decretos de abolicion de la Inquisicion* (Santiago [1813], SHM, Colección del Fraile, t. 230, fol. 90).

99. [José Antonio Saenz de Sta. María], *Segunda representacion que ha hecho el obispo de Segovia al Augusto Congreso Nacional sobre la Inquisicion . . .* (Cádiz, 1813, SHM, Colección del Fraile, t. 650, fol. 122).

100. E.g., D.F.A. y B., Filósofo de Antaño, *Prodigiosa vida, admirable doctrina preciosa, muerte de los venerables hermanos los filosofos liberales de Cádiz* (Cádiz, 1813); and Anon., *Decreto definitivo sobre la Inquisicion al gusto de los liberales* (Cádiz, 1813), which accuses the Liberals of being secretly in league with Napoleon.

101. *A los prelados y cabildos de España, La Regencia del Reyno* (Cadiz, 1813), copy in AHN, Estado, Leg. 745.

102. [Agustín Abad y Sierra], *Copia de la representacion del M. R. Obispo de Barbastro* (Cadiz, 1813).

103. *Felicitacion a la Córtes Generales y extraordinarias* (Palma, 1813).

104. AHN, Estado Libro 12, "Actas del Consejo de Estado 29 de Febrero 1812 [to May 23, 1814]" reports from the provinces of León, Seville, Cordoba, and Granada, Apr. 3, Apr. 21, Nov. 29, 1813 and Apr. 23, 1814.

105. *Constituição politica da Monarchia Portugueza* (Lisbon, 1822). It copied some features of the Spanish constitution but was essentially an original document.

106. The texts are in A. Aquarone et al., eds., *Le Costituzioni italiane* (Milan, 1958), 461–505 and 507–52.

107. Frank Safford, "Politics, Ideology and Society in Post-Independence Spanish America," in *CHLA*:361–63.

108. Ibid., 367–68.

109. See Callahan, *Church, Politics*, 216–20.

110. E. Christiansen, *The Origins of Military Power in Spain 1800–1854* (London, 1967), is comprehensive but I believe overrates the role of military men in ordinary political life.

111. Texts in *Constituciones de España 1808–1978*; and translations in Verduin, *Spanish Constitutions*.

112. 1837, art. 2; 1845, art. 2; 1856, art. 3; 1869, art. 17; 1873, preamble; 1876, art. 13.

113. 1869, arts. 17, 7; 1876, arts. 13, 7.

114. Martínez Marín, *Derecho parlamentario* 2:709–10.

115. 1869, art. 93.

116. 1837, art. 11; 1845, art. 11.

117. 1856, art. 14.

118. 1869, art. 21.

119. 1873, arts. 34, 35.

120. 1876, art 11.

121. See the forthcoming book by Carolyn Boyd on Spaniards' interpretations of their historical past.

122. This is my name. I develop its origin and nature in *An Historical Essay on Modern Spain* (Berkeley, 1974), chap. 7.

123. The standard work on *caciquismo* is José Varela Ortega, *Los amigos políticos* (Madrid, 1977). My understanding of *caciquismo* is explained in my chapter "Spain" in David Spring, ed., *European Landed Elites in the Nineteenth Century* (Baltimore, 1977), 98–126.

124. See Stanley G. Payne, *Spanish Catholicism, an Historical Overview* (Madison, WI, 1984), chap. 3.

125. John F. Coverdale, *The Basque Phase of Spain's First Carlist War* (Princeton, NJ, 1984), esp. chap. 9. On language see 185, on violence 211. See also Stanley G. Payne, *Basque Nationalism* (Reno, NV, 1975), chap. 2.

126. In 1906 the Catalan leader Enric Prat de la Riba used the term "nacionalidad" to apply to both the Catalan and Basque peoples, quoted in Jordi Solé-Tura, *Catalanismo y revolución burguesa* (Madrid, 1970), 163.

CHAPTER 3

1. For more on the philosophical underpinnings of the Spanish colonial system, see Colin M. MacLachlan, *Spain's Empire in the New World: The Role of Ideas in Institutional and Social Change* (Berkeley, 1988), 1–19.

2. Irving A. Leonard, *Baroque Times in Old Mexico: Seventeenth-Century Persons, Places, and Practices* (Ann Arbor, MI, 1959), 24–25.

3. C. H. Haring, *The Spanish Empire in America* (New York, 1962), 194.

4. Ibid., 165.

5. Mark A. Burkholder and D. S. Chandler, *From Impotence to Authority: the Spanish Crown and the American Audiencias* (Columbia, MO, 1977), 145.

6. John Lynch, "The Institutional Framework of Colonial Spanish America," *Journal of Latin American Studies* 24, Quincentenary Supplement (1992), 73–77.

7. Haring, *The Spanish Empire*, 169.

8. For a good review of the history of slavery in Latin America, with many comparative observations, see Herbert S. Klein, *African Slavery in Latin America and the Caribbean* (New York, 1986).

9. For more, see Henry Kamen, *The Spanish Inquisition* (New York, 1965).

10. For more on Humboldt in Spanish America, see D. A. Brading, *The First America: The Spanish Monarchy, Creole Patriots, and the Liberal State, 1493–1867* (Cambridge, 1991), 514–34.

11. Arthur P. Whitaker, ed., *Latin America and the Enlightenment*, 2d ed. (Ithaca, NY, 1961).

12. MacLachlan, *Spain's Empire in the New World*, 81.

13. For more on the role of the press in this period, see José Torre Revello, *El libro, la imprenta y el periodismo en America durante la dominación española* (Buenos Aires, 1940). For a discussion of the impact of newspapers in both North and South America prior to independence, see Benedict Anderson, *Imagined Communities*, rev. ed. (London, 1991), 61–64.

14. MacLachlan, *Spain's Empire in the New World*, 85–86.

15. Richard Graham, *Independence in Latin America: A Comparative Approach* (New York, 1972), 7.

16. For more, see Magnus Mörner, ed., *The Expulsion of the Jesuits from Latin America* (New York, 1965).

17. John Lynch, "The Origins of Spanish American Independence," in *CHLA*, 10–11.

18. Haring, *The Spanish Empire*, 322–23.

19. Doris M. Ladd, *The Mexican Nobility at Independence, 1780–1826* (Austin, TX, 1976), 96.

20. John J. Johnson (with the collaboration of Doris M. Ladd), *Simón Bolívar and Spanish-American Independence: 1783–1830* (Princeton, NJ, 1968), 26.

21. Lynch, "The Origins of Spanish American Independence," 36.

22. For a detailed case study, see John Lynch, *Spanish Colonial Administration, 1782–1810: The Intendant System in the Viceroyalty of the Río de la Plata* (London, 1958).

23. Lynch, "Institutional Framework," 81.

24. Ladd, *Mexican Nobility*, 29.

25. Mark A. Burkholder and Lyman L. Johnson, *Colonial Latin America* (New York, 1990), 267.

26. This is a major theme traced in Brading, *The First America*.

27. Víctor Andrés Belaunde, *Bolívar and the Political Thought of the Spanish American Revolution* (Baltimore, 1938), 13.

28. For more, see Harry Bernstein, "Some Inter-American Aspects of the Enlightenment," in Whitaker, ed., *Latin America and the Enlightenment*, 53–69.

29. As quoted in Belaunde, *Bolívar*, 33.

30. These developments are detailed in Frank Moya Pons, "Haiti and Santo Domingo: 1790– c. 1870," in *CHLA*, 237–75.

31. Louis A Pérez, Jr., *Cuba: Between Reform and Revolution* (New York, 1988), 100.

32. See Roderick J. Barman, *Brazil: The Forging of a Nation, 1798–1852* (Stanford, 1988), 37; and Maria Odila Silva Días, "The Establishment of the Royal Court in Brazil," in A. J. R. Russell-Wood, ed., *From Colony to Nation: Essays on the Independence of Brazil* (Baltimore, 1975), 100.

33. Ricardo Levene, *A History of Argentina*, trans. and ed. William Spence Robertson (New York, 1963), 191–202.

34. For example, see *CHLA*, 51–275; Graham, *Independence in Latin America*; John Lynch, *The Spanish American Revolutions, 1808–1826* (New York, 1973); William Spence Robertson, *Rise of the Spanish-American Republics As Told in the Lives of Their Liberators* (New York, 1960); and Russell-Wood, ed., *From Colony to Nation*.

35. Belaunde, *Bolívar*, pref. For more on this most important leader of the wars of independence, see Johnson, *Simón Bolívar and Spanish American Independence*; and Gerhard Masur, *Simón Bolívar* (Albuquerque, 1948).

36. For more, see Hugh M. Hamill, *The Hidalgo Revolt: Prelude to Mexican Independence* (Gainesville, FL, 1966); Timothy E. Anna, *The Fall of the Royal Government in Mexico City* (Lincoln, NE, 1978) and the same author's "The Independence of Mexico and Central America," in *CHLA*, 51–94. See also Ladd, *The Mexican Nobility at Independence*, 105–31.

37. For more, see J. M. Miguel i Verges, *La independencia mexicana y la prensa insurgente* (Mexico City, 1941).

38. Levene, *History of Argentina*, 264–66.

39. Simon Collier, *Ideas and Politics of Chilean Independence, 1808– 1833* (Cambridge, 1967), 97.

40. Brading, *The First America*, 544–45.

41. Leslie Bethell, "A note on the Church and the Independence of Latin America," in *CHLA*, 230.

42. David Bushnell, *The Santander Regime in Gran Colombia* (Newark, DE, 1954), 196.

43. Timothy E. Anna, *The Mexican Empire of Iturbide* (Lincoln, NE, 1990), 4.

44. Eugene M. Wait, "Mariano Moreno: Promoter of Enlightenment," *Hispanic American Historical Review* 45, 2 (August 1965): 361.

45. Belaunde, *Bolívar*, 32.

46. Lynch, *The Spanish American Revolutions*, 172–79. For the role of Cochrane in Brazil, see Neill Macaulay, *Dom Pedro: The Struggle for Liberty in Brazil and Portugal, 1793–1834* (Durham, NC, 1986), 138–67.

47. Brading, *The First America*, 607. See also, Alfred Hasbrouck, *Foreign Legionaries in the Liberation of Spanish South America* (New York, 1928).

48. John J. Johnson, *The Military and Society in Latin America* (Stanford, 1964), 23.

49. Bushnell, *The Santander Regime*, 249.

50. David Bushnell, "The Independence of Spanish South America," *CHLA*, 150–53.

51. Bushnell, *The Santander Regime*, 289.

52. For more on Bolívar's political ideas, see Belaunde, *Bolívar*, 231–58.

53. For more, see Anna, *The Mexican Empire of Iturbide*.

54. For more, see Macaulay, *Dom Pedro*; and Russell-Wood, *From Colony to Nation*. For an insightful analysis of Brazilian independence and subsequent developments, see Emilia Viotti Da Costa, *The Brazilian Empire: Myths and Histories* (Chicago, 1988).

55. Frank Safford, "Politics, Ideology and Society in Post-Independence Spanish America," in *CHLA*, 358.

56. Claudio Véliz, *The Centralist Tradition of Latin America* (Princeton, NJ, 1980), 151.

57. Bushnell, *The Santander Regime*, 31.

58. Ibid., 268–69.

59. Emilia Viotti Da Costa, "The Political Emancipation of Brazil," in Russell-Wood, ed., *From Colony to Nation*, 86.

60. Bushnell, *The Santander Regime*, 177.

61. Safford, "Politics, Ideology and Society," 387–88.

62. Charles Hale, *Mexican Liberalism in the Age of Mora, 1821–1853* (New Haven, CT, 1968), 124.

63. Belaunde, *Bolívar*, 417–18.

64. Anna, *The Mexican Empire of Iturbide*, 57.

65. Hale, *Mexican Liberalism*, 98–107.

66. Ibid., 16–17.

67. Bushnell, *The Santander Regime*, 62.

68. Collier, *Ideas and Politics of Chilean Independence*, 162. See also, the extensive listing of Santiago newspapers and journals of the period on 372–76.

69. Luis Valencia Avaria, comp., *Anales de la República: Textos consti-*

tucionales de Chile y registro de los ciudadanos que han integrado los poderes ejecutivo y legislativo desde 1810 I (Santiago de Chile, 1951): 46.

70. Ibid., 160–85.

71. For the importance of Bulnes in consolidating Chilean constitutional government, see Arturo Valenzuela, *Political Brokers in Chile: Local Government in a Centralized Polity* (Durham, NC, 1977), 174–83.

72. Paul Vanorden Shaw, *The Early Constitutions of Chile* (New York, 1930), 167.

73. As quoted in Johnson, *Simón Bolívar*, 112.

74. For a further discussion of these and other points of contrast, see Kenneth W. Thompson, ed., *The U.S. Constitution and the Constitutions of Latin America* (Lanham, MD, 1991), especially 54–75.

75. The classic analysis of the rise of *caudillismo* in Argentina is Domingo Sarmiento, *Life in the Argentine Republic in the Days of the Tyrants: or, Civilization and Barbarism* (New York, 1868). A less passionate analysis is provided in John Lynch, *Argentine Dictator: Juan Manuel de Rosas, 1829–1852* (Oxford, 1981).

76. For an insightful discussion of machismo and the caudillo, see Glen Caudill Dealy, *The Public Man: An Interpretation of Latin America and the Other Catholic Countries* (Amherst, MA, 1977), 53–70.

77. John Lynch, *Caudillos in Spanish America, 1800–1850* (Oxford, 1992), 182.

78. Richard M. Morse, "The Heritage of Latin America," in Louis Hartz, *The Founding of New Societies: Studies in the History of the United States, Latin America, South Africa, Canada, and Australia* (New York, 1964), 157–69. See also Frank Safford, "The Problem of Political Order in Early Republican Spanish America," *Journal of Latin American Studies* 24: 83–97.

79. Lynch, *Caudillos in Spanish America*, 35.

80. A good overview of the phenomenon is provided by Hugh M. Hamill, ed., *Caudillos: Dictators in Spanish America* (Norman, OK, 1992).

81. Samuel P. Huntington, *Political Order in Changing Societies* (New Haven, CT, 1968), 264.

82. Safford, "Politics, Ideology and Society, 375.

83. Martin C. Needler, "Ideas and Interests in the Struggle for Democracy in Latin America," in Thompson, ed., *The U.S. Constitution and the Constitutions of Latin America*, 144.

84. See, for example, "Colonial Institutions and Contemporary Latin America," reprinted in Lewis Hanke, ed., *Readings in Latin American History* 3 (New York, 1966): 18–37; and Stanley J. and Barbara H. Stein, *The Colonial Heritage of Latin America: Essays on Economic Dependence in Perspective* (New York, 1970), vii. For a view that emphasizes some of the changes that occurred as a result of independence, see Charles C. Griffin, "Economic and Social Aspects of the Era of Spanish-American Independence," in Hanke, ed., *Readings in Latin American History* 3:1–9.

85. For an overview, see Magnus Mörner (with the collaboration of Harold

Sims), *Adventurers and Proletarians: The Story of Migrants in Latin America* (Pittsburgh, PA, 1985).

86. Tulio Halperín-Donghi, *The Aftermath of Revolution in Latin America*, trans. Josephine de Bunsen (New York, 1973), 89.

CHAPTER 4

1. Conor Cruise OBrien, *The Great Melody. A Thematic Biography of Edmund Burke* (London, 1992), 3–86.

2. L. G. Mitchell, ed., *The Writings and Speeches of Edmund Burke* 8 (Oxford, 1989): 17–28; Isaac Kramnick, *The Rage of Edmund Burke: Portrait of an Ambivalent Conservative* (New York, 1977), 180–85; Gary Kelly, "Revolution, Crime, and Madness: Edmund Burke and the Defense of the Gentry," *Eighteenth-Century Life* 9 (1984): 16–32; F. P. Lock, *Burke's Reflections on the Revolution in France* (London, 1985), 134–36.

3. I. D. McCalman, "Prophesying Revolution: Lord George Gordon, Edmund Burke and Madame La Motte," in Ian Dyck and Malcolm Chase, eds., *Learning and Living. Essays in Honour of John Harrison* (Aldershot, Hants, 1996).

4. Robert Kent Donovan, "The Military Origins of the Roman Catholic Relief Programme of 1778," *Historical Journal* 28 (1985): 79–102; Colin Haydon, "The Gordon Riots in the English Provinces," *Historical Research* 63 (1990): 354–59.

5. McCalman, "Prophesying Revolution," passim.

6. O'Brien, *Great Melody*, 452.

7. Ibid., 479–80.

8. Ibid., 566–92.

9. For a brilliant synoptic analysis of modern British-Irish relations, see Oliver MacDonagh, *States of Mind. A Study of Anglo-Irish Conflict 1780–1980* (London, 1983).

10. James Vernon, *Politics and the People. A Study in English Political Culture c. 1815–67* (Cambridge, 1993), 1–11, 295–330; James A. Epstein, "The Constitutional Idiom: Radical Reasoning, Rhetoric and Action in Early Nineteenth-Century England," *JSH* 23 (1990): 553–74; Gareth Stedman Jones, *Languages of Class. Studies in English Working Class History 1832–1982* (Cambridge, 1983), 16–24, 90–178; James Epstein, *Radical Expression. Political Language, Ritual, and Symbol in England, 1790–1850* (Oxford, 1994); Jonathan Fulcher, "Contests over Constitutionalism: The Faltering of Reform in England, 1816–24" (Cambridge PhD diss., 1993).

11. Fulcher, "Contests," 290–327.

12. E. P. Thompson, *The Making of the English Working Class* (Harmondsworth, 1968), 668–779; D. G. Wright, *Popular Radicalism. The Working Class Experience 1780–1880* (London and New York, 1988), 64–82; I. D. McCalman, *Radical Underworld. Prophets, Revolutionaries and Pornographers in London 1795–1840* (Oxford, 1993), 97–177; Epstein, *Radical Expression*, 29–69.

13. Epstein, *Radical Expression*, 3–28.

14. I. D. McCalman, "'Erin go Bragh': the Irish in British Popular Radicalism c. 1790–1840," in Oliver MacDonagh and W. F. Mandle, eds., *Irish-Australian Studies. Papers Delivered at the Fifth Irish-Australian Conference* (Canberra, 1989), 167–84; A. D. Harvey, *Britain in the Early Nineteenth Century* (London, 1978), 220–50; J. Dinwiddy, "Sir Francis Burdett and Burdettite Radicalism," *History* 65 (1980): 17–31.

15. McCalman, *Radical Underworld*, 97–151; John Belchem, *"Orator" Hunt. Henry Hunt and English Working-Class Radicalism* (Oxford, 1985), 91–162.

16. Kevin Gilmartin, *Print Politics: Writing and Radical Opposition in Early Nineteenth-Century England* (Cambridge, forthcoming). I am grateful to Dr. Gilmartin for allowing me to cite his manuscript.

17. See, for example, Thomas Laqueur, "The Queen Caroline Affair: Politics as Art in the Reign of George IV," *JMH* 54 (1982): 417–66; Anna Clark, "Queen Caroline and the Sexual Politics of Popular Culture in London, 1820," *Representations* 31 (1990): 31–68; Leonore Davidoff and Catherine Hall, *Family Fortunes. Men and Women of the English Middle Class 1780–1850* (London, 1987), 149–55; Craig Calhoun, *The Question of Class Struggle* (Chicago, 1982), 105–15. For the best discussions of the Diamond Necklace affair, see Robert Darnton, *The Literary Underground of the Old Regime* (Cambridge, MA, 1982), 1–40; Lynn Hunt, ed., *Eroticism and the Body Politic* (Baltimore, 1991), 63–89, 108–30; Sarah Maza, *Private Lives and Public Affairs. The Causes Celebres of Prerevolutionary France* (Berkeley, 1993), 167–211.

18. McCalman, *Radical Underworld*, 163–71. For an excellent and influential example of such contemporary romances, see Thomas Ashe, *A Concise Abridgement of the Popular and Interesting Work. The Spirit of "The Book"* (London, 1812).

19. Paul Johnson, *The Birth of the Modern. World History 1815–30* (London, 1991), 553.

20. McCalman, *Radical Underworld*, 176.

21. Laqueur, "Queen Caroline Affair," 417.

22. Henry Mayhew, *London Labour and the London Poor*, 4 vols. (London, 1861, repr. 1986), 1:200; 2:468.

23. John Belchem, "Henry Hunt and the Evolution of the Mass Platform," *EHR* 93 (1978): 739–73.

24. Oliver MacDonagh, *O' Connell. The Life of Daniel O'Connell 1775–1847* (London, 1991), chaps. 1–7.

25. Ibid., chaps. 8–12.

26. M. Beames, *Peasants and Power: The Whiteboy Movements and Their Control in Pre-Famine Ireland* (New York, 1983); S. Clark and J. S. Donnelly, eds., *Irish Peasants. Violence and Political Unrest, 1780–1940* (Madison, 1983), 64–101.

27. J. C. D. Clark, *English Society, 1688–1832: Ideology, Social Structure and Political Practice during the Ancien Regime* (Cambridge, 1985), 393–99.

28. E. J. Hobsbawm and George Rude, *Captain Swing* (Harmondsworth, 1973); Stanley H. Palmer, *Police and Protest in England and Ireland 1780–1850* (Cambridge, 1988), 50–57, 386–87.

29. James Epstein, "Understanding the Cap of Liberty: Symbolic Conflict and Social Conflict in Early Nineteenth-Century England," *Past and Present* 122 (1989): 75–118; T. M. Parssinen, "Association, Convention, and Anti-Parliament in British Radical Politics, 1771–1848," *EHR* 88 (1973): 504–33.

30. Epstein, "Constitutional idiom," 566–69.

31. Hevda Ben-Israel, *English Historians on the French Revolution* (Cambridge, 1968), 101–4.

32. Stedman Jones, *Languages of Class*, 173–75.

33. Vernon, *Politics and the People*, 15–47. This essential argument was made many years earlier by Norman Gash, *Politics in the Age of Peel* (London, 1953), 86–101.

34. John Prest, *Liberty and Locality: Parliament, Permissive Legislation and Ratepayers' Democracies in the Nineteenth Century* (Oxford, 1990); F. O'Gorman, *Voters, Patrons and Parties. The Unreformed Electoral System of Hanoverian England 1734–1832* (Oxford, 1989); J. A. Phillips, *Electoral Behaviour in Unreformed England, 1761–1802* (Princeton, 1982).

35. Vernon, *Politics and the People*, 16–31.

36. MacDonagh, *States of Mind*, 32, 53; Palmer, *Police and Protest*, chaps. 8–9; K. T. Hoppen, *Elections, Politics and Society in Ireland, 1832–85* (Oxford, 1984).

37. MacDonagh, *O'Connell*, chaps. 19–21.

38. James Epstein, *The Lion of Freedom. Feargus O'Connor and the Chartist Movement, 1832–1842* (London and Sydney, 1982); John Belchem, "'1848: Feargus O'Connor and the Collapse of the Mass Platform," in James Epstein and Dorothy Thompson, eds., *The Chartist Experience. Studies in Working-Class Radicalism and Culture, 1830–1860* (London, 1982), 269–310.

39. Dorothy Thompson, *The Chartists. Popular Politics in the Industrial Revolution* (New York, 1984), chaps. 2–3, 5–9; David Jones, *Chartism and the Chartists* (London, 1975), chaps. 1, 3–4; E. Royle, *Chartism* (London, 1980); Asa Briggs, ed., *Chartist Studies* (London, 1959); Patricia Hollis, ed., *Class and Class Conflict in Nineteenth-Century England, 1815–1850* (London, 1973).

40. D. J. V. Jones, *The Last Rising: The Newport Insurrection of 1839* (Oxford, 1985); David Goodway, *London Chartism, 1838–1848* (Cambridge, 1982), 32–33.

41. Malcolm I. Thomis and Peter Holt, *Threats of Revolution in Britain 1789–1848* (London and Basingstoke, 1977), 100–116.

42. Edward Royle and James Walvin, *English Radicals and Reformers 1760–1848* (Brighton, 1982), 160–80; J. F. C. Harrison, *The Common People. A History from the Norman Conquest to the Present* (London, 1984), 260–70.

43. D. G. Wright, *Popular Radicalism. The Working Class Experience, 1780–1880* (London, 1988), 142–44.

44. MacDonagh, *O'Connell*, 510–18.

45. Thompson, *Chartists*, chaps. 5–9; Eileen Yeo, "Christianity in Chartist Struggle, 1838–42," *Past and Present* 91 (1981): 109–39.

46. Jones, *Chartism*, 188.

47. R. F. Foster, *Modern Ireland 1600–1972* (London, 1988), 313–15.

48. Jones, *Chartism*, 182.

49. Ruth L. Smith and Deborah M. Valenze, "Mutuality and Marginality: Liberal Moral Theory and Working-Class Women in Nineteenth-Century England," *Signs: Journal of Women in Culture and Society* 13 (1988): 277–98.

50. Anna Clark, "The Rhetoric of Chartist Domesticity: Gender, Language, and Class in the 1830s and 1840s," *Journal of British Studies* 31 (1992): 62–88. On this related theme, see also Joan W. Scott, *Gender and the Politics of History* (New York, 1988), 53–67; Catherine Hall, *White, Male and Middle Class. Explorations in Feminism and History* (Cambridge, 1992), 124–50.

51. I am grateful to Anna Clark for allowing me to read chapter 8, from the manuscript of her *The Struggle for the Breeches* (Chicago, 1995). See also, McCalman, *Radical Underworld*, 182–95.

52. I. D. McCalman, "Females, Feminism and Freelove in an Early Nineteenth-Century Radical Movement," *Labour History* 38 (1980): 1–25; Dorothy Thompson, *Outsiders*, 77–102.

53. Clark, "Chartist Domesticity," 80–82.

54. Hall, *White, Male and Middle Class*, 131; Dorothy Thompson, "Women in Radical Politics: a Lost Dimension," in Juliet Mitchell and Ann Oakley, eds., *The Rights and Wrongs of Women* (Harmondsworth, 1976), 122–38.

55. Hall, *White, Male and Middle Class*, 94–107, 151–71; Scott, *Gender and Politics*, 53–67.

56. Joel H. Wiener, *Radicalism and Freethought in Nineteenth-Century Britain. The Life of Richard Carlile* (Westport, CT, 1983); I. D. McCalman, "Popular Radicalism and Freethought in Early Nineteenth-Century England: A Study of Richard Carlile and his Followers, 1800–32," (Australian National Univ., MA thesis, 1975).

57. Epstein, *Radical Expression*, 100–46.

58. McCalman, "Females, Feminism and Freelove," 1–25.

59. Adrian Desmond, *The Politics of Evolution. Morphology, Medicine, and Reform in Radical London* (Chicago, 1989), 101–51.

60. I. D. McCalman, "Popular Irreligion in Early Victorian England: Infidel Preachers and Radical Theatricality in 1830s London," in R. W. Davis and R. J. Helmstadter, eds., *Religion and Irreligion in Victorian Society* (London, 1992), 51–67.

61. J. F. C. Harrison, *Quest for the New Moral World. Robert Owen and the Owenites in Britain and America* (New York, 1969).

62. Barbara Taylor, *Eve and the New Jerusalem* (London, 1983); Smith and Valenze, "Mutuality and Marginality," 289–90.

63. Gregory Claeys, *Citizens and Saints. Politics and Anti-Politics in Early British Socialism* (Cambridge, 1989), chaps. 1, 8; id., *Machinery, Money*

and the Millennium. From Moral Economy to Socialism, 1815–60 (Oxford, 1987), 184–95.

64. Noel W. Thompson, *The People's Science. The Popular Political Economy of Exploitation and Crisis, 1816–34* (Cambridge, 1984), 219–28; Gertrude Himmelfarb, *The Idea of Poverty: England in the Early Industrial Age* (New York, 1984), 230–52; Patricia Hollis, *The Pauper Press. A Study in Working-Class Radicalism of the 1830s* (Oxford, 1970), chaps. 6–7.

65. McCalman, *Radical Underworld*, chaps. 5–7.

66. Marilyn Butler, *Romantics, Rebels and Reactionaries. English Literature and its Background 1760–1830* (Oxford, 1981), chaps. 5–6.

67. J. R. Dinwiddy, *Radicalism and Reform in Britain, 1780–1850* (London, 1992), 217–23.

68. Margot C. Finn, *After Chartism. Class and Nation in English Radical Politics, 1848–1874* (Cambridge, 1993), 60–104.

69. Dinwiddy, *Radicalism and Reform*, 228.

70. Malcolm Chase, *The People's Farm. English Radical Agrarianism 1775–1840* (Oxford, 1988), chaps. 6–7.

71. Foster, *Modern Ireland*, 310–17; MacDonagh, *States of Mind*, 76–77.

72. John Saville, *1848. The British State and the Chartist Movement* (Cambridge, 1987); Palmer, *Police and Protest*, 430–81.

73. MacDonagh, *States of Mind*, 108–13.

74. Dorothy Thompson, *Outsiders*, 134–63.

75. Patricia Hollis and Brian Harrison, "Chartism, Liberalism and the Life of Robert Lowery," *EHR* 82 (1967): 503–35; Thomis and Holt, *Threats of Revolution*, 116.

76. Patrick Joyce, *Work, Society and Politics: The Culture of the Factory in Later Victorian England* (Brighton, 1980).

77. J. Foster, *Class Struggle and the Industrial Revolution: Early Industrial Capitalism in Three English Towns* (London, 1974), chaps. 4–5; E. J. Hobsbawm, *Labouring Men* (London, 1964), 272–315.

78. G. Crossick, *An Artisan Elite in Victorian Society. Kentish London 1840–1880* (London, 1978), chaps. 6–7, 10; R. Q. Gray, *The Labour Aristocracy in Victorian Edinburgh* (Oxford, 1976), 165–75; Neville Kirk, *The Growth of Working-Class Reformism in Mid-Victorian England* (London, 1985), chaps. 3–5.

79. Finn, *After Chartism*, 88.

80. Ibid., chaps. 2–4.

81. F. B. Smith, "The View from Britain I: 'Tumults abroad, Stability at home'," in Eugene Kamenka and F. B. Smith, *Intellectuals and Revolution. Socialism and the Experience of 1848* (London, 1979), 115–18; Frances Elma Gillespie, *Labor and Politics in England 1850–67* (London, 1966), chap. 2.

82. Finn, *After Chartism*, 197–99; Eugenio F. Biagini, *Liberty, Retrenchment and Reform. Popular Liberalism in the Age of Gladstone, 1860–1880* (Cambridge, 1992), chap. 3.

83. Finn, *After Chartism*, 84.

84. Ibid., 209.

85. Ibid., 211–12.

86. Biagini, *Liberty, Retrenchment*, chaps. 1–5; Eugenio F. Biagini and Alistair J. Reid, eds., *Currents of Radicalism. Popular Radicalism, Organized Labour and Party Politics in Britain, 1850–1914* (Cambridge, 1991), chap. 1; Vernon, *Politics and the People*, 295–339.

87. Biagini and Reid, *Currents of Radicalism*, chaps. 5, 8, 10.

88. Vernon, *Politics and the People*, 251–91; Biagini, *Liberty and Retrenchment*, 369–85.

89. Vernon, *Politics and the People*, 321–22.

90. Gregory Claeys, "Mazzini, Kossuth and British Radicalism 1848–1854," *Journal of British Studies* 28 (1989): 225–62.

91. Royden Harrison, *Before the Socialists. Studies in Labour and Politics, 1861–1881* (London, 1965), 53–64; Cf. Biagini, *Liberty, Retrenchment*, 72–83.

92. Miles Taylor, "The Old Radicalism and the New: David Urquhart and the Politics of Opposition, 1823–67," and Rohan McWilliam, "Radicalism and Popular Culture: the Tichborne Case and the Politics of 'Fair Play', 1867–86," in Biagini and Reid, *Currents of Radicalism*, 21–64.

93. Michael Roe, *Kenealy and the Tichborne Cause. A Study in Mid-Victorian Populism* (Melbourne, 1974).

94. MacDonagh, *States of Mind*, 80–85; Foster, *Modern Ireland*, 390–95; T. W. Moody, ed., *The Fenian Movement* (Dublin, 1968).

95. F. S. L. Lyons, *Culture and Anarchy in Ireland, 1890–1939* (Oxford, 1982), chap. 1.

96. Dorothy Thompson, "Ireland and the Irish in English Radicalism before 1850," in Epstein and Thompson, eds., *Chartist Experience*, 120–51; J. H. Treble, "O'Connor, O'Connell and the Attitudes of Irish Immigrants towards Chartism in the North of England 1838–48," in J. Butt and I. F. Clarke, eds., *The Victorians and Social Protest: A Symposium* (Newton Abbott, 1973), 33–70.

97. Kirk, *Working-Class Reformism*, 337–38; E. H. Hunt, *British Labour History 1815–1914* (London, 1981), 158–75.

98. Finn, *After Chartism*, chaps. 4–5; Hall, *White, Male*, chaps. 9–10.

99. Dorothy Thompson, *Queen Victoria: Gender and Power* (London, 1990), chaps. 5–6.

100. Marc Brodie, "Politics and the Unskilled Poor in Mid Nineteenth-Century London," (Melbourne Univ. MA thesis, 1993), 45–64.

101. Himmelfarb, *Idea of Poverty*, 435–52; Anne Humpherys, "G. W. M. Reynolds: Popular Literature and Popular Politics," in Joel H. Wiener, ed., *Innovators and Preachers. The Role of the Editor in Victorian England* (London, 1985), 3–21.

102. Roe, *Kenealy*, 165–89.

103. Patrick Joyce, *Visions of the People: Industrial England and the Question of Class, c. 1848–1914* (Cambridge, 1991), 329–42; R. McKibbin, "Why was there no Marxism in Great Britain?" *EHR* 99 (1984): 297–331.

104. Vernon, *Politics and the People*, 336–39.

105. F. B. Smith, "Some British Reactions to the Commune," in Eugene Kamenka, ed., *Paradigm for Revolution? The Paris Commune 1871–1971* (Canberra, 1972), 65–90; Harrison, *Before the Socialists*, 232–37.

106. Biagini, *Liberty, Retrenchment*, 65.

CHAPTER 5

1. For a discussion of a useful model of the revolutionary process, see James Rule and Charles Tilly, "Political Process in Revolutionary France, 1830–32," in John M. Merriman, ed., *1830 in France* (New York, 1975); Charles Tilly and Lynn H. Lees, "The People of June, 1848," in R. D. Price, ed., *Revolution and Reaction* (London, 1975).

2. Ronald Aminzade, *Class, Politics, and Early Industrial Capitalism: A Study of Mid-Nineteenth-Century Toulouse, France* (Albany, NY, 1981), esp. chap. 9.

3. H. A. C. Collingham, *The July Monarchy: A Political History of France 1830–1848* (New York, 1988), 103.

4. William H. Sewell, Jr., *Work and Revolution in France: The Language of Labor from the Old Regime to 1848* (New York, 1980), esp. chap. 9. For a strident critique of Sewell's book see Lynn Hunt and George Sheridan, "Corporatism, Association, and the Language of Labor in France, 1750–1850," *JMH* 58 (Dec. 1986): 813–44.

5. Gordon Wright, *France in Modern Times* (3d ed., New York, 1981), 105.

6. Pamela Pilbeam, *The 1830 Revolution in France* (London, 1991).

7. See John M. Merriman, *The Red City* (New York, 1985), chaps. 1 and 2.

8. See Charles Tilly, "The Changing Place of Collective Violence," in Melvin Richter, ed., *Essays in Theory and History* (Cambridge, MA, 1970) and "Food Supply and Public Order in Modern Europe," in Charles Tilly, ed., *The Formation of National States in Western Europe* (Princeton, NJ, 1975). See Paul Gonnet, "Esquisse de la crise économique et sociale en France de 1827 à 1832," *Revue histoire économique et sociale* 33 (1955), esp. 271–72; Pilbeam, *1830 Revolution*, chap. 3.

9. See Sherman Kent, *The Election of 1827 in France* (Cambridge, MA, 1975).

10. John M. Merriman, "The Norman Fires of 1830: Incendiaries and Fear in Rural France," *FHS* 9, 3 (1976): 451–66. In fact, insurance agents trying to stoke up their business probably set some of them, using inflammatory balls that would catch fire in straw at the peak of the day; ordinary people settling scores certainly set some others.

11. David H. Pinkney, *The French Revolution of 1830* (Princeton, NJ, 1972), 18–19.

12. About 1,000 insurgents and troops had been killed, and about 4,800 wounded, the vast majority on the side of the now victorious Parisians.

13. Roger Price, "Popular Disturbances in the French Provinces After the July Revolution of 1830," *European Studies Review* 1, 4 (1971): 323–55.

14. Collingham, *July Monarchy*, 70.

15. Pilbeam, *1830 Revolution*, 86–87.

16. Karl Marx, *Class Struggles in France, 1848–1850* (New York, 1934), 34; a view shared by Jean Lhomme, *La grande bourgeoisie au pouvoir, 1830–80* (Paris, 1960).

17. Alexis de Tocqueville, *Selected Letters on Politics and Society*, ed. Roger Boesche (Berkeley, 1985), 16, 66. See also Adeline Daumard, *Les bourgeois de Paris au XIXe siècle* (Paris, 1970).

18. Most notably, by David H. Pinkney in "The Myth of the French Revolution of 1830," in David H. Pinkney and Theodore Ropp, eds., *A Festschrift for Frederick B. Artz* (Durham, NC, 1964), 52–71, and *The French Revolution of 1830*. Pinkney concludes that the revolution of 1830 was something of a Bonapartist revolution. The stirring of nationalist sympathies encouraged a widespread revival of the cult of Napoleon. The elections of 1831 did not bring a flood of businessmen into the Chamber of Deputies. Pamela Pilbeam's recent *1830 Revolution* adds little of significance to what Pinkney wrote twenty years earlier, while oddly dismissing his account as an "American" one.

19. See André-Jean Tudesq, *Les Grands notables en France, 1840–49*, 2 vols. (Paris, 1964).

20. Wright, *France*, 112–13.

21. Christopher Johnson, "The July Revolution in French Economic History," in Merriman, ed., *1830 in France*.

22. Collingham, *July Monarchy*, 178.

23. James Cuno, *Charles Philipon and La Maison Aubert: The Business, Politics, and Public of Caricature in Paris, 1820–1840* (Ann Arbor, MI, 1985), 108; John Merriman, "Introduction," in Elise K. Kenney and John M. Merriman, eds., *The Pear: French Graphic Arts in the Golden Age of Caricature* (South Hadley, MA, 1992).

24. Alfred Cobban, *A History of Modern France* (Harmondsworth, 1970), 2:131.

25. Ibid., 84–88.

26. Robert Justin Goldstein, *Censorship of Political Caricature in Nineteenth Century France* (Kent, OH, 1979), 132. The image of Louis-Philippe as a pear, a soft and bulbous piece of fruit, one that easily became rotten, became both an emblem and a metaphor, a deflating image of contempt, appearing as early as November 1830. More than this, James Cuno notes that "*poire*" was commonly taken to be an obscene image, its phallic associations, linked to prostitution, understood by the middle-class market for political caricature.

27. Beginning in several border departments, nationalists early in 1831 formed "national associations" intending to defend France should the Congress powers, made anxious by events in Belgium, decide to try to enforce the settlements of 1815. Following the Saint-Germain l'Auxerrois riots, the government dissolved the national associations in 1831; a few survived as revolutionary clubs (Pilbeam, *1830 Revolution*, 154–60).

28. See Sherman Kent, *Electoral Procedure Under Louis Philippe* (New Haven, CT, 1937).

29. Sewell, *Work and Revolution*, 209: "It was in this confluence of corporate and republican agitation in the fall of 1833 that the Parisian workers developed the idiom of association into a coherent framework of collective action."

30. *Le Moniteur Universel*, Dec. 22, 1831. See James Rule and Charles Tilly, "Political Process in Revolutionary France, 1830–1832," in Merriman, ed., *1830 in France*.

31. See Sewell, *Work and Revolution*; Christopher H. Johnson, *Utopian Communism in France* (Ithaca, NY, 1975); Bernard Moss, *The Origins of the French Labor Movement* (Berkeley, 1976).

32. Of the men interviewed after the revolution when they stepped forward to ask for rewards, 76 percent said they had fought for "liberty" and 29 percent for "the nation" (Edgar Leon Newman, "What the Crowd Wanted in the French Revolution of 1830," in Merriman, ed., *1830 in France*, 17).

33. Sewell, *Work and Revolution*, 196.

34. Ibid., 195–96.

35. Ibid., 201.

36. Ibid., 201–18.

37. Ibid., 194–96.

38. Ibid., 33–35.

39. See Price, ed., *Revolution*; and Rule and Tilly, "Political Process."

40. See John M. Merriman, "The 'Demoiselles' of the Ariège, 1829–1831," in Merriman, ed., *1830 in France*; François Baby, *La Guerre des Demoiselles en Ariège (1829–1972)* (Montbel, 1972); and Peter Sahlins's recent *Forest Rites: The War of the Demoiselles in Nineteenth-Century France* (Cambridge, MA, 1994). In Alsace, and other regions as well, the loss of forest rights generated considerable resentment.

41. Sewell, *Work and Revolution*, chaps. 4–6.

42. See Suzanne Coquerelle, "Les droits collectifs et les troubles agraires dans les Pyrénées en 1848," *Actes du 78e Congrès National des Sociétés Savantes* (1953), 345–63; and M. E. Meaume, *Des droits d'usage dans les forêts de l'administration des bois communaux et de l'affouage* 1 (Paris, 1851).

43. Merriman, "The Demoiselles," 92–99.

44. Archives départementales de l'Ariège, Pe 45, prefect to minister of the interior, Mar. 8, 1830, and prefect to the bishop of Pamiers, June 30, 1829; bishop, letter to prefect, Sept. 10, 1829.

45. Natalie Zemon Davis, "The Reasons of Misrule," "Women on Top," and "The Rites of Violence" in *Society and Culture in Early Modern France* (Stanford, 1975), 97–187. The war of the demoiselles can be characterized as a "*révolte carnavalesque*," a "drama of social vengeance," a sort of psychodrama or "social exorcism," complete with sexual overtones as peasants, male and cuckolded, but disguised, attempt to retake possession of the forest, to which is assigned feminine characteristics, from the "outsiders," the

forest guards and charbonniers who have violated it. See Baby, *La Guerre*, 126–39 and Peter Sahlins, *Forest Rites*.

46. André Jardin and André-Jean Tudesq, *Restoration and Reaction, 1815–1848* (Cambridge, 1983), 109.

47. Sewell, *Work and Revolution*, 196; Collingham, *July Monarchy*, 159–60; Jardin and Tudesq, *Restoration*, 114–15.

48. See Oliver Larkin, *Daumier: A Man of His Time* (Boston, 1966), 27–28.

49. Marrinan, *Painting Politics*, 5.

50. Patricia O'Brien, "*L'Embastillement de Paris*: The Fortifications of Paris during the July Monarchy," *FHS* 9, 1 (1975): 63–82.

51. Collingham, *July Monarchy*, 146.

52. O'Brien, "*L'Embastillement*," 68–69.

53. Collingham, *July Monarchy*, 292–93. In 1840–41, France, by virtue of supporting Mehemet Ali of Egypt against the Turks in the so-called Eastern Question, faced the threat of war against England and continental allies.

54. John M. Merriman, *The Margins of City Life: Explorations on the French Urban Frontier, 1815–51* (New York, 1991). Paris grew from 785,866 in 1831 to 900,000 just five years later and reached 1,053,000 in 1846. The inner suburbs, with 75,000 inhabitants in 1831, had 173,000 in 1846. See Louis Chevalier, *Laboring Classes and Dangerous Classes in Paris During the First Half of the Nineteenth Century* (London, 1973), 182.

55. Robert J. Bezucha, *The Lyon Insurrection of 1834* (Cambridge, MA, 1974), 135; see Pilbeam, *1830 Revolution*, 166–67.

56. James Cuno, *Philipon*, 108. Article Seven of the constitution followed its predecessor in stating: "All Frenchmen have the right to publish and have printed their views in conformity with the laws," to which was added "Censorship will never be re-established."

57. Goldstein, *Censorship of Political Caricature*, 133.

58. Ibid., 128–29, 137–41, and 146–47; Cuno, *Philipon*, 153–54.

59. Sewell, *Work and Revolution*, 249.

60. Peter H. Amann, *Revolution and Mass Democracy: The Paris Club Movement in 1848* (Princeton, NJ, 1975), argues that clubs characterize "societies in transition," before the rooting of permanent political parties.

61. Tilly and Lees, "People," 179. Estimates twice as high by other sources include papers of a single sheet, many of which appeared only once or twice.

62. Remi Gossez, *Les ouvriers de Paris* (Paris, 1971), 9.

63. Ibid., 40.

64. John M. Merriman, *Agony of the Republic: The Repression of the Left in Revolutionary France, 1848–51* (New Haven, CT, 1978).

65. For a revisionist view of the combatants in the June Days, see Marc Traugott, *Armies of the Poor* (Princeton, NJ, 1985), who argues that those fighting on the side of "order" were essentially the same in social composition as the insurgents. Certainly some younger workers, including artisans, fought alongside unskilled proletarians in the Mobile Guard. They were less likely to have been integrated into a trade.

66. Louis Napoleon won 5.4 million votes to 1.45 million for Cavaignac, 370,000 for Ledru-Rollin, and a mere 18,000 for Lamartine.

67. See Edward Berenson, *Popular Religion and Left-Wing Politics in France, 1830–1852* (Princeton, NJ, 1984).

68. Maurice Agulhon describes the diffusion of the ideas presented by *Le Démocrate du Var* in one bourg of 1,800 people, although only 8–10 copies of each paper arrived: "La Diffusion d'un journal montagnard: *Le Démocrate du Var* sous la Deuxième République," *Provence historique* 10, 39 (jan.-mars, 1960): 16.

69. Merriman, *Agony of the Republic*, 30–31.

70. Ibid., 31.

71. AN, BB18 1470C, report of the *procureur-général* of Douai, Feb. 16, 1850; *procureur-général* of Colmar, Mar. 11, 1849.

72. AN, BB18 1494, *procureur-général* of Lyon, Oct. 21, 1849; minister of justice to minister of interior, Nov. 5, 1849; *procureur-général* of Besançon, Mar. 6, 1850; *procureur-général* Nancy, May 1, 1851 and esp. *procureur-général* of Metz, June 24, 1850.

73. Expression of *procureur-général* of Limoges, AN, BB30 378, dossier 6, Dec. 21, 1848. See also AN, BB18 1470C, *procureur-général* of Aix, Apr. 14, 1849; AN, BB30 368, dossier 2, *procureur-général* of Bourges, Nov. 1849; Alexandre Zévaès, "La Propagande socialiste dans les campaignes en 1848," *Révolution de 1848* (juin-août, 1934), 80–81; G. Rocal, *1848 en Dordogne* (Paris, 1934), 1:52.

74. See Roger McGraw, "Pierre Joigneaux and Socialist Propaganda in the French Countryside, 1849–51," *FHS* 10 (Fall, 1978): 599–640.

75. AN, BB18 1474A.

76. Merriman, *Agony of the Republic*, chap. 3.

77. Ibid., 66–82.

78. Ibid.; and Bernard Moss, "Parisian Producers' Associations (1830–51): The Socialism of Skilled Workers," in Price, ed., *Revolution*.

79. Ibid., 70–78.

80. Agulhon, *République*, 346.

81. AN, BB18 1474B, prefect of the Rhône, Aug. 22, 1849.

82. Merriman, *Agony of the Republic*, 73–77.

83. AN, BB18 1468, June 13, 1850.

84. The number of men who lost their right to vote was 3,126,823, 31.4 percent of those previously eligible.

85. AN, C 977, "Tableau comparatif de nombre des maires et adjoints en fonctions au février, 1848 et du nombre de ces fonctionnaires qui ont été réélus par les conseils municipales" (32,657 of 65,231, or 50.05 percent).

86. Merriman, *Agony of the Republic*, 107–18, daily correspondence of the ministry of war, F1 32, 36, 38, 42; AN, BB18 1480; and J. Dagnan, *Le Gers sous la Seconde République* (Auch, 1928), 330–31.

87. AN, BB18 1496, *procureur-général* of Montpellier, May 5, 1851.

88. AN, C 977, "Résumé des décisions rendues par le conseil d'état sur les

propositions de révocations depuis son entrée en fonctions le 18 avril, 1849 jusqu'à 28 février, 1851."

89. Max Ferre, *Histoire du mouvement syndicaliste révolutionnaire chez les instituteurs* (Paris, 1954), 19; Dagnan, *Le Gers*, 168, 294, 299.

90. Paul Gerbod, *La Condition universitaire en France au XIXe siècle* (Paris, 1965), 257–63.

91. AN, F9 423, correspondence.

92. AN, F9 422, "gardes nationales, dissolutions."

93. AN, BB30 364, *procureur-général* of Poitiers, Feb. 15, 1850.

94. AN, BB18 1481; Merriman, *Agony of the Republic*, 97–101.

95. Archives de la Guerre (Vincennes), MR 258, dossier Saison.

96. Ted W. Margadant, *French Peasants in Revolt: The Insurrection of 1851* (Princeton, NJ, 1979), 130–31.

97. Ibid.

98. The fact that, following the coup d'état, peasants were the largest social group participating in the resistance of over 125,000 people is bad news for Eugen Weber's view, in *Peasants into Frenchmen* (Stanford, 1978), that peasants could not become interested in politics until "modernization"— railroads, education, military conscription—had turned them into "Frenchmen," which he argues occurred between 1880 and 1914. Weber's analysis misses the very structure of rural society and of manufacturing in France. For a critique, see Charles Tilly, "Did the Cake of Custom Break?" in John Merriman, ed., *Consciousness and Class Experience in Modern Europe* (New York, 1979).

99. Theodore Zeldin, *The Political System of Napoleon III* (New York, 1958).

100. Jean-Claude Dalotel, Alain Faure, and Jean-Claude Freiermuth, *Aux origines de la commune: le mouvement des réunions publiques à Paris, 1868–1870* (Paris, 1980).

101. Denis Poulot, *Le sublime ou la travailleur comme il est en 1870, et ce qu'il peut être*, repub. with an intro. by Alain Cottereau (Paris, 1980).

102. Robert Tombs, *The War Against Paris 1871* (Cambridge, 1981), 34–36, 53.

103. The arrondissement numbers changed on Jan. 1, 1860, when the inner suburbs were annexed to Paris.

104. Tombs, *War Against Paris*, 90, writes that the army's weakness "continued to influence the whole conduct of the war, and of the repression that followed."

105. Stewart Edwards, ed., *The Communards of Paris, 1871* (London, 1973).

106. Stewart Edwards, ed., *The Paris Commune 1871* (Paris, 1971), 218; Roger L. Williams, *The French Revolution of 1870–1871* (New York, 1969), 139–40.

107. Alain Corbin, *The Village of Cannibals* (Cambridge, MA, 1992).

108. Jeanne Gaillard, *Communes de province, commune de Paris 1870–1871* (Paris, 1971).

109. Louis M. Greenberg, *Sisters of Liberty: Marseille, Lyon, Paris and the Reaction to a Centralized State, 1868–1871* (Cambridge, MA, 1971). For example, in Limoges, Greenberg's thesis works nicely for the moderate republican club; its rival, the Société populaire, had considerably more radical goals (Merriman, *The Red City*, chap. 5).

110. Tombs, *War Against Paris*, 145 ff. He notes that within the troops of Versailles, some were sympathetic to the cause of the Communards and many more "were strongly opposed to involvement in civil war" (107) but that "the pressures of military discipline reinforced by propaganda" explains "the way in which the army performed its task of attacking Paris."

111. Ibid., 164, 167–80.

112. Prosper-Olivier Lissagaray, *Histoire de la Commune de 1871* (Paris, 1990), 371.

113. Jacques Rougerie, *Paris libre 1871* (Paris, 1971), 253–57. There were 17,000 inhumations. Tombs, *War Against Paris*, writes that "The total number of Parisians killed could therefore be anything between 10,000 and 30,000, with the most probable figure about halfway between" (191).

114. See Tilly, "The Changing Place of Collective Violence in France," in Richter, ed., *Essays in Theory and History*.

115. See John Merriman, *Aux marges de la ville: faubourgs et banlieues en France 1815–1870* (Paris, 1994), chap. 10.

116. Rougerie, *Paris libre*, 19, 66, 104–5, 229.

117. Tombs, *War Against Paris*, 199.

118. Quoted by David Harvey, *Consciousness and the Urban Experience* (Baltimore, 1985), 229–30.

119. Gérard Jacquement, "Belleville aux XIXe et XXe siècles: une méthode d'analyse de la croissance urbaine à Paris," *Annales* 33 (1975): 182.

120. Louis Lazare, *Les quartiers pauvres de Paris: le XXe arrondissement* (Paris, 1970), 34. In 1866, some residents of the twentieth arrondissement had petitioned for another church, pointing out that the 30,000 residents of Ménilmontant had only one small one, barely more than a chapel, Notre-Dame-de-la-Croix (1865).

121. R. P. Jonquet, *Montmartre autrefois et aujourd'hui* (Paris, 1919), 98: "Et puis, quel emplacement! Quel féerique panorama! Du haut de Montmartre, nous dominons tout Paris," continued the report.

122. Harvey, *Consciousness*.

123. François Furet, *Revolutionary France 1770–1880* (Oxford, 1992), 537.

124. Furet, ibid., 509; Maurice Agulhon, *The French Republic 1879–1992* (New York, 1993), 40.

125. Agulhon, *French Republic*, 25; Wright, *France*, 225–29.

126. Furet, *France*, 533.

127. Charles Tilly, *European Revolutions, 1492–1992* (Oxford, 1993), 145; Furet, *France*, 535. The disappearance of the national guard, which had proven ineffective and, even more, unreliable during the Second Republic and the Commune, also symbolized the victory of state centralization and republican social conservatism. The Third Republic would readily use the

army against strikers, notably in 1905 and 1907. Fearing the state's monopoly over coercive power in the name of social order, the socialist Jean Jaurès called for the establishment of a civilian force.

128. Furet, *France*, 522.

129. Agulhon, *French Republic*, 27.

CHAPTER 6

I am indebted to the other contributors to this volume, especially Isser Woloch and Sergio Luzzatto, and to David Caputo, Alice Kelikian, Sidney Tarrow and Richard Davis for errors corrected, erudition appended, and stimulating criticisms not always adequately used.

1. For an admirably informed, even-handed, and insightful review of recent literature, see John A. Davis, "Remapping Italy's Path to the Twentieth Century," *JMH* 66 (1994): 291–320.

2. There were revolts in Corsica against Genoa in 1730 and by Paoli in 1768. Ferrari's figure is cited by Benedetto Croce, *Storia della storiographia italiana nel secolo decimono* (Bari, 1947), 2:12–13.

3. John A. Davis, *Conflict and Control: Law and Order in Nineteenth-Century Italy* (Atlantic Highlands, NJ, 1988), 71–90.

4. A police official in Rimini lamented in 1845 that there revolution had become an "idea fissa," Franco della Peruta, *Mazzini e i rivoluzionari italiani* (Milan, 1974), 426.

5. Luigi Bulferetti, *Socialismo risorgimentale* (Turin, 1949), is devoted to this case.

6. Gaetano Salvemini, *Mazzini* (London, 1956), 67–73; della Peruta, *Mazzini*, 77–81.

7. Carlo Ghisalberti, *Le Costituzioni "Giacobine" (1796–1799)* (Milan, 1957), 135.

8. Sismondi made the distinction very clearly in J. C. L. de Sismondi, *A History of the Italian Republics: A View of the Origin, Progress, and Fall of Italian Freedom* (London, 1907), 324–30, first published in 1832.

9. John A. Davis, "1799: The 'Santafede' and the crisis of the 'ancien régime' in southern Italy," in John A. Davis and Paul Ginsborg, eds., *Society and Politics in the Age of the Risorgimento* (Cambridge, 1991), 1–25.

10. Bulferetti, *Socialismo risorgimentale*, 66–69.

11. Nello Roselli, *Carlo Pisacane nel Risorgimento italiano* (Milan, 1958), 223.

12. Raymond Grew, "Garibaldi come soggetto di storia sociale," in Aldo A. Illola, ed., *Garibaldi Generale della Libertà* (Rome, 1984), 551–68.

13. Kent Roberts Greenfield, *Economics and Liberalism in the Risorgimento: A Study of Nationalism in Lombardy, 1814–1848* (Baltimore, 1965), 238–39.

14. Alexis de Tocqueville, *The Old Régime and the French Revolution*, Stuart Gilbert, trans. (Garden City, NY, 1955), 12–13.

15. Carlo Ghisalberti, *Storia costituzionale d'Italia, 1849–1948* (Bari, 1974), 1.

16. See the discussion in Denis Mack Smith, *Modern Sicily After 1713. A History of Sicily* (New York, 1968), 415–26.

17. Clara M. Lovett, *Carlo Cattaneo and the Politics of the Risorgimento, 1820–1860* (The Hague, 1972), 76–78.

18. Assessing revolutionary failures, Pisacane wrote that "Foreign bayonets did not destroy a revolution, that would have been impossible, but the forces of some individuals won," Roselli, *Pisacane*, 154.

19. A. Aquarone, M. d'Addio, G. Negri, eds., *Le Costituzioni italiane* (Milan, 1958), 159.

20. Benedetto Croce, *Storia della storiographia*, 1:121 makes this point and lists important Catholic historians, among the most important propagandists of a conception of revolution, who held revolutionary office. He includes Manzoni, Troya, Cappoini, Balbo, Gioberti, Tosti, Tommaseo, and Tabarrini, a remarkable group.

21. Clara M. Lovett, *The Democratic Movement in Italy, 1830–1876* (Cambridge, 1982), 3, 35.

22. Franco della Peruta, "War and Society in Napoleonic Italy: The Armies of the Kingdom of Italy at Home and Abroad," in Davis and Ginsborg, *Society and Politics*, 41–42.

23. Benedetto Croce, *Storiographia italiana*.

24. Paul Ginsborg, *Daniele Manin and the Venetian Revolution of 1848–49* (Cambridge, 1979), makes the strongest case for that view.

25. Benedetto Croce, *La Storia del Regno di Napoli* (Bari, 1953), 239; on Masaniello, 142–44. Compare Nello Roselli's belief as an antifascist in 1932 that Pisacane's martyrdom lived on and that his dream provided a foundation for Italy, Roselli, *Pisacane*, 336–37.

26. Antonio Monti, "Il Quarantotto nei Ricordi dell'Ambasciatore Austriaco, G. A. von Hübner," in Ettore Rota, ed., *Il 1848 nella storia italiana ed europea* (Milan, n.d. [1948]), 409–10.

27. Ernestina Monti, "I Teatri Milanesi nel 1848," in ibid., 726–49; Leopoldo Marchetti, "I Moti di Milan e il Problema della Fusione col Piemonte," in ibid., 666–87.

28. Pietro Nurra, "Genova nel 1848," in ibid., 766–67.

29. Ginsborg, *Manin and the Venetian Revolution*, 75–81, 109.

30. Raymond Grew, "How Success Spoiled the Risorgimento," *JMH* 34 (1962): 239–53.

31. Raymond Grew, *A Sterner Plan for Italian Unity: The Italian National Society in the Risorgimento* (Princeton, NJ, 1963), 167–90.

32. Lovett, *Democratic Movement*, 72–76.

33. Carlo Botta's entry in the competition for the best essay on the government most suitable for Lombardy, Armando Saitta, ed., *Allo origini del Risorgimento: I testi di un "celebre" concorso (1796)* (Rome, 1964), 1:21–22.

34. Giuseppe Ferrari, "La Révolution et les Réformes en Italie," *Revue des*

Deux Mondes, Nov. 16, 1844, and Jan. 1, 1848, cited in Clara M. Lovett, *Giuseppe Ferrari and the Italian Revolution* (Chapel Hill, NC, 1977), 42.

35. The life of David Levi offers an ideal example; see Bulferetti, *Socialismo risorgimentale*, 81–94; but the entire volume in a sense illustrates this point.

36. Antonio Gramsci, *Quaderni del carcere* (Turin, 1975), edizione critica dell'Istituto Gramsci, Valentino Gerratana, ed., 1766–67.

37. Ibid., 814–16.

38. In 1993, upon his release from prison, the leader of Italy's Red Brigades replied to an interview's question by explaining, "There has never been a revolution in Italy . . . There was no bourgeois revolution, no industrial revolution, and no modern revolution." *Newsweek*, May 17, 1993, 54.

39. Ghisalberti, *Storia costituzionale*, 2–3. The Tuscan constitutions were proposed in 1782 and 1793, Corsica's in 1794. Others can of course be added to the list, including the Piedmontese republic of 1796 and Corfu in 1803, Aquarone et al., *Costituzioni italiane*, 3.

40. Antonio Marongiu, *Il parlamento in Italia nel medio evo e nell'età moderna* (Milan, 1962).

41. Including the 1835 essay *Progetto di costituzione per l'Itala fatta libera ed independente all'anno 1835*, reprinted in Aquarone et al., *Costituzioni italiane*, 744 ff; Carlo Boncompagni's *Della monarchia rappresentiva* (Turin, 1848), the beginning of a long career as government official and professor of constitutional law; and P. Peverelli, *Commenti intorno allo Statuto del Regno di Sardegna* (Turin, 1849).

42. R. R. Palmer, *The Age of Democratic Revolution*, 1. *The Challenge* (Princeton, NJ, 1959), 18–19; 2. *The Struggle* (Princeton, NJ, 1964), 293.

43. Carlo Ghisalberti, *Le Costituzioni "Giacobine" 1796–1799* (Milan, 1957), 119–22.

44. Ibid., 101–11.

45. "A new state created in the midst of so much political commotion, cannot all at once leap to that level of consistency, of perfection, of strength," Aquarone et al., *Costituzioni italiane*, 322.

46. Ibid., 39–40, 83–84.

47. Ibid., 308.

48. Ghisalberti, *Costituzioni "Giacobine"*, 147–49, 163–64; Palmer, *Democratic Revolution* 2:275–76; 303–4.

49. Ibid., 9–10, 17–21, 141–43.

50. The statement, in N. Palmieri, *Saggio storico e politico sulla costituzione di Sicilia nel 1816* (Lausanne, 1847), is cited by Enzo Sciacca, *Riflessi del costituzionalismo Europeo in Sicilia (1812–1815)* (Catania, n.d. [1966?]), 16.

51. Benedetto Croce, *Storia del Regno di Napoli* (Bari, 1953), 259.

52. The Piedmontese version was a literal translation intended primarily as proof of commitment to the idea of a constitution; in the Kingdom of the Two Sicilies, however, provisions specific to their needs were added. Richard Herr points out, for example, the sentence added to article 353 specifying that girls will be taught the domestic arts, whereas the Spanish version stops

with the requirement of elementary schools in every commune to teach reading, writing, counting, and the Catholic catechism. Carlo Ghisalberti, *Dall'Antico regime al 1848: Le origini costituzionale dell'Italia moderna* (Bari, 1974), 128–40, shows the importance of the efforts in the decade 1821–31 to establish constitutions in Naples, Sicily, Piedmont, and the Papal States.

53. Ghisalberti, *Storia costituzionale*, 14–20. Giuseppe Maranini, *Storia del potere in Italia, 1848–1967* (Florence, 1967), 8–114, although highly critical of the Risorgimento, emphasizes the importance throughout the period of demands for a constitution and memories of historical precedents.

54. The rebellion in Sardinia in 1847 abolished the traditional *stamenti* there, Daniele Petrosino, "National and Regional Movements in Italy: The Case of Sardinia," in John Coakley, ed., *The Social Origins of Nationalist Movements: The Contemporary West European Experience* (London, 1992), 125.

55. Aquarone et al., *Costituzioni italiane*, 563, 565.

56. Ibid., 599.

57. Ibid., 623.

58. Ibid., 632.

59. Ibid., 818.

60. Ibid., 830–31.

61. Francesco de Feo, ed., *Atti della Reale Consulta di Stato del Granducato di Toscana, settember 1847–aprile 1848* (Milan, 1967).

62. Some were officially promulgated or adopted, some just official projects; the figure includes the two constitutions written for Sicily, two for the Kingdom of the Two Sicilies, two for the Papal States, and one each for Parma, Tuscany, Modena, and Piedmont. Monaco would make an eleventh.

63. Aquarone et al., *Costituzioni italiane*, 310.

64. Giuseppe Ferrari, "La Philosophie Catholique en Italie," *Revue des Deux Mondes* Mar. 15 and May 15 1884, cited in Lovett, *Ferrari*, 43.

65. Ghisalberti, *Costituzioni "Giacobine"*, 190–93.

66. On the importance of administrative law, see Ghisalberti, *Storia costituzionale*, 16–17 and the bibliography there.

67. Adrian Lyttleton, "The Middle Class in Liberal Italy," in Davis and Ginsborg, eds., *Society and Politics*, 228, 234–37; Gramsci was sufficiently struck by the point to write out the statistics showing that Italy had twice as many lawyers per capita as France and three times as many as Germany at the end of the century, *Quaderni del carcere*, 948–49.

68. Bulferetti, *Socialismo risorgimentale*, 199–200; this failure added ambiguity to the democrats' acceptance of Piedmont's leadership in the Risorgimento and lessened the monarchy's claim to legitimacy.

69. Guido di Ruggerio, *Storia del liberalismo europea*, 5th ed. (Bari, 1949), 311, notes the lack of originality.

70. Raffaele Romanelli, *Il Commando impossibile: Stato e società nell'Italia liberale* (Bologna, 1988), 163–69.

71. The phrase is R. R. Palmer's, *Democratic Revolution* 2:310ff.

72. Candeloro considered this characteristic of liberals, cited in Lovett, *Democratic Movement*, 113. But note also the very limited interest in the American constitution, Raymond Grew, "One Nation Barely Visible: The United States as Seen by Nineteenth-Century Italy's Liberal Leaders," in Emiliana P. Noether, ed., *The American Constitution as Symbol and Reality* (Lewiston, NY, 1989), 119–34.

73. In Aquarone et al., *Costituzioni italiane*, 270.

74. Ibid., 579.

75. Ibid., 614.

76. The more conservative constitution of Lucca was unusual in not beginning with any list of general principles; in the Kingdom of Italy, the Consulta di Stato, while adopting a fully Bonapartist position in 1805, nevertheless included "civil and political liberty" as one of the desiderata of constitutional government. Aquarone et al., *Costituzioni italiane*, 213, 324.

77. Benedetto Croce, *Storia del Regno di Napoli* (Bari, 1953), 259.

78. *L'Italie au dix-neuvième siècle ou de la nécessité d'accorde en Italie le pouvoir avec la liberté* was written by Francesco Saverio Salfi, a Neapolitan who served Napoleon and was one of Confalonieri's teachers, cited by Emilia Morelli, "La Costituzione americana e i democratici italiani dell'ottocento," *Rassegna Storica del Risorgimento* 86 (Oct.-Dec. 1989): 432.

79. Ghisalberti, *Constituzioni "Giacobine,"* 87–88.

80. Something like it was promised Sicily by a Neapolitan regime in crisis in 1848, one more promise never carried out.

81. The explanation of Giuseppe Pecchio cited in Morelli, "La Costituzione americana," 428.

82. Antonio Gramsci, *Quaderni del carcere*, 1051.

83. Aquarone et al., *Costituzioni italiane*, 832; after 1848 Mauro Macchi also thought the two forms not so fundamentally different, Lovett, *Democratic Movement*, 41. This tradition further limited the appeal of Sonnino's cry toward the end of the century for a return to the Piedmontese Statuto, to a more literal and conservative interpretation of Italy's constitution.

84. Often, at the sacrifice of some political liberty, de Ruggiero, *Storia del liberalismo*, 307.

85. Ghisalberti, *Storia costituzionale*, 91–92.

86. Gramsci, obviously thinking of Italy, noted that the principle of the division of powers incorporated a liberal ideology that permitted the bureaucracy to become a caste. His solution was equally Italian: a permanent constituent assembly. Gramsci, *Quaderni del carcere*, 752.

87. A quality shared with the Spanish constitution of 1812, with its requirement of patriotism (pointed out to me by Richard Herr), which was carefully repeated in the Italian versions.

88. Aquarone et al., *Costituzioni italiane*, 14.

89. Ibid., 160.

90. Ibid., 650–54.

91. Despite the threat of excommunication as many as 70 percent of adult

males voted in some Roman electoral colleges in 1848, Lovett, *Democratic Movement,* 137.

92. The famous essay contest in Milan in 1796–97 on the form of government that Italy should have was part of a program of public instruction; and more than a century later Gramsci could write that constitutions are instructional texts, "piú che altro 'testi educativi' ideologici," Gramsci, *Quaderni del carcere,* 1666.

93. Saitta, ed., *I Testi di un "celebre" consorso* 1 : vii–xii.

94. Ghisalberti, *Costituzioni "Giacobine",* 177–84.

95. Federico Chabod, *L'Idea di nazione* (Bari, 1961), 66.

96. Ibid., 77–79.

97. Ibid., 72–75.

98. Norberto Bobbio, "Gramsci and the Concept of Civil Society," in John Keane, ed., *Civil Society and the State* (London, 1988), 89–92.

99. Saitta, ed., *I Testi di un "celebre" concorso* 1 : 105; Botta also envisioned a revival of the Olympic games, ibid., 166.

100. Joseph LaPalombara, *Democracy Italian Style* (New Haven, CT, 1987), 25–29, uses the quotation to make the further point that Leopardi in practice rather liked the very qualities of Italian society he denounced; and LaPalombara notes in particular its great tolerance, the belief that all conflicts can be adjusted, and the conviction that nothing in public life is quite what it seems; the citation from Leopardi is from his "Discorso sopra lo stato presente dei costumi degli italiani," in Francesco Flora, ed., *Tutte le opere di Giacomo Leopardi* (Milan, 1940).

101. Leonardo Olschki, *The Genius of Italy* (Ithaca, NY, 1954), 450.

102. Significantly in an essay entitled, "Qualche idea sopra una costituzione nazionale," Chabod, *L'Idea di nazione,* 71.

103. Sydel Silverman, *Three Bells for Civilization: The Life of an Italian Hill Town* (New York, 1975), passim.

104. Sergio Luzzatto drew my attention to the passage in Jules Michelet, "Introduction à l'histoire universelle," in id., *Oeuvres Complètes,* Paul Viallaneix, ed. (Paris, 1972), 2 : 284.

105. Ibid., 149.

106. Provocatively discussed in Mario Isnenghi, *L'Italia in piazza: I luoghi della vita publica dal 1848 ai giorni nostri* (Milan, 1994).

107. Giandomenico Romagnosi, *La Scienza della Costituzioni* (Turin, 1848), pt. 3, bk. 4, chap. 5, 420–38.

108. Ibid., 91–116.

109. Gramsci, *Quaderni del carcere,* 117–18; and in a related note comments on the distinction between *Italia legale* and *Italia reale* by Catholic critics of the liberal state.

110. Grew, *Sterner Plan,* 261–76; *Quaderni Storici* 47 (Aug. 1991), esp. Paolo Subacchi, "Il Mutamento guidato, Associazioni, Comitati Elettorali e formazione delle canditature a Piacenza negli anni sessanta del ottocento," 493–506. Robert Putnam, *Making Democracy Work: Civic Traditions in*

Modern Italy (Princeton, 1993), 138–62, sees this flowering as a significant bridge between the civic traditions of Italy's city states and Italian politics today, contributing to the political differences between north and south.

111. His speech of 1867 at the University of Padua.

112. The phrase is Eugenio Curiel's, *Classi e generazioni nel secondo Risorgimento* (Rome, 1955), 130. Italy's suffrage, extended to all of Italy when Piedmont's Statuto became the national constitution, was from 1859 to 1882 narrower than that of Spain or Austria, *Compendio delle statistiche elettorali italiane dal 1848 al 1934* (Rome, 1896), 70–71.

113. Piero Gobetti, *Coscienza liberale e classe operaia*, Paolo Spriano, ed. (Turin, 1951), 38.

114. Romanelli, *Il Commando impossibile*, 151–201.

115. A major theme of the Risorgimento, de Ruggerio, *Storia del liberalismo*, 311–13.

116. Denis Mack Smith, "Francesco De Sanctis: the Politics of a Literary Crisis," in Davis and Ginsborg, *Society and Politics*, 255–56, notes De Sanctis's belated acceptance of a two-party system.

117. Raymond Grew, "Il Trasformismo: Ultimo Stadio del Risorgimento," in Vittorio Frosini, ed., *Il Risorgimento e l'Europa* (Catania, 1970).

118. Lovett, *Democratic Movement*, 188–226.

119. Michela de Giorgio, *Le Italiane dall'Unità a oggi* (Bari, 1992), 126.

120. Salvemini, *Mazzini*, 30.

121. de Giorgio, *Le Italiane*, 6–13.

122. Jane Schneider and Peter Schneider, *Culture and Political Economy in Western Sicily* (New York, 1976), 153–60.

123. Romagnosi, *Scienza della Costituzioni*, pt. 3, bk. 4, chap. 5, 417–18.

124. Morelli, "La Costituzione americana," 428–29.

125. The point is made by Lucy Riall, "Elite Resistance to State Formation: the Case of Italy," in Mary Fulbrook, ed., *National Histories and European History* (Boulder, CO, 1993), 63.

126. Olschki, *Genius of Italy*, 433.

127. A little over half the eligible voters went to the polls from 1861 to 1904, Maranini, *Potere in Italia*, 254.

128. Raymond Grew, "Italy," in Raymond Grew, ed., *Crises of Political Development in Europe and the United States* (Princeton, NJ, 1978), 27, 96.

129. Even after World War 2, one of Italy's leading legal theorists began his course on the founding of the modern Italian state with Roman law and ended the term without getting to the French Revolution. Guido Astuti, *La formazione dello Stato moderno in Italia: Lezioni di storia del diritto italiano* (Turin, 1967).

130. It is the focus of much of the literature on civil society, René Gallissot, "Abus de société civile: étatisation de la société ou socialisation de l'Etat," *L'Homme et la Société* 4 (1991): 3; the entire number is very telling on the multiple uses of the concept of civil society.

131. Norberto Bobbio, *Liberalism and Democracy* (London, 1990), 71–72, cites De Sanctis on Mazzini and Mazzini himself.

132. Although American and English scholars have been prominent in the spread of this view, it has been shared by a number of Italian scholars such as Carlo Tullio-Altan. For a useful recent review of some of this literature, see Robert Cartocci, "Fra vecchie e nuove fratture culturali in Italia," *Affari Sociali Internazionale* 21 (1993): 57–75; Franco Paroncello, "The Roots of Discontent. The Nature and Dynamics of Political Disaffection in Italy" (PhD diss., Univ. of Michigan, 1984).

133. Steven Hughes finds that of the duels fought between 1879 and 1889, one-third were responses to newspaper articles. Old forms of honor were being used to discipline new public forums because private honor and public knowledge were inseparable. "Honor in Modern Italy and the *Codice Cavalleresco* of Iacopo Gelli," unpubl. paper.

134. Silverman makes the similar point about public life and festivals generally, *Three Bells*, 16–17, 35–41, 122, 228–30.

135. Discussed in Raymond Grew, "The Nineteenth-Century European State," in Charles Bright and Susan Harding, eds., *Statemaking and Social Movements: Essays in History and Theory* (Ann Arbor, MI, 1984), 100–106.

136. Steven Soper, "The Liberal State in Nineteenth-Century Italy," unpubl. paper.

137. Chabod, *L'Idea di nazione*, 79–91.

138. Guiseppe Prezzolini, who had an alchemist's genius for making clichés glitter like fresh coins, offered a particularly telling example in his essay, "Il Regionalismo," in id., *La Cultura Italiana* (Milan, 1938), 29–40.

139. Eric W. Cochrane, *Tradition and Enlightenment in Tuscan Academies, 1690–1800* (Chicago, 1961). While insisting on the ideological importance of Tuscan writers who praised peasant culture and collections of peasant songs and poems (he cites a half dozen authors), Umberto Carpi sees this interest as an exercise in moderate hegemony, noting their omission of traditions of resistance and little attention given peasants by the party of action, id., "Egemonia moderata e intellettuali nei Risorgimento," in Corrado Vivanti, ed., *Storia d'Italia*, Annali 4, *Intellettuali e potere* (Turin, 1981), 430–71. For comments on some southern writers later in the century, also from a Gramscian perspective but with a different emphasis, see Alberto Mario Cirese, *Intelletuali, folklore, istinto di classe* (Turin, 1986).

140. Mariella Columni Camerino, *Idillio e propaganda nella letterature sociale del Risorgimento* (Naples, 1975), 257–60 and 37–79, 106–71.

141. Gramsci's aphorism is autobiographical, *Quaderni del carcere*, 1514.

142. Ibid., 117.

143. Ibid., 2011–15; Bobbio, "Gramsci and the Concept of Civil Society," 89–92.

144. Gramsci, *Quaderni del carcere*, 1540.

145. On holidays the republican catechism was to be read to assembled school children, and there was to be an elected court in every canton to judge the non-democratic behavior of those who put on airs ["userà dei modi superbi ed insolenti e contro equaglianza"]. In Aquarone et al., *Costituzioni italiane*, 295.

146. Marchetti, "I Moti di Milano," 697–709.

147. A consistent concern, see Steven C. Hughes, *Crime, Disorder and the Risorgimento* (Cambridge, 1994).

148. From his speech in 1867 on accepting his professorship at the University of Padua, cited in Luigi Luzzatti, *Memoire* (Bologna, 1931), 1:261–62. I owe the reference to Steven Soper.

149. Lovett, *Democratic Movement*, 37, 44.

150. Carlo Sforza, *The Real Italians: A Study in European Psychology* (New York, 1942), 132.

151. Prezzolini, *Cultura italiana*, 18, includes this in a long description of the Italian character.

152. "La Cultura Politica," in Paolo Spriano, ed., *Pietro Gobetti, Coscienza liberal e classe operaia* (Turin, 1951), 35; the essay was first published in 1923.

CHAPTER 7

1. See Reinhart Koselleck, "Revolution," in Otto Brunner et al., eds., *Geschichtliche Grundbegriffe*, 6 vols. (Stuttgart, 1972–90), 5:653–56, 725–88.

2. Hans-Ulrich Wehler, *Deutsche Gesellschaftsgeschichte*, 3 vols. (Munich, 1987–95), 1:35.

3. Ralf Dahrendorf, *Society and Democracy in Germany* (Garden City, NY, 1967).

4. Whether Germany followed a "special path" [*Sonderweg*] to modernity has been one of the most contested issues in modern German historiography. For a guide to the debate see Robert Moeller, "The Kaiserreich Recast? Continuity and Change in Modern German Historiography," *JSH* 17 (1984): 655–83; and James Retallack, "Social History with a Vengeance? Some Reactions to H-U. Wehler's 'Das deutsche Kaiserreich," *German Studies Review* 7 (1984): 423–50.

5. The quote is from Marx's *Eighteenth Brumaire of Louis Napoleon*, reprinted in Robert C. Tucker, ed., *The Marx-Engels Reader*, 2d ed. (New York, 1978), 595.

6. Alexis de Tocqueville, *The Ancien Regime and the French Revolution* (Garden City, NY, 1955), 1, 8, 277.

7. Generations of German historians have viewed these bureaucratic institutions as the most significant source of political modernization. For a classic statement of this position see Otto Hintze, *The Historical Essays* (New York, 1975). In his influential study *Bureaucracy, Aristocracy, and Autocracy: The Prussian Experience, 1660–1815* (Cambridge, MA, 1958), Hans Rosenberg accepts the main lines of Hintze's analysis but reverses its ideological valience. For a spirited critique of the idea that bureaucratic modernization was the "German revolution," see Wehler, *Gesellschaftsgeschichte* 1:36ff.

8. Jürgen Schlumbohm, *Freiheit. Die Anfänge der bürgerlichen Emanzipationsbewegung in Deutschland im Spiegel ihres Leitwortes, ca. 1760–*

ca. 1800 (Düsseldorf, 1975); Manfred Riedel, "Bürger, Staatsbürger, Bürgertum," in Brunner, ed., *Grundbegriffe* 1:672–725.

9. Tocqueville, *Ancien Regime*, 228–30. For an example of the gap between absolutist intentions and reality, see Walter Mertineit, *Die friedericianische Verwaltung in Ostpreussen* (Heidelberg, 1956).

10. James Allen Vann, *The Making of a State: Württemberg, 1593–1793* (Ithaca, NY, 1984). For other examples of polities that do not fit the Prussian model, see Mack Walker, *German Home Towns: Community, State, General Estate, 1648–1871* (Ithaca, NY, 1971).

11. William Hagen, "The Junkers' Faithless Servants. Peasant Insubordination and the Breakdown of Serfdom in Brandenburg-Prussia, 1763–1811," in R. J. Evans and W. R. Lee, eds., *The German Peasantry* (London, 1986), 71–101. See also Edgar Melton, "*Gutsherrschaft* in East Elbian Germany and Livonia, 1500–1800: A Critique of the Model," *CEH* 21 (1988): 315–49.

12. Immanuel Kant, "What is Enlightenment?" in Hans Reiss, ed., *Political Writings* (Cambridge, 1970). On the public see Rudolf Vierhaus, "Politisches Bewusstsein vor 1789," *Der Staat* 6 (1967): 175–96; and Lucian Hölscher, *Öffentlichkeit und Geheimnis. Sprache und Geschichte* (Stuttgart, 1979).

13. Wehler, *Gesellschaftsgeschichte* 1:347ff., is especially good on the impact of the American revolution in Germany; the quote is from 349. On the impact of the French Revolution, see James J. Sheehan, *German History, 1770–1866* (Oxford, 1989), chap. 4; the quote from Gentz is on 211.

14. T. C. W. Blanning, *Reform and Revolution in Mainz, 1743–1803* (Cambridge, 1974). On Saxony, see Klaus Epstein, *The Genesis of German Conservatism* (Princeton, NJ, 1966), 441ff.

15. For a contemporary analysis of the German situation, see Alfred Freiherr von Knigge, "Über die Ursachen, warum wir in Deutschland vorerst wohl keine gefährliche politische Haupt-Revolution zu erwarten haben," *Schlesig'sches Journal* 2 (1793): 273–90. See also Volker Press, "Warum gab es keine deutsche Revolution? Deutschland und das revolutionäre Frankreich, 1789–1815," in Dieter Langewiesche, ed., *Revolution und Krieg* (Paderborn, 1989), 67–86. On the scarcity of great revolutions, see Seymour Drescher, "'Why Great Revolutions will become Rare': Tocqueville's Most Neglected Prognosis," *JMH* 64 (1992): 429–54.

16. The best account in English is T. C. W. Blanning, *The French Revolution in Germany: Occupation and Resistance in the Rhineland, 1792–1802* (Oxford, 1983).

17. I develop this argument somewhat more fully in "State and Nationality in the Napoleonic Period," in John Breuilly, ed., *The State of Germany* (London, 1992), 47–59.

18. On the reforms see Sheehan, *German History*, chap. 5. My interpretation is most influenced by Reinhart Koselleck, *Preussen zwischen Reform und Revolution* (Stuttgart, 1967).

19. The standard work on the formation of the Confederation is Enno Kraehe, *Metternich's German Policy*, 2 vols. (Princeton, 1963–84). See also

Wolf Gruner, "Die deutsche Einzelstaaten und der Deutsche Bund," in A. Kraus, ed., *Land und Reich/Stamm und Nation* (Munich, 1984), 3:19–36.

20. Peter Thielen, *Karl August von Hardenberg, 1750–1822* (Cologne and Berlin, 1967), 207.

21. The standard account of German constitutionalism is E. R. Huber, *Deutsche Verfassungsgeschichte*, 3d ed., 8 vols. (Stuttgart, 1967–90). The Bavarian, Badenese, and Württemberg constitutions are reprinted in Huber, ed., *Dokumente zur deutschen Verfassungsgeschichte*, 3 vols. (Stuttgart, 1956–57), 1:141–200.

22. Hartwig Brandt, *Landständische Repräsentation im deutschen Vormärz: Politisches Denken im Einflussfeld des monarchischen Prinzips* (Neuwied, 1968). On public life between 1815 and 1848, see Sheehan, *German History*, chaps. 7 and 10; Heinrich Lutz, *Zwischen Habsburg und Preussen. Deutschland, 1815–1866* (Berlin, 1985); and Thomas Nipperdey, *Deutsche Geschichte, 1800–1866: Bürgerwelt und starker Staat* (Munich, 1983).

23. On German liberalism, see James J. Sheehan, *German Liberalism in the Nineteenth Century* (Chicago, 1978); Dieter Langewiesche, *Liberalismus in Deutschland* (Frankfurt, 1988); Dieter Langewiesche, ed., *Liberalismus im 19. Jahrhundert: Deutschland im europäischen Vergleich* (Göttingen, 1988); Wolfgang Schieder, ed., *Liberalismus in der Gesellschaft des deutschen Vormärz* (Göttingen, 1983).

24. In addition to the works cited in n. 23, see the articles on "Freiheit," "Bürger," and "Volk" in Brunner, ed., *Grundbegriffe*.

25. John Breuilly, *Nationalism and the State*, 2d ed. (Manchester, 1993), 2. On German nationalism, see the essays in Breuilly, ed., *State of Germany*.

26. There are some useful treatments of liberalism's social base in Lothar Gall, ed., *Liberalismus* (Cologne, 1976).

27. On popular politics in the first half of the nineteenth century, see the general introduction in Charles Tilly et al., eds., *The Rebellious Century, 1830–1930* (Cambridge, MA, 1975); Rainer Wirtz, *"Widersetzlichkeiten, Excesse, Crawalle, Tumulte, und Skandale." Soziale Bewegung und gewalthafter sozialer Protest in Baden, 1815–1848* (Frankfurt, 1981); Hans-Gerhard Husung, *Protest und Repression im Vormärz. Norddeutschland zwischen Restauration und Revolution* (Göttingen, 1983).

28. Quoted in Rudolf Muhs, "Zwischen Staatsreform und politischen Protest. Liberalismus in Sachsen zur Zeit des Hambacher Festes," in Schieder, ed., *Liberalismus*, 194.

29. Rotteck quoted in Muhs, "Staatsreform," 213. Guido de Ruggiero described the relationship between liberalism and democracy as being one "at once of continuity and of antithesis." *The History of European Liberalism* (Boston, 1959), 370.

30. Nipperdey, *Deutsche Geschichte*, 403–51, provides a good introduction to the problem of religion. See also Jonathan Sperber, *Political Catholicism in Nineteenth-Century Germany* (Princeton, NJ, 1984) and the long review of Sperber by Margaret L. Anderson, "Piety and Politics: Recent Work on German Catholicism," *JMH* 63 (1991): 681–716.

31. See Husung, *Protest*, especially chaps. 5 and 6; Wirtz, "*Widersetzlich-keiten*", chap. 5.

32. For a sample of contemporary opinion, see Carl Jantke and Dietrich Hilger, eds., *Die Eigentumslosen: Armutsnot und Arbeiterschicksal in Deutschland in zeitgenössischen Schilderungen und kritischen Beobachtungen bis zum Ausgang der Emanzipationskrise des 19. Jahrhunderts* (Munich, 1965).

33. Sheehan, *German History*, 645; Hermann Beck, "State and Society in Pre-March Prussia: The Weavers' Uprising, the Bureaucracy, and the Association for the Welfare of Workers," *CEH* 25 (1992): 303–32.

34. Sheehan, *German History*, 621–54.

35. Jonathan Sperber, *Rhineland Radicals. The Democratic Movement and the Revolution of 1848–1849* (Princeton, NJ, 1991), chaps. 3 and 4.

36. For an excellent brief account of the European situation on the eve of the revolution, see Jonathan Sperber, *The European Revolutions, 1848–49* (Cambridge, 1994).

37. The most recent general survey is Sperber, *European Revolutions*.

38. There are general accounts of the German revolution in Sheehan, *German History*, chap. 11; Lutz, *Zwischen Habsburg und Preussen*, chap. 4; Nipperdey, *Deutsche Geschichte*, chap. 5; and Wehler, *Gesellschaftsgeschichte* 2:703–79. Wolfram Siemann's *Die deutsche Revolution von 1848/49* (Frankfurt, 1985) is a good short history.

39. Richard Tilly, "Popular Disorders in Nineteenth-Century Germany: A Preliminary Survey," *JSH* 4 (1970): 221. On industrial workers and the revolution, see Sperber, *Rhineland Radicals*, 223ff.

40. There is an excellent regional analysis of the elections in Sperber, *Rhineland Radicals*, 173–84. On the suffrage and its administration, see Theodore Hamerow, "The Elections to the Frankfurt Parliament," *JMH* 33 (1961): 15–32.

41. The standard work in English is Frank Eyck, *The Frankfurt Parliament, 1848–49* (London, 1968).

42. Sperber, *Rhineland Radicals*, examines the growth of participatory politics; chap. 4 of his *European Revolutions* puts the German situation in a European context.

43. P. H. Noyes, *Organization and Revolution: Working Class Associations in the German Revolution of 1848–49* (Princeton, NJ, 1966); on the political mobilization of Catholics, see Manfred Botzenhardt, *Deutscher Parlamentarismus in der Revolutionszeit, 1848–50* (Düsseldorf, 1977), 335ff.

44. In addition to Sperber, *Rhineland Radicals*, see Joachim Paschen, *Demokratische Vereine und preussicher Staat. Entwicklung und Unterdrückung der demokratischen Bewegung während der Revolution von 1848–49* (Munich and Vienna, 1977). On women in the revolution, see Stanley Zucker, *Kathinka Zitz-Halein and Female Civic Activism in Mid-Nineteenth Century Germany* (Carbondale, IL, 1991).

45. Sperber, *Rhineland Radicals*, chaps. 9–11; Christoph Klessmann, "Zur Sozialgeschichte der Reichsverfassungskampagne von 1849," *HZ* 218 (1974): 283–337.

46. Engels quoted in Lutz, *Zwischen Habsburg und Preussen*, 319. See Michael Neumüller, *Liberalismus und Revolution. Das Problem der Revolution in der deutschen liberalen Geschichtsschreibung des neunzehnten Jahrhunderts* (Düsseldorf, 1973).

47. Charles Tilly, *European Revolutions, 1492–1992* (Oxford, 1993), 5 and 189.

48. There are general accounts of the post-revolutionary era in Sheehan, *German History*, chap. 14; Lutz, *Zwischen Habsburg und Preussen*, chap. 6; and Nipperdey, *Deutsche Geschichte*, chap. 6.

49. Sheehan, *German Liberalism*, chap. 3.

50. Toni Oppermann, *Arbeiterbewegung und liberales Bürgertum in Deutschland, 1850–1863* (Bonn, 1979); Wolfgang Schwentker, *Konservative Vereine und Revolution in Preussen, 1848–49: Die Konstituierung des Konservatismus als Partei* (Düsseldorf, 1988); Sperber, *Political Catholicism*, chaps. 2 and 3.

51. Quoted in Otto Pflanze, *Bismarck and the Development of Germany*, 2d ed., 3 vols. (Princeton, NJ, 1990), 1:184.

52. For some thoughtful reflections on these issues, see Dieter Langewische, "'Revolution von oben?' Krieg und Nationalstaatsgründung in Deutschland," in Langewiesche, ed., *Revolution*, 117–34.

CHAPTER 8

1. The only (somewhat) recent, comprehensive history of the 1848–49 revolutions in the Habsburg monarchy is Rudolf Kiszling, *Die Revolution im Kaisertum Österreich, 1848–1849*, 2 vols. (Vienna, 1948), which, however, concentrates on military events. Other works of interest are R. John Rath, *The Viennese Revolution of 1848* (Austin, TX, 1957); Maximilian Bach, *Geschichte der Wiener Revolution im Jahre 1848* (Vienna, 1898), a still valuable liberal interpretation; István Deák, *The Lawful Revolution: Louis Kossuth and the Hungarians, 1848–1849* (New York, 1979); László Deme, *The Radical Left and the Hungarian Revolution of 1848*, East European Monographs, 19 (Boulder, CO, 1976); Stanley Z. Pech, *The Czech Revolution of 1848* (Chapel Hill, NC, 1969); Paul Ginsborg, *Daniele Manin and the Venetian Revolution of 1848–49* (Cambridge, 1979); and Alan Sked, *The Survival of the Habsburg Empire: Radetzky, the Imperial Army, and the Class War, 1848* (London and New York, 1979). Two general histories of the revolutions: François Fejto, ed., *The Opening of an Era 1848: An Historical Symposium*, intro. A. J. P. Taylor (New York, 1966); and Priscilla Robertson, *Revolutions of 1848: A Social History* (Princeton, NJ, 1952), contain valuable chapters on the events in the Habsburg monarchy.

On the economic causes of the 1848 revolutions, see Julius Marx, *Die wirtschaftlichen Ursachen der Revolution von 1848 in Österreich* (Graz and Cologne, 1965).

2. Among the best histories of the Habsburg monarchy in English are Oscar Jászi, *The Dissolution of the Habsburg Monarchy* (Chicago, 1929;

2d ed., Chicago, 1961); Barbara Jelavich, *The Habsburg Empire in European Affairs, 1814–1918* (New York, 1975); Robert A. Kann, *A History of the Habsburg Empire, 1526–1918* (Berkeley, 1974); C. A. Macartney, *The Habsburg Empire, 1790–1918* (London, 1968), which is also available in a condensed form as *The House of Austria: The Later Phase, 1790–1918* (Edinburgh, 1978); Alan Sked, *The Decline and Fall of the Habsburg Empire* (London and New York, 1989); Victor L. Tapié, *The Rise and Fall of the Habsburg Monarchy*, trans. Stephen Hardman (New York, 1971); and A. J. P. Taylor, *The Habsburg Monarchy, 1809–1918: A History of the Austrian Empire and Austria-Hungary* (New York, 1965). Although greatly stimulating, Taylor's book must be used with caution because of its many inaccuracies.

On the Habsburg dynasty, see Adam Wandruszka, *The House of Austria: Six Hundred Years of a European Dynasty*, trans. Cathleen and Hans Epstein (Garden City, NY, 1964), and Dorothy G. McGuigan, *The Habsburgs* (New York, 1966).

There are quite a few useful histories of Hungary in English, such as C. A. Macartney, *Hungary: A Short History* (Chicago, 1962); Péter Hanák, ed., *One Thousand Years: A Concise History of Hungary* (Budapest, 1988); and Peter F. Sugar, ed., *A History of Hungary* (Bloomington, IN, 1990). The most original piece of writing on modern Hungary is Andrew C. Janos, *The Politics of Backwardness in Hungary, 1825–1945* (Princeton, NJ, 1982).

Some other valuable national historical surveys are Norman Davies, *God's Playground: A History of Poland*, 2 vols. (Oxford, 1981); A. H. Hermann, *A History of the Czechs* (London, 1975); Jörg K. Hoensch, *Geschichte Böhmens* (Munich, 1987); Vlad Georgescu, *The Romanians: A History* (Columbus, OH, 1991); and Fred Singleton, *A Short History of the Yugoslav Peoples* (Cambridge, 1985).

3. To be precise, between 1740 and 1815, the Habsburgs lost most of the great Duchy of Silesia, the so-called German Vorlände, and the Austrian Netherlands, or Belgium; on the other hand, they gained the Kingdom of Galicia and Lodomeria, the Duchy of Bukovina, the Kingdom of Dalmatia, the former Republic of Venice, the archepiscopal see of Salzburg, and the episcopal sees of Brixen and Trent in what is today northern Italy.

4. On the post-1867 history of the Habsburg monarchy, see especially Arthur J. May, *The Hapsburg Monarchy, 1867–1914*, 2d. ed. (Cambridge, MA, 1965).

5. Alexius von Fényes [Elek Fényes], *Statistik des Königreichs Ungarn*, 3 tomes in 1 vol. (Pest, 1843–49), 1:133.

6. There appears to be no comprehensive history, in any language, of the very large and influential Habsburg high aristocracy or of the central European nobility in general. István Deák, *Beyond Nationalism: A Social and Political History of the Habsburg Officer Corps, 1818–1918* (New York, 1990), chap. 9, and Solomon Wank, "Aristocrats and Politics in Austria, 1867–1914: A Case of Historiographical Neglect," *East European Quarterly* 26 (Summer, 1992): 133–48, might serve as useful introductions to the subject. See also the essays of István Deák, Mirjana Gross, and Andrzej Kamin-

ski in Ivo Banac and Paul Buskovitch, eds., *The Nobility in Russia and Eastern Europe* (New Haven, CT, 1983) as well as Solomon Wank, "Some Reflections on Aristocrats and Nationalism in Bohemia, 1861–1899," *Canadian Review of Studies in Nationalism* 20, 1–2 (1993): 21–33; and Nikolaus von Preradovich, *Die Führungsschichten in Österreich und Preussen 1804–1918, mit einem Ausblick zum Jahre 1945* (Wiesbaden, 1955). Josef Polišensky, *Aristocrats and the Crowd in the Revolutionary Year 1848: A Contribution to the History of Revolution and Counter-revolution in Austria*, trans. Frederick Snider (Albany, NY, 1980) deals mostly with the Bohemian aristocracy.

7. On the post-revolutionary trials of the Hungarian officers and politicians, see, among others, Deák, *The Lawful Revolution*, 329–37; Kiszling, *Die Revolution im Kaisertum Österreich* 2:291–94; and the following documentary collections: Gyula Tóth, ed., *Küzdelem, bukás, megtorlás. Emlékiratok, naplók, az 1848-1849-es forrradalom és szabadságharc végnapjairól* (Struggle, defeat, and retribution. Memoirs and diaries from the last days of the 1848–49 revolution and war of independence), 2 vols. (Budapest, 1978); and Tamás Katona, ed., *Az aradi vértanúk* (The Arad martyrs), 2 vols. (Budapest, 1979), especially 1:209–10 and 227–28. Count Batthyány's trial and execution are well told and superbly documented in Árpád Károlyi, *Németújvári gróf Batthyány Lajos első magyar miniszterelnök főbenjáró pöre* (The trial for high treason of the first Hungarian prime minister, Count L. B.), 2 vols. (Budapest, 1932).

8. Historical literature on the Habsburg monarchy in the eighteenth century is relatively scarce. Among the best works are Charles W. Ingrao, *The Habsburg Monarchy, 1618–1815* (New York, 1994); Ernst Wangermann, *The Austrian Achievement, 1700–1800* (London, 1973); T. C. W. Blanning, *Joseph II and Enlightened Absolutism* (London, 1970); S. K. Padover, *The Revolutionary Emperor: Joseph II of Austria* (2d ed.; London, 1967); Adam Wandruszka, *Leopold II*, 2 vols. (Vienna-Munich, 1963–65); George Barany, "Hoping against Hope: The Enlightened Age in Hungary," *AHR* 79 (1971): 319–57; Béla K. Király, *Hungary in the Late Eighteenth Century: The Decline of Enlightened Despotism* (New York, 1969); Henrik Marczali, *Hungary in the Eighteenth Century* (Cambridge, 1910); and Robert J. Kerner, *Bohemia in the Eighteenth Century* (New York, 1932).

9. On censorship in Austria, see Julius Marx, *Die österreichische Zensur im Vormärz* (Munich, 1959).

10. The outstanding intellectual qualities and simultaneous pettiness of the Josephinian bureaucracy in Austria is well described in Waltraud Heindl, *Gehorsame Rebellen: Bürokratie und Beamte in Österreich, 1780–1848* (Vienna, 1991).

11. On Jacobinism in the Habsburg monarchy, see Ernst Wangermann, *From Joseph II to the Jacobin Trials* (Oxford, 1959); Peter F. Sugar, "The Influence of the Enlightenment and the French Revolution in Eighteenth Century Hungary," *Journal of Central European Affairs* 17, 4 (1958): 331–55; Denis Silagyi, *Ungarn und der Geheime Mitarbeiterkreis Kaiser Leopold IIs*

(Munich, 1961); and id., *Jakobiner in der Habsburger Monarchie* (Munich, 1962). The story of the Austrian secret police is told in Donald E. Emerson, *Metternich and the Political Police: Security and Subversion in the Habsburg Monarchy, 1815–1830* (The Hague, 1968).

12. The most important work on the Transylvanian peasant revolt in 1784 is David Prodan, *Rascoală lui Horea* (The revolt of Horea), 2 vols. (Bucharest, 1979).

13. On Andreas Hofer, see F. Gunther Eyck, *Loyal Rebels: Andreas Hofer and the Tyrolean Uprising of 1809* (Lanham, 1986).

14. Nationalism and the nationality question has been studied by many historians. Some of the more important writings are Jászi, *The Dissolution of the Habsburg Monarchy*; Robert A. Kann, *The Multinational Empire: Nationalism and National Reform in the Habsburg Monarchy, 1848–1918*, 2 vols. (New York, 1970); Hans Kohn, *The Idea of Nationalism: A Study on Its Origins and Background* (New York, 1948); and Peter F. Sugar and Ivo J. Lederer, eds., *Nationalism in Eastern Europe* (Seattle, WA, 1969). Also of considerable interest are George Barany, *Stephen Széchenyi and the Awakening of Hungarian Nationalism, 1791–1841* (Princeton, NJ, 1968); Stanley Z. Pech, "The Nationalist Movement of the Austrian Slavs in 1848: A Comparative Sociological Profile," *Histoire sociale/Social History* 9 (Nov. 1976): 336–56; Joseph P. Zacek, *Palacky: the Historian as Scholar and Nationalist* (The Hague, 1970); and Peter Brock, *The Slovak National Awakening* (Toronto–Buffalo, 1976) as well as Peter Brock and Gordon Skilling, eds., *The Czech Renaissance of the Nineteenth Century* (Toronto, 1970); Duncan Wilson, *The Life and Times of Vuk Stefanović Karadžič, 1787–1864: Literacy, Literature and National Independence in Serbia* (Oxford, 1970); Elinor M. Despelatović, *Ljudevit Gaj and the Illyrian Movement* (Boulder, CO, 1975); Keith Hitchins, *The Rumanian Movement in Transylvania, 1781–1849* (Cambridge, MA, 1969); and finally, vol. 3 of the *Austrian History Yearbook* (1967), in 3 tomes, all of which is devoted to the problem of nationalisms in the region.

15. Reliable figures on literacy in the mid-nineteenth century are very hard to come by. Clearly, however, it ranged from well over one half in the German- and Czech-inhabited provinces to below 10 percent in Dalmatia, along the Adriatic coast. However, compulsory primary school education was progressing by leaps and bounds at that time. In 1850–51, up to 60 percent of the school age children actually went to school. But here, too, great differences still prevailed between west and east. In Lower Austria, which included Vienna at that time, almost 100 percent of the school-age children went to school. The situation was only slightly less good in the other German Austrian and the Czech provinces. But in Hungary 61 percent of the children attended primary school; in Galicia 14 percent, and, surprisingly, in Venetia, only 30 percent. Source: Elek Fényes, *Az ausztriai birodalom statisztikája és földrajzi leírása* (The statistics and geographic desciption of the Austrian Empire), 2 tomes in 1 vol. (Pest, 1857), 1:181.

16. The Serbo-Croatian literary language, created in the first half of the

nineteenth century by a handful of Orthodox (Serbian) and Catholic (Croatian) intellectuals out of the so-called Stokavski dialect spoken by many Orthodox and fewer Catholic South Slav peasants, stands as a classical example of this type of nation-building. Today most Serbs, Croats, Bosnian Muslims, and Montenegrins speak the Serbo-Croatian literary language, which, as we know only too well, has not led to the creation of a unified South Slav nation.

17. The concept of a three-stage process in the development of nationalism stems from the Czech historian Miroslav Hroch in his *Social Preconditions of National Revival in Europe*, trans. Ben Fowkes (Cambridge, 1985).

18. On the so-called Wenzelsbad or St. Vaclav Committee, see Pech, *The Czech Revolution of 1848*, chap. 2.

19. Frederick Engels, *Germany: Revolution and Counter-revolution* (London, 1933), 57. Note that while it was Engels who actually wrote the articles on Central Europe that appeared over Marx's name in *The New York Daily Tribune* in 1851 and 1852, Marx contributed his views and edited Engels's writings. Thus it is appropriate to consider these articles as their joint product.

20. Miklós Wesselényi, *Szózat a magyar és szláv nemzetiség ügyében* (Memorandum with regard to the Hungarian and Slavic nationalities) (Leipzig, 1843). In 1815, approximately 21 percent of the inhabitants of the monarchy spoke German, 16 percent Czech and Slovak, 14 percent Italian, 13 percent Hungarian, 8 percent Ukrainian or Ruthene, 7 percent Romanian, 6 percent Polish, 4 percent Croatian, 4 percent Serbian, 3 percent Slovene, and 4 percent some other language. With the loss of most of the Italian possessions in 1859 and 1866, the acquisition of Cracow in 1846 and of Bosnia-Hercegovina in 1878, as well as the demographic advances made by the Hungarians through assimilation, the proportions changed considerably. In 1910, out of 51.4 million inhabitants, 23.4 percent spoke German, 12.5 percent Czech and 3.8 percent Slovak, 1.5 percent Italian, 19.6 percent Hungarian, 7.8 percent Ukrainian or Ruthene, 6.3 percent Romanian, 9.7 percent Polish, 8.5 percent Serbo-Croatian, 2.4 percent Slovene, and 4.5 percent some other language. (Source: Erich Scheithauer et al., *Geschichte Österreichs in Stichworten. Teil IV: von 1815 bis 1918* [Vienna, 1976], 30; and Deák, *Beyond Nationalism*, 25.)

Jews who spoke Yiddish figured in the statistics as German-speakers, unless they insisted—in Austria—that their everyday language was Polish or Czech, or—in Hungary—that their mother tongue was Hungarian, or Slovak, or some other language. In 1850–51, the monarchy had 36.5 million inhabitants. Of these, 7.9 million lived in Hungary, 4.5 million in Galicia, and 4.4 million in Bohemia. The military, which was counted separately, numbered 739,000 at that time. (Source: Fényes, *Az ausztriai birodalom statisztikája* 1:23. *Statistik des Königreichs Ungarn*, 3 tomes in 1 vol. [Pest, 1843–49].)

21. *Grenzboten* 2 (1846): 106. Reprinted in Otto Frass, ed., *Quellenbuch zur österreichischen Geschichte*, 3 vols. (Vienna, 1956–62), 3: 166–67.

22. Alphons Danzer et al., *Unter den Fahnen. Die Völker Österreich-Ungarns in Waffen* (Prague-Vienna-Leipzig, 1889), 152–57.

23. Similar to the revolt of the Galician peasants in 1846, the hunger-inspired revolts of the Vienna artisans and industrial workers in the terrible years from 1845 to 1848 had no ethnic connotation. But the peasants in northeastern Hungary who in 1831 killed Hungarian officials and landowners as well as Jewish innkeepers were by religion and language generally different from their victims. This was during a cholera epidemic, when a quarantine was imposed on the region and when bismuth and chloride of lime was dumped into the local wells. For the peasants, this was a clear case of conspiracy by aliens to clear them off the land and to replace them with sheep. So they went on a rampage against the suspected enemy. On the cholera epidemic in northeastern Hungary in 1831, see Deák, *The Lawful Revolution,* 21–22; and István Barta, *A fiatal Kossuth* (The young Kossuth) (Budapest, 1966), 46–59.

24. Note that the terms "historic" and "unhistoric" (or "a-historic") nations, so often employed in central Europe and in historical literature, are useless in making distinctions between the Germans, Hungarians, Croats, Czechs, and Poles on the one hand, and such people as the Slovaks, Slovenes, and Ruthenes on the other hand. Nor is it any better with the frequent attempts to distinguish between "dominant" and "oppressed" nations. All ethnic groups have had a "history," and no nation has ever been "dominant" in its entirety. Those using such terms ignore the fundamental difference between the pre-modern and modern meanings of the word "nation." Before the nineteenth century, Czech-speaking great landowners were part of the nobility of the Kingdom of Bohemia and hence of the Holy Roman Empire of the German Nation. Slovak-speaking landowners, on the other hand, were part of the "Natio Hungarica," the nobility of the Hungarian kingdom. Only in the nineteenth century, and then very slowly, did the meaning of the term "nation" expand to include all the citizens of a specific country.

It is even more absurd to assume that the peasants and urban poor have ever been part of a "dominant nation." There is no evidence to show that German factory workers in Bohemia derived any material benefits from not being Czech, or that Hungarian-speaking peasants were better treated by the Hungarian authorities than non-Hungarian speaking peasants were. Yet the thesis of dominant versus oppressed nations was fully accepted by the peacemakers in Paris after both World War 1 and World War 2, and the peace treaties they imposed on the defeated countries were based on the premise that the oppressed central and east European nations had to be freed from the yoke of the dominant nations.

At the other end of the spectrum, one finds the no less dangerous argument, voiced by many nationalist leaders, that the majority population they represent is the exploited and oppressed victim of one or another minority in its own country. This argument, in the past, "legitimized" the persecution of Jews; today it "legitimizes" the oppression of the Muslims and Albanians by the Serbian leaders of Rump-Yugoslavia.

25. On Habsburg finances and the economy of the Habsburg monarchy in the nineteenth century, see, among others, David F. Good, *The Economic*

Rise of the Habsburg Empire, 1750–1914 (Berkeley, 1985); and John Komlos, *The Habsburg Monarchy as a Customs Union: Economic Development in Austria-Hungary in the Nineteenth Century* (Princeton, NJ, 1983). The most substantial work on the subject is Alois Brusatti, ed., *Die wirtschaftliche Entwicklung* (Vienna, 1973).

26. See Deák, *The Lawful Revolution*, xvii–xviii and 140–41.

27. On the Pillersdorf Constitution and the suffrage laws of May 11 and 16, see Macartney, *Habsburg Empire*, 355–56.

28. On the Austrian elections in June-July 1848, see ibid., 372–73. According to the *Oesterreichischer Kalender* for 1849, which is cited ibid., 373 n., the Reichstag included 20 priests, 19 higher nobles, 27 lesser nobles, 18 industrialists, 9 merchants, 48 advocates, 74 officials, 33 doctors, 13 journalists, 22 miscellaneous bourgeois occupations, 94 peasants, and 9 of unknown occupation.

29. On the resignation of Ferdinand, see Macartney, *Habsburg Empire*, 407–8; and Adolph Schwarzenberg, *Prince Felix zu Schwarzenberg: Prime Minister of Austria, 1848–1852* (New York, 1946), 33–37.

30. The making of the Kremsier Constitution is best discussed in Macartney, *Habsburg Empire*, 422–23 and passim.

31. On the Stadion Constitution, see ibid., 423–25. There is a detailed discussion of both constitutions in Schwarzenberg, *Prince Felix zu Schwarzenberg*, 37–49.

32. On the April Laws in Hungary, see Deák, *The Lawful Revolution*, 91–106. Also, *Kossuth Lajos összes munkái* (The complete works of Lajos Kossuth), vol. 11, *Kossuth Lajos az utolsó rendi országgyűlésen, 1847/48* (L.K. at the last estates' diet, 1847–48), ed. István Barta (Budapest, 1966); and Ervin Szabó, *Társadalmi és pártharcok a 48–49-es magyar forradalomban* (Social and political party struggles in the revolution of 1848–49) (Vienna, 1921, and Budapest, 1949).

33. On the 1848 elections in Hungary and the new national assembly, see János Beér, ed., *Az 1848/49. évi népképviseleti országgyűlés* (The representative assembly in 1848–49) (Budapest, 1954), which contains both text and documents; and Andor Csizmadia, *A magyar választási rendszer 1848–1849-ben: Az első népképviseleti választások* (The Hungarian electoral system in 1848–1849: the first elections to a representative assembly) (Budapest, 1963).

34. For Marx's and Engels's dire views on the prospects of the Czech nation see, among others, Engels, *Germany: Revolution and Counterrevolution*, 57.

35. A summary of the events in Milan, Vienna, and Budapest in March 1848 is in Robertson, *The Revolutions of 1848*, chaps. 10–19.

36. On the workers in Vienna, see Wolfgang Häusler, *Von der Massenarmut zur Arbeiterbewegung. Demokratie und soziale Frage in der Wiener Revolution von 1848* (Vienna, 1979).

37. Documents of the spring 1848 pogroms and the Hungarian government's answer to them are in Jenő Zsoldos, ed., *1848–49 a magyar zsidóság*

életében (1848–49 in the lives of the Hungarian Jewry) (Budapest, 1948), 47–107. See also Imre Deák, ed., *1848: A szabadságharc története levelekben, ahogy a kortársak látták* (The history of the war of independence as seen by contemporaries) (Budapest, 1942), 69–70; Dénes Pap, ed., *Okmánytár Magyarország függetlenségi harczának történetéhez 1848–1849* (Documents on the history of Hungary's war of independence), 2 vols. (Pest, 1868–1869), 1:59–60; and Salo W. Baron, "The Impact of the Revolution of 1848 on Jewish Emancipation," *Jewish Social Studies* 11, 3 (July 1949): 195–248.

38. The role of Romanians in the events of 1848–49 is described in Victor Chereșteșiu, *Adunarea națională de la Blaj* (The Blaj national assembly) (Bucharest, 1966); Silviu Dragomir, *Avram Iancu* (Bucharest, 1965); Keith Hitchins, *The Rumanian National Movement in Transylvania, 1848–1849* (Cambridge, MA, 1969); I.D. Suciu, *Revoluția de la 1848–1849 in Banat* (The revolution of 1848–49 in the Banat region) (Bucharest, 1968); Zoltán Tóth, *Az erdélyi és magyarországi román nemzeti mozgalom, 1790–1848* (The Romanian national movement, 1790–1848) (Budapest, 1959).

On the Transylvanian Saxons, see Carl Goellner, *Die Siebenbürger Sachsen in den Revolutionsjahren 1848–1849* (Bucharest, 1967); Zoltán Sárközi, *Az erdélyi szászok 1848–1849-ben* (The Transylvanian Saxons in 1848–49) (Budapest, 1974); and Otto Folberth, *Der Prozess Stephan Ludwig Roth: Ein Kapitel Nationalitätengeschichte Südosteuropeas im 19. Jahrhundert* (Vienna, 1959). The events in southern Hungary are discussed in József Thim, ed., *A magyarországi 1848–49-iki szerb fölkelés története* (The history of the Serbian uprising in Hungary, 1848–49), 3 vols. (Budapest, 1930–40), which contains both text and documents.

39. On Vienna in October 1848, see, among others, Heinrich Friedjung, *Österreich von 1848 bis 1860*, 2 vols. (Stuttgart-Berlin, 1908–12); Bernard Isaacs, ed., *The Revolution of 1848–49: Articles from the "Neue Rheinische Zeitung" by Karl Marx and Friedrich Engels*, trans. S. Ryazanskaya (New York, 1972), 138–39, 146–49, 255–65 and passim.

40. On the battle at Pákozd, see Ferdinand Hauptmann, ed., *Jelačić's Kriegszug nach Ungarn 1848*, 2 vols. (Graz, 1975), which contains both text and documents.

41. On the Austrian and Hungarian armies during and after the revolutions of 1848–49, see Deák, *Beyond Nationalism*; Antonio Schmidt-Brentano, *Die Armee in Österreich. Militär, Staat und Gesellschaft 1848–1867* (Boppard am Rhein, 1975); *Sechzig Jahre Wehrmacht 1848–1908* (Vienna, 1908); and Alphons Freiherr von Wrede, *Geschichte der k.u.k. Wehrmacht. Die Regimenter, Corps, Branchen und Anstalten von 1618 bis zum Ende des XIX. Jahrhunderts*, 5 vols. (Vienna, 1898–1905).

42. On the desertion of Italian troops from Field Marshal Radetzky's army in the spring of 1848, see Sked, *The Survival of the Habsburg Empire*, chap. 3.

43. On Italian patriotic propaganda among the Italian soldiers in the Austrian army, see ibid.

44. On Hungarians, Croats, Frenchmen, Piedmontese, etc. in the war of

1859, see István Deák, "Defeat at Solferino: The Nationality Question and the Habsburg Army in the War of 1859," in Béla K. Király, ed., *The Crucial Decade: East European Society and National Defense, 1859–1870* (New York, 1984), 496–516.

45. On the question of Italian and Austrian atrocities in Brescia, see *Biografie des k.k. Feldzeugmeisters Julius Freiherrn von Haynau von einem seiner Waffengefährten* (Graz, 1853)

46. On the doubtful loyalty of many counties in Hungary to Kossuth's cause, see Deák, *The Lawful Revolution*, 227–228.

47. On neo-absolutism in Austria, see, among others, Heinrich Friedjung, *Österreich von 1848 bis 1860*, 2 vols. (Stuttgart and Berlin, 1908); and György Szabad, *Hungarian Political Trends Between Revolution and Compromise* (Budapest, 1977).

48. On Austrian foreign policy in the early 1850s, see Heinrich Friedjung, *The Struggle for Supremacy in Germany, 1859–1866*, trans. A. J. P. Taylor and W. L. McElvee (New York, 1966); id., *Der Kriemkrieg und die österreichische Politik* (Stuttgart-Berlin, 1907); Schwarzenberg, *Prince Felix zu Schwarzenberg*, chap. 3 and passim; and A. J. P. Taylor, *The Struggle for Mastery in Europe, 1848–1918* (Oxford, 1954).

49. The most recent biographies of Francis Joseph are by Jean-Paul Bled, *François-Joseph* (Paris, 1987); and Alan Palmer, *Twilight of the Habsburgs: The Life and Times of Emperor Francis Joseph* (New York, 1994).

CHAPTER 9

1. For a precise definition of the sovereign's absolute power, see "Miatezh," in *Ugolovnoe ulozhenie: Proekt redaktsionnoi komissii i ob"iasneniia k nemu* (St. Petersburg, 1897), 2:34.

2. Volker Rabe, *Der Widerspruch von Rechtsstaatlichkeit und strafender Verwaltung in Russland 1881–1917: Motive, Handhabung und Auswirkungen der administrativen Verbannung von Revolutionären*. Wissenschaftliche Beiträge Karlsruhe, no. 14 (Karlsruhe, 1985), 143–56.

3. The picture became more foreboding in the decade after 1905; see the classic Leopold H. Haimson, "The Problem of Social Stability in Urban Russia, 1905–1917," 1, *SR* 23, 4 (1964): 619–42; 2, *SR* 24, 1 (1965): 1–22.

4. See contradictions in the text of her Instruction: Paul Dukes, ed., *Russia under Catherine the Great*, vol. 2, *Catherine the Great's Instruction (Nakaz) to the Legislative Commission, 1767* (Newtonville, MA, 1977).

5. Gary Marker, *Publishing, Printing, and the Origins of Intellectual Life in Russia, 1700–1800* (Princeton, NJ, 1985).

6. Paul Avrich, *Russian Rebels, 1600–1800* (New York, 1972), 195–96, 203–5, 217–21, 233, 235. My interpretation of Pugachev follows Avrich.

7. Ibid., 242.

8. Quoted in R. V. Ovchinnikov, "Sledstvie i sud nad E. I. Pugachevym," *Voprosy istorii*, no. 3 (1966), 126–28 (quotes, 128); also ibid., *Voprosy istorii*, no. 9 (1966), 141 and 145; and Avrich, *Russian Rebels*, 243.

9. Document in Ovchinnikov, "Sledstvie," *Voprosy istorii*, no. 9, 146.

10. Dmitriev's memoirs, quoted in Alexander Pushkin, *The History of Pugachev*, trans. Earl Sampson (Ann Arbor, MI, 1983), 108.

11. Decree no. 10101 (1753), *Polnoe sobranie zakonov Rossiiskoi imperii* (St. Petersburg, 1830), 13:838–39. Also embodied in law of Sept. 30, 1754 (no. 10306); see N. S. Tagantsev, *Russkoe ugolovnoe pravo: Lektsii* (St. Petersburg, 1902), 2:973–74. Also, Peter Liessem, "Die Todesstrafe im späten Zarenreich: Rechtslage, Realität und öffentliche Diskussion," *Jahrbücher für Geschichte Osteuropas* 37, 4 (1989): 493.

12. Cesare Beccaria, *An Essay on Crimes and Punishments*, trans. from the Italian of Beccaria with the commentary by Voltaire, trans. from the French, 5th ed. (London, 1801), 95, 76, 100. See T. Cizova, "Beccaria in Russia," *Slavonic and East European Review* 40 (1961/1962): 392, 396.

13. On interpretation, see D. N. Bludov, "Obshchaia ob"iasnitel'naia zapiska," in *Proekt ulozheniia o nakazaniiakh ugolovnykh i ispravitel'nykh, vnesennyi v 1844 godu v Gosudarstvennyi Sovet, s podrobnym oznacheniem osnovanii kazhdogo iz vnesennykh v sei proekt postanovlenii* (St. Petersburg, 1871), li; also Tagantsev, *Russkoe ugolovnoe pravo* 2:975.

14. Count Dmitrii Bludov, author of the revised criminal code of 1845, noted that the death penalty was necessary to produce a "salutary psychological effect" (spasitel'no deistvovat' na umy): Bludov, "Obshchaia ob"iasnitel'naia zapiska," lii.

15. Before the use of corporal punishment was severely restricted in 1863 and 1871, culprits often died from its physical effects. See Donald Rawson, "The Death Penalty in Late Tsarist Russia: An Investigation of Judicial Procedures," *RH* 11, 1 (1984): 29–52; and Tagantsev, *Russkoe ugolovnoe pravo* 2:977–79.

16. Remarks of a contemporary, quoted in Roderick Page Thaler, "Introduction," in Aleksandr Nikolaevich Radishchev, *A Journey from St. Petersburg to Moscow*, trans. Leo Wiener, ed. Roderick Page Thaler (Cambridge, 1958), 11.

17. See Thaler, "Introduction," 11–12; also, D. S. Babkin, *Protsess A. N. Radishcheva* (Moscow-Leningrad, 1952), 56–59, 268, 271–72, 276–77. Babkin does not mention a public ceremony of dishonor in his heavily ideological account of Radishchev's heroic suffering.

18. Thaler, "Introduction," 14, 16–19. On Radishchev's suicide and the Roman model, see Iurii M. Lotman, "The Poetics of Everyday Behavior in Eighteenth-Century Russian Culture," in Iurii M. Lotman, Lidiia Ia. Ginsburg, and Boris A. Uspenskii, *The Semiotics of Russian History*, ed. Alexander D. and Alice Stone Nakhimovsky (Ithaca, NY, 1985), 90–92. Political suicide was a theatrical gesture that had gained currency in France during the Revolution, where the practice drew on the same classical and Enlightenment sources that inspired Radishchev. See Dorinda Outram, *The Body and the French Revolution: Sex, Class, and Political Culture* (New Haven, CT, 1989), 90–105; also Andrzej Walicki, *A History of Russian Thought: From the Enlightenment to Marxism* (Stanford, 1979), 39.

19. For documents, Marc Raeff, *The Decembrist Movement* (Englewood Cliffs, NJ, 1966); for standard account, Anatole G. Mazour, *The First Russian Revolution, 1825* (Stanford, 1937). On official projects for reform, see S. V. Mironenko, *Samoderzhavie i reformy: Politicheskaia bor'ba v Rossii v nachale XIX v.* (Moscow, 1989).

20. Lotman, "The Decembrist in Daily Life," in Lotman et al., *Semiotics.*

21. Richard Wortman, *Scenarios of Power: Myth and Ceremony in Russian Monarchy*, vol. 1, *From Peter the Great to the Death of Nicholas I* (Princeton, NJ, 1995), has argued that Peter the Great set a pattern by which acts of founding violence became central to the symbolics of imperial legitimation. Thanks to the Decembrists, this pattern was replicated even for Nicholas, the ideological conservative who reigned in the name of dynastic continuity, not rupture.

22. Mazour, *First Russian Revolution*, 205–9. Among the investigators were close friends and associates of the accused. For that reason it was hard for the prisoners to see their questioners as enemies or political abstractions. Lotman, "Decembrist," 143.

23. Mazour, *First Russian Revolution*, 210–14. The information accumulated by the prosecution constitutes the basis of what we know about the event, and much of what we know of the conspirators' ideas, but it was not available to contemporaries. For Nicholas's belief that the Decembrist trial had convinced the world of Russia's respect for legality, see A. A. Kizevetter, "Imperator Nikolai I, kak konstitutsionnyi monarkh," in *Istoricheskie ocherki* (Moscow, 1912; rpt. The Hague, 1967), 405.

24. Mazour, *First Russian Revolution*, 220; Herzen cited, ibid., 214.

25. Radishchev's exile and his sister-in-law's decision to follow him to Siberia had made no such impression on his contemporaries and exercised no enduring fascination. In the space of 30 years, as Lotman notes ("Decembrist," 121–22), formerly neutral gestures had acquired new meaning.

26. On codification under Nicholas I, see A. A. Kizevetter, "Vnutrenniaia politika v tsarstvovanie imperatora Nikolaia Pavlovicha," in *Istoricheskie ocherki*, 494–97.

27. See articles 241–52 in *Ulozhenie o nakazaniiakh ugolovnykh i ispravitel'nykh 1885 goda*, ed. N. S. Tagantsev (St. Petersburg, 1901), 253–59.

28. "Miatezh," in *Ugolovnoe ulozhenie* 2:10, 16–20, 24–25, 40–41, 45–46. For the origins of this legal tradition, see N. N. Evreinov, *Istoriia telesnykh nakazanii v Rossii* (St. Petersburg, [1913]), 23, 25; and James Cracraft, "Opposition to Peter the Great," in *Imperial Russia, 1700–1917: State, Society, Opposition*, ed. Ezra Mendelsohn and Marshall S. Shatz (DeKalb, IL, 1988), 23, 25–26.

29. On political divisions within the Polish elite before incorporation into the Russian Empire and on Polish attitudes toward the constitution of 1815 at the time it was introduced, see Andrzej Walicki, *Russia, Poland, and Universal Regeneration: Studies on Russian and Polish Thought of the Romantic Epoch* (Notre Dame, IN, 1991), 5–6.

30. Norman Davies, *God's Playground: A History of Poland* (Oxford, 1981), 2:321.

31. W. Bruce Lincoln, *Nicholas I: Emperor and Autocrat of all the Russias* (Bloomington, IN, 1978), 138–39. For Constantine's scruples, see Kizevetter, "Imperator Nikolai I." For narrative accounts of 1830, see R. F. Leslie, *Polish Politics and the Revolution of November 1830* (London, 1956), 117–23; Piotr S. Wandycz, *The Lands of Partitioned Poland, 1795–1918* (Seattle, WA, 1974), 105–17; and *The Cambridge History of Poland, from Augustus II to Pilsudski (1697–1935)*, ed. W. F. Reddaway et al. (1941; rpt. New York, 1971), 295–310. These accounts do not agree in all details, and none completely elucidates the intricate confusion of events.

32. Lincoln, *Nicholas*, 140–43.

33. See Davies, *Playground* 2:324–25; Leslie, *Polish Politics*, 257; Wandycz, *Partitioned Poland*, 105–17; and Michael T. Florinsky, *Russia: A History and an Interpretation* (New York, 1953), 2:757–64.

34. Davies, *Playground* 2:331–32. For the 250 condemned to death though never executed, see *Protiv smertnoi kazni: Sbornik statei*, ed. M. N. Gernet, O. B. Gol'dovskii, and I. N. Sakharov (Moscow, 1907), 386–94.

35. Lincoln, *Nicholas*, 271–77, 287–89, 313–15, 318–22, 320 (Holy War), 323 (Kavelin on tyranny).

36. Historians have debated to what extent Alexander II was motivated by the specter of peasant violence in finally embarking on emancipation as a way of warding off disorder from below. For the standard Soviet view, see M. V. Nechkina, "The Reform as a By-Product of the Revolutionary Struggle," in *Emancipation of the Russian Serfs*, ed. Terence Emmons (New York, 1970), 66–71. Compare Alfred J. Rieber, "The Politics of Emancipation," in *The Politics of Autocracy: Letters of Alexander II to Prince A. I. Bariatinskii, 1857–1864*, ed. Alfred J. Rieber (Paris, 1966), 15–58.

37. See Terence Emmons, "The Peasant and the Emancipation," in *The Peasant in Nineteenth-Century Russia*, ed. Wayne S. Vucinich (Stanford, 1968), 41–71, esp. 48–50, 54–55; and the wonderful account in Daniel Field, *Rebels in the Name of the Tsar* (1976; rpt. Boston, 1989), 31–111.

38. On 1863, see Florinsky, *Russia* 2:909–18; Wandycz, *Partitioned Poland*, 155–79; Reddaway et al., eds., *Cambridge History*, 365–86.

39. Bazarov was the hero of Turgenev's novel *Fathers and Sons* (1862). On the concept of the intelligentsia, see Martin Malia, "What is the Intelligentsia?" *Daedalus* (Summer 1960): 441–58; and Michel Confino, "On Intellectuals and Intellectual Traditions in Eighteenth and Nineteenth Century Russia," *Daedalus* (Spring 1972): 117–49. The men of the 1840s are conventionally described as the first generation of the intelligentsia, and the men and women of the 1860s as the second. Michael Confino ("On Intellectuals") argues, however, that only the generation of the 1860s fits the strict definition of the intelligentsia, characterized by a sense of social estrangement and intense moral commitment to civic or political action.

40. See the brilliant discussion in Irina Paperno, *Chernyshevsky and the*

Age of Realism (Stanford, 1988), 21 (Chicherin quoted), 22 (arrest). For specific charges, see *Vedomosti S.-Peterburgskoi gorodskoi politsii*, 17 maia 1864, no. 108, quoted in *Gosudarstvennye prestupleniia v Rossii v XIX veke: Sbornik izvlechennykh iz offitsial'nykh izdanii pravitel'stvennykh soobshchenii*, ed. B. Bazilevskii [B. Bogucharskii] (St. Petersburg, 1906), 1:123.

41. Nicholas Ishutin, sentenced to hard labor for his part in the attempted assassination of the tsar in 1866, considered Chernyshevskii one of the world's three great men, along with Jesus and St. Paul. Franco Venturi, *Roots of Revolution: A History of the Populist and Socialist Movements in Nineteenth Century Russia*, intro. Isaiah Berlin, trans. Francis Haskell (New York, 1966), 331.

42. Term "edifying" (pouchitel'noe) used by the 1864 judicial reform commission complaining that this effect was no longer produced: quoted in N. V. Murav'ev, "Obriad publichnoi kazni" (*Iuridicheskii vestnik*, 1874, no. 7 and no. 8), repr. in *Iz proshloi deiatel'nosti* (St. Petersburg, 1900), 1:19.

43. Quoted in Venturi, *Roots*, 240 (trans. modified).

44. Eyewitness account in *Protsess N. G. Chernyshevskogo: Arkhivnye dokumenty*, ed. N. A. Alekseev (Saratov, 1939), 354–55.

45. A note on the ambiguities of status and the discord between juridical and cultural meanings in late tsarist Russia: Although Chernyshevskii, in his modest personal demeanor and clerical family background, represented the archetypal intellectual-commoner, he was legally a member of the nobility. Having earned the civil service rank of *tituliarnyi sovetnik*, which conferred the status of "personal" nobility, he was entitled to have a sword broken over his head as a token of civic degradation. Nikolai Gogol's famous downtrodden hero, the clerk Akakii Akakevich in "The Overcoat" (1842), an object of universal derision, belonged to the same rank. See Seymour Becker, *Nobility and Privilege in Late Imperial Russia* (DeKalb, IL, 1985), 91, 95, 97.

46. Murav'ev, "Obriad," 42.

47. Yarmolinsky, *Road*, 82.

48. Quoted in Murav'ev, "Obriad," 19.

49. On reaction to Pugachev, see Pushkin, *History*, 106–7. Local citizens watched impassively the civil execution of three of Nechaev's followers: Venturi, *Roots*, 775. The crowd at Nechaev's own ceremony was hostile: ibid., 387; and N. A. Troitskii, *Tsarskie sudy protiv revoliutsionnoi Rossii: Politicheskie protsessy 1871–1880 gg.* (Saratov, 1976), 150. No one gathered to consecrate Karakozov's death, but the civil execution of Dolgushin's followers in 1875 provided an occasion for public theater similar to the performance at Chernyshevskii's "execution" ten years before: see N. A. Troitskii, *Tsarizm pod sudom progressivnoi obshchestvennosti, 1866–1895 gg.* (Moscow, 1979), 132; also Venturi, *Roots*, 500–501. On the case, see Bazilevskii, ed., *Gosudarstvennye prestupleniia* 1:254–318.

50. Murav'ev, "Obriad," 48.

51. For comments on the changed moral impact of public executions as one of the reasons for their removal from public sight after 1881, see "Nakazaniia," in *Ugolovnoe ulozhenie* (1897), 1:124.

52. Venturi, *Roots*, 260–64, 275, 285–99.

53. Ibid., chap. 14; Bazilevskii, ed., *Gosudarstvennye prestupleniia* 1: 135–51.

54. "Revolutionary Catechism" (1869), quoted in Venturi, *Roots*, 365.

55. Ibid., 369.

56. See ibid., chap. 15.

57. Quoted in Troitskii, *Tsarskie sudy*, 150.

58. "Obriad publichnoi kazni nad S. G. Nechaevym," *Krasnyi arkhiv* 1 (1922): 280–81. See also Murav'ev, "Obriad," 40–41.

59. Quoted in Venturi, *Roots*, 364. On Nechaev and his relation to Bakunin, see Michael Confino, "Introduction," *Violence dans la violence: Le débat Bakounine-Nečaev* (Paris, 1973), 13–93.

60. See Andrzej Walicki, *The Controversy Over Capitalism* (Oxford, 1969); id., *History of Russian Thought*, chap. 10; also Martin Malia, *Alexander Herzen and the Birth of Russian Socialism* (Cambridge, 1961).

61. Articles 1030–32, 1050, 1055–56, "Ustav ugolovnogo sudoproizvodstva, Razdel vtoroi: O sudoproizvodstve po gosudarstvennym prestupleniiam," in *Rossiiskoe zakonodatel'stvo X–XX vekov*, vol. 8, *Sudebnaia reforma*, ed. B. V. Vilenskii (Moscow, 1991), 220–21, 223. Also, Troitskii, *Tsarskie sudy*, 107, on closed doors.

62. Committee of Ministers, opinion of March 1875, quoted in Venturi, *Roots*, 585. This opinion was expressed after some of the rules had already been changed to limit the impact of trials but before the two major trials of 1877 and 1878, which did the greatest damage from the government's point of view.

63. Troitskii, *Tsarskie sudy*, 127–28, 133, 135, 137–38; also Bazilevskii, ed., *Gosudarstvennye prestupleniia* 1:159–227.

64. Laws of May 19, 1871 (transfer inquiry) and June 7, 1872 (Osoboe prisutstvie pravitel'stvuiushchego senata): Troitskii, *Tsarskie sudy*, 99 and 101. The law of Feb. 4, 1875, imposed further limitations on published accounts: ibid., 107–8.

65. Ibid., 147–50. It was the first time a tsar had intervened to increase the severity of a sentence (even Nicholas I had exercised his imperial prerogative to mitigate the sentences imposed on the Decembrists).

66. See Venturi, *Roots*, 586.

67. Troitskii, *Tsarskie sudy*, 187–90.

68. Bazilevskii, ed., *Gosudarstvennye prestupleniia* 3:3–4. The Judicial Statutes of 1864 in fact provided for closed trials in just such cases.

69. "Troitskii, *Tsarskie sudy*, 194–95. Translation, modified, from Venturi, *Roots*, 590.

70. Troitskii, *Tsarskie sudy*, 196–98.

71. A. F. Koni, "Vospominaniia o dele Very Zasulich," in *Sobranie sochinenii* (Moscow, 1966), 2:63–64. The acquitted remained in St. Petersburg and spoke of their experiences, increasing public indignation: ibid., 78.

72. For the circumstances and official justification of the trial, including suppression of its political motives, see ibid., 66–67, 73, 75.

73. Troitskii, *Tsarskie sudy,* 216.

74. Venturi, *Roots,* 605. Koni remarks that according to law, Zasulich should have been convicted, then given a mild sentence in recognition of the nature of her motives. Since Trepov remained unpunished for his misdeed, the jury violated the letter of the law to compensate for the government's disregard of justice: Koni, "Vospominaniia," 74–75.

75. Koni, who had rejected the request by the minister of justice to manipulate the outcome of the trial, now refused to be pressured into resigning. See Koni, "Predislovie," *Sobranie sochinenii* 2: 15–16; id., "Vospominaniia," 202–12; Troitskii, *Tsarskie sudy,* 217–18.

76. Quoted in Troitskii, *Tsarskie sudy,* 226.

77. Venturi, *Roots,* 610.

78. Quoted in Troitskii, *Tsarizm,* 185.

79. Quotes in ibid., 212 and 206. Although the transfer to military courts violated the 1864 statutes and the rules governing military justice according to the 1881 decrees were harder on civilian defendants than the statutes governing the regular courts, military lawyers nevertheless adhered to standards of professional conduct and respected the procedural framework in which they worked: see William C. Fuller, Jr., *Civil-Military Conflict in Imperial Russia, 1881–1914* (Princeton, NJ, 1985), 124–27.

80. Quoted in Troitskii, *Tsarizm,* 219.

81. The question of women, as actors and icons, in the Populist movement is an important one. For self-portraits of female activists, see Barbara Alpern Engel and Clifford N. Rosenthal, eds., *Five Sisters: Women Against the Tsar* (New York, 1975). For attitudes toward women radicals and on the question of whether female culprits should be subjected to corporal punishment, see Koni, "Vospominaniia," 47–48. On images of sexual purity and pollution, see Troitskii, *Tsarizm,* 214, 218; and id., *Tsarskie sudy,* 191.

82. Troitskii, *Tsarizm,* 228.

83. Quotes in ibid., 221–22 (Aleksandrov), 223 (D. M. Gertsenshtein). Just as Aleksandrov had once left the prosecutor's bench for the bar, two of the prosecutors in the Zasulich trial resigned to work for the defense.

84. Quoted in ibid., 230.

85. Ibid., 52, 107, 109–10, 123–28; also Troitskii, *Tsarskie sudy,* 267–68.

86. Ibid., 224–29.

87. Ibid., 131, 133, 137; also Troitskii, *Tsarskie sudy,* 271.

88. Troitskii, *Tsarskie sudy,* 229.

89. Venturi, *Roots,* 614–15, 629–56.

90. Moving political cases to military courts had begun in 1878; see Rawson, "Death Penalty," 38. The exceptional laws of 1881 allowed administrative authorities to transfer civilian cases to military courts operating under the laws of wartime, which greatly extended the number of cases in which the death penalty could be imposed. See Fuller, *Civil-Military Conflict,* chap. 4; also Tagantsev, *Russkoe ugolovnoe pravo* 2:978–79.

91. On this period, see Norman M. Naimark, *Terrorists and Social Demo-*

crats: The Russian Revolutionary Movement Under Alexander III (Cambridge, MA, 1983), 5–7, 14, 35–38.

92. On the formation of a working class and urban-rural interaction, see Robert Eugene Johnson, *Peasant and Proletarian: The Working Class of Moscow in the Late Nineteenth Century* (New Brunswick, NJ, 1979). On changes in rural culture, see Ben Eklof, *Russian Peasant Schools: Officialdom, Village Culture, and Popular Pedagogy, 1861–1914* (Berkeley, 1986); and Jeffrey Brooks, *When Russia Learned to Read: Literacy and Popular Literature, 1861–1917* (Princeton, NJ, 1985).

93. On growth of a professional class, see V. R. Leikina-Svirskaia, *Intelligentsia v Rossii vo vtoroi polovine XIX veka* (Moscow, 1971); Nancy Mandelker Frieden, *Russian Physicians in an Era of Reform and Revolution, 1856–1905* (Princeton, NJ, 1981); Richard S. Wortman, *Russian Legal Consciousness* (Chicago, 1976).

94. See Venturi, *Roots*, chap. 19.

95. On society's involvement in the labor question, see Reginald E. Zelnik, *Labor and Society in Tsarist Russia: The Factory Workers of St. Petersburg* (Stanford, 1971); on links between radicals and bureaucrats, see the case described in E. Willis Brooks, "The Improbable Connection: D. A. Miljutin and N. G. Cernysevskij, 1848–1862," *Jahrbücher für Geschichte Osteuropas* 37, 1 (1989): 21–44.

96. See Naimark, *Terrorists*, 34–35.

97. See Terence Emmons, *The Russian Landed Gentry and the Peasant Emancipation of 1861* (Cambridge, 1968).

98. The tsar had helped endow the Bulgarian people with a political constitution after liberating them from Turkish rule. Why, asked a group of zemstvo men from Tver, did he deny Russians the same "opportunity to progress along the path of gradual and lawful development." Shmuel Galai, *The Liberation Movement in Russia, 1900–1905* (Cambridge, 1973), 10–13, 16 (quote).

99. See Heidi Whelan, *Alexander III and the State Council: Bureaucracy and Counter-Reform in Late Imperial Russia* (New Brunswick, NJ, 1982).

100. For the work of these commissions, see Laura Engelstein, *The Keys to Happiness: Sex and the Search for Modernity in Fin-de-Siècle Russia* (Ithaca, NY, 1992), 22–23; and William G. Wagner, *Marriage, Property, and Law in Late Imperial Russia* (Oxford, 1994).

101. Naimark, *Terrorists*, 21–22, 42 (almost 6,000 members of Narodnaia volia were sentenced from 1881 to 1894).

102. On the debate on capitalism among Populists and Marxists, see Walicki, *Controversy*.

103. On the split, see Leopold H. Haimson, *The Russian Marxists and the Origins of Bolshevism* (Cambridge, MA, 1955).

104. Quoted in Venturi, *Roots*, 640. On examples from the 1870s, see Field, *Rebels*, chap. 3.

105. On the pogroms, see John D. Klier and Shlomo Lambroza, eds., *Po-*

groms: Anti-Jewish Violence in Modern Russian History (Cambridge, 1992), especially chapters by Michael Aronson, Erich Haberer, Shlomo Lambroza, and Hans Rogger.

106. E. P. Thompson, *Customs in Common: Studies in Traditional Popular Culture* (New York, 1993), 188–91, 260, 336, 340, 344.

107. For a brilliant analysis of these issues, see Reginald E. Zelnik, "Russian Workers and the Revolutionary Movement," *JSH* 6, 2 (1972–73): 214–36.

108. Adam Ulam has argued, for example, that the Russian revolution was not a product of class formation and class conflict, as Marxists would like to believe, but a product of retarded social development, a symptom of the very incompleteness of Russia's economic development in the early twentieth century: see Adam B. Ulam, *The Unfinished Revolution: An Essay on the Sources of Influence of Marxism and Communism* (New York, 1960).

109. See Reginald Zelnik, "The Peasant and the Factory," in Vucinich, ed., *The Peasant in Nineteenth-Century Russia;* id., *Labor and Society,* chap. 9; Johnson, *Peasant and Proletarian,* chap. 7; Timothy Mixter, "The Hiring Market as Workers' Turf: Migrant Agricultural Laborers and the Mobilization of Collective Action in the Steppe Grainbelt of European Russia, 1853–1913," in *Peasant Economy, Culture, and Politics,* ed. Esther Kingston-Mann and Timothy Mixter (Princeton, NJ, 1991).

110. See *A Radical Worker in Tsarist Russia: The Autobiography of Semen Ivanovich Kanatchikov,* trans. and ed. Reginald E. Zelnik (Stanford, 1986); Reginald E. Zelnik, "Russian Bebels: An Introduction to the Memoirs of Semen Kanatchikov and Matvei Fisher," *Russian Review* 35, 3 (July 1976): 249–89 and 35, 4 (Oct. 1976): 417–47; and id., "'To the Unaccustomed Eye': Religion and Irreligion in the Experience of St. Petersburg Workers in the 1870s," *RH* 16, 2–4 (1989): 297–326; Allan K. Wildman, *The Making of a Workers' Revolution: Russian Social Democracy, 1891–1903* (Chicago, 1967).

111. See Jeremiah Schneiderman, *Sergei Zubatov and Revolutionary Marxism: The Struggle for the Working Class in Tsarist Russia* (Ithaca, NY, 1976); Gerald D. Surh, "Petersburg's First Mass Labor Organization: The Assembly of Russian Workers and Father Gapon," *Russian Review* 40, 3 (1981): 241–62 and 40, 4 (1981): 412–41; and Laura Engelstein, *Moscow, 1905: Working-Class Organization and Political Conflict* (Stanford, 1982), 59–62, 79–81.

112. Mark Steinberg, *Moral Communities: The Culture of Class Relations in the Russian Printing Industry, 1867–1907* (Berkeley, 1992), following E. P. Thompson's argument for the paternalism of the eighteenth-century moral economy.

113. See Charters Wynn, *Workers, Strikes, and Pogroms: The Donbass-Dnepr Bend in Late Imperial Russia, 1870–1905* (Princeton, NJ, 1992), chap. 7.

114. Lenin solved the problem of the masses' unreliability by substituting party domination for the spontaneous impulses of the crowd. But this was a radical solution, not fulfilled in practice before 1917 even by the Bolsheviks

themselves, and rejected by most Social Democrats as contrary to the movement's values as well as its ideas. See Zelnik, "Russian Workers."

115. See Scott J. Seregny, "Peasants and Politics: Peasant Unions During the 1905 Revolution" in *Peasant Economy, Culture, and Politics*, ed. Kington-Mann and Mixter, 341–77; also id., *Russian Teachers and Peasant Revolution: The Politics of Education in 1905* (Bloomington, IN, 1989), chaps. 7 and 8. For more on peasant political activity, see Maureen Perrie, "The Russian Peasant Movement of 1905–7: Its Social Composition and Revolutionary Significance," in *The World of the Russian Peasant: Post-Emancipation Culture and Society*, ed. Ben Eklof and Stephen P. Frank (Boston, 1990); and Robert Edelman, *Proletarian Peasants: The Revolution of 1905 in Russia's Southwest* (Ithaca, NY, 1987).

116. John Bushnell, *Mutiny and Repression: Russian Soldiers in the Revolution of 1905–1906* (Bloomington, IN, 1985).

117. See Galai, *Liberation*, 144–55.

118. On the second wave of terror, see Anna Geifman, *Thou Shalt Kill: Revolutionary Terrorism in Russia, 1894–1917* (Princeton, NJ, 1993).

119. On student unrest, see Galai, *Liberation*, 90–91. See also Samuel D. Kassow, *Students, Professors, and the State in Tsarist Russia* (Berkeley, 1989).

120. Recent scholarship on the social dynamics of the revolution includes Henry Reichman, *Railwaymen and Revolution: Russia, 1905* (Berkeley, 1987); Gerald D. Surh, *1905 in St. Petersburg: Labor, Society, and Revolution* (Stanford, 1989); Steinberg, *Moral Communities*; Wynn, *Workers, Strikes, and Pogroms*; Robert Weinberg, *The Revolution of 1905 in Odessa: Blood on the Steps* (Bloomington, IN, 1993). For an excellent overall narrative, see Abraham Ascher, *The Revolution of 1905: Russia in Disarray* (Stanford, 1988).

121. This is the argument of Engelstein, *Moscow, 1905.*

122. On the political fragmentation of the industrial bourgeoisie, see Alfred J. Rieber, *Merchants and Entrepreneurs in Imperial Russia* (Chapel Hill, NC, 1982); also Ruth Amende Roosa, "Russian Industrialists, Politics, and Labor Reform in 1905," *RH* 2, 2 (1975): 124–48.

123. Bulgakov, quoted in Galai, *Liberation*, 181.

124. See Engelstein, *Moscow, 1905*, 121.

Index

In this index an "f" after a number indicates a separate reference on the next page, and an "ff" indicates separate references on the next two pages. A continuous discussion over two or more pages is indicated by a span of page numbers, e.g., "57–59." *Passim* is used for a cluster of references in close but not consecutive sequence.

Library of Congress Cataloging-in-Publication Data
Revolution and the meanings of freedom in the nineteenth century /
edited by Isser Woloch.
 p. cm. –(The making of modern freedom)
Includes bibliographical references and index.
ISBN 0-8047-2748-1 (cloth : alk. paper)
ISBN 0-8047-4194-8 (pbk. : alk. paper)
 1. Revolutions—History—19th century. 2. Liberty. 3. Constitutional history. I. Woloch, Isser. II. Series.
D359.7R48 1996
303.6'4'09034—dc20
95-43721   CIP

⊗ This book is printed on acid-free, recycled paper.

Original printing 1996
Last figure below indicates year of this printing:
05 04 03 02 01